IRISH ON THE INSIDE

IRISH ON THE INSIDE

In Search of the Soul
of Irish America

—————————◆—————————

TOM HAYDEN

VERSO
London • New York

First published by Verso 2001
© Tom Hayden 2001
Paperback edition first published by Verso 2003
© Tom Hayden 2003
All rights reserved

1 3 5 7 9 10 8 6 4 2

The moral rights of the author have been asserted

Verso
UK: 6 Meard Street, London W1F 0EG
USA: 180 Varick Street, New York, NY 10014–4606

Verso is the imprint of New Left Books
www.versobooks.com

ISBN 1–85984–477–4

British Library Cataloguing in Publication Data
A catalogue record for this book is available from the British Library

Library of Congress Cataloging-in-Publication Data
A catalog record for this book is available from the Library of Congress

Typeset by M Rules
Printed by R R Donnelley & Sons, USA

Contents

Part III Recovering the Irish Soul

Introduction and Acknowledgements

As this book was being finished, the City of New York was creating a memorial to millions of Irish people forced by the Great Hunger of 1841–55 to become exiled immigrants to America. The memorial would include native sod, as imagined in the dream that concludes this book. It was a sign that the fog of amnesia might be lifting. Until lately, there have been virtually no monuments in the USA to the Famine immigrants whose suffering – perhaps the greatest displacement of nineteenth-century Europe – devastated Ireland while at the same time giving rude birth to Irish Catholic America. For generations, Irish Americans – like many other Americans – have embraced an assimilation process that requires a forgetfulness of ethnic roots and a misleading Anglicized version of the ongoing conflict in Ireland. I was one of those assimilated ones, learning nothing of my Irish heritage from my family, or from schools and universities, until I was forced to confront my identity in 1968. This is a story of how assimilation can go too far, and why. It is a story of recovering invisible roots, opening closets in our consciousness, in order to become fuller, more grounded, human beings, able to assimilate not only into the highest levels of the English-speaking world but also the depths of the impoverished, ex-colonial world from which we come.

I am thankful to Niamh Flanagan and Dr Robbie McVeigh for their steadfast personal support as I reconstructed this Irish past. Both are independent Irish republicans, from Fermanagh and Omagh respectively, who live in Northern Ireland. They arrived at their proud Irish identities from "the two traditions," a euphemistic term for colonialist (unionist and usually Protestant) and colonized (nationalist and usually Catholic). My gratitude goes as well to Dr Garrett O'Connor, of Derry and Los Angeles, a therapist with years of experience in addressing the phenomenon of personal and collective denial of the past. And to Peter Quinn, once the speechwriter for Mario Cuomo and author of the novel *The Banished Children of Eve*, for the elegant insights and support he has given. Also to John Waters, Nell McCafferty and Mary Moore, historians Andrew Wilson, John Duffy Ibson, Terry Golway, David Lloyd, Eric Foner, and Kerby Miller, the artist Trisha Ziff, poets Eavan Boland and Nuala Ni Dhomhnaill, novelists James Carroll and Sean Kenny, actors Gabriel Byrne and Fionualla Flanagan, and writer-commentators Tim Pat Coogan and Luke Gibbons, who have helped me understand the consequences of colonialism and the Famine on Irish identity. Thanks to Patricia Harty, the Irish-born editor of *Irish America*, a magazine which has done wonders to chronicle Irish American achievements and history. I am also appreciative of numerous government officials and sources in Washington, Dublin, Belfast, and London, including Senator George Mitchell, the Hon. Marjorie "Mo" Mowlam, and the family of the late Robert F. Kennedy, Jr. The former Northern Ireland editor of the *Irish Times*, Deaglan de Breadun, provided me with candid and independent analysis of the peace process. The researchers at the West Belfast Economic Forum – Charlie Fisher, Fionna McIlduff, Caroline Nolan, Denis O'Hearn, and Mike Tomlinson – were always helpful with original data. So was the staff of the political section of the Belfast Linen Hall Library. The editors of the *Andersonstown News*, Máirtín Ó Muilleoir and Robin Livingston, were always generous with insight and support. Thanks also to Mike Davis for his comments on the manuscript at a critical stage, and to Colin Robinson, who had confidence in the project from the start. Amy Scholder, my editor at Verso, walked into my life at just the right moment with encouragement, empathy, and a proposal for organizing the manuscript properly. Pat Harper and Jane Hindle, also at Verso, did superb jobs as well in editing and organizing the material. They made the book happen. Thanks as well to my assistant in Sacramento, Mary Burbidge.

There are many others to thank whose views are quoted or profiled in the pages herein. To all those in the throes of bringing a just peace to Northern Ireland, those in Belfast, Derry, and south Armagh with whom I spent countless hours during fifteen visits since 1993, my deepest thanks and hopes that this book will tell a story that challenges the conventional media narratives. I have benefited deeply from being around the likes of Tom Hartley, Gerry Adams, Martin McGuinness, Danny Morrison, Bairbre de Brún, Laurence McKeown, Deirdre McManus, Don Mullin, Inez McCormack, Mitchel McLaughlin, and Rita O'Hare. To the staff of the Tyrone Guthrie Centre at Annaghmakerrick, my thanks for the power generator during those dark and freezing nights while I finished the final draft. Thanks to my family – my wife Barbara, son Troy, daughter Vanessa, and new son Liam – for accompanying me on this journey into the borderlands of our identity. And to all my lost ancestors from the land of Cuchulainn to the fields of Wisconsin, so they may be remembered in dignity.

Tom Hayden
Los Angeles, California
June 2001

PART I

Irish on the Inside

To be the present of the past. To infer the difference
with a terrible stare. But not feel it. And not know it.

Eavan Boland, Irish poet[1]

I think they are hoping we will just give up on this and go away,
but we can't. All this talk of peace is good, but it makes people
want to forget what the RUC have done. The Patten Commission
are supposed to investigate the RUC but don't want to hear. How
can you learn from the past if you're not told what they have
done?

Diane Hamill, sister of Robert Hamill, kicked to
death by loyalists in Portadown, 1997[2]

In the coming generation it is likely that those persons who have
the fewest conventional Irish attachments will become the most
conscious of their Irish heritage.

Daniel Patrick Moynihan, 1963[3]

Prologue

"White, non-Hispanic." That was my designation on the year 2000 United States census form. Angrily, I penciled over the box (and one marked "other") and wrote in: "Irish, born in the United States, American citizen." I don't know if my form was counted or cast into a reject file. But I didn't want my census label to be "white, non-Hispanic" and I shuddered at the thought that the identity of the Irish could be whited out, so to speak, by checking this bureaucratic box. While some historians were writing about "how the Irish became white," I wanted more white people to become Irish, and non-white people were welcome to Irishness, too.

Or whatever hyphenated description that best identifies the hybrid blend of culture, race, and history that says who we are. "White ethnic" won't do, and nor will "Anglo." WASPs, of course, are never called "ethnics" because their tradition is still considered the foundation of core values. They remain the standard by which the assimilation of the rest of us is judged. To be "white ethnic" provides the illusory self-esteem and privileges that flow from whiteness, but remains a lesser category of identity below WASP predominance. White ethnics don't make the Social Register. Their tribes are too swarthy, their blood too hot. If the US is no longer "a Protestant nation for a Protestant people" (to borrow a one-time Unionist Party slogan for Northern Ireland), WASPs still dominate the citadels of power and define elite pedigrees. Of fifty-three American presidents, all but one – John F. Kennedy – have been white male Protestants. All our vice presidents have been white male Protestants. In our national immigrant myth of the melting pot, numerous presidents are celebrated as Irish (and others, like Richard Nixon, are forgotten Irishmen), but all of those (except Kennedy) were Scots-Irish Protestant descendants of Britain's Ulster plantation.

I was born a white American, first generation middle class. Middle American, Middle West too. I can't remember how I became self-consciously white, or how I was imprinted with such vivid stereotypes of people of color. My parents sent me to a Catholic grade school in the fifties, when pundits claimed that all religions were blending into a new creed of "Americanism." My parents, intent on becoming postethnic, never mentioned their Irish roots or the pain concealed in these genealogies.

Then the sixties erupted, and this cultural consensus was challenged by a succession of movements reclaiming stolen and closeted identities they considered more real. At first, it was the Negroes who redefined themselves as black, then African American; soon after, the Hispanics became chicanos, then Latinos. Then women claimed sisterhood. American Indians became native Americans, then indigenous, then tongva. Asians transformed into subidentities such as Pacific Islanders. Homosexuals redefined themselves as gays, lesbians, transsexuals, queers. I was none of these, and as these rebels recaptured identities of their own, the assimilated American identity proudly constructed by my parents was hollowed out and near collapse. After a decade in the civil rights movement, I associated being "white" with either supremacy or emptiness. Then, in 1968, accused of being less than a red-blooded American by the authorities, having been beaten up and indicted in Chicago, having been targeted for "neutralization" by J. Edgar Hoover, I saw marchers in Northern Ireland singing "We Shall Overcome" and, in an epiphany, discovered that I was Irish on the inside.

This is the story of my struggle to understand what it means to be Irish in America, which is also my discovery of what it means to be an American. It is an autobiography of an identity, one that was lost through assimilation and found only after I realized assimilation lacked meaning. It is meant as a contribution to the debates on multiculturalism in the USA as this country evolves towards a demographic majority of non-white, non-Anglo Saxon people. Finally, it is a reflection on being Irish in an age of US-led globalization that threatens to assimilate Ireland itself.

Liberal historian Arthur Schlesinger and conservatives like William Bennett fear the unraveling of America in the face of what they call a new ethnic tribalism. In such views, the secret ingredient holding together American civilization is "putting the past behind us," forgetting bitter racial memories, trading in our original ethnicity for a new American one, as smoothly as we buy a new model automobile. Even when a Colin Powell or Michael Dukakis emerges on the national scene, they are obliged to explain their racial or ethnic past as a stepping stone preparing them for Americanism. Like John Kennedy in 1960, they must attend all the right institutions, such as Harvard or West Point; they have the proper zip code, such as Georgetown or Cambridge; they are vetted by a blue-blooded WASP such as Warren Christopher or the senior George Bush. The result is the appearance of racial or gender diversity in the cabinet or in corporate boardrooms, but it's old-school at the core.

Others think multiculturalism is only about the inclusion of racial minorities and women, and therefore white groups like the Irish are excluded. Because whiteness is privileged, according to this argument, the Irish don't count in the ranks of the underrepresented, a category limited to people of color. This division of white from nonwhite also ignores Jews, Italians, Armenians, and others whose histories include racial profiling, repression, or genocide. All whites are "honkies." Because Irish Americans and the Irish have discriminated against blacks and immigrants, they forfeit the right to be considered a subject people themselves. Thus, when the Dublin band the Commitments, in Roddy Doyle's novel of the same name, declare themselves "black and proud" as "the niggers of Europe," they are only deluded white men seeking to appropriate an identity not their own.[4]

I propose an alternative to both of these perspectives. In the first place, for thousands of years the Irish were never considered white or privileged. Noted British authorities and popular commentators described the Irish as subhuman, apelike. The Irish "became white" in America by virtue of voting rights that Africans did not have, but at the same time they were subjected systematically to second-class treatment amounting to racial profiling. The Irish have been both victims and victimizers on the basis of race. Their racial attitudes have been aggravated by their class position as competitors with minorities at the bottom of the ladder. Their racism grew with their assimilation. The history of antiracist Irish and Irish American rebels, moreover, has been minimized or erased from the assimilation story. The Irish experience is therefore invaluable for examining how racial attitudes are formed, not from a genetic disposition but from particular conditions, like a virus needing a host culture. Because the Irish harbor a racial memory, however fogged by amnesia, of what it means to be treated as nonhuman, there still remains the possibility of Irish solidarity with people of color. When the Irish leave whiteness, there goes the neighborhood. America will become a community of ethnicities, no longer a white society with minorities.

Vivid media models of the desired role for assimilated Irish Americans are portrayed in films such as *Patriot Games* and *The Devil's Own* where Irish Americans representing law and order thwart the revolutionary designs of the IRA. The character Jack Ryan in Tom Clancy's *Patriot Games* makes the point explicitly: proud but assimilated Irish Americans are "the glue that holds society together." In other words, assimilation has invigorated America with new patriots while at the same time dissolving the ancient bonds of revenge and violence that have always bedeviled the Irish. The irony is that popular films commonly portray a multicultural America – with police and intelligence agencies led by Irish Americans, African Americans and women – against new alien scapegoats, most often narco-terrorists or shadowy Arab fanatics.

I take pride in what Thomas Keneally calls "the triumph of the Irish in the English-speaking world,"[5] but I would dispute any notion that our Irish destiny is to mimic and outachieve the English. To be genuinely Irish is to challenge WASP dominance and to assimilate ourselves not only into advanced Western societies but also into the nonwhite, non-English-speaking world. That the Irish are white and European cannot erase the experience of our having been invaded, occupied, starved, colonized, and forced out of our homeland. This history of our degradation is not a shame to conceal or shovel into a dustbin. It is a reminder that while some might believe Irish Americans fit snugly into the "emerging Republican majority," Irish America's history includes ties to radical labor movements, the liberal wing of the Democratic Party, Catholic draft resisters, and crusaders for human rights in Central America. The history of oppression is not a burden to erase for our children, but a powerful source of energy to use as we face the twenty-first century.

Of course there is no such thing as a "pure" Irish person. As a result of invasions and emigrations, we are a mixture of blood and culture from all over the European continent and perhaps beyond. Such inter-mingling caused James Connolly, the trade unionist and leader of the Easter 1916 uprising, to link his nationalism with internationalism: "Let no Irishman throw a stone at the foreigner; he may hit his own clansman. Let no foreigner revile the Irish; he may be vilifying his own stock."[6]

Thomas Cleary, in his "In Search of the Irish Soul," notes that "the original Irish culture is older than the English or even imperial Roman cultures" and is embedded in legends going back to Greek Scythia, to nomads "in contact with both Asiatic and European cultural basins." The whole history, as narrated in the fifth-century Book of Invasions, appears to be one of "migrations and amalgamations" producing an awareness by the Irish that "dispersal is not a recent event or an anom-alous condition, but a primal theme and recurrent experience . . . [The] poignancy of the human condition reminds the wearied soul that all life on earth is exile from our origin."[7]

Being Irish, therefore, is a "continuity of consciousness" flowing from multiple, migratory streams, of dreaming, of remembering, as much as it is a literal genealogy. The epic heroes of James Joyce, for example, are Stephen Daedelus, who bears an ancient Greek name, Leopold Bloom, a Jew, and Molly Bloom, from Spanish Gibraltar. In the continuum of Irish consciousness, the most characteristic abiding experience is the struggle to maintain an independent spirit and culture against oppres-sion, exile and "colonization of the mind." In his works *The Druids* and *The Celtic Empire*, Peter Beresford Ellis compares this threat of Irish ethnocide to that of the American Indians.[8]

This latent consciousness is most manifest where the Irish language is spoken, where Celtic spirituality flourishes (both outside or inside insti-tutional churches), where traditional music is played, and where resistance to British rule is a way of life. In the middle ground on this continuum of identity – the postcolonial – the Irish consciousness becomes modified as people blend or identify with non-Irish (British, WASP, and European) governing structures or cultural norms. The modified culture is less independent, more sentimental, at times so Anglicized that the adherents are labeled "West Brits." At the dead end of the Irish continuum are many Irish Americans, who identify Irishness as a heritage filled with nostalgia but little more. They are interested in family trees, they celebrate St Patrick's Day, they make self-deprecating jokes, they believe it is Irish to drink and, when they visit Ireland, they explore pubs, graveyards, scenic attractions, and avoid the North as a frightening reminder of how lucky they are to be Yanks.

A central theme of this book is that the most independent Irish consciousness is rooted in the North of Ireland (known officially as Northern Ireland), where the ancient and enduring conflict between Irish nationalism and British colonialism is most stark. Irish Americans, for example, should visit Belfast, Derry and Crossmaglen to find their deepest cultural roots, not simply the Blarney Stone. Instead, the North is erased from the tourist's map of Ireland as alien and forbidding, trapped in ancient quarrels. Instead a new Ireland, one more civilized, more European, is offered as the modern touchstone of Irish identity. A popular book extolling this "new Ireland" at great length, for example, manages to avoid a single reference to the North, as if it is a leper colony.[9]

Admittedly, this is a simplified overview. For example, about 900,000 people born and raised in Northern Ireland identify themselves as "British." One of their wall murals in east Belfast proclaims "Irish Out!" a puzzling proclamation to the visitor not familiar with basic identity distinctions. These 900,000 people are self-described Ulster unionists and loyalists, who trace their roots to the English military invasions and Scottish Presbyterian land seizures (the Ulster plantation) of centuries ago. To honor this coexistence, the North is often described as a place of "two traditions," Catholic/nationalist and Protestant/unionist. The "two traditions" formula is meant to convey respect to both sides of the divide, but it also smooths over the fact that the unionists represent the colonial tradition, while the nationalists are the colonized.

Unionists in Northern Ireland occupy a role similar in some respects to threatened and privileged white people in America. To identify with the Union with Britain – as with whiteness – is to embrace economic, political, and cultural advantage. Such a narrow definition of Britishness clashes with traditions of democracy, liberty, and dissent in which Protestants have played important historic roles. If and when unionism identifies with those nationalist democratic traditions, coexistence between the "two traditions" will become more viable. It is not clear how people who define themselves as British will ever feel comfortable in Irish skin, any more than white people will ever feel comfortable as equals of nonwhite people. But if they do, the Northern Irish Protestants could contribute significantly to breaking the narrow and conservative Roman Catholic structures in which many northern Catholics have taken refuge.

But peace and equality will be achieved only if those who identify as British in Northern Ireland and those who identify as white in Irish America reappraise their roots; if not voluntarily, then perhaps they will do it out of necessity. Northern Ireland will eventually have a nationalist and Catholic majority, as the USA will soon have a nonwhite majority. The question for unionists in the North and whites in America is whether to cling at all costs to a structure of privilege, unleashing a backlash against the inevitable, or to accommodate to or even embrace a new world brought about by demographic change and democracy.

My great-grandparents were Irish Famine immigrants to America, a fact I never was told. They left behind other relatives of mine whose names I will never know, who died of the diseases of colonialism, fever and starvation. Others survived, but wept to the heavens when they watched their children sail off to America. Their mournful keening reminded a visitor, the freed slave Frederick Douglass, of the "wild notes" of African mothers during the slave trade.[10]

The native Irish were subject to a centuries-long racism, based not on skin color but on an analysis of their racial nature. This mentality was expressed thus by *The Times* of London in 1847, during the worst of the Famine, or Great Hunger, of the 1840s: "by the inscrutable but invariable laws of nature, the Celt is less energetic, less independent, less industrious than the Saxon. This is the archaic condition of his race."[11] During the seventeenth century, when the English "transported" tens of thousands of Irish to American colonies and to Barbados, a Puritan broadside declared that the Irish were descended from "maneaters," the "very offal of men," the "dregs of mankind." The Puritan sword should be "cursed" if not "drunk with Irish blood."[12]

Two centuries before the Great Hunger of the 1840s these Irish came to the Americas as indentured servants and slaves. The distinction between these forms of degradation, which blurred in practice, was that the first were in a bondage which they could theoretically end by means of their wages – by using their wages to pay off their indentures – while the slaves were permanent property. Indentured servants could not leave their plantations without a pass, could not marry without an owner's permission, could not vote, and could be sold, gambled away, or used as security on a loan. Any children born out of wedlock or in poverty could be bonded to an owner until the age of twenty-one. According to African-American historian Lerone Bennett, Irishmen were sold in North Carolina for thirty-five barrels of turpentine in the 1640s.[13] In 1714, the prominent Boston merchant Samuel Sewall placed an advertisement in the local newspaper selling

> several Irish maid servants time
> most of them for five years one
> Irish man servant who is a good
> Barber and wiggmaker, also four
> Or five likely Negro boys.[14]

As Thomas Addis Emmet – who, we shall see, was my namesake – wrote later, these Irish were "sent abroad into slavery in the West Indies, Virginia and New England, that they might thus lose their faith and all knowledge of their nationality, for in most instances even their names were changed."[15] They were branded with the initials of the ships that transported them, which in some cases were the same ships that carried African slaves to the West Indies. Some became runaway slaves with the Africans and natives in southern swamps and forests. In the West Indies in 1686, they conspired with African slaves to seize the islands, and were charged with "being concerned with or privy to an intended rising of negroes to destroy all their masters and mistresses." They were among thirty-six alleged leaders who were captured, hung, drawn, and quartered.[16]

George Washington was among those who bought white indentured servants, likely including Irishmen, among the 80,000 imported by Virginians alone during the Colonial period. The offenses that led to their being transported included stealing bread, joining early trade unions, being members of secret societies, or being anti-social types defined in Elizabethan law as "rogues and vagabonds . . . Schollers going about begging . . . minstrels . . . juglers . . . tynkers . . . pedlers . . . [and] wandering persons." All were rounded up and shipped to the colonies as His Majesty's Seven Year Passengers.[17]

Another wave of Irish, mostly Presbyterian, came to America in the late eighteenth century in flight from religious persecution. The swelling ranks of these "wild Irish" (as they were described on the floor of the US Congress), including rebellious United Irishmen, so threatened the Anglophile Federalists that the Alien and Sedition Acts were rushed into law. In a famous denunciation, Representative Harrison Gray Otis in 1797 declared that he did not "wish to invite hordes of wild Irishmen, nor the turbulent and disorderly of all parts of the world, to come here with a view to disturb our tranquility."[18]

But it was the Great Hunger that created Irish America, or at least Catholic Irish America, as two million people began a forced exodus in the 1840s that did not abate for decades. It was the largest population upheaval of nineteenth-century Europe. According to one famine expert, "in no other famine in the world was the proportion of people killed as large as in the Irish famines in the 1840s."[19]

This was the story I was never told. In the apt phrase of an old friend, the writer Paul Cowan, about growing up Jewish, I was an "orphan in history."[20] My parents never told me of their grandparents' traumatic coming to America. I don't know if they themselves were aware of it, for they died before I knew what questions to ask. Often the Irish are described as "burdened by history," but there are millions like myself whose greater burden is amnesia. For these Irish Americans, the Atlantic was an ocean of silence. To be sure, there were those who remembered, and their memory became rebellion. But even today there are thousands of unmarked Famine graves under the celebrated green fields of Ireland,

and the assimilation of Irish America has been achieved through either forgetting or the sentimental rewriting of the past.

Experiencing amnesia as a coping mechanism is not unique to the Irish. To my surprise, in the immediate years after World War Two many Jewish Americans experienced a similar reluctance to face the trauma of the Holocaust. And, according to the historian Charles Johnson, "in the black communities for many years after emancipation there was great shame and embarrassment about the memory of enslavement. Rather than admit and accept the past, children were raised to deny their slave bloodlines."[21] Interviewing African American students at Emory College in 2001, I found the same response. "We have been raised to believe that other, lower types of blacks were slaves, while our families were not," was a typical comment. "It's about shame, and about feeling weak if you were made into a slave," was another.

I focus on the Irish Famine of the 1840s because of its impact on my own history and that of Irish America. But before that famine there were other famines, and other brutal invasions from the Anglo-Normans in 1169 to Oliver Cromwell in 1649, disasters that tore apart the world of my ancestors, even threatening its survival. There were Irish uprisings as well, failures that became a tradition of courage. Ireland survived, but even today its population is half that of 150 years ago. If we concentrate on the Famine of the 1840s in this long-suffering context, the question is, Why is the trauma so forgotten, or supplanted by the comforting melting-pot mythology of Irish triumph? (Why, for that matter, was the genocide of the American Indian rationalized in the myth of American democracy?) There is a human need to block the pain, not transfer it to one's children. There is survivor guilt, the *Sophie's Choice* syndrome. There is complicity as well: the Irish gentry benefited from the Famine, which exterminated a class – the Irish-speaking landless peasantry – more than the Irish as a race. But power also is operative in the neglecting of this history. The power to oppress others remains insecure without the power to impose forgetting.

Ireland's first Famine museum, a modest facility in remote County Roscommon, opened only in the 1990s, just in time for the 150th anniversary of Black '47, remembered as the worst of the Famine years.

Almost a century had passed before the Irish government ordered a folk history to be recorded of the Famine before its last remaining survivors passed away. There was virtually no Irish academic or published intellectual work on the Famine until 1962, when Ms Cecil Woodham-Smith, the Irish daughter of a colonial general, published *The Great Hunger, Ireland 1845–1849*, which unexpectedly became a best-seller.[22]

Despite its immense popularity in Ireland, Woodham-Smith's book was debunked by a generation of academics who became known as "revisionists," who sought to revise a folkloric nationalism, taught by the Christian Brothers, that the Famine was a case of England's genocidal attitudes towards Irish Catholics. If there was any legitimacy to this revisionism, it was to transport the Famine story from mythic memory to the framework of academic debate and research. But little if any original academic research was published from the 1930s until the Troubles of the 1960s. The real thrust of revisionism was "a kind of intellectual counterinsurgency," in the phrase of the eminent journalist Tim Pat Coogan.[23] Revisionism was designed to discredit the nationalist claim of genocide as opined in the fiery nineteenth-century tract of the exiled Fenian John Mitchel, *The Last Conquest of Ireland (Perhaps)*. Mitchel's charge was that millions of Irish died or emigrated because of "hunger in the midst of abundance," and he concluded that while "the Almighty indeed sent the potato blight . . . the British created the Famine."[24] The academic counterinsurgency was necessary even one century later to discredit the rationale for revolutionary violence by the IRA, for if the British were brutal, indifferent colonialists, public sympathy would tolerate armed struggle. Woodham-Smith's *The Great Hunger*, according to one revisionist account, provoked too much "ungoverned passion" in Ireland.[25] The British were in fact "genuinely good men" who simply failed "to act in a generous manner" because of the laissez-faire "conventions of the larger society," declared the foreword to the revisionist classic by R. Dudley Edwards and T. Desmond Williams, *The Great Famine: Studies in Irish History* (1956).[26] As late as 1986, during the height of the war in the North, an insipid text by the historian Mary Daly concluded that "it does not appear appropriate to pronounce in an unduly critical fashion on the limitations of previous generations."[27] The Irish had made too many earlier appeals to "British generosity," Daly opined, and thus London's "goodwill eroded." The argument has resonance today for those whose grievance goes like this: If those whining Irish (blacks) hadn't tested our patience by demanding the dole (welfare) we might have been more generous. "Anti-Irishness is a core part of British culture," argues Dr Robbie McVeigh, a Protestant from Omagh. At its worst, he says, "academia in Ireland is still like a colonial Big House . . . it often prefers to deconstruct pop songs or provide an analysis of James Joyce's favorite ice cream than engage with the huge problems of poverty, homelessness, and unemployment that structure contemporary Irish life."[28]

While this cultural amnesia blanketed Ireland in the twentieth century, a parallel academic lack of interest was evident in the schools and universities I attended. The Irish people were subjects of derision and racism for many of the great thinkers we studied. Edmund Spenser had advised Queen Elizabeth in 1598 that "Until Ireland can be famished, it cannot be subdued."[29] Malthus wrote in 1826 that "we should facilitate . . . the operations of nature in producing this mortality . . . and if we dread the frequent visitation of the horrid form of famine, we should . . . encourage . . . forms of destruction [for example] make the streets narrower, crowd more people into houses, and count on the return of the plague."[30] Nathaniel Hawthorne labeled the Irish immigrants "maggots"; Ralph Waldo Emerson said the Irish, along with Africans and Chinese, could never "occupy any high place in the human family." Instead, he wrote, "before the energy of the caucasian race all the other races have quailed and done obeisance."[31]

When I was at the University of Michigan in the sixties, a historical text by Samuel Eliot Morrison taught that the Irish had "added surprisingly little to American life, and almost nothing to American intellectual life." Similarly, in the influential 1963 book *Beyond the Melting Pot*, Daniel P. Moynihan disparaged the Irish culture by saying that two generations in the slums of New York killed any respect for learning "if it ever existed."[32] In a statement perhaps more about himself than about the Irish, Moynihan lamented the failure of Irish Americans to "attain a degree of cultural ascendancy" which he attributed to their parochial and peasant-rooted attitudes. Accordingly I decoupled what was intellectually inspiring from what was Irish. When I read and re-read one of the most influential books of my life, James Joyce's *A Portrait of the Artist as a Young Man*, I understood it only in the context of my Catholic upbringing, as a struggle between individual freedom and Church authority, not as an insight into the Irish soul.

School curriculums in the USA continued to be devoid of Irish content throughout the 1990s. How else to explain the recent *Oxford History of the United States* by Joy Hakim, which taught public school students that the Irish, like the Germans and the Chinese, "are ambitious, or they wouldn't have made the big journey to the 'New World'. They are the kind of people who don't mind moving – and moving again once they are in America." (Former British prime minister Margaret Thatcher repeated the stereotype in a television interview in 2001: "The Irish are used to movements of population – if the Northern population wants to be in the South, why don't they just move over there?")[33] Ambition? My God, what a plucky people we must have been. If there was an ambition, it was to survive, even as animals, and if we kept moving it was because of those signs saying "No Irish Need Apply." Nevertheless, the Irish stereotype was integral to the dominant image of America, expressed by Lynne Cheney, wife of vice president Dick Cheney, when she was director of the National Endowment for the Humanities under Ronald Reagan in the 1980s. Of the sanitized American immigrant story, she said, "I find it hard to imagine that there's a story more wonderful than being driven by the desire to worship freely, to set off across that ocean, to make a home out of this wild and inhospitable land."[34] In this rhapsody, the Irish were driven by "desire," not by starvation, and not by colonialism. They were not exiles but emigrants. Who, after all, would "desire" to live in Ireland? And so they "set off across the ocean" like a World Cup team, not like emaciated victims in the overcrowded holds of coffin ships. And upon arrival, it's best to forget they were revisited by new fevers, hungers, and mental disorders in squalid tenements; Cheney would have us substitute the mellow vision of settling down at "home," ignoring the additional untidy fact that the land already was inhabited by others, and the Irish immigrants would have to inflict what was inflicted on them to push out the "wild and inhospitable" Indian tribes.

So furious was I at reading the sanitized, romanticized material in the *Oxford History* that in 1997 I prepared California legislation requiring that references to the Irish Famine be included in the next cycle of social science texts. Lobbyists for the British government immediately showed up in Sacramento to protest that there be no teaching of the Famine as genocide, a demand that was surfacing in several other states. I agreed, it being enough for me that students debate whether it was genocide, a well-intended catastrophe, or a mishap of history. At least our trauma would be recognized alongside those of African Americans, the Jews, the Armenians, and others who had demanded a place in classroom texts. As I lobbied for the bill, however, I noticed that many of my colleagues, including my closest allies, shook their heads, chuckled, asked why the Irish didn't just go fishing (as if the Irish peasants had oceangoing craft or access to the landed gentry's salmon streams). They universally accepted the notion that "the potato famine," as they called it, was a freak accident of nature rather than the consequence of poverty, land-lessness, and colonial rule. In the end, however, they voted for the bill. Then Governor Pete Wilson, harboring presidential aspirations, signed the measure and immediately took his first trip to Ireland, where he took credit for the legislation and claimed his newfound ancestry. Wilson was a perfect example of the strangely disconnected Irish American, claiming his own roots among Irish immigrants to America with genuine feeling as well as for political gain, while at the same time campaigning with an anti-immigrant television commercial showing Mexicans cross-ing the US border, with the inflammatory headline "They're Coming" emblazoned across the footage. This dissociation between past and pres-ent was more than political opportunism, it was the outcome of what the American educational system and media had promoted.

California's universities were equally barren of Irish studies, in contrast to the academic incorporation of programs in gender, African American,

Latino, Asian American, Native American, and gay/lesbian studies. In response to my letter of inquiry, UC Berkeley touted its Celtic Studies Program, which had awarded just fifteen bachelor degrees between 1997 and 2000. The program, incidentally, was within the Department of Scandinavian, with a focus on language and literature (including "advanced Breton"). There were no other Celtic Studies programs in the nine-campus University of California system, but there were scattered courses on Joyce, Yeats, Swift, and Old Irish. Aside from a rare visiting lecturer, there were no courses on the Famine or Irish American history, and virtually none on contemporary Irish nationalism and the Troubles – this at a time when the Irish conflict was on the front pages as a major foreign policy focus of the Clinton Administration. By comparison, in the 1998–99 academic year, there were bachelor degree programs in women studies on eight of the nine UC campuses, African American studies on six campuses, Latino studies on eight, and Asian studies on eight.[35] Why the lack of Irish studies? After all, not only did Northern Ireland become a major focus of US foreign policy in the 1990s, but Gerry Adams became an international celebrity, Seamus Heaney won the Nobel prize for literature, John Hume and David Trimble shared a Nobel for their peace efforts, and *Riverdance*, U2 and *Angela's Ashes* enjoyed mass audiences. Was this not enough to attract academic attention? Clearly not. The presumption, I suppose, was that the Irish were already absorbed in Western civilization as a whole and therefore needed no special attention, or perhaps were an asterisk to the body of Greek, Roman, and British thought known as "the canon." Father Andrew Greeley recounts the story of an academic colleague who went to the US Office of Education to ask for funding for Irish studies. Rebuffed, the scholar was told that it was "Because the Irish don't count."[36]

In short, the 135,000 students annually enrolled by the University of California system, our state's best and brightest, who will go on to high positions in government, business, and the professions, will do so thinking, if they think about it at all, that the Irish are a quaint, fiddle-playing, hard-drinking people who might be irrelevent today were it not for their famous authors, many of whom were drunks themselves. If that seems a stretch, consider the unconsciously bigoted performance of the Stanford University marching band during a football game with arch-rival Notre Dame in October 1997. The band staged a parody of the Famine featuring one "Seamus O'Hungry," described to the fans as the representative of "a sparse cultural heritage [that] consisted only of fighting, then starving" and producing "stinking drunks."[37] The band, which refused to apologize for what it believed to be "funny" to many Irish people, was banned from future games with Notre Dame for three years.

The same stereotyping of the Irish in popular culture was evident in the Hollywood version of Frank McCourt's best-selling autobiography *Angela's Ashes*, in which a Limerick life of poverty, abuse, alcoholism, and seemingly permanent rain gives way to the movie's only scene with sunlight, as the young Frank McCourt sails into the New York harbor and sees the glowing Statue of Liberty. The luck of the Irish, it seems, is to become American. Similarly, Tim Pat Coogan's account of the Irish in America ends with the familiar story of John F. Kennedy at the Atlantic's edge, saying, "To think my grandfather came here from Ireland with nothing more than a pack upon his back."[38] This crediting of America for Irish success needs reappraisal. The lesson was that the Irish were able to prove their potential when given an opportunity in America which was denied them in Ireland. But the same story implied that the Irish could not and would not succeed in their own land, but only by leaving it behind. "The adoration of JFK and Grace Kelly reinforced the self-hatred – you had to get out of Ireland to be rich, successful, and have two kids," the Irish researcher Niamh Flanagan once said.[39]

But it wasn't only the Irish stereotyping that gave *Angela's Ashes* its appeal. Along with its sequel *'Tis*, it remained a best-seller in America longer than any other book about Ireland because the writing is pitch-perfect in capturing the simultaneous melancholy and humor of Irish storytellers. Frank McCourt may represent in part the tradition of the stage Irish since, as Moynihan once noted, there is "a touch of Sambo in the professional Irishman; he was willing to be welcomed on terms that he not forget his place."[40] But there was something deeper occurring in the reception to the book: the ability of Frank McCourt to step out of the closet and honestly tell a story of secret shame and poverty, and the hunger of the audience to receive it. This level of candor might have been embraced at an Alcoholics Anonymous meeting but not, until recent years, among the Irish American book-buying public. The same honesty is present in popular Irish novels on rape, abortion, domestic violence, and official hypocrisy such as Roddy Doyle's *The Woman Who Walked into Doors* (1996) and Edna O'Brien's *Down by the River* (1997).

Indeed, in the past five years there have been stunning signs that the Irish are emerging in greater confidence from 150 years of amnesia. In the 1990s they elected as Ireland's president a human rights lawyer, Mary Robinson, who spoke repeatedly about the Famine legacy, patronized the first Famine museum, visited Famine graves in Canada and the US, and wept openly on a state visit to famine-ridden Ethiopia. Her presidency seemed to symbolize a deeper thaw in the Irish. She was not alone in her personal interest in the Famine. During the period 1995–2000 more books were written about the Famine than in the previous century. In the same period, groups like U2 and the musical play *Riverdance* became global sensations. The musical not only united Ireland and its Diaspora, but revealed a new sensuality long hidden or repressed by the Catholic Church. The fabled Irish step dance, for example, was a legacy of post-Famine Church sexual morality that insisted on limiting the body's movement to below the knees. *Riverdance* unveiled and unbottled the sexual energy locked within the step dance, and freed an uninhibited dimension of the Irish soul. On opening night, Mary Robinson wept again, as did many Irish Americans, perhaps at feelings we did not know we harbored.

The emergence of a new Irish self-confidence was evident as well in the economic phenomenon dubbed the "Celtic Tiger," as the Irish Republic's economy for the first time grew more rapidly than England's, and the Republic replaced its dependency on London with a new role in the European Community. California's Silicon Valley began investing heavily in the Irish Republic, which became one of the world's leading centers of high-tech assembly. Ireland was not entirely comfortable riding this tiger, as we shall see. Suddenly Dublin was filled with BMWs and stockmarket capitalists, while unemployment, poverty, and drug addiction deepened in urban and rural districts. Racial violence flared against new immigrants from starving African nations. The toxic waste of the pharmaceutical and electronics industries polluted the rivers. Corruption scandals consumed most of the government's time and the media's attention. Moral questions were raised: What would happen to Irish spirituality and culture as the country became a platform for multinational corporations seeking an advantage in the European market? But none of these shadows eclipsed the fact that the Irish were finally building a modern competitive economy after nearly a century of a gnawing inferiority complex caused by the colonial legacy and reinforced by decades of emigration to Britain and the USA. Even many of the Irish in New York were returning home.

The greatest single factor in the thaw was the emergent peace process in Northern Ireland. Thirty years of war, euphemistically labeled the "Troubles," had cast multiple shadows over the Irish future. Investment in civilian employment was inhibited by the military conflict. So were tourism and community development in the North. But more important was the war's effect on the politics and culture of the island. Since the British-imposed partition in 1922, the Irish Republic had steadily evolved towards a concept of modern statehood that left behind the ancient conflict with England and its continuing manifestation in the North of Ireland. The Southern state developed a "national" interest in achieving a stability of its own. This required coexistence with the British state and a political and cultural distancing from Northern nationalists. The Southern Irish began internalizing the British stereotype of a North populated with primitive tribes, utterly alien from the civilized Dubliners who were busy becoming modern. This distancing was reinforced by a state censorship which prohibited any interviews with representatives of Sinn Féin or the Irish Republican Army. In time, the Republic became like Mexico, a nation-state wrapped in the rhetoric, symbols, anthems, and colors of the very revolution it had abandoned. Anyone, especially intellectuals, who seemed critical of this Southern drift, could be deemed a "sympathizer with IRA terrorists" and marginalized, even criminalized, as an enemy of the state. The chill extended across the sea as well, where the Irish American political establishment routinely denounced Sinn Féin and the IRA with a stridency comparable only to the McCarthy period of anticommunism in the fifties. Throughout this period, the US government consistently supported and cooperated with the British military establishment, viewing the North as an "internal affair" of the so-called United Kingdom of Britain and Northern Ireland. The United States, once a center of nationalist rebellion against precisely the same British occupation, now held London in an embrace which took precedence over such uncomfortable humanitarian issues as human rights' violations in Belfast.

But the peace process thawed these long-frozen equations. The peace process would end the demonizing of Northern republicans as nothing more than hooded terrorists. Leaders like Gerry Adams and Martin McGuinness could speak and be heard. Calls for investigations into British or loyalist violence could no longer be treated as fronting for the IRA. Mary Robinson could venture North and shake Gerry Adams's hand. So would President Clinton and, in time, prime minister Tony Blair. Restrictions by the American State Department on travel by Adams and Sinn Féin to the United States were lifted, thus allowing Irish Americans to have first-hand contact with representatives of an Irish nationalist cause which called out for completion.

Perhaps what was happening overall was a relaxation of the hardened personal and institutional habits built up to ensure Irish survival against the decimating tendencies of famine, eviction, emigration, and war, including civil war. The world was becoming a safer place for the Irish soul to emerge.

The Irish today, in America and at home, are somewhere between memory and forgetting. Amnesia and denial, whether self-induced or engineered by technicians of power, are being challenged by a rising hunger to reclaim a real identity free of hype, stereotype, and shame.

Che Guevara, C. Wright Mills, and the Problem of Split Identity

The effects of alienation from one's Irish identity are multiple and serious. First, it steadily reduces the number of Irish – or those who think of themselves as Irish – in the world. Second, the assimilation or decoupling process results in a minimal or conservative Irish identity, one reduced to St Patrick's Day parties, Irish police fraternities, and Catholic men's clubs. And finally, those of Irish descent who are activists, radicals, freethinkers, or secular liberals often feel divided, having to dissociate their moral and political views from being Irish, an ethnicity they consider irrelevant or reactionary. In the process, Irish identity steadily erodes to, at best, a sentimental link to an imaginary past. Thus, many sixties radicals who were Irish didn't think of their ethnicity as a strength, a rich tradition to draw upon, but as a legacy to escape and overcome. Take two examples who loomed large over the sixties: Ernesto "Che" Guevara and C. Wright Mills. Both were heroes of mine, both had closeted Irish identities, and both led lives that would be better understood if their Irishness had not been concealed from themselves and the world.

The great-grandfather of Che Guevara was Patrick Lynch, identified in Che's biographies only as having "fled from England to Spain," and from there to Argentina where he became a local governor. Why did he flee? No one has answered that question, but it likely was related to persecution for being Catholic or Irish or both. Che's paternal grandmother, Ana Lynch, born in California in 1868, was a "liberal and iconoclast," according to one historian. His father, Ernesto Guevara Lynch, may have been caught up in Catholic nationalism in Argentina. He was, according to Jorge Casteneda, "very eccentric," filled with phobias and superstitions. He was expelled from college to become a civil engineer whose projects repeatedly failed, as did his business ventures.[41] As for Che, his first girlfriend came from an Anglophile family. Che wore a dirty nylon shirt to dinners at their house and once called Winston Churchill "another ratpack politician" to their horror.[42] Che was an adventurer who traveled through Latin America on a motorcycle before he became engaged in revolutionary politics. His life as a global revolutionary, an internationalist, a diarist, an intellectual, and, finally, a martyr followed the arc of many Irishmen. In the end, Che was a transcendent individual without a country. He was not the first Latin American revolutionary of partial Irish descent, but Che was totally detached from his heritage. He once characterized his forebears as "members of the great Argentine cattle-raising oligarchy," nothing more. If Che instead had internalized and cited his Irish family's original flight from persecution, he still would have been primarily a Latin American revolutionary but he would also have been a living representative to young people like myself of what the hidden Irish heritage was about. Instead, he was viewed as an "other" from a radically different culture than our own (white) one.

C. Wright Mills was the American intellectual who had the single greatest impact on the New Left. He authored a series of books and tracts that explained the American power elite and the mostly white-collar society from which a majority of activists emerged. He tried to resurrect an idealistic Marxism from the bureaucratic clutches of Stalinist states. He was an individual of extreme and restless passion, engaged in endless polemics against complacent intellectuals, and who incidentally rode a motorcycle to his office at Columbia University. A typical Mills performance was described in a Columbia University student paper as follows: "Mills strides excitedly up and down the room . . . He pauses to glare at his towering bookcase. 'It's a writer's responsibility to orient modern publics to the catastrophic world in which they live,' he says. 'But he cannot do this if he remains a mere specialist. To do it at all, he's got to do it big!'" He collapsed and died of a heart attack in the prime of his life, in 1962.[43]

Mills was Irish in his origins and style. But as an iconoclastic American he replaced ethnic heritage as an explanatory category with issues of class, status, and power. Mills was a descendant of Irish Famine immigrants from County Leitrim. In a 1963 letter, Mills's mother described the family forebears – the Gallaghers and McGinnisses – not primarily as Irish but as Catholics "driven from

Ireland in 1840 by persecution from England on account of their religion."[44] They were seventeen years old when they arrived in Galveston Bay after a three-month voyage of "cold, hunger, storm and sickness." They then drove "through the wilderness" by oxen team to a small Irish settlement in south Texas. In all of Mills's work, he never discussed his Irish roots, except in a 1943 personal letter to his friend the sociologist Hans Gerth:

> Last Friday I was working at the office at night on motives chapter and sort of collapsed emotionally and "spiritually." For about two hours, I realized later, I just sat and stared at the row of books, with the light on in the office and the rest of the building all dark. It was the oddest feeling and I can't explain it. Like a trance, only all the time I was thinking about war and the *hopelessness of things*. It was as if you were thinking – yes, you have to use that word – with a *sequence of moods*. The polarity was probably between *helplessness* and *aggressiveness* and both were, I think, rather relished! Also for the first time, except in what was, explicitly at least, in fun, I had a self-image of being very *Irish*. I did not realize it at first but that came through very clearly. *I do not know why because I do not know anything about "the Irish"* and I have never, to my knowledge, been stamped as Irish by anyone particularly. Anyway, there I was alone, *helpless, aggressive, and Irish!* I think maybe it is all because of the *inarticulate feelings of indignation* that come up when I confront politics in any serious way and because I cannot locate and denounce (with all the energies I've available and eager for the job) such enemies as are available. Living in an atmosphere soaked in lies, the man who thinks, at least, that he knows some of the truth but would lose his job were he to tell it out and is not man enough to do it anyway . . . if such a man has built such a life around finding out the truth and being aggressive with it, *then he suffers*. I wrote a lot more, and even began a short story, or what might turn out to be one: here is a passage from some of that tripe . . . :

What happened was that the *self-distance and the use of self for objective work* which was usual with him had collapsed. It collapsed and he saw *another self* for a while. And what he saw was a political man. He had not known before that the *well of indignation* which had become his basic political feeling was masking such strong political urges . . .[45]

I have italicized the specifically Irish moods and Mills's ability to dissociate from them in this remarkable passage. It is regrettable that this was the only time in twenty-five years of writing that Mills contemplated his Irish identity. Clearly it was a "wellspring" of his indignation at "the hopelessness of things," and of his alternating moods of helplessness and aggression. A deeper understanding might have been medicine for his rootless, nomadic sense of loneliness. Instead his "psychology of the outlander," as noted by a biographer, was considered a Texas trait, not an Irish one. Mills was assimilated unconsciously, devoting his academic life to analyzing rootless, alienated individuals unable to connect their personal troubles to larger structures of power and oppression. His assimilation blocked his ability to see that their loss of ethnic roots, their own assimilation, not only prepared them for the mass society but prevented them from building identities able to resist its robotizing pressures. Except for a heavily academic dissertation on New York's Puerto Ricans in the labor movement (*The New Men of Power*, written with Gerth in 1948), Mills never addressed the issues of race and ethnicity, never wrote about the civil rights movement, apparently believing these issues to be secondary to class, status, and power. Though he wrote extensively of the personal "milieux" of individuals in mass society, the milieux lacked an ethnic ingredient that might have explained feelings of shame, inferiority, and helplessness. In this omission, he encouraged the tendency of the original New Left to ignore the ethnic or racial dimension of identity. It would have made an enormous difference if he had called for a New Left built not only on class but also on the radical strains in ethnic histories that were repressed by the manipulators of power. Many would have been inspired – or threatened – by the notion that Mills and Che Guevara had Irish souls.

What is an Irish Soul?

Part I of this book, *Irish on the Inside*, explores how the dynamics of assimilation into America and the modern world either repress or omit the Irish struggle to forge an independent nation and culture in the world. Why has so little about the Great Hunger been written or transmitted across the generations? Why has the struggle of republicans in the North of Ireland – including that of the Irish Republican Army – to complete the reunification of Ireland been subject to official censorship and to a stereotyping that borders on demonization? Why have Irish American rebels in the Molly Maguires, the Land League, the Fenians, the Wobblies, and twentieth-century movements for peace and justice been marginalized or erased from history? Does the loss of these Irish memories create an Irish American failure to connect with people of color and immigrants reliving elements of the Irish experience today? Does assimilation into a new social order require a masking that becomes permanent? Why are forgetting the past and "moving on" such important preconditions of being accepted?

Being absorbed into the assimilation process is not natural, nor is losing one's identity an accident. The disappearace of the Irish character has been sought for centuries. Usually it has been accomplished militarily, or as the result of the Famine and emigration; in America it has happened through planned assimilation. In my parents' youth, Harvard's president, Abbott Lawrence Lowell, declared that "what we need is not to dominate the Irish but absorb them." By becoming middle-class, Lowell argued, they would come "to share our sentiments." Lowell was clear that assimilation did not apply to "tribal Indians," "Chinese," or "negroes under all conditions," but only to "our own race, and to those people we can assimilate rapidly."[46] Unlike the Jews, the Irish were Christians who could become so merged into American culture that they would not be "distinguished as a class."[47] In addition to the racial and religious prejudice revealed in this prescription, note the casual elitism and arrogance that assumes that Irish culture has no intrinsic value worth saving or nurturing.

The story of the assimilation of Irish America told in this book revolves around a personal narrative: the loss of my own Irish roots in the process of assimilation, and their recovery in the search for identity in the sixties. The Ireland that I believe is repressed and forbidden in the assimilation process is the nationalist struggle in Northern Ireland, which I discuss in the second part of this book. My view is that the Irish character contains seeds of rebelliousness rather than conformity, of moral idealism rather than amoral materialism, of communal ethics rather than individualistic ones, of mysticism and even otherworldliness that challenge modernity. These qualities, like an ancient forest, should not be clearcut in the name of progress, to be replaced by a middle-class robo-culture and an "old country" that is marketed as a theme park for tourism with an economy of Laptop Men – the phrase is Tim Pat Coogan's – serving the global interest of American multinationals, and thus becoming assimilated into America's version of the New World Order.

In an age of globalization, the missionary modernizers ask why are small nations like Ireland important at all? Why not apply the melting-pot model to the future of the whole world? A responsible answer has to transcend narrow national chauvinism. It has to be based on the belief that the Irish culture, language, and identity have an intrinsic value expressed over thousands of years, and therefore a right to exist that cannot be annulled by any claimants to empire. Cultural diversity, like biological diversity, maintains the resources needed for a balanced life on earth.

Second, the next generation will have to assess and revise the creation stories of the Irish and the Irish Americans. These stories, as defined by Thomas Berry, constitute not only the written history but the deepest archetypes that shape the identity of individuals and nations. The Irish creation story is a contested one, with colonizers categorizing the native Irish as primitive and backward until "civilized" by outside powers. From a nationalist standpoint, on the other hand, the Irish experienced a golden age before they were sullied, impoverished, and brutalized by occupying powers. In any event, the creation story of the Irish nation is still being written in the continued unfolding of the so-called Troubles of the past three decades. Irish people and Irish Americans can participate in the resolving of this national story in the coming generation.

Creation stories involve controversies over matters of religion as well, as the bloody history of Ireland shows so clearly. But beyond the conventional Catholic–Protestant divide is another issue: the indigenous, pre-Christian spirituality of the early Irish. This longer-lasting tradition focused on the universe, on creation itself, on the inherent sacred quality of sun, moon, earth, forests, mountains, rivers, and other living things. The world of Newgrange, of supernatural beings, and of shamanic druids was replaced, though never eliminated, by the Christian world with its focus on guilt, redemption, and the afterlife. As John Muir, the great environmentalist, who was of Celtic origins and an exile from Puritanism, noted in the nineteenth century, the new image of God "became very much like an English gentleman [who] believes in the literature and language of England, is a warm supporter of the English constitution and Sunday schools and missionary societies."[48] Will the next generation resurrect, incorporate, and blend their indigenous spiritual heritage into the ethos of modern Christianity? Or will the rush to marketplace amorality eliminate the last traces of indigenous Irish spirituality and marginalize an already declining church?

Finally, the creation story of Irish America desperately needs rewriting. If we are to believe the conventional story, the Scots Irish fled to the New World, which they found surprisingly like Ireland: a wilderness filled with savages. A manifest destiny dictated that the primitive tribes yield to the planters who, in time, created a new nation-state led by a general who never told a lie. Later, Irish Catholics left their miserable, hopeless, and primitive conditions in the Old Country to fill the frontiers of the New World with fun-loving but industrious laborers who, by embodying the work ethic, lifted themselves by their bootstraps into the middle class and eventually elected one of their own as president. The truth, as this book will show, is otherwise. Continuing to cling to national creation stories that are untenable fairy tales profoundly undermines one's cultural identity. Yet Irish Americans, like all Americans, are expected to internalize these myths as a sign that they are well-adjusted.

Today's Irish Americans face a post-assimilation issue, just as the Irish Republic faces a postcolonial issue. If full assimilation can be defined as electing an Irish Catholic president, the Irish Americans have been assimilated for forty years. Should we not embrace our Americanism and forget the past? Should our Irish heritage be placed on the shelf, a kind of wistful background in our family portrait? Many of us think so or, worse, are so assimilated that we don't recognize the question. But many others maintain at least a sentimental attachment, and rising numbers have a kind of hunger for ethnic identity that Americanism cannot meet except superficially.

How should the Irish American soul be grounded? It is the contention of this book that assimilation, the understandable goal of Irish Americans seeking to survive in a hostile land, can never erase the need for roots. The ultimate design of assimilation, however, is to sever ethnic roots through a complex process of shame and denial, as if they contain no intrinsic worth. Therefore, while recognizing the historic benefit of assimilation, it becomes necessary for this next generation of Irish Americans to find its identity in the rediscovery of our most hidden roots. If we do so, we will realize that to assimilate must mean more than turning into an ethnic ornament in the English-speaking world. It means questioning our status as a "model minority" held out to others – always people of color – as an example of how the melting pot works. It means reassessing our racial identification with "whiteness." It means rejecting displays of self-hatred like drinking to prove ourselves Irish, rejecting the toleration and even perpetuation of anti-Irish stereotypes, and rejecting viewing Ireland as a theme park. In the new Irish revival, we must be deepening our ties with Irish nationalism, understanding why so many of our relations still raise their arms against English occupation, becoming involved in the peace process, and promoting economic and cultural regeneration for the Irish everywhere. Finally, a deeper assimilation will mean assimilation into the nonwhite world with whom we share a common experience of colonialism, starvation, poverty, and threats of extinction.

The only alternative to this reassessment will be our shallow incorporation into the Western establishment. Then we will lose the historic opportunity to play a meaningful role in the emergence of a multicultural America. Whatever the outcome of this reappraisal of who we are, it will affect not only the Irish but America and the world. There are too many of us for it not to.

Growing Up Unconscious

When I was growing up the priests never talked about the Famine. Even two weeks ago when I went to Mass, the priest was reading an encyclical on the Famine saying, "We're not trying to apportion blame, we're here to pray for those experiencing famine today." It was only when I went to Australia that I learned about the Famine. I visited distant family, and they showed me the death certificate of a man from Fermanagh who died in 1848. It made me really sad thinking of people back in Fermanagh living in wee holes separated from their families in Australia. It took six months for the letter to arrive from Ireland. When I realized the crap I was taught, it made me really angry. They wanted to colonize Van Dieman's Land and who better than the Coolies of the West?

Niamh Flanagan, County Fermanagh, 1998[49]

Just as many people avoid showing off their poor relations, the colonized in the throes of assimilation hides his past, his traditions, in fact all his origins which have become ignominious. . . . The first ambition of the colonized is to become equal to that splendid [colonial] model and to resemble him to the point of disappearing in him.

Albert Memmi[50]

. . . individuals, families or societies that willfully suppress their history will face a season of reckoning, one certain to arrive

obliquely, in a dark place, at a hostile hour, with consequences for
the innocent as well as for the conspirators.

William Kennedy[51]

Irishness did not evaporate in the United States, but instead was
forced underground, often retreating to the level of unconscious-
ness.

John Duffy Ibson[52]

My life is an exercise in learning to know what I don't know, and inquir-
ing why. My family ancestors lived in the borderlands of Ireland, in
Monaghan, south Armagh, Cavan and north Louth. Great megalithic
structures and caverns exist there as mute evidence of a disappeared
past. Long before the present partition was carved through these lands,
they were contested zones between the English Pale and the Gaelic world.
They were the lands of Cuchulainn, hero of the pre-Christian Irish epic
the *Tain Bo Cuailgne*. In the nineteenth century they were the homelands
of Olwells, Garitys (Geraghtys), McGees, Duceys, Foleys, Clintons,
McKennas, and Murrays who formed the matrix of the families from
which I descended. Hayden was my father's family name, Norman in
origin, Garity my mother's. In the Irish language they carry ghostly meanings that were never passed down to me until one day when they were
translated by an Irish friend. In Irish, he noted, "Hayden" is from
Ó hAodain which, deconstructed further, means "the person of the
flame," while Garity, originally Mac Garity or Mag Oireachtaigh, means
"the assembly man." What to make of this? While I don't believe destiny
is coded in a name, it is part of my repressed genealogy. We who wish to
know our ancestry are doomed to fragments, hints, associations, a birth
certificate here, an obituary there, a ship's log, a family tale. Poverty,
famine, and emigration take a toll on family records.

Landlords in those times organized "assisted passage" schemes to
remove people from their lands in order to replace them with the more
profitable cattle. The records of these immigrant families from Monaghan
remain buried in repositories in Northern Ireland where someday they

may be catalogued. What I know is that my great-grandparents took ships from Liverpool across the Atlantic, arrived mainly in Canada, and found their way to the farmlands of Wisconsin. Their death certificates list such occupations as farmer, day laborer, buttermaker, and railroad brakeman. My Irish great-grandfather, Thomas Emmet Hayden, was born in the year the Famine began, 1845, and married Alice Foley, who was three years younger than himself. Their son Thomas was born in 1868, just after the Civil War, and lived until 1941, a period spanning the industrial revolution and the post-Famine immigration of the Irish to America. That Thomas Hayden was a lawyer, tax assessor, justice of the peace, and director of the local Building and Loan Association in Milwaukee's Third Ward at a time when the Irish machines were ascendant. He married Mary Agnes Ducey, and their child, my father John Francis, was born in Milwaukee in 1906. Mary Agnes died suddenly when my father was five years old. My grandfather lived silently and alone until his passing in 1941, supporting his children but saying little that they remembered.[53]

On my mother's side, my great-grandfather was Emmet Owen Garity, who married Mary Ethel Olwell. He survived the coffin ships to land in Canada, perhaps at the quarantine island called Grosse Île in the St Lawrence River, where many thousands died from spending weeks in the squalid, overcrowded chambers of the ships. Some of the Garitys arrived in Caledon, not far from Toronto, where they awaited the chance to obtain land in the United States. Emmet finally came to pastoral Sullivan, Town 6 North, in Jefferson County, Wisconsin, which today sits time-lessly next to the interstate between Madison and Milwaukee. On April 30, 1853, Emmet Owen Garity paid $50 for forty acres of wooded lands, and gradually assembled more. It appears that the Garitys arrived not long after the indigenous people, the Winnebago, had been forced to cede their hunting grounds in 1832. In short, the Garitys, displaced from Ireland, inherited the lands of displaced Indians through the US government's homesteading policy. What the Garity clan thought of this fateful irony is unrecorded. But I did discover in the family archive compiled by Mormons that the Garity homestead was a secret station on the underground railroad for African slaves escaping from the Confederacy. Three of Emmet Garity's sons served in the Union army: Bernard and James, both of whom died of wartime tuberculosis, and George, who died in a disabled veterans' home.

These ancestors of mine came from the greatest single upheaval of nineteenth-century Europe, the Great Hunger, to an America descending into civil war. How I would like to know more about them! Why did Emmet Garity harbor fugitive slaves and send his sons to war? What did Thomas Hayden in Milwaukee think about the Democratic Party, which offered the Irish immigrants economic opportunity but which supported slavery and Jim Crow? Their lives were part of a larger turning point in American history in which the flood of Irish immigrants challenged the Protestant character of the nation. The immigrants were hardly welcomed as a positive ingredient, as the melting-pot story would have us believe. In fact, thousands went back home to Ireland, a story never told. The two million who stayed faced systemic discrimination and suffered the rise of a massive Protestant "Know Nothing" movement. In many ways, the immigrants faced conditions not unlike those they left behind. Those who survived the journey to the New World faced a life expectancy of only six years.[54] Infants died by the tens of thousands. Fevers continued to be the leading cause of death in the tenements described in Jacob Riis's 1890 classic *How the Other Half Lives*. Riis observed that "hundreds of men, women and children are every day slowly starving to death in our tenements."[55] In New York, 30,000 people "lived below ground level in cellars often flooded with rainwater and raw sewage."[56] A majority of the inmates in mental hospitals in New York and Massachusetts were Irish. Schizophrenia was commonly called an Irish disease. Catholic girls became prostitutes to survive. Alcoholism was epidemic. Crime and violence were rife. The police "paddy wagon" was named for the Irish. The Irish constituted the first American underclass, and were considered a degenerate, hopeless threat to the American future.

America, however, had a key advantage over Ireland: the right of white male immigrants to vote. And so it became possible for my grandfather in Milwaukee to become a ward heeler, a man who organized the

Irish vote and distributed services. The political opportunity, however, was not granted so much as it was taken. In New York and across the country, the Irish vote was solicited by politicians, but the Irish themselves had no power in the Democratic Party until they seized it, sometimes through physical confrontations. Along with their dominance in workingmen's associations and later trade unions, the Irish were able to translate their massive numbers into political and economic power at municipal levels.

A fundamental identity change was required of these Irish ancestors. The Irish "became white," in the phrase of historian (and former sixties activist) Noel Ignatiev.[57] Their enfranchisement as voters was based on their racial classification as white, a privilege which guaranteed an advantage over the Africans in occupations ranging from domestic servants to dockworkers. As Frederick Douglass and W. E. B. DuBois lamented, there was a psychic "wage" of whiteness as well.[58] Douglass, who had visited Ireland for the abolition cause, issued a prophetic curse.

> Perhaps no class of our fellow citizens, and no people on the face of the Earth, have been more relentlessly persecuted and oppressed on account of race and religion than have these same Irish people. The Irish who, at home, readily sympathize with the oppressed everywhere, are instantly taught when they step upon our soil to hate and despise the Negro. . . . The Irish American will one day find out his mistake . . .[59]

My library in Los Angeles is filled with artifacts celebrating Irishness, with one exception. There is a framed drawing from the *Illustrated London News* dated August 8, 1863, depicting an Irish mob lynching a black man on Clarkson Street in New York City. I can identify eighty-three distinct people in this lifelike sketch, half men and half women, and at least ten children. Six of the men are holding sticks in the evening air, three are waving their hats, and one is holding back a black man seeking to reach the victim. In the background are the masts of the ships that brought the Irish to America. The riots of 1863 were against conscription into the Union army (which the wealthy could avoid by paying a sum of money) but also against the blacks who were perceived to be taking "Irish" jobs.

How to explain this transformation of the Irish immigrants, the oppressed in their homeland only a decade before, into a lynch mob in America? The legacy of racism weighs heavily on Irish America. It was a principal reason that activists like myself were alienated from our Irish roots in the sixties. Coogan's uncharacteristically vague statement – "on the Confederate side, the Irish did not join up because they wished to maintain slavery, but because they had adapted to Southern life" – didn't do this issue justice.[60] What was the difference between slavery and "Southern life"? And what of the Northern Irish? That they joined the Union army and sacrificed themselves in huge numbers still leaves open the question of their hostility to the abolitionists. The leading Catholic clergyman in America, Bishop John Hughes in New York, opposed an anti-slavery appeal from Daniel O'Connell and 15,000 Irish signatories on the grounds that it "emanated from a foreign source."[61] Foreign? Hughes's congregants themselves were only recent arrivals from the same "foreign" land. What had happened?

Others, like Noel Ignatiev, treat the subject as if it were ultimately a moral one. Instead of fighting racism, he writes, the Irish Americans opted for the privileges of whiteness.[62] And thus today, 150 years later, those of Irish descent remain categorized as white ("non-Hispanic") on the official census forms.

I agree with neither the economic nor the moral explanations. My ancestors who hid slaves were not an isolated fringe. Emmet Garity's neighbors, the residents of Jefferson County, Wisconsin, supported Abraham Lincoln in 1860 with the largest majority in the county's history. We need more understanding of those Irish newcomers who resisted being reduced to whiteness, however many they were. And we need to understand what the Irish therapist Garrett O'Connor calls the "toxic transmission of shame" as a possible diagnosis of racist behavior. The Irish were classified as subhuman simians at the moment they came to

America. Charles Kingsley wrote in 1860 that the peasants of Ireland were "human chimpanzees": "To see white chimpanzees is dreadful; if they were black, one would not feel it so much, but their skins, except where tanned by exposure, are as white as ours."[63]

The race theories of eugenics were articulated in America at the same time. In 1863, the year of the New York riots, Charles Loring Brace, founder of the Children's Aid Society, published *Races of the Old World*, which recapitulated the Victorian theory that intelligence was measured by skull size. The Irish, he asserted, were in between the Anglo-Saxons and the Africans. With drawings of the Irish as ape-like creatures, Brace claimed that the "difference between the English and Irish skulls is nine cubic inches, and only four between the average African and Irish."[64] Many of the destitute Irish must have internalized these colonial images, welling up with shame. Arriving in America, traumatized and penniless, they transferred their shame upon those below them. To avoid being categorized as aliens, they became super-Americans. To show their patriotic loyalty, they became policemen and soldiers in disproportionate numbers. Remembering the times when they were powerless to prevent starvation, they seized the opportunity to vote and build political machines. In time they repressed the trauma of being classified as chimpanzees by transferring it to others they could police or exclude. In my father's generation, for example, James T. Farrell's fictional Irishman Studs Lonigan sat on his porch complaining with his neighbors thus:

> I know what we ought to do. Put all the foreigners we got taking jobs away from Americans, pack them in boats, and say to them, "now, see here, America belongs only to the Americans."
>
> It's only right, America is America, and it should be for Americans, Studs said.
>
> You're damn right it should be. And you know who's going to wake Americans up? It's men like Father Moylan who speaks on the radio every Sunday. He tells 'em and he talks straight.
>
> And he's a Catholic, too, Studs said proudly.[65]

That radio priest was a fictional version of Father Charles Coughlin, in whose parish I was enrolled as a young boy. But I'm getting ahead of the story.

Excavating Identity

> By blandly insisting that we leave the past behind us, we prevent ourselves from doing so.
>
> *Irish Times* columnist John Waters[66]

At the end of the sixties, I briefly changed my name to Emmet Garity – combining my middle name and my mother's name – to live anonymously in Venice, California, while studying Irish history for the first time. I didn't know that there was an Emmet Garity in my family, my grandfather, until years later, since he died in a cannery accident when my mother was a little girl. And it was not until March 2000, coincidentally on the day our baby Liam was born, that I discovered my great-grandfather Emmet Garity's family plot beneath a worn Celtic cross in St Mary's church graveyard in Sullivan, Wisconsin. Buried with him are a whole family of lost Famine ancestors – his wife Catherine, and children Patrick, Margaret, George, Mary, John, Rosie, Bernard, and Eugene, who lived between 1846 and 1934.

Down the road five miles is Oconomowoc, population 10,000, where the Garitys moved and set down roots, proving themselves not so "ambitious" and "adventurous" as the *Oxford History of the United States* would suggest. In compensation for my grandfather's death, the Carnation corporation provided my Nanny $5,000 on which to raise twelve children, including my mother Gene, through the Great Depression. They lived in a big farmhouse with fields, a water tower, lakes and railroad tracks nearby. They had a classic small-town life, their time spent in churches, parks, bowling alleys, out fishing, on golf courses, in bars, drugstores, and big porches on which to rock and gossip. They produced sixty cousins for me to play with during summertime vacations. While I remember vividly how Catholic they were, everyone attending the ancient St Jerome's in the center of town, everyone abstaining from meat on Fridays, avoiding bad language, and while I remember how the drink flowed freely (because they were Irish, and because the beer barons ruled the state), what strikes me today is their silence about being Irish. They would not consider renouncing their religion, around which their life revolved, but their Irishness became "baggage" which could be left behind. Years later, when the Irish had more cultural currency and I spoke at an Irish Festival in Milwaukee, my eighty-four-year-old aunt Mary sat mystified and told me, "You know, there wasn't any advantage to being Irish back in my day."

The author James T. Farrell, creator of Studs Lonigan, represented their generational silence. "The effects and scars of immigration are upon my life. The past was dragging through my boyhood and adolescence. . . . But for an Irish boy born in Chicago in 1904, the past was a tragedy of his people, locked behind the silence of history."[67] Even in Ireland, where the past was present in a more palpable way, silence was a heavy curtain. One day several years ago I visited the great Irish novelist John McGahern at his remote farm in the border country, expecting him to contribute something about the Famine legacy for a book I was editing. In his novel *Among Women,* McGahern had written about a "silent father" of the post-Famine generation whose "racial fear of the poorhouse or the famine was deep," and I hoped he would amplify.[68] He asked me to take a walk through the afternoon rain to a corner of his farm within view of his window. There was an indent in the ground, perhaps twenty-five feet in circumference, where the bodies of Famine dead were left behind. Silenced by the starkness of the sight, I felt for the first time the difficulty, a moral and imaginative difficulty, of putting the meaning of what I was seeing into words. It did not surprise me when, weeks later, I received a terse note from John saying there was nothing he wanted to write.

The poet Brendan Kennelly had attempted to articulate this silence as well. The popular culture of song in the Irish countryside, as described in books like George Petrie's nineteenth-century collection of the ancient music of Ireland, was terminated by the Famine. Ireland became "the grave of song," in Kennelly's phrase,[69] because the desolation of the Famine silenced the popular imagination for decades:

> When winds of hunger howled at every door
> She heard the music dwindle and forgot the dance.[70]

According to Petrie's 1850s eyewitness account, "the land of song was no longer tuneful; or, if a human sound met the traveller's ear, it was only that of the feeble and despairing wail for the dead. This awful unwanted silence struck more fearfully upon their imaginations,"[71] causing what cultural critic Terry Eagleton terms a "traumatized . . . muteness."[72] In a later poem, Kennelly summoned the image of an "awful absence":

> Skeletoned in darkness, my dark fathers lay
> Unknown, and could not understand
> The giant grief that trampled night and day
> The awful absence moping through the land. . . .
> No dancing feet disturbed its symmetry
> And those who loved good music ceased to sing.[73]

I believe every Irish person has stories of such family silence, deriving from ancient traumas of famine and emigration. The silence itself has been a way of expressing the unspeakable.

One root of my lost family is from County Monaghan, in old Ulster, but divided by partition to become a border county in the Republic. Monaghan town, population 5,000, perfectly resembles the rural Wisconsin to which the Garitys emigrated. The town is a small and charming nexus of traditional shops and churches with a circle in the center, now becoming unbalanced by the siting of an American-sized Dunne's department store. It is a republican enclave, and was the target of a huge loyalist bomb which claimed thirty-three lives in 1974. It has elected the first Sinn Féin representative to the Republic's parliament since partition, a solid, attentive local politician named Caoimhghín Ó

Caoláin. There are dreams of making the place a heritage region complete with a causeway named after the Black Pig of Celtic mythology. There is even the classic Leslie Castle, where Mick Jagger once ran naked across the grounds to the border with the North. When I first visited Monaghan, in 1976, I wandered the streets, tried to imagine the past, stared at local faces in the small town center, and simply pondered why and how history cast us apart. Years later, I sought my ancestors in the county museum, but was overwhelmed at the task. A friendly curator, Padraig Long, took me into a basement storage room with shelves of boxes containing thousands of letters written during the Famine. I chose to browse the official records of the year 1849, shortly after many of my ancestors left. The records appeared to be an accounting of cattle herds, not human beings. In carefully penciled handwriting there was a record of "Paupers who were admitted into, or discharged from, the Workhouse; and the Number of the Sick, and the number Born, or who died therein, during the week ended Saturday —, day of —." Below this explanation are columns marked "Admitted," "Discharged," "Died," and the count of "Sick and Lunatic Paupers." In June 1849, the workhouse overflowed with 2,000 people. The stone building was allowed to deteriorate and collapse because people suspected it was still contagious.

Monaghan lost 40 percent of its population, about 60,000 people, during the Famine decade, the most of any county in old Ulster. According to an out-of-print history, *The Monaghan Story*, the local people called the blight "the Blackness."[74] How to recall "blackness"? The records yield little. There were four workhouses in Monaghan, in which the inmates were separated from their families and performing hard labor, while hungry and fevered, for two meals a day. According to a 1845 Monaghan county history, these institutions were "repulsive to the habits and feelings of a people." The "intolerable overcrowding" was relieved in only two ways: through forced emigration, or "when death helped to empty the workhouses through fever and disease."

The story of Mary Ann McDermott of Monaghan, who supported her two children by doing chores rather than submit to the workhouse, told of a fierce, frugal pride. "On Friday, March 12, 1847," the local history says that Mary "walked from Killeveen to Clones on an errand for which she received a cupful of meal which she divided among her children. . . . She returned from Clones and got weak and sat down. . . . [Someone] gave her food but she was unable to eat it. She died on the spot of starvation."[75]

There was callousness recorded too. The Famine "changed the whole attitude of people to their neighbors. Peter Coogan of Cornamucklagh carried out the beggar, Laurence Daly, first from his own house and then from the house of his cottier, Terry Hughes, and dumped him on the roadside to die. This was a change in Ireland."[76]

In 1995, I decided to search out the grave sites of the "disappeared" Famine victims of Monaghan. I found the local genealogist, Theo MacMahon, a distinguished silver-haired man sitting at his computer in a small flat along the main road. He was a man accustomed to occasional interruptions by visiting Americans hurriedly checking on their roots. He quickly agreed to my request.

Theo had never looked for the Famine graves of Monaghan though he had dedicated his life to exploring Irish roots. He plunged into the task, driving us up a winding road above the modern town, to a place where white, two-story stucco housing units give way to rolling hillside farms reminding me of my pastoral summers. We strolled up a gravel driveway to a flattened field of stone rubble and, lost, returned to the street to stop an elderly passerby. It was as if the neighbors were waiting for someone to ask for the directions. The field of rubble, he said, was the forsaken site of the old Monaghan fever hospital. More neighbors stepped from their kitchens to point farther into the distance. The grave sites were over there, they said, pointing across two small hills into a little tree-lined knoll by a stream. "And what's being done about it?" they asked. Were we from the government? I was taken aback, then realized that from a Catholic viewpoint, Famine victims could not be included in the annual blessing of the graves and therefore were barred from Heaven. The Famine haunted them beyond death.

I climbed a fence and started walking across the wet hillside, seeing indentations that might have been potato beds but now were trails for cattle in search of water. The cows were trekking over a field of the dead, dropping dung on Irish ancestors. My eyes kept trying to focus on signs of the mounds the villagers were pointing to. Obviously it was misleading to look for marked, individual "graves." I was looking for the remains of multiple bodies taken by wagon from the fever hospital, perhaps across this very trail, covered with lime to protect the gravediggers, and deposited in crude trenches dug in the earth. No names, no crosses, no flowers would mark the place of shame.

Theo saw them before I did, and simply said "There they are," pointing into the grove at scattered mounds, some alone, some below bushes, some with small trees growing from their centers. Not distinct mounds like the elevated graves in a cemetery, but the shape of bodies just under the blanket of green grazing grass. Piles of hardened cow dung rested alongside the mounds. So here they were, my ancestors, as close as I could come to them. I had finally traced my family tree to this shaded resting place on a muddy, degraded, abandoned slope. No gravestones or flowers. I sat on the wet ground, knelt involuntarily it seemed, as if I were in church for the first time in years. I took photos, and placed a small rock in my pocket. Except for dizziness, I could not feel the emotions I wanted to feel. Like the history buried under those slopes, my emotions couldn't be brought to the surface.

The Long Day's Journey to Success

Turning lower middle class is a painful process for a group such as the Irish who, as stevedores and truck drivers, made such a grand thing of a Saturday night. Most prize fighters and a good many saloon fighters die in the gutter – but they have moments of glory unknown to accountants . . . a good deal of color goes out of life as a group begins to rise. A good deal of resentment enters.

Daniel Patrick Moynihan[77]

One can never underestimate the way the American Irish shunned anything improper . . . propriety has been the curse of the Irish

since they came to America . . . they often fight so hard to be
accepted that they can never be themselves at all.

John Corry[78]

My father, who fit the stereotype of Daniel Patrick Moynihan's accountant, had little glory and a good deal of resentment in his life. He was
cynical and thrived on black humor. Though a law-and-order
Republican, he took no interest in politics. Though Catholic, he seemed
to attend Mass for my sake only, and I don't know if he took confession.
Once, late in his life, he went down in the cellar and brought up a
sheathed four-foot Knights of Columbus sword he wanted to bequeath
to me. It symbolized his pride in assimilation. The Knights had originated as an Irish Catholic society "proclaiming American patriotism,
urging uplift and assimilation . . . [and] being conspicuously patriotic in
wartime."[79] When my father was four years old, his mother died suddenly. His father raised four children on his own. As a young man my
father worked as a doorman at a Milwaukee hotel. Eventually he became
a career accountant at the Chrysler Corporation. He loved fishing and
the outdoors, read passionately, but disciplined himself to white-collar
life, accepting dullness for security, always keeping nearby a boxful of
sharpened pencils with which he wrote precisely. The high point of his
life, I believe, came in 1944 when we moved to San Diego where he spent
one year as a marine. Though he was never sent to the war zone, he had
done his American duty and internalized the World War Two generation's belief in their country, right or wrong. When the war ended, he
took almost another year to hitchhike alone back to Detroit while my
mother and I rode the train. At five, I was too young to realize there was
something strange about this separation. I think those few months were
the closest my father ever got to freedom.

When he returned from military life, he was not the same. He drank
constantly, mostly with his buddies at the local American Legion hall. I
remember him driving the family Plymouth on vacations holding a full
glass of beer in his right hand. As a boy, I noticed it seemed to make him
funny for a while, and then silently distant, but seemingly content.

When I was ten, he walked into my darkened bedroom, sat on the edge of the bed, told me he was divorcing my mother, kissed me on the cheek for the first time I could remember, and walked out. I was shocked, my chest was locked in pain, and I stared at the wall trying to understand. The only incident I could remember that foretold this family crisis was when one night I heard him staggering up the stairs yelling something at my mother, who was crying behind their locked bedroom door. He smashed it open with a hammer. She was screaming. I never asked what happened, and it was never mentioned. A few months later, I saw my father at a golf course – I had gone to watch Ben Hogan – with another woman on his arm. He introduced her as "Esther" with a big smile, as if it was a natural development I should understand or even appreciate. It made me sick, and I never asked him about it, and never told my mother. My dad and Esther eventually married and had a child, my half-sister Mary, in 1963, a cute, funny little child I loved to play with when I was in town. But as I became more radical in my politics, my dad stopped talking to me, and raised Mary without the knowledge that I was her brother. The silent treatment lasted sixteen years, during which time I replicated his ability to repress and compartmentalize a painful secret. The relationship thawed and began to heal only when I was married to Jane Fonda, we had a child of our own, and Esther starting yelling at him, "You stubborn Irishman, pick up that phone and call your son!" Instead of calling, he sent a one-line note with his phone number. It worked. We were reconciled. He said he was proud of me. I told him I loved him.

My mother came of age in the so-called "flapper" generation of the 1920s, at the buoyant moment women's suffrage was achieved. She moved up to Milwaukee, then a big city in comparison with Oconomowoc, took secretarial classes and became a working girl. There she met and married my father. I never asked, but I feel certain he was the first man she slept with. They moved to Detroit, where I was born, and then to Royal Oak, a suburb twelve miles out of Detroit, where we moved in the late forties. Royal Oak gained some fame in recent times, becoming a key stop on Bill Clinton's successful 1994 campaign to win back Michigan's "white ethnics." It is becoming a trendy center of coffee shops and the gay subculture. Dr Jack Kervorkian's office happens to be on Main Street. But the Royal Oak I grew up in was an early suburb, including a Catholic stronghold dominated by Father Charles Coughlin.

Even today, my parish priest is remembered with indignation among Jews and embarrassment among some Catholics for his fiery and often anti-Semitic radio crusades. Next to Franklin Roosevelt and Huey Long, Father Coughlin was one of the most powerful voices in America during the Depression. Week after week, Catholic families listened over the radio to his booming denunciations of international bankers who controlled the government and drove workers and farmers into debt. His social gospel demanded unemployment insurance, social security, and the right to unionization at the time of the historic Flint auto strikes. But his populism was anti-Jewish and anticommunist as well. "Must the entire world go to war for [the] Jews in Germany who are neither American, nor French, nor English citizens, but citizens of Germany?" he asked in 1939.[80] So inflammatory were his sermons that the Vatican, under pressure from the US State Department, muzzled his political pronouncements.[81]

My parents told me nothing of this controversy. Once I remember my mother suggesting with a raised eyebrow that there was a "problem" with Father Coughlin, but she gave no explanation. Appearances were more important than nasty truths. My parents regarded it as a significant achievement that they were members of his famous parish, and that I attended his Mass on school days and Sunday mornings. The church, the Shrine of the Little Flower, which still stands at the corner of Woodward Avenue and Twelve Mile Road, remains one of the most impressive in the world. Father Coughlin's radio broadcasts were made from a 130-foot granite Crucifixion tower, and Mass occurred in a circular chamber seating 3,000 people around a central altar made of Italian marble weighing eighteen tons – still the largest monolith in the USA.

Delivered in a deep brogue, Father Coughlin's theology was a stern, repetitive warning about the eternal fires of hell. It scared me out of my wits as a boy. The extreme nature of the doctrine is difficult to exaggerate. The Irish therapist Garrett O'Connor has noted how shame-based doctrines can be powerfully transferred from such different places as Famine Ireland to suburban America. The research therapist Monica McGoldrick has written that "more than other ethnic groups, the Irish struggle with their sense of guilt and sin. . . . Irish schizophrenics, for example, are commonly obsessed with guilt for sins that they may not even have committed."[82]

The priests used Saint Thérèse as a model of extreme devotion. Born in France in 1873, she entered a Carmelite convent in Lisieux at age fifteen, where she remained "hidden in prayer" until she died of tuberculosis at age twenty-four. Known as the Little Flower of Jesus, Thérèse was canonized in 1925, and the Shrine of the Little Flower became the first church in North America dedicated to her name and ideal.[83] (By coincidence, as this book was completed, the remains of Saint Thérèse were transported across Ireland, drawing crowds totalling three million.) The Catholic ideal, as I understood it at the time, was that life should be devoted to an intimacy with God gained through self-punishment and abnegation under the sheltering structure of the Church. Or, as Mary Gordon stated it irreverently in her 1978 novel *Final Payments*, Saint Thérèse was "someone who would submit to having dirty water thrown on her by her sisters in Christ and die a perfect death at twenty-four" (a reference to the large number of deaths in convents and schools from tuberculosis, caused by infected water in shared drinking cups).[84] But this ascetic life was at complete odds with the freedom of suburban culture around me. I couldn't believe that God created my Jewish or Protestant friends to fill the quotas of Hell. I couldn't imagine praying twenty-four hours a day. I couldn't grasp tuberculosis as a challenge from God.

Yet the church did inspire awe, with its imposing circular chamber and six-ton statues of saints and martyrs, dimmed lighting and flickering votive candles. In this sacred space, the world had more gravity than the suburban culture outside. Mortality and the eternal were more compelling than sports, shopping, or grades. Most of all, there were role models to emulate; if not Saint Thérèse, there were the martyrs who stood up to the Roman Empire. The church instilled in me the idea that life had its heroic potential. For all these reasons, I considered becoming a priest. But the contradiction of the Catholic Church was that it culti-vated my instinct for learning, for reading, for figuring things out, all the while demanding that I obey hypocritical priests and nuns or face God's wrath. I couldn't question authority and be obedient at the same time. If there was a place for conscientious objectors in the Catholic Church, I might have filled out the application. But there was no room for loyal dis-senters. When as a boy I fooled around in class, the priests made me kneel on the hard floor, arms outstretched until they filled with fiery pain, while my palms were beaten with a hard rod. As Father Coughlin declared himself:

> On this earth you must belong to the church militant or get the hell out of it. That's the right word. You're either with me or against me. There is no middle ground in this battle between Christ and the anti-Christ. If you step out of [the battle], you're worse than those boys who ran off to Norway, Sweden, those boys who deserted the gov-ernment [over Vietnam]. You're deserters, rotten deserters.[85]

This Catholic upbringing consisted of the same fear-based, shame-ridden doctrines of original sin and redemption based on obedience that emerged in Ireland's post-Famine "devotional" revolution and were imported to America with the Famine generation. Historians like Emmet Larkin (1972) estimate that only one-third of Irish Catholics attended Mass before the Famine, and a smaller percentage in the Celtic and rural west. Attendance grew to more than 90 percent after the calamity. The Church leadership "patently derived very great advantage from the pyschological impact the famine had . . . the growing awareness of a sense of sin already apparent in the 1840s was certainly deepened as God's wrath was made manifest in a great natural disaster that destroyed and scattered his people," in the standard thinking of the time. "Most of the two million Irish who emigrated between 1847 and 1860 were part of the pre-famine generation of nonpractising Catholics, if indeed they were Catholics at all," writes Larkin. But once they settled in New York or Boston, the Church became their shelter from the storms of poverty and persecution. Following them to America were nuns and priests trained in Ireland. With their Irishness criminalized in Ireland, and with pressures to abandon their language and Gaelic identity in America, Larkin goes on: "Irishmen who were aware of being Irish were losing their identity, and this accounts in large part for their becoming practising Catholics."[86] The historian Terry Golway also notes that "until the late 1840s and early 1850s, Irish Catholics in America were not particularly church-going," but the number of New York City parishes doubled between 1845 and 1863 and Mass attendance tripled.[87]

By the American 1950s, the sense of being Irish had receded entirely in my schooling at the Shrine, but not the Catholic doctrines that grew from the Irish Famine experience. It was no wonder that the tortured devotional emphasis was losing its appeal, and becoming a disincentive to Catholics like myself. Even my parents were more formal than devout. We were turning into secular Catholics, blending into American society by disconnecting from our fading Irishness. Even as assimilation proceeded, however, I was jolted by reminders that there were different religions. I was once jumped and beaten for being Catholic by a Protestant school jock. My first high-school girlfriend was Protestant, from a higher-class neighborhood, whose parents couldn't wait until she broke up with me. (She did.)

Then there were the Jews, living in a neighborhood of their own just across Woodward Avenue from the Shrine. I gravitated towards them as fellow outsiders in public high school, where we shared an interest in the student newspaper, plays, and offbeat intellectual discussions at the local pizza parlor. I heard the first comment about Jews not from Father Coughlin, but from my mother when I was very little. She was sweeping the kitchen floor and stopped to listen to the radio announcer call a home run by her hero, Hank Greenberg, the Detroit Tigers' slugging first baseman, who had just returned from military service. She looked at me and whispered a little secret between us: "He's Jewish, you know." Why did she have to whisper? To her mind, this must have been controversial.

Jews were demonized in Roman Catholic history for centuries, a prejudice seemingly spliced into Irish culture. At the height of the Famine, a future Archbishop of Dublin, Dr Paul Cullen, was blaming Jewish bankers in London for "fattening" on the starving Irish.[88] When czarist-instigated pogroms drove Jews into forced flight from Poland and Russia in the 1880s, the economic "threat" combined with Catholic teaching to foster anti-Semitism in Ireland. In 1904, anti-Jewish riots broke out in Limerick.[89] The hero of Joyce's *Ulysses* was a wandering Jew, Leopold Bloom, who was bombarded with anti-Semitic accusations by a Sinn Féin nationalist in Barney Kiernan's pub. Joyce, who chose a life of exile himself, identified with the double-bind of Bloom who, in spite of being an assimilated Jew, could never be accepted as an Irish Dubliner. For Joyce, the Jews of Europe were cousins in marginality. Through Bloom Joyce said, "it's no use . . . force, hatred, history, all that." When Bloom adds that a "word known to all men," love, is "really life," the hard bartender in Barney Kiernan's dismisses him as just "a new apostle to the gentiles." Though a nationalist himself, Joyce was troubled deeply by the ways nationalism could be racialized or essentialized to exclude others. Part of his anger against the Catholic Church was its anti-Semitism, and "his reading of Arthur Griffith's *United Irishmen* provided him with an example of anti-Semitism at the heart of Sinn Féin nationalism." Griffith, for example, sided with the French army during the Dreyfus affair, criticizing "the white-washing of a Jew Officer."[90]

In Ireland, the Jewish population never exceeded 3,000 (it is only 1,500 today), but from its ranks came Chaim Herzog, a future president of Israel, Robert Briscoe, a lord mayor of Dublin, and several members of the Dáil.[91] In America, Jewish and Irish youth might have fought on New York street corners, but both communities also cooperated in the labor movement, urban politics, and the New Deal.[92] But Father Coughlin's views predominated in my mother's world, and would resonate in Ireland's official neutrality during World War Two, when Eamon de Valera visited the German embassy to express condolences at the death of Adolf Hitler. Was this neutrality the result of a claustrophobic Catholicism, or had the Irish grievance against the British been turned into a blind belief that "the enemy of my enemy is my friend"? De Valera believed that if Neville Chamberlain could allow Hitler to occupy the Czech Sudetenland, England might also be pressured to accept de Valera's claims on Northern Ireland. Hitler himself noted the Irish obsession with England in 1939: "I have just read a speech by de Valera, the Irish Taoiseach, in which, strangely enough, and contrary to Roosevelt's opinion, he does not charge Germany with oppressing Ireland but he reproaches England with subjecting Ireland to continuous aggression."[93] Needless to say, there were thousands of Irishmen, Protestant and Catholic, who fought against the Axis powers in World War Two. But in Ireland, in America, and in the Vatican, there were forces of anti-Semitism which obliged my mother to whisper in her own kitchen.

Suburban Dreams

Side by side with the belief in sin . . . is the Irish belief in dreams . . . life is organized around one's dreams.
Monica McGoldrick, John K. Pearce, and Joseph Giordano[94]

[The Irish have a] shrewd knowledge of the world and a strange reluctance to cope with it.
Sean O'Faolain[95]

Oh the dreaming! The dreaming! The torturing, heartscalding, never satisfying dreaming!
George Bernard Shaw[96]

I became a nonconformist in response to the Catholic pressures for obedience to parents, priests, nuns, and teachers. Obedience was a kind of forced assimilation. After eight years at the Shrine, I shifted to public high school where my circle of friends was an underground before there was an underground subculture, identifying with the Alfred E. Newman character in *Mad* magazine. His idiotic motto "What, me worry?" described the cheerful apathy of students preparing to enter the middle-class American dream. At the other end of this spectrum were the cliques

of rich WASPs from suburbs like Birmingham who dominated student ath-
letics and government. They were sexy, sophisticated girls in pleated skirts,
tight cashmere sweaters, with aloof smiles that said Stay Away. The guys
were the types who never showed any evidence of sweating after a tennis
match. They had convertibles. My mother let me use her Nash Rambler.

Suburbia was the promised land of assimilation. From farms to cities
to the suburb of Royal Oak was the trajectory of our family. We were
neither shanty Irish nor lace-curtain; we would settle happily for the
venetian blinds of the suburbs. Detroit was the last stop before my family
made it to Royal Oak, the site of the first regional shopping center in
America. Detroit had a social history I never learned from my parents,
who came with thousands of people from the Midwest and South seeking auto industry and wartime jobs. It was also a seething center of
social, economic, and racial unrest. While Father Coughlin was attacking Jews, Henry Ford was proposing an American Nazi Party, and
pro-Hitler espionage units were penetrating the military plants. In 1942,
FBI raids seized hundreds of cameras, shortwave radios, and weapons
from the pro-Axis underground. But there were deeply progressive Irish
Americans in Michigan, too. Frank Murphy, a former mayor, governor,
and US Supreme Court justice, was organizing an official national committee against Nazi genocide. In 1942 and 1943, massive race riots
shook the city as white workers opposed blacks working next to them on
the assembly lines. The three-day 1943 riots left thirty-four dead and the
city under martial law imposed by Irish American Governor Harry Kelly.
Detroit's police force, all-white and significantly Irish, was accused of terrible brutality by an army general sent to Detroit.[97]

When the war finally ended, it was Murphy again who tried to elevate
the civic society by warning that victory would be empty unless "we
stand guard against those in our midst who have been nurtured on the
myths of superior and inferior races and who practice discrimination
against fellow Americans because of the color of their skin."[98]

These sentiments aside, racial tumult was all around me, not only in
Detroit but in San Diego close by my father's marine base, where US ser-
vicemen brutalized Mexican "zoot suiters" in riots still remembered

today in the barrios of southern California. Amazingly, however, I didn't learn about any of this growing up, not in my family or in school. The subtle mechanism of denial and silence remained intact. What I remember is the formation of racist stereotypes in my child's mind. One image is of three black youths surrounding me, dressed in black clothes, looking exactly like large spiders. I also recall my first image of a Mexican, conjured perhaps on a trip with my parents to Tijuana, as a sly, dark-skinned, mustached man holding a dagger.

Though it was never made explicit, we ran from the blacks to the suburbs, from our past in ethnic enclaves to a future of shopping malls. I never saw a black face again until I entered the University of Michigan. Although the US Supreme Court struck down racial housing covenants in 1948 in a case involving Detroit, Royal Oak seemed to maintain the practice invisibly.

Not that the Irish Catholic entry into the suburbs was effortless. The doors to the promised land had to be knocked open, just as the doors of the Democratic Party had required some hammering the century before. That is the reason, I am convinced, that the Catholics stayed loyal to Father Coughlin. He was sent to start a parish in Royal Oak in 1926, at a time when anti-Irish, anti-Catholic sentiment was raging. It was the Prohibition era, a WASP crusade aimed primarily at the Irish Catholics. Politically, the same establishment was vilifying and undermining the emergence of the first Irish Catholic presidential candidate, the liberal governor of New York, Al Smith. In places like Royal Oak, it was a time of increasing anti-Catholic virulence by the Ku Klux Klan, who burned down Father Coughlin's first church. It is a great mystery how the priest stood up to the Klan and managed to construct his Shrine of the Little Flower. Did the ex-boxer face them down? Did he propose coexistence based on mutual hostility to Jews and blacks? No one knows, but the Shrine was built and the suburban gates to assimilation were finally opened to families like mine.

My mother was a little woman, never more than five feet tall and perhaps 100 pounds, a lifetime sufferer from scoliosis. Like my father, she rarely if ever revealed her Irish past (although when my son Troy was born in 1973, she produced to my surprise a sterling silver shamrock to place over his crib). She was a Democrat, warmer and more liberal than my father. I think she took the 1928 defeat of Al Smith as a crushing blow, because I remember her shaking her head and saying that "they" destroyed him, a disaster she never explained further. It would have been helpful, of course, if she had expressed these feelings and reactions in the context of an Irish heritage, but that was impossible for her. After the divorce, I lived alone with my mother in Royal Oak; my father joined us for silent dinners on weekends. In the summers, I lived in Oconomowoc with my mother's extended family and went fishing in upper Michigan and the Canadian wilderness with my father. Fishing was the perfect activity because we could bond without words.

The sociological priest Andrew Greeley once wrote that since the Famine, "both Irish and Irish American women and men have had a much harder time being affectionate than they used to . . . romanticism seems to have been pretty well crushed out by the famines and the penal laws."[99] And as a result of sexual repression, McGoldrick has added, the Irish also tended to avoid tenderness and intimacy.[100] My mother was attracted to men, gossiped about them, but as far as I know she never had another date after my father walked out. She took a job as a film librarian in the local school system, the only intellectual challenge available to a high school graduate, and went to work every day, rain or shine, sick or well, for twenty-seven years before retiring. I don't remember ever seeing my parents kiss, except on the cheek. Many years later, I found a honeymoon telegram from them to my grandmother, written with my father's permanent sarcasm: "Married a week and still happy." I keep it for remembrance of the love that created me but which I rarely saw.

Unlike my father, my mother never severed our relationship when I became involved in the movement. But neither could she understand the sixties. She lived her life in acute shame at what she believed the neighbors were saying and what the government might do. When the local papers reported my radicalism, she sometimes went into hiding in motels or left the state. She lived with other fears as well, too deep for me to understand at the time. When she died in 1984, I discovered that she had carefully placed a modest $6,000 in life savings in three separate Oconomowoc banks. Inside the bank walls, inside the vaults and safety deposit boxes, she had wrapped her money in tinfoil to protect against an unnamed catastrophe she must have feared. A catastrophe that only an immigrant subconsciousness could imagine.

My parents believed that the world was harsh. The prayers of the Church conveyed that life was about "mourning and weeping in this valley of tears." Not even the neighbors could be trusted, for they would take advantage if they could. Safety lay in assimilation, blending in, preserving appearances of success and respectability. My mother often whispered "shhh" while holding one finger to her lips, even when no one was around. She didn't always trust her own sisters. To the end of their lives, she and my father suspected that everyone was out to take advantage of me, to steer me from the path of success. Theirs was a post-Famine distrust described by Kerby Miller as a "covert competitiveness which found poisonous expression in . . . incessant gossip and obsessive attention to the most minute indices of comparative status or respectability . . . [W]hat will the neighbors think? became lace-curtain Irish America's secular catechism."[101] I would only add that this obsession was just as great among the first-generation middle-class parents who could afford only venetian blinds. Respectability was the end of the rainbow for my parents, and it was defined as sending me to the University of Michigan (my father took two years of community college classes in Wisconsin). What drove them other than Famine memory? I think they were struggling with a subconscious immigrant nightmare, respectability's dread opposite, which is shame. Making it in America was the solution to this shame. Indeed, respectability was the achievement that would not only end their secret insecurity but terminate the Irish "problem" in America as well. A confident *Atlantic Monthly* editorial in 1896, the decade before my parents' births, had predicted that "the Irish, before many years are past, will be lost in the American. . . . There will no longer be an 'Irish question' or an 'Irish vote.'"[102] Assimilation, in this view, was peaceful ethnocide, and the wretched Irish would be the better for it.

The prediction appeared to be coming true in my parents' time. The nightmare of Ireland seemed to be over, the dream of America was being realized. Irish American nationalism ebbed with time and the establishment of a twenty-six-county Republic under a tricolour across the sea. The IRA's border campaign of the fifties collapsed of its own weakness. Normalcy beckoned after the seeming eternity of trauma. The Ancient Order of Hibernians was putting up American flags in every parochial school classroom. Few were singing the old Irish republican anthems, at least not in the suburbs. My mother and I faithfully watched the televised broadcasts of Bishop Fulton J. Sheen, who once described the Irish identity as composed of "love of a fight, humor and blarney."[103] We listened to a blue-eyed Bing Crosby croon "When Irish Eyes are Smiling." At first the song seemed to confirm the new story of the satisfied Irish soul, but there was an unexplained immigrant sadness in the lyrics, which began

> There's a tear in your eye
> And I'm wondering why
> For it never should have been there at all . . ."

Respectable assimilation was still a mask for other longings.

I mirrored my parents' subconscious messages. The silence over what happened to them never lifted, because I never knew to ask. I simply assumed that these silent family failures were normal, or perhaps the price to pay on the long day's journey to success.

Drinking, Sexuality, and Assimilation

Every time they make an agreement to do it, they're like a couple of drunks walking out of the bar for the last time – when they get to the swinging door they turn around and go back in and say I just can't quite get there.

President Bill Clinton, October 9, 1999[104]

That such a sophisticated student of human nature as Bill Clinton would use a drinking analogy to describe the Irish peace process indicates how deeply and pervasively the world associates the Irish identity with drunkenness.

Drinking was the only Irish legacy passed along to me. You drink because you're Irish, I learned, which soon became you're Irish because you drink, an assertion of your heritage. For thirty-three years I drank, sometimes a fifth of bourbon a night, thinking my need was genetic. In the ghettos where I organized, I saw the connections between poverty, alienation, destroyed self-esteem and alcohol, but never applied the analysis to myself. I simply thought all Irish people drank liquor the way Mexicans were said to eat tacos or blacks ate greens. St Patrick's Day celebrations reinforced the idea that heavy drinking was the way to express Irishness. Along with millions of Irish Americans, I was celebrating a degrading caricature of myself. Assimilation left us drunkenness as an acceptable way to be Irish in America. In Alcoholics Anonymous terms, it was called "CIA," for Catholic Irish Alcoholism, a syndrome involving "shame, guilt, and a mortal fear of being exposed as inherently bad."[105] For me, it was a coping mechanism, an illusory way to overcome repression while actually serving to avoid inner feelings. Writ large, it was a coping mechanism for the Irish as a whole.

More recent data are unavailable, but studies through the 1970s showed steep levels of alcohol problems among Irish American Catholics, a pattern which had prevailed for generations. As late as 1988, Niall O'Dowd reported studies showing that Irish American men drank "nearly every day," twice the figure for WASPs or Jews. John Waters calculates that alcohol consumption has tripled in Ireland since 1960, despite large numbers of abstainers and people too young to be served.[106] I simply believed I inherited my hard drinking from my father, that is, that it "ran in the family." Convictions for being drunk and disorderly among the New York Irish were twice that of any other ethnic group in the 1850s. A century later, in the 1950s, Irish Americans predominated among white male and female admissions for alcoholic psychosis to New York mental hospitals.[107]

Father Andrew Greeley once wrote that it is easier and safer "to explain Irish drinking as the result of Catholic sexual repression than as the result of English political repression."[108] I was conditioned to believe that you drank to have sex, to overcome a girl's inhibitions as well as your own, and to provide an excuse for the morning after. If anyone had told me the British made us drink, I would have thought they were wallowing in victimization. But Irish drinking reminds me of Native Americans on reservations, or aboriginals in Australian ghettos. There is something self-destructive that goes far beyond sexual repression. Alcohol numbs depression and keeps a broken personality afloat.

Studies indicate that there are structural dimensions to alcoholism. For example, Irish drinking escalated after the Famine, presumably in response to all that had to be forgotten or repressed. "The Great Famine made Guinness and Co.," wrote Derek Wilson, in a history of the Guinness family. Before the Famine, Guinness was a "moderately successful local brewery" that nearly closed down on one occasion. But it "burgeoned quite spectacularly in [the Famine's] aftermath."[109] Employers were all too willing to subsidize drinking as well. In the wake of the industrial revolution, according to O'Connor, "it became customary for employers to subsidize hard drinking by laborers as a way of keeping them mindlessly at work under appalling conditions which they would probably not have tolerated sober . . . [thus] making permanent drunkenness readily affordable."[110] All the Irish sorrow and silence were captured best in O'Neill's *Long Day's Journey into Night* when the Tyrone son says to his father, "Well, what's wrong with being drunk? It's what we're after, isn't it? Let's not kid each other, Papa. We know what we're trying to forget."[111] The only difference between that father–son exchange and my relation with my own drinking father is that neither of us knew what we were trying to forget.

I finally stopped drinking in 1990, though at the time I didn't understand why I had to. Perhaps I stopped because subconsciously I was feeling a greater shame than that which drinking was supposed to cure: the shame of setting a destructive example for my son and loved ones, the shame of damaging my career and the issues I had dedicated my life to. But it was also because I was learning to apply to myself the connection between despair and alcoholism that I saw in the underclass. Alcoholism wasn't simply a personal problem or congenital disease; it was a way to fill a void in my soul that assimilation had caused. As Mary Cavan Tyrone lamented in *Long Day's Journey into Night*, "I've never understood anything about it, except that one day long ago I found I could no longer call my soul my own."[112]

I was also a casualty of repressed sexuality. If my parents had been my only role models, I would have had no idea that sex or physical affection were part of the human experience. I learned about sex like most young men, from my bragging peers who, in this case, were invariably Protestant. They spoke of girls as meat, and used baseball analogies for sex, which at first I didn't understand. At Catholic school, I learned that what these Protestant boys were talking about was a sin, so of course I kept those secrets to myself. I was embarrassed to discuss them in the confessional with a priest who himself was supposedly celibate. Given this culture of sin, sex was difficult to consummate except at the price of guilt. For the Irish Catholics I grew up with, a friend of mind has said, sex was never a full-body experience. It occurred between the knees and the navel, preferably in darkness, and terminated quickly.

I learned about sex from non-Catholic, non-Irish girls, who gave me permission to explore sexual feelings with less shame. They were either WASPs who represented status and achievement, or non-Catholic "exotic" women who represented sin without guilt. Reflecting over my lifetime, I realize that none of my lasting relationships has been with an Irish Catholic woman. I internalized WASP standards of sexual attractiveness, and was controlled by them. I was sexually colonized. The rejection of Irish Catholics was an indicator of unconscious self-hate. My attraction to blue-eyed blonde WASPs was based on the dominance of cultural standards of superiority that are deeply, invisibly internalized by most of us in this culture, no matter what our racial or ethnic backgrounds may be. This form of colonialism, like all the rest, works most successfully when the master's standards are internalized by the native as if they were natural, no longer foreign, their own. The resultant loss of self-esteem in both men and women is a powerful reinforcement of a whole social system of status, privilege and entitlements.

The pre-Christian Irish seem to have enjoyed sex without guilt in an "open, earthy society – an agricultural society dependent on the fertility of land and animals," according to Brian Lacey, a museum curator in Derry.[113] Many contemporary scholars are discovering and celebrating ancient "lovesongs [that] are saturated with passion and heartbreak in an intense direct language." For at least one thousand years, the pre-Christian Irish allowed divorce in their system of Brehon laws. The very term for Irish gatherings, from those of the kings of Tara to modern political conventions, is *fheis*, which translates literally as "sleeping with a person." Ancient gatherings at Tara included fertility ceremonies. The cycles of nature and procreation were a paradigm for social relationships which the Church mercilessly denounced as pagan. The sheela-na-gig, widely sold as a cultural souvenir, is a stone carving of a Celtic goddess squatting in an openly sexual pose. Joyce's heroine Molly Bloom, who takes lovers freely in addition to her husband, is reminiscent of many Irish fertility and sovereignty goddesses beginning with the story of Queen Medb who offered her "friendly thighs" to numerous consorts in the saga of the *Tain Bo Cuailnge*.[114]

Neither Patrick nor the institutional Church was able fully to stamp out these "wild Irish" behaviors. But the Famine was a decisive turning point. The widespread British and clerical belief was that the promiscuous and lazy Irish brought on the Famine themselves, a notion that was reinforced in the Catholic Church with the rise of the self-blaming doctrines of a seventeenth-century French bishop, Cornelius Jansen. The Jansenists emphasized the consequences of original sin, dooming human beings to a permanently fallen state. Human nature, specifically promiscuous sexual desire, was the cause of overpopulation and famine. Only strict obedience to a punishing Church could prevent such calamities. The Jansenists had been expelled from France after the French Revolution, but were recruited to the Irish seminary at Maynooth. In the Jansenist view, the Famine was a punishment for the immoral, pagan ways of the Irish peasantry. The post-Famine solution was to promote celibacy, to prohibit sex outside of marriage, and to delay marriage and childbirth as long as possible. As a result, according to Brian Lacey, "fewer and fewer people got married, the age at which they got married rose, and many thousands of people remained celibate all their lives."[115] The adverse psychological effects of these shame-induced sexual attitudes were incalculable. But the Irish population fell by half while the rates of mental illness tripled between the Famine and 1914, the time of my parents' childhood.[116]

Long before the Famine, of course, there was a Catholic (and Calvinist) tradition of considering the body the domain of the Devil, a factory producing sinful impulses round the clock. Too much attraction to the temporal sensations diverted from the proper emphasis on the eternal. The most essential Catholic commitment was to the celibate life, for without priests and nuns there would be no Church at all. The New Testament story itself said that Mary was a virgin bride, Joseph a sexless male. Jesus, while experiencing close relationships with all sorts of women including Mary Magdalen, was assumed to be celibate too. He was the most charismatic man of all time, according to the story, but essentially was a spirit made apparent in flesh. To live like Him was to experience and reject sexual and material temptation of every kind. That is what Stephen Hero was taught in Joyce's *A Portrait of the Artist as a Young Man*, that is what I was taught at the Shrine of the Little Flower, that is what Irish Catholics were taught in suburbs across America. Marriage was a permit to sin. Sex should be limited to procreation. Family therapists coined the joke that sex was the "lack of the Irish."[117]

While many acknowledge this psychic burden, at least in the 1950s, of growing up Catholic in America or Ireland, they also assume that 1960s liberal reform lifted this weight of sexual repression. I agree that attitudes shifted in Ireland, and even more so in the United States, but the legacy of sexual repression carries the weight of ten centuries and was not overcome in a decade. In fact, the ongoing controversies in Ireland over abortion, divorce, contraception, not to mention persistent scandals over sexual abuse and alcoholism involving priests themselves, indicate that the issues will cast a long shadow over Ireland's future. Even Sinn Féin and the Irish Republican Army, despite Church denunciations and excommunications, are careful about challenging the clerical influence over many of their traditional Catholic supporters. Sinn Féin avoids taking a clear position on abortion. Its newspaper has begun reporting on gay rights. The struggle against the Church's authoritarian power may rest more on women, students, intellectuals and civil libertarians in the Republic, not on Northern nationalists needing Church tolerance of the struggle for a united Ireland. When Sinn Féin leaders visit New York City, for example, they seek support from the conservative Catholic hierarchy and march in St Patrick's Day parades that traditionally have excluded Irish gays and lesbians.[118] Liberalization has not much altered the traditional Catholic moral obligations and the guilt felt for sexual and other transgressions by Irish Catholics on either side of the ocean. Liberalism itself remains an internally controversial notion in the Church, which has recently reaffirmed the prohibition on women conducting Mass, declared the doctrinal superiority of the Catholic faith, endorsed papal infallibility, and retreated from 1960s versions of liberation theology.

While there may be consensus on the repressive legacy of the Church, many people see no connection to British colonial rule. Among critics in the Republic and especially the United States, it is more common to define the Irish problem as religious in nature, not one of colonialism. This is the main reason that American liberals and radicals, feminists, gays and lesbians, black civil rights leaders and Jewish progressives generally remain on the sidelines when it comes to the Irish question. They may oppose human rights abuses in the North, support the Irish peace process, but generally perceive Irish nationalists and republicans as conservative Catholics who would create a traditional Catholic state. Many liberals of Irish descent consider their activism to be non-Irish in nature, since "Irish" is assumed to be a parochial, even reactionary cultural legacy. Anticolonial movements are seen as the province of people of color, which rules out the Irish and consigns their struggle to the realm of tribal religious conflict.

But there is a deep connection between colonialism and religion in

Ireland. Historically, during the period of the Penal Laws (1695–1709) the British government criminalized, even attempted to exterminate, the Catholic presence in Ireland, thus creating a longterm fusion between the Catholic religion and nationalism which secular progressives either discount or fail to understand at all. But the British also pursued a strategy of co-opting Catholicism when persecution failed. In pastorals that won favor from the British, the Irish Church denounced "levellers" and other "disturbers of the public peace and tranquillity" during the Penal Laws period.[119] The Irish bishops opposed the rising of the United Irishmen in 1798, and supported replacing the Irish parliament with the Act of Union. In 1795, they sought and received British funding to train Catholic priests in Ireland, in the seminary at Maynooth, to better avoid the radicalism spreading across the European continent. Starting in 1831, the British financed the Church's control of the national educational system for Catholics. In 1844, at the critical juncture between the British repression of O'Connell's Repeal movement in 1843 and the onset of massive famine and starvation (1845–51), the Vatican reprimanded the Irish clergy on behalf of the British. Priests were instructed to "separate themselves from all secular concerns, and by work and example to inculcate subjection to the temporal power in civil matters and to dissipate popular excitements."[120] At the same time, the British prime minister Lord John Russell opined, "We have tried to govern Ireland by conciliation and have failed. No other means are now open to us except those we are resolved on using, namely, to govern Ireland through Rome."[121]

The Famine strengthened the Church's role and its shame-based theology for future generations not only in Ireland, but in the United States to which the institution was literally exported with the Famine immigrants. Arriving in chaos, the Irish poor were organized in parishes more than precincts. They built cathedrals, including the magnificent St Patrick's in New York City in 1879, when they were too poor to buy homes. They built schools while their children slept in tenement shelters. The Church was their protection against nativist mobs, their welfare system, their charitable benefactor. But the Church also exported its shame-based doctrines concerning sexuality, temperance, and obedience, with thousands of Irish-born priests to teach and enforce them. Their goal was to achieve Catholic acceptability, both in the United Kingdom and the United States, by pacifying the "wilder" tendencies of the Irish immigrants, above all their sexual appetites. Over time, the struggle against the Protestant power in London and America would decline. But the battle against the pagan instinct, the Devil in the flesh, the old goddess figures of the Celtic world, would be prosecuted so fiercely that the Irish were instilled with a deepening self-hate. Guilt for original sin, guilt for the Famine, guilt for challenging authorities, were combined with rewards for blending in, for disengaged piety, for identifying with the empire, even for collaborating with the regime of power. Joyce was fascinated with self-hate as a factor undermining nationalism; "in Ireland, just at the right moment," he wrote, "an informer always appears."[122] Through this process, the hegemony of British rule was assured, by a mental and emotional, rather than military, occupation of Irish sensibility.

Worldliness and Its Skeptics

Another powerful but invisible shadow on the Irish psyche is ambivalence towards success. My life has been haunted by the Irish trait that Sean O'Faolain called a "shrewd knowledge of the world and a strange reluctance to cope with it," and which Moynihan was identifying when he wrote that "the Irish were distinguished by qualities which tend to make men interesting rather than prosperous."[123] Many scholars have commented on this subject, defined sometimes as a lack of ambition, or a moody fatalism summarized by Moynihan's remark at John Kennedy's funeral: "I don't think there's any point in being Irish if you don't know that the world is going to break your heart eventually." This ambivalence towards success is a many-sided phenomenon, usually oversimplified to define the Irish as "begrudgers." Some trace the mood to the Jansenism transmitted through Maynooth, and its emphasis on the inherent sinfulness of human beings and denial of the Enlightenment concept of progress. But the Irish didn't need Jansenism to become skeptical towards worldly success. They had centuries of military occupation, brutal landlords, traitorous countrymen, famine, and poverty; they had risen countless times in brave but futile combat against their occupiers; and survival was their only success. Their orientation was the opposite of the Protestant ethic of self-made men. The Irish exhibited all the signs of helplessness, defeatism, and lack of achievement always associated with the underclass. What their critics, and often the Irish themselves, could never understand was that this ambivalence towards modern success lay in the very cultural core of the race.

In his classic on the Boston Irish, Oscar Handlin wrote that they "were completely alien to the idea of progress and necessarily antagonistic to the spirit of the age."[124] In more recent times, Harvard researcher Stephan Thernstrom (an author of *The Bell Curve*) mused that might there be something in "the characteristic life styles and values of some groups that impeded their adaptation to American society – or, if you like, that inoculated them against the competitive virus that infected most of the population."[125]

I first experienced this ambivalence, though on an unconscious level, during my years as a student journalist. The *University of Michigan Daily* was an extremely respected paper, and its editor was considered a major campus leader with bright career prospects. I gravitated to journalism as early as high school, dreaming of a future as a foreign correspondent. So when I enrolled at the university I immediately signed up as a *Daily* reporter. I rose in the ranks, as they say, and by my junior year I was considered likely to become the editor. I became a candidate for one of the secret societies that groomed the elite of campus leaders from fraternities, athletic teams, and the student government. It happened that the secret society for promising juniors was called the Druids, an inversion of the ancient Irish sorcerers and wise men into American achievers. I can remember my sense of excited expectation that these Druids would recruit me, lift me up, make me one of the chosen. I waited in nervous expectation for the Druids to come in the night, drag me off for a ceremonial hazing, kick me, crack eggs on my hair, paint my body, roll me in the dirt, and display me half-naked on campus the next day.

I did become a Druid, and the editor of the *Daily* as well, but I didn't respond to success as I expected to. I wanted to run the paper, write the editorials, have an impact. But I realized that at bottom I was a journalist because I wanted to investigate, to be a critic of these secret societies and their counterparts in the world. I was accepted in the upper circle of status – Big Man on Campus – but personally I remained an outsider, maybe even a misfit. So when the secret society for seniors, known by the Indian name Michigauma, came to "tap" me into their special circle, I evaded them. They hunted all night for me while I hid in a friend's apartment. They assumed my disappearance was a misunderstanding. No one had rejected Michigauma in the history of the Ann Arbor campus.

But I didn't feel proud of rejecting the prevailing measure of status and success. I remember feeling that there was something wrong with me, that I had a self-sabotaging streak. Combined with my moral and journalistic resistance to being a member of the secret elite was a gnawing sense that I'd blown my future by running away. I was ashamed to admit my feelings of inferiority. While to all appearances I was making it, achieving the success my parents devoted themselves to, I never really could address, much less transcend, the ancient unspoken feeling that I was an unworthy outsider.

When my early, incoherent alienation grew into intellectual and political radicalism, my parents were baffled. They had striven faithfully for the American dream from the years when Woodrow Wilson railed against "hyphenated Americans" to the 1950s when the so-called Americanizing of religion was complete. In the same year I became a university senior, John Kennedy was elected president. But at this pinnacle of assimilation for Irish Americans, the contradictions of the American dream were revealed by black students battling segregation in the South. It was a time when idealism challenged apathy for the attention of young people. I turned down a possible journalism career at the *Detroit News*, fell in love with a Southern civil rights activist, and drove away to

Atlanta in the station wagon my parents gave me as a graduation present. My father figured I was throwing my life away, and a few years later told a reporter, "I don't know what influenced him when he went away, but it's not the way he was raised." I am sure those "influences" included an Irish dimension which Americanism was supposed to have severed. My first act in the civil rights movement consisted of driving from Ann Arbor to Fayetteville, Tennessee, bringing a carload of food to black sharecroppers who had been evicted from their land. The mission was successful, though we were chased out of town by a violent mob. Was it only coincidental that I responded to a crisis reminiscent of my evicted, starving Irish ancestors? So effective was the assimilation process that my parents couldn't comprehend why I would risk a career to prevent hunger, eviction, and prejudice. I was Irish on the inside though I couldn't name it at the time.

My Irishness was a hidden magnet drawing me towards dreams, underdogs, lost causes, and crusades, to acts of defiance against hopelessness, to the courage of the student movement in the American South, to poets and singers at coffeehouses, to women and men wearing shapeless black clothes, to wild and mindless romance, to existentialists and prophets of the absurd.

I was lost in books at an early age, and have lived my life surrounded by them. In second grade, I was reading weighty theological passages of Saint Thomas Aquinas, my patron saint, to beaming nuns and parents. I was like young Frank McCourt in Limerick whose teacher said, "Your mind is a treasure house that you should stock well and it's the one part of you the world can't interfere with."

Instead of seeking employment in the Kennedy Administration, I went to jail in Georgia on my twenty-first birthday. I am drawn to battles where the likelihood of winning is remote and the penalty of losing is high. Where does this orientation come from? One theory suggests it's in the genes, the secret machinery of one's physical being and therefore not subject to questions. It's been suggested that I was a spoiled only child insistent on being right. Still others offered the notion that I was well educated in democratic ideals and driven by Catholic guilt at their failed realization. I have been wondering about this question for forty years. Since my heart has been broken many times over, why hasn't burnout enveloped my spirit? The reason, I believe, is that I have an Irish propensity to fight for lost causes.

Many immigrants, women, minorities, and poor people suffer from hidden psychic injuries that block their ambition. They expect to lose. It is their lot. How many times I have been approached by people who say, "Tom, you're the first candidate I ever voted for who won!" When I think of a specifically Irish tendency to fight for lost causes, however, I don't mean a sense that failure is inevitable. There is a deeper reason to fight for causes that may not succeed. The reason is that the world would be worse off if no one did. Imagine a world without troublemakers and you have defined a WASP paradise. Imagine a world without dissenters, revolutionaries, jesters, or dreamers and you have imagined a world that is not human. The existence of evil requires a consciousness of good. The Irish view is that life is about spiritual as well as material matters, about the soul as well as the pocketbook. When you fight for a cause that is labeled lost by the temporal power, you are still expressing a fundamental quality of being human. Our genetic makeup is narrowly defined as chemical or material, but it is also the source of our creativity, and the gift of being an absolutely unique individual in communal dependency with all living things. Irish people have always believed in an "otherworld," not only the Christian view of an "afterlife," but a world of the spirits in the here and now, not simply in caves or rivers but in our own personalities. One can act in the name of spiritual motivation that has nothing to do with pragmatism. And if no one did, if everyone put pragmatism first, how would our deepest values be sustained? There is a role for keepers of the flame.

In 1960, the politics of pragmatism and assimilation triumphed in America. The immigrant success story climaxed in the election of John Kennedy who, in a major speech shortly thereafter, pronounced that American social problems could be solved, that only technical fixes were needed to realize the American dream for all. New Frontier planners believed that the remaining battles against racism and poverty were simply mopping-up operations. Kennedy's election, in the mind of Irish America, righted the wrong done to Al Smith three decades earlier, and confirmed the triumph of the Irish over their tragic past. During the campaign, I considered the Southern Baptist attacks on Kennedy's Catholicism as obsolete, irrelevant echoes from a past that no longer mattered, just as the rhetoric of Southern racists would soon be filed in the dustbin of history. I was so Americanized that I felt no ethnic heartbeat, only a flutter of idealism I associated with Kennedy's youth.

Not having a connection to the Irish past, I had to assume that my friends and I were misfits, maladjusted rebels caught up in Freudian dramas with our fathers. I had no historic rationale for why I was rebelling against my parents' achievement of respectability and middle-class comfort. There was no one teaching the Irish dimension of my radical discontent, in contrast to Jews and blacks who were instilled with values of their ancestors. There was the Irish Catholic socialist Michael Harrington, who drank at the White Horse in Greenwich Village (the same Irish watering hole as Frank McCourt). He quoted James Connolly. But the Irish tradition he represented seemed more past than present, more sentimental than serious, more Catholic than political. His uniqueness reinforced the view that I was postethnic in an ethnic world. My destiny was to establish an identity beyond assimilation.

Emmet and Paine: My Irish Radical Past

Years later, I found fragmentary hints at the ethnic roots of my radicalism. For instance, an Irish genealogy text given me by Patricia Harty, the editor of *Irish America*, contained a startling reference to "Hayden":

> O Headon, Oh Eideain, in Irish . . . is of frequent occurrence in the Ormond Deeds from the year 1374 . . . Peter Hayden of Boleycarrigan, Co. Wicklow . . . elected captain of the insurgents . . . was with 35 other prisoners killed . . . in 1798.

Who was this "insurgent" Hayden, killed in the rising of the United

Irishmen in 1798? For the first time, I had an image of a Hayden who stayed and fought, who didn't make the melting pot. I am a believer in invisible ancestral influences, not simply the immediate parental influences so central to current psychological models. Assessing the impacts of one's ancestors is part of the challenge of recovering repressed cultural memory. Where the trail of evidence disappears, where intellect fails, one must rely on imagination, on possibilities that are technically unprovable. I know that my ancestors experienced the 1798 United Irish uprising in which 30,000 were slaughtered, but I may never know what their experience was. An identical name – Peter Hayden – is trace evidence, nothing more. But it is a tantalizing alternative to imagining nothing at all, or internalizing an empty immigrant fairy tale.

The African Nobel laureate Wole Soyinka has written of archetypal "essence ideals" in the collective memory of the Yoruba.[126] The African scholar Clyde Ford asserts that "as long as the name of a departed ancestor can be called, that ancestor is not dead in some final sense of the word." These unseen ones can be "forces in the lives of the living" and accessible in dreaming.[127] Significantly, Ford adds, "mythology has rarely, if ever, entered the modern discourse on race."[128] Irish racial memory is a powerful, unseen force in contemporary Irish life. If there is a consensus that the traumas of our parents directly affect our psyche, how much more powerful are the traumas experienced by our ancestors who imprinted their legacy on descendants in a chain finally leading to ourselves? In addition, there is a symbolic legacy contained in the naming ritual. A Gaelic name, whether that of a warrior, goddess, or martyr, shapes the self-perception of the individual who is named; similarly, the lack of a Gaelic name simplifies the identity transition from traditional to modern, ethnic to assimilated. Naming one's child after a black nationalist like Malcolm X will have a different effect than, say, an Anglo-Irish name like Colin Powell.

I was named after the most respected Irish American of the early immigrants, Thomas Emmet, a leader of the United Irish uprising who was deported to America while his brother, Robert, was hanged in Dublin in 1803. I am Thomas Emmet Hayden the Fourth, suggesting that someone in my family was named for Thomas Emmet while he was a living legend among the Irish Americans. But when I asked my mother who were the other Thomas Emmet Haydens, all she replied was "the first, the second and the third." She had never heard of Thomas Emmet, the exiled Irish nationalist who did more than anyone to organize the Irish immigrant welfare societies that helped my own ancestors with settlement difficulties.

I have tried to imagine, to call the name of, Thomas Emmet because he surely can be an important force in the lives of the living today. He was a Protestant lawyer who joined forces with the Irish Catholics to free the Irish nation from British rule. The uprising was crushed. Tens of thousands died. But modern Irish republicanism was born. Emmet hoped, he wrote, that an alliance with the Catholics would lead to an "identity of views and interests" instead of "fearing each other," but his dream was in vain. It was the collapse of the United Irish rebellion of 1798 that led the British to subordinate Ireland to the Act of Union in 1802, effectively denying the Irish any governmental representation during the Famine crisis of four decades later. Emmet and other accused United Irishmen were blocked from entering the United States by the US Administration of John Adams, just as Sinn Féin leaders were banned from American soil during the so-called Troubles. The American Federalists, following the spirit of Alexander Hamilton, chose to maintain the British connection for commercial reasons but also to prevent the spread of revolutionary republicanism from France and Ireland. It was the 1800 election of the Republican candidate Thomas Jefferson, with Irish emigrant votes, that opened the doors of America to Emmet and the United Irish exiles – just as the election of Bill Clinton nearly two centuries later led to visas for Gerry Adams.

Emmet came to America to realize the dreams the United Irishmen had lost in Ireland. In time he became Attorney General of New York state and a close ally of Thomas Jefferson. When Jefferson won, the New York Irish cheered for "Emmet and liberty" outside loyalist mansions.[129] In 1824, the Orange Order, then a potent force in the so-called nativist movement, organized an intimidating anti-Catholic march through Irish ghettos in today's Greenwich Village. The Irish battled the Orangemen in the streets, in exactly the scenario still played out at Drumcree and other flashpoints in Northern Ireland today. Emmet led the movement in New York City to ban the Orange parades through Irish Catholic communities on the basis that they were racist and triumphalist, the same arguments made by current residents' groups in Northern Ireland. (And like the contemporary conflict, the Orange parades were violent encounters. In 1871, the New York governor permitted the National Guard to accompany the Orangemen on their July 12 march, leading to an encounter in which the Seventh Regiment shot and killed up to sixty people, nearly all Irish Catholics.)[130]

Emmet was an exception who symbolized the possibility of a progressive Irish American role model. He never wavered on the issue of Irish freedom, while at the same time throwing himself into the democratic struggles of his new homeland. His first court appearance was to plead the case of a fugitive slave. Emmet rejected the gradualist arguments for emancipation of the slaves. "Some supposed [of the Irish]," he said, "what has also been asserted of the Negro race, that the Irish were an inferior, semi-brutal people, incapable of managing the affairs of their country."[131]

As a prophet of multicultural equality, Emmet was attacked by the conservative Irish as harmful to their efforts to assimilate. As David Wilson recounts in his history *United Irish, Irish America*, one anti-Emmet tract raised questions that still have resonance for American identity: "Can America after this [the election of Jefferson] be said to have a character as a nation? . . ." went the diatribe, which bemoaned "a multifarious, heterogeneous compound – a Gallo-Hibernico-Hispanico-Corsicano race, living where once lived Americans."[132]

This namesake of mine was also an intimate ally of the most progressive voice of the American Revolution, Thomas Paine. *The Rights of Man* was read on the streets of Belfast and Dublin with the same fervor it generated in America.[133] Forty thousand copies of *The Rights of Man* were sold in Ireland, more than twice the total in England. In 1792, Paine was named an honorary member of the United Irishmen. The osmosis between the thinking of Paine and the United Irish circle was illustrated by the Gaelic code words of the Ancient Order of Hibernians, taken from *The Rights of Man*: *codromaght* (equality) and *saoirseaught* (liberty).

During the same year Dublin Castle was paranoid with reports that Paine was secretly conspiring with the United Irishmen in Belfast. He surfaced instead in revolutionary France, where he joined the conspiratorial circle of exiled Irishmen. He lobbied the French foreign minister to send an expeditionary force to Ireland. When he was tried *in absentia* and burned in effigy in London in September 1792, the Irish papers printed the entire trial transcript, a proscribed offense which led to indictments and persecutions of the publishers. After the election of Jefferson, Paine called for the USA to liberate Ireland by force, but Jefferson resisted the advice and instead allowed the United Irishmen to take refuge in America. There, in 1804, the exiled Thomas Emmet met Tom Paine, who returned in the same year from France. They become close associates and friends.

Paine's dream of international revolution had failed to materialize. England wanted his head. The French had expelled him. Ireland was subjugated by the Act of Union. He was too radical for Jefferson. He died in 1809, lonely, broken, and in debt. There was no state funeral for the man who inspired the Revolution. He was buried in New Rochelle in what a friend of Paine described as "an obscure grave on an open and disregarded bit of land."[134] Not long after, his bones were excavated by an English fortune hunter and apparently lost at sea. The conventional history of this tragic life blames Paine for becoming an alcoholic and angry man in his later years. His intimate connection to Irish republicans like Emmet is not mentioned in standard works such as Fruchtman's *Thomas Paine, Apostle of Freedom* (1994). The best account is in an obscure essay by David Dickson in a 1993 collection by Lilliput Press, Dublin. But there is another way to understand Paine's late-life disillusionment. His heart was broken because the revolutions for which he had fought were compromised. Only the Irish understood his bitterness. "It was Paine's Irish friends, old and new, the émigré United Irishmen – including

Thomas Addis Emmet, whom he made his executor – who befriended him to the bitter end," according to Dickson.[135]

This was the story my mother never told me because she herself did not know that my namesake Thomas Emmet was Thomas Paine's closest ally and executor of Paine's will. Emmet devoted his life to creating democratic republics in Ireland and America, just as Paine was devoted to revolution in America, England, Ireland, and France. Understanding their intertwined lives could have provided a foundation – for myself and for countless Irish Americans – for what it means to be American and what it means to be Irish. Instead, like Paine's bones lost at sea, the stories disintegrate, are bleached and difficult to recover in the tides of assimilation. Even my name drifted atop the surface of my being, its origins indiscernible, by my parents' time.

The Forgotten San Patricios

Many other chapters of Irish radicalism in America were forgotten or erased by the time I was growing up. It is not necessary to explore the tradition in detail to understand how its virtual absence shaped my sense of identity as well as protecting the myth of Irish America, though several stories stand out. One example is the case of the San Patricio Brigade, an Irish detachment of three hundred men who mutinied and deserted the US army to fight on the side of Mexico in 1847.[136] There was significant American opposition to this war, for example by Abraham Lincoln and Henry David Thoreau, but dissension among the heavily immigrant ground forces was an especially grave threat. Led by Private John O'Reilly of Galway (and later Michigan), the San Patricios were Irish Famine immigrants conscripted into the Anglo-led armed forces shortly after arriving in America. Their rebel ranks included several escaped African slaves as well. The immigrants joined for a chance to prove their patriotism and make $7 per month, but soon found themselves suffering a familiar abuse under their Protestant superior officers, including instances of being branded on the face with a "D" for desertion or whipped at the stake. Finally, they chose to fight on the side of a Mexican Catholic peasantry that reminded them of home. With typical Irish bravado, the San Patricios proved to be fighters of great valor under a flag that combined the cry "Erin Go Bragh" with the Mexican eagle. O'Reilly's men defeated the US 1st Dragoons at the battle of Buena Vista in January 1847, but the war turned steadily against the Mexican side. Facing certain death if captured, on one occasion they defended their positions even when the Mexican troops attempted to surrender. Finally, in 1847, the surviving San Patricios were defeated at the battle of Churobusco convent. O'Reilly was branded and lashed, his flesh described by one observer as "a pounded piece of raw beef, the blood oozing from every stripe as given." The survivors were taken to Mexico City with ropes around their necks, and after the US victory at Chapultepec Castle were hanged. O'Reilly himself was spared on a technicality, disappeared, and was never seen again. In some tales, he married a Mexican woman and lived in the mountains. Others claimed he returned to Michigan, and still others, to Galway.

The emphatic nature of the San Patricios' punishment, which was described by one stunned officer as "the most cruel and sanguinary scene that was probably ever enacted in a war," was accompanied by vilification and ultimately erasure of the episode from the history books. The San Patricios are remembered, if at all, as eccentrics, lunatics, drunkards, Irish Catholic peasants lured away by seductive Mexican women.

Why are the San Patricios important to our understanding of the Irish? The episode vividly illustrates how the immigrant Irish were treated even during military service to their country. The suppression of their revolt, not only in military but in political histories, illustrates the importance of molding Irish America as a model minority lest it become a threat to the established order. Most significant, however, is the treatment of the San Patricios in Mexico and Ireland today, where, unlike the United States, they are officially commemorated as heroes in annual celebrations and even on postage stamps. In Mexico, all children learn of the San Patricios in their classrooms. The result is a cultural bond between the Irish and the Mexicans that excludes Irish Americans. The "gut level affinity" is based on a common experience of colonization, religious and spiritual similarities, and what one historian calls a "cavalier attitude towards central governments."[137] Indeed, the British Communist Party in the 1930s denounced the Irish for being "too Mexican" to be good communists![138] In 1999, the president of Ireland, Mary McAleese, visited the San Patricio monument in Mexico City and quipped to an applauding, overflow crowd that "if the Irish and the Mexicans got together they could take over the US" (*Irish Times*, April 8, 1999). To recognize the San Patricios as anything but crazed Irishmen would force an uncomfortable reappraisal of US–Mexican history. It might undermine the historical legitimacy still given the US–Mexico war, recognize a continuing Mexican grievance, perhaps recast the North American understanding of Mexico as a second-class nation, and even shed a different light on the unfinished battle for land and indigenous rights by the Zapatistas in Chiapas state today, where subcommandante Marcos spoke admiringly of the San Patricios on St Patrick's Day 1995.[139] Most important, it might realign Irish America to a new understanding of the similarities between its immigrant past and that of today's Mexican immigrants in their former homelands of Texas, Arizona, Colorado, New Mexico, and California.

The Molly Maguires

Another severed root of Irish rebel history is that of the so-called Molly Maguires, many of whom originated in my ancestral county of Monaghan as an underground movement taking violent vengeance against landlords for evictions and starvation and who appeared as underground saboteurs against the mining companies in the coal regions of Pennsylvania in the 1870s. The image of the Famine Irish as helpless, starving victims of overpopulation who were saved by American assimilation rests on the erasure of resistance movements like the Molly Maguires. Where mentioned at all in American histories, the Irish Mollies were categorized to reinforce the image of the violent, drunken wild Irish. By analogy, their removal from popular history would be equivalent to leaving the Black Panthers, Brown Berets, Young Lords, and Weather Underground out of the history of the American sixties.

But the Irish did not progress towards better living standards and suburban assimilation just by obediently observing the law and English manners; nor did they by religious appeals to conscience. They had to overcome conditions in Ireland and America where political and labor rights were nonexistent, and where Crown forces backed the landholders. Until the English conquest and beyond, the rural peasantry of Ireland spoke the Irish language, and lived in communities (clachans) in the midst of communal lands (rundale), not unlike indigenous people anywhere. That way of life was disrupted by the new agrarian capitalism forcibly introduced under colonial rule. The centuries of anti-Irish persecution in the countryside produced a tradition of rebel secret societies known as Whiteboys or Ribbonmen, groups which took on an additional Catholic identity after the failure of the United Irishmen in 1798. These clandestine organizations raided landlords' estates, cut the fencing, killed cattle, burned down big houses, and at times killed the owners, most famously Major Denis McMahon of Roscommon in 1847, whose former manor house is the site today of Ireland's only Famine museum. W. Steuart Trench, author of *The Realities of Irish Life*, and a land agent in County Monaghan, was the first to name the Molly Maguires, in 1843. Whether they called themselves the Molly Maguires, or whether it was a label affixed by others, is open to question, but these raiders called themselves "Molly," and disguised themselves as women to signify "the passionate, the disorderly, the violent and chaotic side of human nature," according to historian Kevin Kenny.[140] Among those in Monaghan might have been my own ancestors. These were the "aboriginal Irish," in the illuminating phrase of an 1845 English observer, those whose primary language was Irish, who were targeted not only by the landlords but by the Church hierarchy for conversion in the so-called "devotional revolution" after the Famine.[141]

Eventually, from counties like Donegal, Sligo, and Monaghan, they became part of the uprooted who arrived in the harsh coalfields of

Pennsylvania, undertaking brutish work for employers and overseers who treated them as wild animals. What became the industrial labor movement was just emerging as the Workingman's Benevolent Association, with even its legal, peaceful forms being met with venomous hostility by the owners. The Catholic Church, moreover, provided little direct protection since it leased its land in the coalfields from the same owners. And so the Mollies – now considered a Fenian conspiracy against all America – struck back with industrial sabotage and were eventually accused of seventeen vengeance killings of mineowners, superintendents, foremen, and police. They were infiltrated by a Pinkerton agent named James McParlan, himself an Irish immigrant, and fifty were indicted on evidence supplied by Pinkerton agents. Their state prosecutor, Franklin B. Gowen, had been president of the Philadelphia & Reading Railroad Company. Twenty Molly Maguires were hanged, ten on June 21, 1877, a date which became known as Black Thursday. Though later research revealed the indictments to be flimsy or manufactured, the image of the Mollies was conflated with and reinforced the image of the Irish as primitives capable of sudden and savage violence. That their violent resistance, whether moral or not, bore a certain logic given Irish history, was hardly considered in the rush to demonize and punish. Of course, the legalized violence of the landlords, mineowners, and Pinkertons was not considered savage at all.

Whether or not my ancestors include the Molly Maguires, I have a little Molly in my blood, an empathy for their experience, like that of the San Patricios, and for so many doomed martyrs of Irish history. At many points in my life, before and into the seventies, I had to express, or cope with, uncontrollable feelings of rage, at times spilling over into violent confrontations with authority. Where did these depths of alienation originate? My background was a comfortable one, yet I identified with underdogs who, despite hopeless odds, would sacrifice themselves in a confrontation. Such rage is dismissed today as sociopathic. But even the most apparently irrational act may have explicable origins, however buried. For example, the *New York Times* writer Fox Butterfield once researched the entire ancestry of a young African American convict in a

New York prison, Willie James Bosket, Jr, whose short lifetime of violent crimes – he claimed to have committed two hundred armed robberies and twenty-five stabbings by age fifteen – provoked a sensational public outcry by politicians who branded him a "mad dog killer." Bosket, who had a near-genius IQ, believed that his violence came from sources long before his birth. Butterfield gradually traced the ancestry of Bosket back to the violence of slavery in South Carolina which had produced a long line of blacks who in each generation resisted their chains and, in the absence of meaningful alternatives, became "bad" black men. Butterfield's narrative also suggested that such violence was transmitted across generations not because of a "violence gene," but because of the continual reproduction of threats to annihilate a sense of black manhood. Bosket's ancestors were uprooted people, whose very names and identities were erased by slavery, whose families were torn apart, whose lands were taken and never restored, whose manhood was feared and denigrated, who couldn't vote or work for a living wage, and who were defined as barbarians rather than human beings. "Becoming a man meant becoming a criminal," Butterfield concluded.[142]

I believe the Molly Maguires were very much in the same tradition, that their violence can be understood as a response to history, and therefore must be addressed with historical understanding rather than demonization. To shun and dissociate from the "demonic" young men known today as "superpredators" may serve a desire for order, respectability and a scapegoat, but that very distancing contributes to the sense of powerlessness and violation that leads certain individuals to violence. Instead of severing the pathways to our roots, I would rather recognize the Molly Maguire – or the Willie Bosket – in each of us.

Gangs are Us

Few Irish Americans recall or wish to recall that we have had our share of Willie Boskets. The phenomenon of violent street gangs did not begin in Compton or Pico Union in the sixties, and is hardly confined to

African Americans or Mexicans. The Irish underclass of the 1850s gave rise to gangs as feared and bloodthirsty as any gangsta rappers of the current era. In New York, there were the Plug Uglies and Roach Guards, and individual professional heavies with names like Hoggy Walsh, Slops Connolly, and Piker Ryan. They were paid $2 to beat someone up, $15 for chewing off an ear, and $100 for "doing the big job" (killing someone for pay). The police dockets were filled with Irish names.[143] Through the Prohibition period, Irish gangs "had to be crazier than everybody else because we were Irish guys," recalled a hit man for the Westies of Hell's Kitchen in New York.[144] One of the gangsters, Vincent "Mad Dog" Coll, was so bloodthirsty that he was killed for "giving the underworld a bad name." Mad Dog was set up by an Irishman, Owney Madden, and killed in a phone booth by a fusillade from Thompson submachine guns.[145]

Mad Dog was the Willie Bosket of the Irish. Born in Donegal, in one of the poorest agricultural districts of Ireland, Vincent Coll was raised in "an essentially violent society," according to one history.[146] Local landlords had attempted to displace and evict so many people in the parish that "widespread anarchy" required three hundred policemen to keep order in the 1860s. Land agitation in the following decades included the bludgeoning to death of a policeman trying to arrest the parish priest for "incitement" of the villagers. The Coll family tried to emigrate to America at the turn of the twentieth century, but gave up in the face of anti-Irish prejudice and returned. Finally, in 1909, they returned with Vincent, then three, to a Bronx whose streets were filled with notorious gangs and "droves of filth-encrusted kids . . . hawking petty goods, pickpocketing, keeping pigeons on tenement roofs and taking an occasional dip in the Hutchinson and Bronx rivers." The authorities at the time believed that these youths could be cured by shipping them off to Protestant homes in the American West. Vincent, diagnosed as a "constitutional psychopathic inferior," was sent to a reformatory in New York state (as was Willie Bosket). From there he eventually escaped and began his career as a hit man for the Irish mob in New York. It was the time of Prohibition, seen as a WASP repression of the Irish subculture, when the underground economy was more profitable for the Irish poor than the mainstream economy. The parallels with today's underclass violence are pointedly exact.

Even in present times, the glaring evidence of a violent Irish gang headed by James "Whitey" Bulger in Boston is treated by the media and public opinion as an ethnic soap opera in comparison with white attitudes towards black, Mexican or Salvadoran gangs in the inner city. The Bulger brothers – Billy and Whitey – have played a dominant role in Massachusetts politics and society for a generation, Billy as leader of the state senate and president of the University of Massachusetts, and Whitey as a gang leader indicted for twenty-one counts of murder. Whitey, now on America's "Most Wanted" list, has been an FBI inform-ant for twenty-five years, serving his purpose of undermining the Italian mob while obtaining protection from his handlers. Both Bulgers came from the brick tenements of south Boston when crime was one of the few means of winning respect and income. They carried in their bones a memory that three of every ten children in the Boston slums died before they were one year old.[147] "I'll always be a redneck mick from South Boston," Billy said at the height of his power.

If a Whitey Bulger was black or brown, chances are he would be con-sidered a menace to civilization. But, denying the obvious similarities with the black–brown underclass, the Bulger story as written by many journalists reads like an episode of *The Sopranos* or a version of the legend of Robin Hood, a romantic outlaw. Tim Pat Coogan makes the brothers into classic and sympathetic Irish figures. Regarding Billy's political power, Coogan writes: "the fact that his brother might, just might, be lying somewhere in the long grass, served to create a certain, shall we say, circumspection in the minds of opponents."[148] The *Los Angeles Times* described Whitey as a "local pop icon" whose sightings had become "the Boston equivalent of imagined glimpses of Elvis Presley." This Robin Hood-style portrayal was written in October 2000, while several bodies of Whitey's alleged victims were being dug up not far from the campus Billy presided over and where Al Gore and George Bush were debating.

The point I am making is that a racial double standard exists in America's consciousness of gangs. For assimilated Irish Americans (or Italian or Jewish Americans), their cultural roots in the violent underclass have been severed in the process of achieving status and distinction. Their gangster relatives are not only in the family closet, but brilliantly re-invented as sympathetic or tragic heroes in movies and television. It would not be tasteful in light of the Horatio Alger myth to acknowledge that one generation's success was built on an earlier generation's boot-legging, loansharking, money laundering, extortion, and assassinations. The myth of the professional and successful classes is that their achieve-ment rests entirely on the shoulders of hard-working, sacrificing, law-abiding generations that came before them. The truth is often otherwise. But preserving the myth allows the modern white ethnic to project disgust towards members of nonwhite races who learned from the movies that the path towards middle-class status involves drug dealing and drive-by shootings. If Irish Americans could embrace their gangland origins, they would be less likely to see modern street-corner gangsters as unredeemable superpredators fit only for cells on Death Row. They might see the bloody quagmire of the current "war on drugs" as a doomed repeat of Prohibition. They might realize that just as the New Deal, not simply white ethnic pluck, elevated their grandparents to middle-class opportunity, only another New Deal can address the crisis of the inner city.

An Alternative Assimilation

Becoming lace-curtain and respectable was not the only model of assim-ilation possible to imagine. Many nineteenth-century Irish tried to assimilate not into WASP society, but into rebel, democratic, and work-ing-class American traditions, combining the struggles in Ireland and America as one. Such is historian Eric Foner's alternative to the domi-nant notion of assimilation, namely that the Irish eagerly climbed the economic ladder to become middle-class conservative Americans. The hidden history of this Irish American radicalism has been little transmitted until recent publications such as Terry Golway's *Irish Rebel*, and Thomas Keneally's *The Great Shame*, both compelling stories of the Fenian exiles in America. Foner's key point, in a 1980 history of politics and ideology in the age of the Civil War, is that "assimilation" in the United States need not mean only a submission to a dominant culture; it can also mean identification with oppositional working-class or ethnic cultures.[149] Foner focuses on the brief history of the Land League of the 1870s, a movement against both mass evictions in Ireland and the poverty facing the Irish in America during the so-called Gilded Age. Those Irish American supporters of the Land League, like Patrick Ford, the editor of the *Irish World*, "wished to transform their society even as they became a more integral part of it," writes Foner. They identified with American traditions, not simply those of Ireland, including the abolitionist movement, the emerging Knights of Labor, and the radical politics of Henry George. Yet Foner points out that "few histories of the Irish in America contain more than a passing reference" to such subjects. Instead, he goes on, the dominant history of how Irish American nationalism emerged is described as only a response to Protestant nativism. All the Irish sought, in the mainstream history articulated by Thomas N. Brown, was to "be middle class and respectable." According to Brown, "In the Lace Curtain Irishman, the rebel found fulfillment."

The problem with the conventional assimilationist view is that it removes Irish American radicalism from its place in history, viewing it as either marginal or a transitional phase in the march of the Irish to the middle class. Left out are stories of Irish resistance to absorption into the American status quo. The Fenian Brotherhood, formed in 1858, and its 1870s successor Clan na Gael, are seen as irrational, violent, and parochial elements who refused to leave their old country behind or loyally incorporate themselves into the largesse of America. (The same castigation is reserved in modern times for Irish American supporters of the Provisional IRA.) Equally important, Irish Americans like Patrick Ford who sought not only to free Ireland but to bridge the gap with American-born reformers like the abolitionists, or support a progressive income tax and the eight-hour day, are removed from history. Yet the Land League in 1881 had 1,500 branches, and Ford's paper was being read aloud to American cigar-makers as they worked as well as to illiterate blacksmiths and shoemakers in Ireland. The Land League, in Ford's vision, was to become the vanguard in "the war of the great army of the disinherited, in all lands, for their Heaven-willed possessions."[150]

Foner's analysis is an important challenge to the conventional Irish American history. Otherwise, we might believe that ethnic nationalism is simply a stage in becoming American, or, worse, that today's ethnic underclass will eventually lord themselves over the poor of tomorrow, even poor people of their own ethnicity. We might fail to notice that worthy attempts have been made by the Irish, and other ethnic minorities up to the present time, to assimilate into democratic traditions that challenge the status quo. It is not too late, I will argue, for the Irish and Irish Americans today to assimilate culturally and politically with the anticolonial world, or the ranks of racial minorities and immigrants in America, instead of assimilating into the WASP establishment. Foner helps us reclaim this tradition of trying to become part of democratic America without leaving others behind or below us, and reminds us of the progressive role that many Irish Americans played in struggles towards abolitionism, the rights of labor, and ultimately the New Deal. It is this disappeared heritage in which my own political life should have been grounded, but instead I became an American radical thinking that the Irish Americans were inevitable adversaries.

At the same time, Foner's own history shows the limits of such progressive and radical struggles by Irish Americans, and by implication other ethnic or racial minorities, to assert themselves in the face of persistent pressures to conform to dominant values. Vital as it is to reclaim these lost histories and previous lives, it must be acknowledged that for the most part the direction of the Irish in America has been to blend in and support the status quo. Not without reason did the Fenian revolutionary O'Donovan Rossa condemn the prosperous Irish Americans "whose shamrocks blossomed like diamonds," and James Connolly, the leader of the 1916 uprising, describe Irish American politicians as "descendants of the serpents Saint Patrick banished from Ireland." The law of the so-called melting pot may not have worked smoothly, but it has not been suspended either. The historic dynamic can be summarized briefly to bring this story up to the present time. Through strength of numbers, organizational skill, and a powerful survival instinct, the Irish Americans succeeded economically in lifting themselves from unskilled laborers to skilled workers and, in my parents' time, into the professions. They did so through the Church, the trade unions, and the political machines, making themselves a force that had to be accommodated. At the same time, Irish nationalism contributed significantly to the long struggle for Irish independence, which resulted in an appearance of independent, if still partitioned, nationhood in the 1920s. The Irish cause began to subside in America with creation of the twenty-six-county Irish Republic, and was greatly depressed by the subsequent bloody civil war between Irishmen themselves. As the rationale for Irish nationalism ebbed, the possibility of becoming Americans without hyphens opened up. In summary, we succeeded in changing America from a new Ulster, a Protestant country for Protestant people, from puritanism to pluralism, from honoring the rights of capital to protecting the rights of labor as well, from a market society to one in which government plays a positive role. Seen this way, the Irish Americans have a right to celebrate proudly. But the price was a heavy one, if less visible. The Irish became white, became conservative, became super-patriotic, became so assimilated into WASP mentality that we turned indifferent or hostile to any groups that might have reminded us of our former selves. We have made the Irish Republic a tourist attraction while treating the North as another country. Eventually, as I will argue later, Ireland itself might well be assimilated into the American cultural, economic, and political empire.

Perhaps there was a moment, as Foner has noted, when Irish nationalism could have blended permanently into social radicalism in America. I can imagine myself, for example, working for the banished Fenian O'Donovan Rossa when he ran for the New York state senate in 1870. According to Kerby Miller's account, Rossa, a hardline Irish revolutionary, apparently defeated Boss Tweed himself, only to have his election stolen by fraud. In Miller's words, "Irish Americans henceforth voted with their stomachs . . . repeatedly rejecting nationalist pleas to desert and punish the Democratic Party for its indifference or hostility to Irish freedom."[151] And ultimately, who could blame them? When was enough enough? Ethnic, assimilationist politics was a protective reaction against a world in which true justice was impossible but another Famine was preventable. If there was little hope for the redistribution of wealth, the saying went, at least the Irish could redistribute the graft.

Symbolic of the entry of Irish Americans into the mainstream was the difference between Jimmy Cagney's 1931 performance in *The Public Enemy*, about a ruthless and violent Irishman, and his portrayal ten years later of George M. Cohan in *Yankee Doodle Dandy*. For the latter performance, at the outset of World War Two, Cagney received the American Medal of Honor from an appreciative though paternalistic President Roosevelt, who declared that patriotism towards America was "what I've always admired about you Irish Americans." Cagney in turn extolled the Horatio Alger era.[152]

The Sixties Made Me Irish

In 1960 the Irish immigrant success story culminated in the election of the first Roman Catholic, John Fitzgerald Kennedy, to the American presidency. It was the first time in my life that I actually heard the subject raised of whether Irish Catholics were "qualified" and "loyal," an echo of the virulent nativism of past generations. I dismissed these attacks on Kennedy's religion as obsolete, irrelevant refrains from a past that no longer mattered. My primary connection with John F. Kennedy was generational, not Irish. I covered the 1960 Democratic convention in Los Angeles, and was moved by the possibility of the New Frontier energizing a new student movement. There I casually met Robert Kennedy for the first time, marveling at his youth rather than his Irishness. I identified myself more with Martin Luther King and the black students picketing the convention for a civil rights platform than with the historic ascension of an Irish Catholic on the inside. Later in October, when I was at John Kennedy's side as a student reporter, while he declared himself for a Peace Corps, the excitement I felt was for my generation, not my tribe.

It was not simply my cultural assimilation that prevented an Irish identification with John Kennedy, but his own successful effort to present his Irish heritage in the most acceptable terms to America. This meant masking it. Kennedy's glamorous appearance was that of an Anglo. His wife was a cultured Frenchwoman. While his large family of birth fit the Irish stereotype, his having only two children himself showed "progress" towards the American norm. His courage in war, his Harvard credentials, and his US Senate experience all accentuated his acceptability as well. He was not an ethnic politician like Al Smith or others produced by the big-city Irish. John Kennedy presented himself as a Yankee.

But he was not. The price of assimilation, the very question of assimilation itself, continues to be measured in the unfolding of the Kennedy story. "What the hell do I have to do to be an American?" his father Joseph Kennedy once screamed out.[153] The answer seemed to be: whatever it took. The Kennedys built a family fortress from which one child after another would challenge the barriers of a hostile world. To state that they would become overachievers is to understate their daring. They received virtually Olympic training in physical, intellectual, and political pursuits. Their mother, Rose Fitzgerald, was a controlling Irish woman, their father Joseph a driven businessman and, among other occupations, a bootlegger, who became US Ambassador to the Court of St James ("a helluva way from east Boston," he called it). Aside from an analysis by John Duffy Ibson, the psychic toll of climbing from the Irish bog to the US White House has not been narrated as a calamity of assimilation.[154] During his brief presidency, John Kennedy was advised against indulging his desire to visit Ireland once in his life. His Boston Irish advisers told him there were "no political or diplomatic advantages to be gained" by what they dismissed as a "sentimental excursion."[155] But the President apparently could not repress his "sentimental" Irishness any longer, and decided to follow the advice of

Robert Frost, who urged him at his inaugural to be "more Irish than Harvard."[156] So it was in 1963 he visited the cottage of his great-grandfather Patrick, an 1848 Famine emigrant from Dunganstown. Upon leaving, the President promised to return, quoting a poem about an exile's pain:

> 'Tis the Shannon's brightly glancing stream,
> Brightly gleaming, silent in the morning beam
> Oh! The sight entrancing.
> Thus return from travels long, years of exile,
> Years of pain
> To see old Shannon's face again,
> O'er the waters glancing.

Just how powerful was the hidden Irish side of this man who presented himself as representative of modernity? Consider this poem written to him by Jackie in the 1950s:

> But part he was of an alien breed
> Of a breed that had laughed on Irish hills
> And heard the voices in Irish rills
> The lilt of the green land danced in his blood
> Tara, Killarney, a magical flood
> That surged in the depths of his too proud heart
> And spiked the punch of New England so tart
> Men would call him thoughtful, sincere
> They would not see through to the Last Cavalier.[157]

John Kennedy met an Irish fate. Was it accident or conspiracy? We may never know, but from an Irish perspective it didn't necessarily matter. Life is not lived until it is understood as a tragedy, said Yeats.[158] And as Moynihan tearfully said at the funeral, the world will break your heart. In Irish karma, too much success is only a prelude to catastrophe. When Kennedy died, I was shaken to my core. The event confirmed my opinion, formed in high school reading Salinger's *The Catcher in the Rye*, that life was absurd. I concluded that the project we called "modernity," the achievement of rational administrative control of all life's contradictions, the New Frontier Kennedy himself had endorsed, was a profoundly false hope. In pondering these notions of fate, I had no idea how Irish was my soul.

Vietnam and the Irish Americans

In the beginning, the American war in Vietnam was an Irish Catholic one. A century of French colonialism left a Catholic imprint throughout Buddhist Vietnam. When the forces of Ho Chi Minh triumphed at Dien Bien Phu in 1954, at the height of anticommunist hysteria in the United States, the French-sponsored Catholics fled the North – with stimulus from the CIA and US naval ships – and became the base of the new regime in the South. Who now would replace the French in supporting this Catholic colonial stratum opposed by communists, nationalists, and Buddhists? The American Catholic Church filled the void. Francis Cardinal Spellman, who celebrated Joseph McCarthy at home, harshly attacked the 1954 Geneva Agreement which promised all-Vietnam elections. The flight of the Catholic refugees from communism was brought to world attention by Irish Catholic missionaries such as Tom Dooley. The future dictator of South Vietnam, Ngo Dinh Diem, was harbored in Spellman's own New York seminary. The heavily Catholic Vietnam lobby built supportive connections between Diem and a young senator from Massachusetts, John F. Kennedy. In time, he would recruit perhaps the most assimilated Irishman of the era, Robert McNamara, to spin technocratic fantasies of progress while shielding the human cost. (In his memoir of Vietnam, James Carroll describes a family argument over whether McNamara was a descendant of "soupers," Irishmen whose forebears became Protestant in exchange for soup from missionaries during the Famine, just as some Vietnamese in the twentieth century turned Catholic for food.)[159] In the arrogance of the era, no one worried about the fact that the privileged Catholics of South Vietnam were less than 10 percent of the population, or that the isolated Diem circle was notoriously repressive and hostile towards a largely Buddhist population.

In the fall of 1963 I participated in my earliest anti-Vietnam war demonstration, against Diem's sister-in-law, Madame Nhu, the "dragon lady" of South Vietnam. Her acerbic comment about the self-immolation of several Buddhist monks, that they were "barbecued bonzes," had shocked international opinion and led to campus protests for the first time. A few weeks later, at the beginning of November, Diem and Nhu were assassinated in a coup approved by the Kennedy Administration. On November 22, John Kennedy was dead. James Carroll, a great novelist of Irish America, later expressed my feelings exactly: "If Kennedy's ascendance epitomized the triumph of American Catholicism, his assassination on the heels of Pope John's death and that of Spellman's protégé, Diem, revealed the hollowness of that triumph, nay, the utter vanity of it."[160]

When I met Robert Kennedy in 1967, he had traveled a long way from his days as staff counsel to Senator Joseph McCarthy. That journey within Bobby Kennedy reflected a larger civil war for the Irish soul that I didn't understand at the time. Opposed to the conservative Spellmans and the Irish cops were rebel Irish American priests like the Berrigan brothers, and believers in liberation theology who volunteered their way to Latin American slums to foster a church of the poor. Since his brother's murder and the rise of civil rights and student movements, Bobby Kennedy was beginning to empathize with the dispossessed. He was contemplating a presidential campaign bridging two poles of the Irish soul: the amoral power machines of the Mayor Daleys and the powerless morality of Irish Catholic opposition to napalm and body counts.

In October 1967, I received a telephone call at my office in the Newark ghetto. "Bobby Kennedy would like to meet with you," said my friend Jack Newfield of the *Village Voice*. I was deeply conflicted. The hope of an antipoverty crusade was being destroyed by the escalation of the Vietnam war. In Newark, I had watched the war come home that August, when thousands of police and guardsmen, driving armored personnel carriers and employing .30 caliber M-1 carbines, had suppressed a spontaneous rising of angry blacks. Law enforcement officials claimed that snipers were to blame, but offered no evidence. The APCs and jeeps mounted with machine guns, they said, were present to build the confidence of the black community. Twenty-five blacks were shot, 1,000 were injured and 1,000 were jailed in quelling the riot. On the final night of violence, at 4 a.m., I was summoned to meet Governor Richard Hughes (a jovial Irish Catholic) in his bunker headquarters downtown. I argued for two hours that the Governor should withdraw the National Guard, a course he ultimately chose. The Vietnam analogy was seeping into my mind. I was convinced that our intervention in Vietnam was boomeranging into a Vietnam in America. And just as the Democratic and Republican parties supported the war abroad, they were politically addicted to law-and-order at home.

The only politician who interested me was Bobby Kennedy. While he seemed too cautious in opposing the Vietnam war, there was something about his silent brooding, like an exiled Irish lord, that seemed very powerful. He was visiting Indian reservations, farmworker hunger strikes, questioning whether the Gross National Product measured progress, and letting his hair lengthen. Behind the scenes, he was aggressively seeking counsel at home and abroad about disengaging from Vietnam. It was no secret that, despite some vacillation, he was preparing a presidential bid.

Another Irish American politician, Senator Eugene McCarthy, had already launched a campaign to challenge Johnson's war in the primaries. Looking back, I realize McCarthy represented an eclectic Irish Catholic intellectual whose opposition to Vietnam was more cerebral, while Kennedy represented a combined passion and gloom that, in spite of his wealth, appealed to the alienated, and certainly to me. We met in Kennedy's Westside condominium at the United Nations Plaza off the East Side Drive. In addition to Newfield, I was accompanied by Staughton Lynd, a Quaker intellectual with whom I had traveled to North Vietnam in 1965. The discussion wandered back and forth between the war and its relation to the crisis in ghettos like Newark. It was my first conversation with a politician, certainly at the national level, in my life, and I was wary of manipulation. Perhaps as a devil's advocate, Kennedy asked critical questions: Could you trust the communists in negotiating? Wouldn't they disregard free elections if they were in power? He asked also about Newark, and spoke of plans to rebuild the Bedford-Stuyvesant ghetto in New York City. Beneath the political discourse, I found myself liking this man. For a public figure, he seemed strangely shy. The only time he seemed really comfortable was when he was chatting with Staughton's ten-year-old boy. We ended the meeting not knowing whether he was running for President or not. But I felt a destiny about him.

In retrospect, the assassination of John Kennedy must have unleashed a sentimental, melancholic, wilder Irish persona in Bobby than the striving, success-driven politician of his earlier years. He was an alienated man in the body of an American success story. He began immersing himself in poetry after 1963. One night in New York, Newfield listened to him read these lines from Emerson:

> Were it not better done,
> To dine and sleep through forty years
> Be loved by few; be feared by none;
> Laugh life away, have wine for tears;
> And take the mortal leap undaunted,
> Content that all we asked was granted?
>
> But fate will not permit
> The seed of gods to die,
> Nor suffer sense to win from wit
> Its guerdon in the sky,
> Nor let us hide, whate'er our pleasure,
> The world's light underneath a measure.

Newfield recalls Kennedy, who was thirty-eight when his brother was assassinated, reciting the final stanza from memory:

> Go then, sad youth and shine,
> Go, sacrifice to Fame;
> Put youth, joy, health upon the shrine,
> And life to fan the flame;
> Being for Seeming bravely barter,
> And die to Fame a happy martyr.[161]

Bobby was becoming a deeper, more contemplative kind of Irish. He spoke of the Great Hunger and its lessons in the first public speech he gave after his brother's murder, to the Friendly Sons of St Patrick, in Scranton, Pennsylvania. The substance of his remarks was lost in the occasion of their deliverance, but they connected Irish suffering with that of blacks and farmworkers in America.

> There was that black day in February 1847 when it was announced in the House of Commons that fifteen thousand people a day were dying of starvation in Ireland. . . . So the Irish left Ireland. Many of them came here to the United States. Many left behind hearts and fields and a nation yearning to be free. It is no wonder that James Joyce described the Atlantic as a bowl of bitter tears. . . . [Today] there are Americans, who – as the Irish did – still face discrimination in employment. . . . There are walls of silent conspiracy that block the progress of others because of race or creed without regard to ability. It is toward concern for these issues and vigorous participation on the side of freedom that our Irish heritage must impel us. If we are true to that heritage, we cannot stand aside.[162]

I saw Robert Kennedy several times during his 1968 campaign, once at his home in Hickory Hill at a dinner of campaign advisers, and a final time in June 1968 just before his death. He seemed battered from relentless campaigning, his face was windburned, and his hands were reddened and scratched from shaking thousands of clinging hands in Watts that day. We were in an elevator. I told him of the plans for demonstrations in Chicago, and the problems we were having obtaining permits from Mayor Daley. See you there, I remember him saying. A few days later he was martyred.

The night his body was flown to New York, I walked with Newfield and others to St Patrick's Cathedral. It was late, well after midnight, Friday June 7. For the first time in my life I was inside the historic chamber, built by impoverished Irish immigrants of the Famine era, who gave their meager earnings, and their brawn, to build this spiritual fortress against the Know-Nothings of the nineteenth century. Its first archbishop, John Hughes, dedicated his church to protecting the Irish on their journey to success. Hughes rejected the Fenians, and there was no doubt in his mind that the Irish should be concerned first and foremost with assimilation into their adopted country. By the 1960s, St Patrick's was the symbol of Irish achievement and power in America and, incidentally, the pulpit for Spellman's Vietnam crusade.

I found an empty pew in the rear of the cathedral. Around me were construction crews building scaffolds for the morning's television cameras. I wore a rumpled corduroy jacket and had a green Cuban cap stuffed in my pocket. I had not noticed the coffin, a modest wooden one, already placed near the altar in the midst of the busy crews. One of Kennedy's aides asked if I would stand by the coffin in a makeshift honor guard. I did so, then returned to the pew and wept alone. I was crying about Bobby, about the war, about the poor, about fate. Life in America was not as my parents promised it would be. Here in the sanctuary of Irish assimilation, another symbol of that success was dead.

I left the cathedral with a hole in my core filling with bitterness. This was the fate of those who tried to change the system from within. The month before, it had been Martin Luther King, whose nonviolent crusade had drawn me to the South. I felt cold, abandoned, not part of America. The next day I was invited to travel to Washington on the train bearing the coffin. I declined.

In retrospect, two lessons can be drawn from the Kennedy era about the theme of assimilation and Irish identity. First, the tragic Kennedy story makes a mockery of the conventional myth of assimilation. The assassinations reinforce Irish notions of character, mysticism, destiny, and death, not a Horatio Alger tale of hard-won achievement by following the straight-and-narrow path. In addition to the assassinations, the Kennedy family story is filled with too many troubles and tragedies to be considered a model of the melting pot. Indeed, the story raises poignant questions about the psychic and human costs of the quest to assimilate. As the family toll has mounted, the media and popular culture have replaced the Kennedy legend of immigrant success with that of a family "tragically" cursed, the Kennedys as a mysterious exception to the assimilation pattern. Few have questioned this preservation of the assimilation myth at the expense of a deeper look at the destructive pressures entailed in becoming acceptable and successful. And with the exception of Moynihan, even fewer have noted how the Kennedy story – of triumph and tragedy – is more fundamentally *Irish* than American.

This refusal to examine the toll of assimilation prevents an understanding of a second lesson: Irish (or racial) identity is usually recovered from forced amnesia through the experience of suffering. Reclaiming our roots is a jarring experience of awakening, not a hobby like learning a new language or buying a new line of clothing. Americanization is a "soul splitting" social process that becomes psychological, in the phrase of Thomas Wheeler.[163] In Jackie Kennedy's poem, John Kennedy came from "an alien breed" whose very blood danced with a Celtic magic. Hiding this element of his character as the price of passing in WASP society must have been crippling on some level, and reclaiming it would mean tearing away masks of respectability. For Bobby Kennedy, surely it was his brother's murder that shattered his identity of privilege and opened his soul to the realities of absurdity and suffering.

I did not appreciate the Irish nature of political rebels like Bobby Kennedy at the time. He seemed like an anti-hero to me, a defector from the establishment to the counterculture, his Irishness merely part of his background. In part, this was because the Kennedys presented themselves as American, not as ethnic politicians, and because I was little aware of my own Irish rebel heritage. The Irish in my life had always been representatives of the status quo against which my generation rebelled. From Father Coughlin forward, the Irish had seemed to be superpatriots, more American than the Americans. The Coughlin spirit was to resurface in the McCarthy era, so named for an Irish Catholic senator from Wisconsin, Joseph McCarthy. McCarthy was born, like my own father, in small-town Wisconsin at the turn of the century. He belonged to the Knights of Columbus and American Legion, and attended Marquette University law school. Later he was a circuit judge, and challenged the famous progressive US senator Robert LaFollette, winning an upset victory in 1946 and launching a domestic cold war against alleged communists and sympathizers. It was a classic case of Irish Catholic dramatics, with attacks on the Anglo-American State Department for harboring alleged subversives in a conspiracy against "ordinary Americans." McCarthy's very Catholic form of superpatriotism and hatred of atheistic communism turned too extreme for most Americans, and the senator's alcoholism proved too much. By 1954, he was censured by the US Senate itself. The image of Irish Catholics as sputtering, drunken, overzealous Cold Warriors was planted in my mind. At home, we watched the hearings and presidential campaigns on our black-and-white television. My mother gushed over Adlai Stevenson and was embarrassed by McCarthy, unlike my staunch Republican father.

Coogan understates this Irish Catholic conservatism by describing McCarthyism as just a "low water mark for the Irish experience," and calling Coughlin a "false prophet" who misled his Catholic followers.[164] The truth is more that McCarthy and Coughlin were fairly representative of Irish Catholic America. Coughlin had as many as 40 million radio listeners, and the disgraced McCarthy was being cheered by Cardinal Spellman at Emerald Society breakfasts with thousands of Irish police officers.[165] By the sixties, the right-wing power centers we opposed were disproportionately commanded by Irish Catholics. The leader of the John Birch Society in 1961 said that half his membership was Catholic.[166] In Selma, Alabama, it was "Bull" Connor who applied the clubs and hoses to civil rights demonstrators. In New York, it was Cardinal Spellman exhorting the United States to military intervention in Vietnam. The Boston Irish were electing Louise Day Hicks to the school board on a racially divisive anti-busing platform. The ranks of police and

FBI agents harassing us were thick with Irish Americans. A key political analyst, Kevin Phillips, wrote a blueprint for the Nixon era called *The Emerging Republican Majority* based largely on the belief that Irish Catholics were leaving the Democratic Party to become law-and-order Republicans. He noted that "of all the Catholic groups, none matched the Irish in Republican impetus."[167] Anticommunism and opposition to Democratic Party liberalism were driving the working-class and lower-middle-class Catholics of the Al Smith era to the Republican agenda.

The most famous of the Irish political machines after Tammany Hall was that of Mayor Richard Daley of Chicago, described by several historians as an extension of the Irish village system. The sociologist and priest Andrew Greeley, for example, described Daley as "an Irish chieftain governing through a complex system of clan loyalty."[168] In his 1963 work on the New York Irish, Moynihan made the same comparison to "an Irish village writ large," noting that Tammany county committees totaled 32,000 individuals who needed Madison Square Garden to hold their mass meetings.[169] These machines, Moynihan continued, were established to create social order and regularity, not social change.

Daley personified for my generation all that was wrong with traditional politics: the emphasis on accumulating power by patronage, the nepotism of bosses and contractors, the resistance to "good government" reform, the marginalizing of racial minorities and women, and a police force composed mainly of Irishmen dealing out street justice to anyone who dissented too loudly. The Black Panthers didn't call such police "pigs" just to be provocative. Many of these Irishmen did seem to have pink, blown-up faces and massive rotund physiques. When they charged at us with clubs, it was like animals breaking out of a pen. Were they berserk, or was someone giving the orders? During our 1969–70 trial, they broke into a Chicago apartment and killed two Black Panthers who were sleeping in their beds. We called them out of control, but in fact history revealed that the brutality was more planned than spontaneous. For example, the journalist John Conroy documented the systemic use of electrodes in a Chicago precinct in the late sixties to burn and scar African American arrestees. Most of the police and city authorities supervising them were Irish Americans. One magistrate openly stated that the critics of Chicago police brutality should focus their attention on Northern Ireland, not his city.[170]

> It is an outrage that this country has to deal with a second front at home against rioters and beatniks when the fighting men are risking death overseas.
>
> editorial, *Chicago Tribune*, April 10, 1968

> The investigation of Hayden, as one of the key leaders of the new left movement, is of prime importance to the Bureau. You will be expected to pursue it aggressively and with imagination.
>
> internal memo from FBI director J. Edgar Hoover,
> May 17, 1968[171]

Hoover's FBI fed false and provocative information to Mayor Daley and his lieutenants. Our eventual prosecutor for an alleged conspiracy to disrupt the 1968 Democratic Convention was US Attorney Thomas Foran, an Irish American and former Daley law partner, who played a central role from planning the initial police response and operating amid police on the streets, to developing our indictment and managing the case in court. What most disturbed the Daley machine and police, records would later show, was not so much the threat of violence as the challenge to proper morals. Yippie proclamations by Abbie Hoffman or Jerry Rubin that LSD would be put in the Chicago reservoirs (technically impossible), promises of nude-ins and fornication on the beach, plans for rock concerts mobbed by potheads, and poetry celebrating homosexuality by Allen Ginsburg caused the most outrage to the Chicago establishment. It was the youthful defiance of authority, from draft resistance to rock and roll, that Mayor Daley most wanted to protect Chicago against. At the deepest level it was a very Irish Catholic response.

It was said that the Daley machine stole a few votes that elected John Kennedy the first Irish Catholic president. If so, it wasn't the first time or the last. Daley routinely took the law into his own hands in defense of morals. During the protests of 1968 and subsequent trial of 1969–70, I took a deepening interest in the paranoia and overreaction emanating from the mayor's office. During the trial, we subpoenaed the mayor to testify. He arrived with his bodyguards in a federal court building already heavily cordoned off. I had never seen him before. The description I later wrote reflected my curiosity toward the man: "A legendary figure, this round, red-faced, 60 year old Irish Buddha was not without a certain charm. We respected his unpolished platitudes, his protection of working people, and his awareness of being one of a kind, a museum piece."[172] Abbie Hoffman stood up and challenged him to a fist fight to settle our conflict. The mayor rolled with laughter.

The fact that Mayor Daley was Irish became interesting to me long after the trial, when I researched a book on the Famine in the mid-nineties. I began to understand Mayor Daley, and others like him, as persons still carrying the psychic burdens of the Famine generation. My first insight came while reading an essay by Peter Quinn, the novelist and historian of the New York Irish, about Tammany.

> Living in a new country, in the aftermath of the Famine, the Irish employed political power as a buckler of community solidarity and survival, a means to shield themselves from the attacks of their enemies, and as a sword with which to strike back.[173]

Daley was born and lived his entire life in the neighborhood of Bridgeport, which was the endpoint for an east–west canal built by Irish Famine labor. Looking at the *Chicago Tribune* of that time, I found condemnations of the Bridgeport Irish such as this: "Why do our police reports average two representatives from Erin [for] every one from any other inhabitable land?" (1853), and this: "Who does not know that the most depraved, debased, worthless and irredeemable drunkards and sots which curse the community are Irish Catholics?" (1855). In 1867, according to Kerby Miller, "the captains of industry called in the state's militia to repress Irish strikers in Bridgeport, a suburb dominated by packinghouses, rolling mills and workers' shanties." One Irish worker quoted by Miller spoke of his conditions as "despicable, humiliating and slavish," and said that in America there was no protection for an

Irishman, who could be "shot down, run down, kicked, cuffed, spat on – and no redress."[174] Bridgeport was also the world of the Studs Lonigan novels, and the source of Peter Finley Dunne's tales of Mr Dooley, the bachelor philosopher from County Roscommon. I could imagine deep in the soul of Richard Daley all this pain, degradation, persistence, and eventual triumph over the Famine legacy. Those original Bridgeport inhabitants had come from a land where they were denied a government of their own. They arrived in a New York seething with prejudice against them. They built cathedrals for religious sustenance, political parties as bucklers and shields of protection, and canals to take them to promised lands. And they became perfectly capable of inflicting on others the abuse that the British and WASPs had imposed on them.

The Irish of Chicago were known as fierce defenders of their hard-won stake in Chicago, but also as particularly vengeful against the British. The secret Irish organization Clan na Gael once even launched a fruitless invasion of British Canada in hopes of bargaining for London's withdrawal from Ireland. Eventually, the people of Bridgeport saw the Irish come to power in Chicago, led by one of their own, Richard Daley. The Daley machine, I now began to realize, was a wrapped fist against the past. The machine was their mechanism for survival, for saying never again. It stood for the stern sexual mores of the Church, for manners and appearances, for defending the flag, for keeping control of the government and police force that once were used against them. All of these attitudes, which seemed philosophically offensive to me in the sixties, unchangeable elements of the Irish Catholic character, now fell into place as reflexive responses to the trauma of Famine, emigration, and anti-Irish repression in America.

The problem for Daley and machine politicians was that times had changed. Neither Famine nor Know-Nothings were a threat any longer. Even the Irish were becoming middle-class. Pope John XXIII's *Pacem in Terris* was liberalizing the Church, and liberation theology was sweeping Latin America. The long-segregated black community in Chicago could no longer be contained. Children of the middle class were resisting the draft, growing long hair, taking advantage of the birth control pill. The political machine had served its purpose for a century after the Famine. When survival was at stake, when no one else would assist the Irish, people would accept, indeed welcome, the tough-fisted discipline of the machine. But now it was fighting a rearguard action, to hold back change. Its purpose was to perpetuate itself against threats to the America in which the Irish had become successful. No threat was more disturbing than that of young men refusing their government's call to war.

After the deaths of Kennedy and King, I sometimes expected my own death in 1968. I don't know if I had this premonition because I was continually walking into danger, an existential response to the murderous time, or because of survivor guilt. On the first day of the Chicago protests that September, I was warned there was a man on the porch wearing a gun. He was an undercover police officer, it turned out, and I disappeared up an alley. During the next five days, I lived in a cat-and-mouse struggle to avoid being neutralized while the demonstrations against the war and racism were going on. Twice the undercover agents captured me from behind, beat me up, and held me overnight. The streets were lit with teargas and bonfires, and occupied by troops fresh back from Vietnam. Machine guns with live rounds were set up at intersections, and jeeps mounted with concertina wire plowed through protesters seeking sanctuary in public parks. As it turned out, only one person was killed, though thousands were gassed and beaten, and six hundred were arrested.

When it was over, I expected to be arrested for violent conspiracy and to spend a significant time in prison. In eight short years, I had gone from civil rights worker with hopes of a liberal realignment to a weary, alienated target of the government. Then, on October 5, 1968, in a scene that eerily resembled Chicago, four hundred civil rights marchers in Northern Ireland were blocked by British armored vehicles from protesting in Derry. They were beaten into the ground, hosed with water cannons like civil rights demonstrators in our South, and began street battles in the Bogside. They were singing "We Shall Overcome." Our marches and civil disobedience helped inspire the demonstrations in Derry and Belfast.

I was transfixed by the sight of it. Suddenly I realized what had been denied, that these marchers were somehow kin to me, that under the void of my identity I was Irish, and that being Irish need not mean identifying with Cardinal Spellman, "Bull" Connor, Charles Coughlin or Mayor Daley. It could mean being an American rebel not in spite of being Irish, but *because* of being Irish.

By its very nature, the repressive drive towards secure assimilation ultimately brought about its own demise in the 1960s. By the end of the sixties, Father Coughlin came out of retirement to attack the Berrigans as "swingers" and "loud-mouthed clerical advocates of arson, riot, and draft card burning." He told an interviewer that while he admired the youth of the sixties, including the Chicago Seven – one of whom, he noted, had attended the Shrine of the Little Flower – the man he admired most on the contemporary scene was Judge Julius Hoffman, the judge who presided over the Chicago Seven trial.[175] Hoffman, it should be noted, spoke often in the courtroom of his pride at being a highly assimilated Jew, and was shocked and embarrassed most of all at the flamboyant behavior of Jewish defendants like Abbie Hoffman and Jerry Rubin. The generational civil war crossed all ethnic and racial boundaries. Those who had become conservative to achieve respectability in America were confronted by a new generation concerned not with fitting in and following orders but with reviving their moral traditions. The social order of my father's generation, built on loyalty to Americanism at the price of ethnic memory, was crumbling as rebel traditions were revived.

Irish families like mine had achieved a level of success in America that permitted a relaxation of the old ways. Obedience to parents, priests, and politicians might have been needed for survival by the struggling immigrant generations, but it was not necessary by the time of the sixties. The rigid conformity demanded by the post-Famine church and political machines conflicted with an underlying Irish soul. At a mystical, unexpected moment in the early sixties, the authoritarian ice started to melt. Pope John XXIII's *Pacem in Terris* found its way into the Port Huron Statement, the founding manifesto of Students for a Democratic

Society. The hardline doctrines of a Spellman were challenged by priests like the Berrigans and politicians like the Kennedys. The Vietnam war was resisted by young men burning their draft cards; the first was burnt by David Miller, a member of the Catholic Workers. The law-and-order machine of Mayor Daley began to dissipate on the streets of Chicago. Backroom bossism in the Democratic Party was replaced by open presidential primaries in 1972. The federal courts tossed out the conviction of the Chicago Seven on grounds that both judge and prosecutor had gone overboard and engaged in misconduct.

By now it was clear that I wasn't simply white, or American, but that I had a bond with those protesters in Northern Ireland, a bond that the assimilation process had almost erased. So who was I? A pale green Irish American? A recovering Irishman trying to apply an ethnic past to the American present? A stranded Irishman – *eireannach eigin* – unable to go home again? I resolved to find out.

PART II

Going North

I am inside someone who hates me.

Amiri Baraka

We are seeing racism here, racism dressed up as sectarianism.

Rosemary Nelson, a human rights attorney
blown up in her car in Portadown by loyalists,
quoted on the day of her death.[1]

Death makes life meaningless unless life achieves a form that death can't alter.

Seamus Deane

Prologue

The war that began in Northern Ireland in the sixties, and which became the peace process in the nineties, was a bloody reminder that amnesia was not an option, that the past was present. While many tried to deny it, inventing the notion that Northern Ireland was an aberration, for many others the conflict marked the beginning of a reversal of the assimilation process. Just when the Irish Americans, and the Irish in the Southern Republic, thought they finally were making it in the modern world, a new generation of Irish rebels was asserting that the fight for Irish freedom was far from over.

In 1969, trying to escape the pressures and notoriety of the Chicago trial, I lived in Venice, California, paying rent under the name Emmet Garity. I was not fooling the FBI or my friendly landlord, but it was a brief flirtation with Malcolm X's strategy: in my case, eliminating my Anglicized name for a more obviously Irish one. I sat on the beach reading Brendan Behan and Lady Gregory's folk tales. I hung out at Molly Malone's bar on Fairfax. One day Larry Levin, a refugee from the Bobby Kennedy campaign, arrived in Los Angeles from Belfast, where he had been living for a year after Bobby's assassination. Larry regaled me with tapes of Bernadette Devlin speeches and scratchy rebel songs, bottles of Jameson's, and contacts with the few Irish republicans in America. The romantic phase of my Irish identification was under way. I had to visit Ireland.

FEDERAL BUREAU OF INVESTIGATION   Dec. 15, 1971

Urgent

To: Director
From: Los Angeles

THOMAS EMMET HAYDEN

SOURCE ADVISED DECEMBER FIFTEEN INSTANT, THOMAS EMMET HAYDEN
DEPARTED LOS ANGELES EVENING OF DECEMBER FOURTEEN LAST, FOR NEW
YORK CITY, ULTIMATE DESTINATION, IRELAND. SOURCE STATED HAYDEN PLANS
ON GOING TO NORTHERN IRELAND THROUGH SOUTHERN IRELAND AND
ANTICIPATES TAKING PART IN PRESENT REVOLUTION. SOURCE STATED HAYDEN
MAY BE UTILIZING THE NAME EMMET GARITY, MAIDEN NAME OF MOTHER.[2]

So it was that my emigrant's return would result in banishment. Not
flogging or repression, mind you, for the authorities were civil, but a
banishment nonetheless. When I landed in Shannon, several gardaí took
me aside for questioning. I had taken precautions, carrying with me letters from Irish American leaders like Paul O'Dwyer in New York and
Senator Edward Kennedy's staff in Washington. But it was no use. The
Irish government was following the advice, or perhaps the orders, of the
intelligence services of Washington and London.

It may seem difficult for an outsider to understand the hostility of the
Dublin establishment to Northern republicans – or their American sympathizers – at the time. The origin of this split was the treaty of 1921
which fostered a Northern state gerrymandered to assure a unionist
majority under British rule, later described by its architects as "a
Protestant state for a Protestant people." The nationalist population
was abandoned by the settlement to second-class status under brutal
Unionist rule. Irish leader Michael Collins, who negotiated the compromise in London, believed that his forces needed a breathing spell, that
partition would be temporary, that the Northern struggle would be

revived with strong support from the new twenty-six-county republic to the south. But only one of his predictions came true: he wrote that he was signing his death warrant. Collins soon was assassinated by opponents of the compromise, and any strategy of continuing the Northern struggle was deferred. The Irish descended into civil war between supporters and opponents of the treaty with Britain, a civil war that cost thousands of lives and sowed bitter antagonisms and a weary self-doubt among the next generations of Irish. An Irish newspaper predicted long-term trauma of "children being born in anxiety, and often in terror, that will bear to their early graves the constitutional traces of pre-natally shattered nerves."[3]

One historian later noted that "the Civil War has always been something 'not talked about', and it was the 1960s before articles began to appear in historical journals about events during that time."[4] It is speculative, but the Irish civil war seems to have reflected the same divisions in the Irish psyche that were apparent in America through the sixties: between compromising and adapting to the requirements of the larger power or resisting that power in the name of an independent Irish identity.

As in Mexico during the same period, the revolutionaries' fate was either repression at the hands of their fellow Irishmen, depression as their dream collapsed, or absorption into the gradual process of building the Irish Free State out of twenty-six counties of Ireland. Also like Mexico, while the official Irish rhetoric, tricolours, and martial anthems remained revolutionary in tone, in truth the new state and political parties were designed to perpetuate their new legitimacy, not subvert the North. Tacitly at first, partition was accepted by the Southern state, even enforced by repressive laws and censorship through the 1980s. Not simply the state but most of the people in the South of Ireland were weary of civil war, and desired a certain normalcy and order in their long-battered lives. They wanted jobs, investment, a secure environment, and assimilation into the modern world. Many would succumb to what Brian Friel called "the London vertigo," a "sudden and dizzy conviction that London is the very heart of style and wit and good fortune and excitement."[5]

This assimilation required a psychic, cultural, and political distancing from the North, as if it were another country. It meant that Southerners would impose on Northerners stereotypes that the British had inflicted on the Irish for many centuries. Northern Catholics became an alien tribe, hopelessly given to primitive bloodletting, manipulated by mafia gunmen, completely unlike the modern, civilized Irish people just south of the border. The Irish soul was being partitioned.

What happened to the 1916 generation is described in gritty detail in Roddy Doyle's novel *A Star Called Henry*. Doyle's epic hero, a street urchin named Henry Smart, grows up to become a loyal Volunteer in the 1916 rebellion.[6] He kills people, from British soldiers to suspected spies, following the orders of his leaders, until he realizes how driven by power they have become. Nationalism turns into chauvinism, anti-Semitism, and power madness. Henry's nemesis, a sinister character named Ivan Reynolds, says the revolution wasn't about Ireland, which is only a "dollop of muck." The revolution was about "control of the island, that's what soldiering's about, not the harps and the martyrs and the freedom to swing a hurley."[7] The new state, composed of men on the make, has no further need of Henry's services. "We needed trouble-makers and very soon now we'll have to be rid of them. And that, Henry, is all you are and ever were. A trouble-maker. The best in the business, mind. But –" And he hands Henry a slip ordering his own death.[8]

An Anglophile *New York Times* review of *A Star Called Henry* claimed that Doyle was acknowledging that the Irish revolution was a mistake. The reviewer, Alan Riding, said Doyle was chipping away at the blarney that "Ireland was actually a better place after its war of independence against Britain."[9] In fact, however, Doyle appeared to be suggesting that the ideal was betrayed, and that its true spirit would be carried into the future. Henry, who will fight no more, who feels mocked by the new state's "stale air," will start his life again as an immigrant to Liverpool. "I didn't know where I was going. I didn't know if I would get there. But I was still alive. I was twenty." His wife, the free-spirited rebel named Miss O'Shea – probably a reference to Mrs "Kitty" O'Shea, the woman at the center of the adultery/divorce scandal that brought down

Home Rule leader Charles Stewart Parnell in the 1890s – is locked up in Kilmainham jail by the Free State government. While behind bars, she has borne them a daughter, named Saoirse (Freedom). In Doyle's presentation of the birth of the Irish state, its ideal – embodied in Henry – is going into exile and prison. Its future is his "daughter called Freedom I'd held only once," during the euphoria of the Uprising.[10]

Even in the era of the Good Friday Agreement, serious Irish commentators sometimes manage to perpetuate this exclusion of the North from their definitions of modern Ireland. As noted earlier, in 1996 the respected Irish author Fintan O'Toole wrote an entire book on the "new Ireland" without any reference to the North at all. The thrust of his argument was that the Republic had modernized, industrialized, and economically outstripped the British in per capita income, rendering "differences between Britishness and Irishness . . . to almost nothing."[11] Such analysis is not so much evidence of assimilation into modernity as it is the triumph of denial. While O'Toole was asserting a fanciful possibility of understanding Ireland "without reference to Britain," the Northern conflict and peace process was very much based on a "reference to Britain," namely the need for complete revision of the colonial connection and official recognition of an Irish national identity, language rights and social equality in the North. The peace blueprint, to be successful, would require an end to decades of avoidance of the North by Southern officials, media, and the public. It soon became apparent that beneath the surface of the South, there was an Irish soul that could be stirred. In an astounding example, Irish public opinion surveys found that the most respected politician in the year 2000 was Gerry Adams, the Sinn Féin leader who had been officially censored by the media and demonized by the authorities as a faceless, voiceless terrorist for the thirty previous years.

When I tried to visit Ireland in 1971, however, Sinn Féin activists like Adams were being interned, incarcerated and, according to later human rights reports, subjected to horrific interrogation techniques usually associated with the Soviet Union and Third World dictatorships. In American terms, a rough similarity could be drawn with the American FBI counterintelligence programs against the Black Panthers or Students for a Democratic Society revolutionaries. The difference was that in America one could appeal to the voting public or find refuge in the independent judiciary, options that were unavailable to Irish nationalists under British rule.

I was excited to be on my first flight to Ireland on Aer Lingus. To be surrounded for the first time by a planeload of Irish people was like reverse immigration, heading back to the home my ancestors left. They definitely were not "white," not in the homogenized American sense. Nor were they alien. There was an earthy conviviality that didn't exist among the silent, stationary American passengers on long-distance flights. These people were up in the aisles, chatting and laughing, some of them during the whole flight. The welcoming accents of the flight attendants were the loveliest rendition of the English language I could want. My romantic enthusiasm aroused, I stayed awake the whole way. When, at dawn, I landed on Irish soil for the first time, I was thrilled even more.

Then the airport police took me into custody. I was diverted from the happy, homesick travelers picking up baggage and hugging their relatives. Instead I was escorted into a gray-walled cubicle with a metal table and empty chair. For several hours, the officers, sometimes joined by a civilian I assumed was from the intelligence service, questioned why I was in Ireland. "Because I am of Irish descent" was not an adequate answer. Nor was "Because I want to see the situation for myself." I was out of answers, but they wanted more. Who had invited me? No one. Whom did I plan to see? I didn't know anyone specifically. What did I plan to do? See first hand, then return home. See what first hand? The North. Who sent you here? I sent myself. We went round and round, while I kept asking my status and who was preventing my travel. They merely shrugged and said we would have to wait and see.

It did me no good to have an open letter of introduction from Paul O'Dwyer, a distinguished Irish-born New York attorney who defended Irish republicans in America. Mentioning my supporters in Senator Kennedy's Washington office drew a more concerned response, but it was not sufficient. Nor were press inquiries from the *Irish Times*. After twenty-four hours, without explanation, I was courteously and firmly escorted onto the next flight back to New York.

The minister signing my deportation order was named Geraghty, my mother's maiden name. At least I'd come across a namesake, a family connection. Dreaming of an exile's return, however, I was reliving for the moment the banishment of my own ancestors. My romanticism began to fade.

I didn't find much sympathy for my Irish identity quest among the New Left (as we were known), which generally excluded Northern Ireland from its menu of progressive causes. Not since the nineteenth century had there been much solidarity between the American left and Irish republicans. The Irish struggle was never a center of left-wing attention like Russia and Mexico in the 1920s, Spain in the 1930s, China in the 1940s, or Cuba and Vietnam in the 1960s. Perhaps in large part this was because the twentieth-century Irish struggle came to be dominated by Catholic nationalism. While it was acknowledged that the Irish had suffered, not only in Ireland but in America, under British colonialism, the American Left distrusted the spirit of Catholic nationalism as inherently claustrophobic, reactionary, anti-Semitic, even fascistic. Irish neutrality in World War Two was a break from the global Left that would not be forgotten.

This left-wing suspicion made a certain sense. If the Irish in the Old Country were anything like their descendants I was encountering in America, who could be enthusiastic about a "cause" that was against secularism, public education, and birth control pills, that was streaked with anti-Semitism and racism, that was associated with riots against busing in Boston, that opposed women's reproductive rights, that was incensed about Irish gays and lesbians marching in St Patrick's Day parades? An example of how American right-wing politics captured Irish American republicanism was that of US Representative Mario Biaggi, who chaired the Congressional Irish National Caucus beginning in the 1970s. Biaggi, an Italian American with a huge Irish constituency in the Bronx and Queens, was an old-fashioned pol who in his career as a New York police officer shot fifteen people and was elected in 1968 on a platform of denouncing black rioters as "subversives."[12] One could support Irish self-determination in principle but any enthusiasm was weakened by its social content. Those who did so unswervingly were limited to Irish immigrants or first-generation Irish Americans usually living in a few square blocks of the Bronx. From the viewpoint of a progressive American like myself, white ethnics like the Irish seemed alien. Instead of marching with the Ancient Order of Hibernians, we were marching against apartheid in South Africa.

Nor was there much support for the Northern republican struggle among the liberal Irish American elite, especially as events turned violent. Dublin foreign minister Garret Fitzgerald "personally directed the government's anti-republican initiatives," including efforts to neutralize or win over Irish Americans.[13] These initiatives were remarkably successful. After an early call for British withdrawal, the key Irish American leader, Senator Edward Kennedy, changed course, accepted the British presence, and denounced the IRA as a "cut-throat terrorist gang" in the influential journal *Foreign Policy*.[14] Kennedy was a pivotal member of the Irish American coalition known as the "Four Horsemen" (the others being Senator Moynihan, New York Governor Hugh Carey, House Speaker "Tip" O'Neill, followed later by Speaker Tom Foley). These individuals, along with a few Church leaders, became the gatekeepers of legitimate opinion on the Irish question, and political advocates of republicanism were not admissible. Summing up the change, the Irish American diplomat and author William V. Shannon wrote a 1977 article called "Change of Heart Among Irish Americans Over Ulster." Most Irish Americans, Shannon wrote, initially supported the Northern civil rights movement with an "instinctive desire" to "kick the British out and reunite the country." But now they were more "conversant with the realities and complexities of the situation" and believed that "if Britain were to withdraw now, there would be more violence."[15]

Shannon did not explain the "realities and complexities" that smothered the "instinctive desire" that these mainstream Irish Americans still retained. As an establishment commentator on the Irish question, he simply assumed the distinction between a "complex" understanding that came with assimilation as opposed to the more "instinctive" (animal) attitudes of those who wanted the British out of Ireland. Presumably those like Shannon were convinced that the British presence was that of a peacekeeper, not a colonial power, keeping the Irish from each other's throats. From that perspective, the Irish American role was to support British (and Dublin's) diplomatic efforts to defuse the crisis, while in the meantime accepting the occupation of Ireland by up to 15,000 British troops (the equivalent of 2.5 million foreign troops occupying America).

In addition, the US Justice Department harassed and indicted pro-republican fundraising groups among Irish Americans. Little has been revealed of clandestine ties between US intelligence agencies and British or Dublin security forces, although the FBI was deeply involved in tracking, indicting, and disrupting the operations of Americans suspected of raising funds for IRA weapons.[16] While attacking and discrediting the handful of American IRA supporters, the US government was actually helping arm the Royal Ulster Constabulary for their brutal war of counterinsurgency. Official State Department policy was to permit the sale of thousands of pistols and rifles from American manufacturers to the RUC in Northern Ireland.[17] In addition, while banning Sinn Féin spokesmen from America, the US government was granting visas in the seventies to leaders of the paramilitary Ulster Defence Association (UDA) and the loyalist Ulster Volunteer Force (UVF), both connected with hundreds of killings in the North.[18]

To achieve this demonization of Irish republicans as the "enemy," the US government complemented Irish censorship policies with the refusal of visas to Sinn Féin spokesmen who could have explained their views in America. Finally, they fashioned an acceptable alternative to republicanism in the person of John Hume and his Social Democratic and Labour Party. Many years later, as the peace process was beginning, the *New Statesman* magazine revealed the hidden hand in the formation of the SDLP. "British intelligence played a vital role in the creation of the SDLP. Dusted off from decolonization strategies of 1960s Africa, the objective was to create an acceptable, moderate alternative to armed militant nationalism. With the benefit of competent leadership and discreet official support, the SDLP has prospered over the decades."[19]

However, John Hume was no puppet. He was a tireless and respected civil rights activist from Derry who professed nonviolence and constitutional politics. It happened that his politics were complementary to US and British interests in launching an alternative to the IRA. To cement his American connections, Hume moved to Harvard University for a period in 1976. The American Ireland Fund was created in the same year to channel fundraising away from militant nationalism towards projects beneficial to moderate alternatives like Hume's or those of the Church. Later in the eighties, on the same day the *New York Times* headlined President Reagan's pledge to extradite IRA fugitives back to Margaret Thatcher's government, a lengthy story noted the funding of Hume through the US National Endowment for Democracy, operated by the former head of the CIA-funded Radio Free Europe. The mission of the endowment was described as to implement the Reagan Doctrine of "aggressively fostering pro-Americanism."[20] Years later, the *Boston Globe* obtained internal Reagan Administration documents that revealed a fervent pro-British commitment as well. During the Irish American protests at the death of hunger strikers in British jails in 1981, Reagan's national security adviser Richard Allen wrote that it was "intolerable that representatives of our staunchest ally in the world are subject to this sort of treatment."[21]

The flaw in this US strategic approach was that it overlooked the basic tenet of nationalism, namely that the British occupiers would have to be forced to withdraw from Ireland. While the flow of government and foundation funding may have materially benefited the Catholic middle class and the Church, which were the base of Hume's party, the same middle class was subject to second-class treatment and the brutal role of British troops, the Ulster Defence Regiment, and the RUC that deepened the alienation of the working class and the permanently unemployed in the ghettos where the IRA drew its support. The blind presumptions were that middle-class Catholics could be weaned off Irishness, that hearts and minds could be won at the point of bayonets, or that the British army and intelligence services could defeat the IRA.

This attitude of the Irish American establishment toward the Northern Irish rebellion can be understood only in the context of assimilation. The newly reconstituted Provisional IRA represented just the Irish image – primitive, bloodthirsty, masked zealots – that Irish America sought to overcome in the quest for acceptance. The IRA were the Fenians, the IRB, Rossa's legion, the Molly Maguires, the wild Irish all over again. Irish America historically was seen, by the British and Dublin, as a stronghold of extreme Irish republicans bent on revenge for their ancestors. There was more than a kernel of truth to this theory in Fenian times, but by the mid-twentieth century the number of Irish republicans in American had dwindled to inconsequential numbers. The real function of this attitude was to provide the British with a comforting "outside agitator" explanation of the events in the North, not unlike Southern American segregationists who blamed "Yankees" (ironically) for stirring up the supposedly contented blacks of Mississippi. The "outside agitator" theory also became the litmus test for defining who was a respectable Irish American, and who was still "bogged" down in primitive ways of thinking.

Thus there were deeper reasons for mainstream Irish America's role during the Troubles, unspoken reasons having to do with ethnic assimilation and respectability. Though most Irish Americans were historical descendants of anti-British rebels, as newly respectable Americans they were in denial of their own heritage. Thus it was no surprise that so many Irish American leaders were indistinguishable from the British government in their attitudes towards the IRA or its American sympathizers. For ethnic comparisons, they resembled the contemporary Mexican American leaders who distance themselves from the Zapatista rebels in Chiapas. In each case, showing the slightest sympathy for either the IRA or the Zapatistas would undermine the respectability of the ethnic politician seeking acceptance. The same politicians might sing songs and raise a glass to the Wolfe Tones and "Wexford boys," or the Pancho Villas and Emeliano Zapatas, while denying any similarities with revolutionaries invoking their names in the present. Such recognition would undermine the legitimacy of institutional arrangements in places like Dublin and

Mexico City as well as the long-sought acceptance of ethnic politicians in America. No one in power wants the ghosts of their revolutionary heritage to break out of the closet and make claims of being spiritually expropriated.

In a classic case of internalized infatuation with the colonizer, US House Speaker Tom Foley became a Knight Commander of the Order of the British Empire "for his services to Britain."[22] In another example, US House Speaker "Tip" O'Neill prohibited the ninety-three-member House Ad Hoc Committee on Irish Affairs from holding public hearings on the 1970s human rights violations in Northern Ireland. He thought it inappropriate to stir things up, even though Amnesty International was documenting cases of British torture at the time.[23] More generally, their affinity for WASP standards blinded many Irish Americans from seeing British colonialism as the source of the violence. Instead, the British were understood as the civilized arbiters of a tribal dispute between Catholics and Protestants that would eventually be ended through assimilation into modernity. A model based on the American civil rights crisis was adopted in place of the colonial model. In the American analogy, Washington DC had been the civilizing arbiter of a violent dispute in the South lingering from the Civil War. For the rest of America, it was believed, racism was a "dark chapter" from the past that still festered only in the backwaters of the old Confederacy. Washington had to use its alliances with Southern segregationists (who were a powerful force in the Democratic and Republican parties) to nudge them into modern times, while also creating safe, nonviolent alternatives like voter registration drives for blacks who might otherwise be drawn to the rhetoric of Malcolm X. In this analogy, the British were the civilizing mediators, loyalists like the Reverend Ian Paisley were the "no surrender" Southerners (in fact, Paisely received a divinity degree from, and remains closely associated with, the historically white-supremacist Bob Jones University in North Carolina), John Hume and the clergy were the moderate reformers, and the IRA was akin to the Black Panthers. The goal was to make it safe to be a Catholic subject of the United Kingdom in Northern Ireland.

The key problem with this analogy was the assumption that the American South was identical to the Irish North. As I have already observed, the analogy rested on a denial of colonialism. In the American case, while blacks were treated in some ways like colonial subjects, they were also American citizens eligible to vote, demonstrate, and sue the government itself. They had allies across the entire nation who could take official action on their behalf. In short, they were outcasts in a democratic society. In the case of Northern Ireland, the nationalists' aspiration conflicted directly with the colonial power based in London. Nationalists by definition were not seeking equal rights as British subjects. And the rest of Ireland in the Republic was powerless in the decision-making process of the North. The United States officially treated the Northern conflict as "an internal matter" of the United Kingdom, not an international anticolonial struggle producing a human rights crisis that demanded at least moral or political intervention.

To identify with the civil rights movement in Northern Ireland was tolerated, but to express any sympathy for those driven to violence against the British was an illegitimate, self-marginalizing viewpoint in America from 1970 to the 1990s. It was not thought proper to call the conflict a "war," for that might suggest that a rebel army was fighting successfully on British soil. Despite the fact that 44 percent of the British MI5 budget went to "Irish terrorism,"[24] the conflict became known as "the Troubles," the better to describe it as another case of Irish pathology needing British case management and American understanding. The British cultivated this viewpoint in America, which has been well documented in Andrew Wilson's *Irish-America and the Ulster Conflict* (1995). The British, according to Wilson, operated a "campaign of misinformation aimed at discrediting the IRA" while "US law enforcement agencies began covert operations against all militant Irish American groups."[25] They even targeted John Lennon, who wrote songs for the 1972 protests in New York against the Bloody Sunday repression in which fourteen people were shot and killed by British paratroopers.[26] The British information service, with a staff of forty-five, spent millions of pounds annually on everything from dinners with American journalists to distribution of thousands of radio "news spots" on a regular basis.[27] They wined and dined American foreign correspondents who rarely left London in their coverage of Northern Ireland. One *New York Times* writer recollected that "American journalists cover Northern Ireland infrequently. . . . Many stories are simply written from London, with no on-the-ground reporting, even though Belfast is just an hour away by shuttle." The journalists frequently took their cues from the Northern Ireland Office and the British Army Information Unit.[28]

The American media were culturally receptive in the first place. Liberal *New York Times* columnists like Gloria Emerson speculated over "something dark, inexplicable and strange in the Irish soul" while Anthony Lewis called for "enlightened colonialism" by the British. The *New York Times* took the British view of Bloody Sunday, reporting the British army's original story of provocation, then claiming the paratrooper shootings were "another landmark in the long history of misunderstanding."[29] Editorially, the *New York Times* supported direct rule from Westminster, as opposed to a British withdrawal, after Bloody Sunday.[30] The *Los Angeles Times* was even more rhapsodically Anglophile in a 1972 Bloody Sunday editorial: "Whatever the past sins of the British government, London is trying, decently and honestly, to tip the scales to the side of peace and justice. It deserves the world's sympathy and understanding in that enterprise."[31]

In response to that editorial, I visited the *Los Angeles Times*'s foreign editor who told several of us that America's interest was in supporting the British against terrorism in Northern Ireland. He received us as a protesting ethnic group, not as serious critics of unbalanced coverage. Years later, of course, numerous investigations, including a British tribunal, revealed that the British paratroopers shot innocent and unarmed demonstrators on Bloody Sunday, then covered up the episode for two decades.[32]

The final pro-London argument shared by many Irish Americans with the State Department was that the British were America's "strategic allies" in the Cold War and their larger quest to shape the world order. To be faithful to America's national interest, therefore, one had to set aside or forget altogether any previous loyalties to one's Old Country. In the most paranoid Anglo-American view, Northern Ireland, after all, could become "another Cuba." This "special relationship" between Britain and the United States has been cultivated for a long time. Britain is the largest source of foreign private investment in the United States, although exact data of these interlocking relationships are closely guarded. Some cite a familial dimension, noting over a hundred marriages between "American money and British nobility" in the twenty years before World War One, including those of Lord Randolph Churchill to Jennie Jerome and the Duke of Marlborough (Jennie's nephew) to Consuelo Vanderbilt.[33] E. Digby Baltzell, who invented the acronym "WASP," wrote in *The Protestant Establishment* that at the turn of the twentieth century "a British-American, White-Anglo-Saxon-Protestant (WASP) establishment, consolidated through family alliances between Mayfair and Murray Hill, involving many millions of dollars, authoritatively ran the world, as their ancestors had done since Queen Elizabeth's time."[34] The reverence of Americans, including Irish Americans, towards the British, seems to derive from a sense that the British Empire was our formative culture. The American Revolution, in this perspective, was a regrettable family dispute.

The US State Department has long been considered the strategic head-quarters of this cultural alliance. World War One, World War Two, and the Cold War sealed this "special relationship" on every level. But this was more than realpolitik. It was a bond of identity and destiny. As prime minister John Major observed, "It is very rare to find any serious diver-gence between the *instinctive* views of the UK and the US."[35] In a 1987 interview, Senator Joseph Biden expressed this affinity: "There is an over-whelming admiration and awe for British majesty and power. As they are in the twilight of their position as a world power, we are reluctant to take issue with them."[36] Asked about Margaret Thatcher's demands for extra-dition of republicans from America to Britain, Senator Biden was circumspectly supportive: "It is something that is not inappropriate to have on the agenda when the United States is dealing with a true, faithful and legitimate real ally."[37] Given this "awe . . . for British majesty and power," how could American leaders think critically about the British role in Northern Ireland?

The tone of abiding good will between the British establishment and mainstream Irish American leaders continued relatively undisturbed through the entire period known as the Troubles. As recently as February 1998, Tony Blair breakfasted in Washington with senators Kennedy, Moynihan, and Christopher Dodd, Congressmen Peter King and Joseph Kennedy and others, urging them to "keep up the pressure on Sinn Féin not to go back to violence" and to give "comfort" and "understanding" to Ulster Unionist Party leader David Trimble, who only recently had done a jig with Ian Paisley on the nationalist Garvaghy Road in Portadown. Notes on the meeting by Blair's secretary stated that "this was a notably successful occasion. The already benevolent mood of those present towards us was further strengthened by the open approach of the Prime Minister. . . . Feedback from those at the breakfast has been universally favourable."[38] The Irish Americans did make constructive proposals to Blair, for example, on police reform. But none questioned his alliance with Trimble, or rejected his request that they "keep up the pressure on Sinn Féin." None represented the position that the British presence was the root cause of the violence. Allowing for a bias in the notes, the meeting's atmosphere seemed politely collaborative, as if everyone was traveling towards the same political objective. By analogy to civil rights in America, Blair's agenda was akin to requesting selected African American leaders to keep the lid on the ghetto while understanding and trying to cultivate the Republican Party "moderates."

When President Bill Clinton pondered his decision to become involved in Northern Ireland, he was vigorously opposed not only by Secretary of State Warren Christopher, his appointees at the Justice Department and FBI, but by House Speaker Foley as well.[39] Clinton went ahead anyway. The British Conservative government of John Major had infuriated him by meddling in the American presidential election on behalf of George Bush. Clinton also remembered being affected by the Irish civil rights movement two decades earlier when he had been a student at Oxford. In addition, Clinton had shrewdly decided to court the white ethnic vote in his quest for a new centrist majority. He had promised Irish American activists a visa for Gerry Adams and a peace envoy for Northern Ireland. Revealingly, none of the Irish American *ad hoc* peace lobbyists were part of the Irish American establishment, although they later recruited senators Kennedy and Dodd to support the Adams visa after the IRA ceasefire. It was not the Irish American political or religious establishment that produced the historic change in American policy towards Northern Ireland in 1993 so much as it was Bill Clinton himself, a man of the sixties, a Southern Protestant with distant ancestral ties to shanty Irish. (I am informed authoritatively that Clinton's father was three-quarters Irish, but that his fabled "Cassidy" family connections in County Fermanagh are unproven. Nevertheless, the myth has been formalized in Irish–America's history of successful assimilation.)

Northern Ireland, September 1976

Oliver Cromwell's mission to Ireland has never been completed. . . . Catholicism as in Cromwell's day has no right to exist in Ireland at all. . . . Expel popery and you will have liberty.
Reverend Ian Paisley, April 1976[40]

. . . conditions can be made reasonably uncomfortable for the population as a whole, in order to provide an incentive for a return to normal life . . .
Frank Kitson, British army counterinsurgency expert, 1971[41]

. . . the notorious problem is how a civilized country can overpower uncivilized people without becoming less civilized in the process.
Sunday Times, 1977[42]

There is no such thing as a humane or civilized war. War may be forced upon a subject race or a subject class to put an end to subjection of race, of class or sex. When so waged, it must be waged thoroughly and relentlessly, but with no delusions as to its elevating nature or civilizing methods.

James Connolly[43]

My first trip to Ireland in 1976 opened my eyes to the realities that assimilation had obscured. There was no such thing as Romantic Ireland. There was war in the North and denial in the South. By now I was respectable enough to enter the Old Country. The Chicago trial was over, ending in acquittals by the higher courts. I was married to a famous actress, Jane Fonda. I was a father, and I wanted to root my three-year-old son in his Irishness as I wished my parents had done for me.

Naming my son Troy O'Donovan Garity was an act of nostalgia. My wife and I did not want to choose between our public last names, so we selected "Garity" to keep alive my mother's plainly Irish one. "Troy" was an Americanization of the name of a young Vietnamese man accused of conspiring to kill US officials. Though I regret the association, if indeed it was true, at that time all I knew of the Vietnamese Troi was that his death was unusually brave, a gesture of sacrifice against overwhelming odds. Troi was lashed to a stake, sentenced to death by firing squad. He asked that his blindfold be removed so that he could face the bullets without fear. He died calling for others to open their eyes.

"O'Donovan" was for a militant nineteenth-century Irishman, O'Donovan Rossa, a post-Famine immigrant to New York, an almost-successful candidate against "Boss" Tweed, and leader of the secret Irish Republican Brotherhood who directed a military campaign against England in the 1880s. What moved me about Rossa was not his militarism but the significance of his 1915 funeral in Ireland. There, amid a throng of thousands, the poet Padraic Pearse gave a powerful oration that anticipated – some say stimulated – the rising of the following year. It is well to read the peroration for which I named my son, along with eyewitness accounts of the moment, one of which begins: "Below the grave he stood, impressive and austere in green, with slow and intense delivery . . ."[44] Pearse said:

This is a place of peace, sacred to the dead, where men should speak with all charity and restraint; but I hold it a Christian thing, as O'Donovan Rossa held it, to hate evil, to hate untruth, to hate oppression, and, hating them, to strive to overthrow them.

Our foes are strong and wise and wary; but strong and wise and wary as they are, they cannot undo the miracles of God who ripens in the hearts of young men the seeds sown by the young men of a former generation. And the seeds sown by the young men of '65 and '67 are coming to their miraculous ripening today. Rulers and Defenders of Realms had need to be wary if they would guard against such processes. Life springs from death; and from the graves of patriot men and women spring living nations.

The defenders of this realm have worked well in secret and in the open. They think they have pacified Ireland. They think that they have pacified half of us and intimidated the other half. They think that they have foreseen everything, think that they have provided against everything.

But the fools, the fools, the fools! They have left us our Fenian dead, and while Ireland holds these graves, Ireland unfree shall never be at peace.

According to the eyewitness, as Pearse "cried aloud upon the fools he threw back his head sharply and the expression seemed to vivify the speech which ended proudly and calmly. He walked home and sat in his study." The Souvenir of the funeral was equally rhapsodic: "Cold, lifeless print cannot convey even an idea of the depth and intensity of feeling in which his words were couched . . . it was the soul of a patriot breathing words of love and devotion."[45]

One year later, in April 1916, Pearse marched into the Dublin General Post Office, proclaimed the Irish Republic, fought the superior British army, was captured, and was executed by firing squad.

I must admit that my blood still heats involuntarily when I read Pearse's oration, in the same way many Americans are roused by hearing our national anthem. (I felt the same reaction towards the "Star Spangled

Banner" once during a soulful rendition by Smokey Robinson.) I was touched by Pearse's summoning of a mystical courage, rooted in an ancient heroic tradition, so lacking in the world I inhabited. That he named a spiritual tradition, not material achievement, as "the soul of Ireland," and that he denounced conventional education as a cultural "murder machine" and called instead for Gaelic renewal, inspired my search for roots. That an intellectual, teacher, and poet could fight the British empire against hopeless odds was fascinating, challenging. Naming a son in Pearse's spirit was a way of commemorating this utopian sacrifice.

But the naming would also mark me in some quarters as an unreconstructed Fenian, the kind of Irish American who applauds the IRA from a safe American armchair. I am mindful of the criticism, and do not celebrate violence even for a just cause. But the violence of April 1916 is singled out for unusual disapprobation. By comparison, the critics of Pearse seem to have no problem with the slaughters of World War One that occurred at the same time. The dead of World War One, thousands of them Irish, were sacrificed for the empire that Pearse and his comrades rose against. But does that make their sacrifice more legitimate? The reason that Pearse remains controversial is that his declamations – that "the fools" thought they had "pacified half of us and intimidated the other half," and that "from the graves of patriot men and women spring living nations" – were as subversive in 1966, at the fiftieth anniversary of the Rising, as they were in 1916. If Pearse was a recognized founding father of the twenty-six-county state, why wasn't it patriotic for the IRA to rise against British rule in the North? If Pearse is considered a great martyr for Ireland, why not Bobby Sands and the IRA hunger strikers? As a popular IRA ballad puts it,

> Terrorists or the dreamers,
> The savage or the brave,
> Depends whose vote you're trying to catch,
> Whose face you're trying to save.[46]

Pearse remains a subject of controversy and discomfort in Irish political history. Obviously he was an icon for republicans, incorporated into the founding myth of the new state. But once the state was formed, its defenders saw no need for another Pearse. There does not even exist a modern, comprehensive collection of his essays and poetry. The last collected works were published in 1917. Five of his short stories were republished in 1968 by Mercier Press, and an eighty-page collection of selected poems was published in 1993.[47] The major biography of Pearse was first published in 1977 by Ruth Dudley Edwards, an arch critic of republican nationalism. The book, well-researched and well-written, interprets Pearse as a "triumph of failure," whose fanatical sacrifice ignited a popular movement for Irish independence which cost thousands of lives. The book sees the desire of Pearse and others to die a martyr's death for Ireland as a morbid glorification of violence – although their fiercest opponents are people who similarly express devotion to the full galaxy of martyrs for Christ. Such "primitivism" is "bloody crazy" and "bloody embarrassing," warns an empathetic introduction by Eugene McCabe to the 1993 selection of Pearse's poetry, as if the verses might ignite violence in the reader.[48] In short, Pearse is either politely admired in an understated way as a founder whose ideals have been achieved by the tricolour flying over the GPO, or he is dismissed as an obsolete psychopath. Like the omission or downplaying of the Famine in conventional history, the marginalizing of Padraic Pearse has been an effort to eliminate a moral or political rationale for the IRA.

For those who see Pearse only as a bloodthirsty fanatic with a death wish, the prison poem he wrote the night before his execution is worth quoting for the Irish sentiment it reveals:

> The beauty of the world hath made me sad,
> This beauty that will pass;
> Sometimes my heart has shaken with great joy
> To see a leaping squirrel in a tree,

Or a red ladybird upon a stalk,
Or little rabbits in a field at evening,
Lit by a slanting sun,
Or some green hill where shadows drifted by,
Some quiet hill where mountainy men hath sown
And soon would reap; near to the gate of heaven;
Or children with bare feet upon the sands
Of some ebbed sea, or playing on the streets
Of little towns in Connacht,
Things young and happy,
And then my heart hath told me:
These will pass,
Will pass and change, will die and be no more,
Things bright and green, things young and happy;
And I have gone upon my way
Sorrowful.[49]

Before he faced the executioners, Pearse had died of a broken heart. As an Irish archetype, he was more poet than guerrilla. Assimilation would kill him a second time.

Today I might not be so propagandistic in the naming of my son. But in the sixties, I needed to wrench control of my own history from oblivion. So it was that I was finally allowed to enter the country, and traveled in 1976 with Troy O'Donovan Garity on the streets and lanes of Ireland, in a quest to reverse my assimilation. When we arrived, I told Troy we were in the land of his ancestors. At first, he took this to mean that we would dig up dead people from their graves and introduce ourselves. Then, in front of the General Post Office where the Easter Rising was launched, without my prompting, he started pointing at passersby and asking if they were our ancestors.

In Monaghan, where at the time I knew no one, we sat on a bench at the Diamond in the town center looking at "ancestors" as well. It struck me that Troy's way of seeing things was as valid as any. While I couldn't grasp my family history, he was simply feeling a childlike relatedness that I never had. It was not a blissful time, however. Only two years before, on May 17, 1974, thirty-three people had been killed by bombs in Monaghan and Dublin by loyalists, with suspected involvement of British military intelligence.[50] I entered and left Monaghan that day without speaking to a soul. I didn't want to be a prying Yank, and couldn't deal with my feelings about coming "home."

Near Derry, a sleepy Troy and I reached the border in our rented car and stopped at a British army checkpoint. All was darkness except the flashlights aimed at our faces. Automatic weapons were pointed at the car, and at Troy, who bolted up. We could see blackened faces of soldiers behind the lights. They motioned to roll down the windows, told us to leave the car while they probed the backseats, the floor, the trunk, our bags. They were young, taut, lethal-looking. We were put back in the car while they ran a license check. We were waved along.

I was wondering whether Troy was my good-luck charm in their decision to let us through, when he burst out, "Dad, don't call me Irish because the soldiers will shoot me." He was learning that his roots could get him killed. I realized why the Irish changed their names, their religion, their country: out of fear, if not for themselves, for their children.

We crossed the border and took the motorway to Belfast, a two-hour drive. I had no idea whom I was looking for, but assumed that I could make contact with Sinn Féin activists on the Falls Road. At the time, republicans were going through a vicious period, tangled in bloody factional and ideological feuds not unlike black revolutionaries in the US. But this was a life-and-death situation with nowhere to hide. British Saracens and foot patrols were in the streets and, often enough, breaking through the doors. If you weren't killed by the Brits, you could be "done" by one of your own. A feud between Official and Provisional factions of the IRA in late 1975 left eleven dead, including a child. Local propaganda organs of the factions were filled with photos of assassinated activists such as nineteen-year-old Hugh Ferguson, with factional epitaphs like "he died so the Irish Socialist Republican Party might live."[51]

It took me two hours driving around central Belfast – including a stop-and-search by the RUC when I kept circling one roundabout – before I found my way to the Falls Road. Maps were useless because street signs were hard to find. Pedestrians I asked gave vague answers. At other street corners I found myself afraid to ask. All in all, a scary place, or so I projected.

But I did somehow find the Sinn Féin office and bookstore on the upstairs floor of a Falls Road building. Carrying Troy, I introduced myself and inquired about a possible place to stay. Someone named Tom – it might have been Tom Hartley, today a Sinn Féin member of the city council – took charge of showing me around. The place reminded me of an SDS office in the sixties, cluttered with radical debris, everyone young and defiantly disheveled, only a peephole in a thick reinforced door.

After some introductory conversation, Troy and I were sent to the flat of Danny Morrison, twenty-three, a Sinn Féin spokesperson, just off the Road. Danny was a targeted man, who had already spent months underground and who later would spend five years in prison. His family, an English wife named Sandra and a infant named Kevin, lived amid a jumble of unmade beds, cups and dishes everywhere, unfinished books cracked open on tables, an environment arranged for life on the run. I contributed to the disorder by mixing brown sauce and tomato ketchup with my meals, an unfamiliar combination that quickly exhausted all supplies. Danny, like myself, was a writer by nature who had been pressed into organizational propaganda for the cause. If the United States had disintegrated into civil war at the end of the sixties, I might have been in the same position. He joined the Provisionals because "they take the risks while others only talk." Somewhat contemptuous of other groups, he believed that a left-wing politics would grow out of the Provisionals' experience, not the study guides of other parties. We talked back and forth about the relationships of community organizing, political campaigns and underground movements, questions that briefly had come to the fore in America but were permanent issues in occupied Belfast. The Provos were "speaking" with weapons because they were voiceless under British colonial rule. But the armed struggle could only undermine the status quo, not replace it. That would take political support, from Ireland and Irish America. If Provo violence was inevitable under the circumstances, it also limited public support in America to a fringe who always supported the IRA, or to those who reacted temporarily to British atrocities like Bloody Sunday. With the British dominating the media and republicans officially censored, how could political organizing and lobbying reach a mass audience? My concerns sounded arrogant, but Danny was a patient listener. From his standpoint, the only politics on offer required an unacceptable oath to the Crown. A radically different politics did not exist. Though he was a writer, he wondered if there were any readers! My reformism sounded empty. In the meantime, bullets were flying.

His wife was less ideological and blamed the community for giving too little support for the Provisionals. Sandra complained that "these boys are not out laughing and rioting, they're not laughing when they come out of the RUC barracks bruised and bleeding. People wouldn't hide one boy recently when he was running right down the street." She wasn't on speaking terms with her father, then serving in the British army in a location outside Northern Ireland. Sandra didn't know how long she could take it. She felt too much tension over what would happen to Danny. She feared for one-year-old Kevin. "I don't want him to grow up in the same situation twenty years from now."

At the time, a popular call for the Provos to cease violence was being generated by two "peace women," Betty Williams and Mairead Corrigan, with huge international support from Dublin, London, the American media, and the singer Joan Baez, a campaign that eventually resulted in a Nobel Peace Prize. The origins of this peace movement, however, lay in a tragedy that was only indirectly attributable to the Provisional IRA. British forces in pursuit of a blue Cortina on the Andersontown Road opened fire and instantly killed the driver, IRA Volunteer Danny Lennon, twenty-three, whose car then swerved into the

Maguire family, killing three children.[52] In the wake of the catastrophe, thousands of Irish people marched to end the killings. But gradually the pacifists shifted to an emphasis on condemning the Provisionals, who were forced to argue that armed resistance was necessary until the British agreed to withdraw. Once again the view that IRA violence was unjustified while state-sponsored British and RUC violence was somehow legitimate infected the public debate. Even today the authoritative *Northern Ireland: A Political Directory* (1999) describes the cause of the children's death as being "struck by a gunman's getaway car" as if the vehicle was driven by an escaping criminal on a solo joyride.[53] Without the British army, there would have been no car chase, no shooting, no deaths of children that day. But given the extraordinary filters on public perception, it was made to appear that the Provos were responsible for killing the Maguire children. Eventually, the Peace People fell apart over just these issues combined with personality clashes over the use of Nobel prize money.[54] Pacifist or one-sided appeals were not enough to end the violence in the North. But given the depth of the anti-IRA, antiviolence orientation in the public and the media, the Provos were disadvantaged in the war for public opinion whatever they did. The British, seen in the Western media as peacekeepers amid sectarian savagery, held the public relations advantage. The republican physical force tradition was just that, a strategy to wear down the British will. But in a television-dominated world feeding on images of violence, the Provos would be known only for their bombs and guns until they created a human face and a political platform. A majority of Irish people preferred the constitutional tradition in politics and were gripped by a schizophrenia towards IRA violence. It had been an armed uprising, after all, that led to creation of the Republic. The national anthem, after all, was "The Soldier's Song," a tribute to IRA volunteers. But the self-hatred traditionally instilled in the colonized also led to Irish civil war in the 1920s and a permanent sense among most Irish people that IRA violence was more shameful than the official violence of the state.

However, the dim beginnings of an alternative form of struggle were present at the time of my 1976 visit. The British had embarked on a so-called criminalization policy, which consisted of refusing political status to republican prisoners. Since British prisons had a long history of being "universities" for the republican movement, the British wanted to undermine the morale of prisoners and squelch any efforts by inmates to organize themselves along republican lines behind bars. If the British granted republicans any rights as political prisoners, or prisoners of war, it would be a damaging admission that the British state was employing repression against an independence movement. In September 1976, as the British were forcing republican prisoners to wear the apparel of common criminals, a republican prisoner named Kieran Nugent refused. Nugent's statement, "Prison garb? The Brits will have to nail it on!" was a battle cry that led to anti-criminalization campaigns from 1976 to 1981.[55] These actions, culminating in fasts to the death by ten hunger strikers in 1981, shifted the onus for violence onto the British. By using their bodies this way, the republican prisoners sent a powerful appeal to public opinion. While at first their political leaders in Sinn Féin had serious doubts about the hunger strike, the moral gesture created the unique political opportunity that previously had eluded republicans. Thirty thousand voters elected a dying Bobby Sands as a Member of Parliament in 1981. Republicans began formulating a new strategy that would involve electoral politics, not yet as a road to power, but as a means of building public support for their views. If elected, they would continue to abstain from taking seats in British institutions or swearing oaths to the Crown. But they would make inroads in local politics and begin to compete for the support of the Northern electorate. Danny Morrison summed it up with a famous assertion that Sinn Féin could struggle "with a ballot paper in one hand and an Armalite in the other." He was denounced by some as a thug and by others for going soft, but his statement nonetheless captured the riddle of republicanism. Armed struggle was the only language the British understood, but it could not by itself create a united Ireland. Constitutional politics, on the other hand, lacked an understanding that partition was in itself a denial of democracy – a denial of the wish expressed by the overwhelming majority in 1918 for Sinn Féin's goal of an independent republic. Pursuing both approaches at the same time might ultimately be self-defeating, but in the short run it allowed Sinn Féin to blossom as a political party, not just a leafleting organization for the IRA or a pacified nationalist grouping at Stormont. (Twenty years later, the same issues endured. The British, the unionists, and some in Dublin were demanding that the IRA begin disarming before being recognized as a party in office. The IRA had created a historic ceasefire, but refused to decommission its weapons before a British decision to withdraw from Northern Ireland. And Danny Morrison had formulated a new phrase to sum up the situation: "an armed peace," *Belfast Telegraph*, July 28, 1999.)

The Irish education of my son Troy continued. Danny's wife Sandra walked us around the Falls, a lively community of shops and strollers, and over to the stark prison on Crumlin Road where republicans were held. We walked through the British patrols and under the army helicopters. Each day Troy and I spent time in a small park where the asphalt was littered with broken glass. We played with kids on swings made of rope and tires, and tried to learn hurling. As the days passed, Troy's fear of saying we were Irish seemed to recede. There were 180 shooting incidents that month in Belfast, according to the *Republican News*.[56] From the media's standpoint, the wild Irish were at it again. From the nationalist standpoint, the old British strategy of divide-and-conquer was in high gear. At the same time, my own personal war with assimilation was deepening. West Belfast was where Irish identity was being contested and reclaimed. Troy was face to face with his heritage. What it meant to be an Irish American between two worlds I would soon find out.

The Falls resembled a vast American ghetto or barrio. The Road was like LA's Central Avenue in the old days of legalized segregation: a packed, thriving, separate community with a history of its own. Families identified with their immediate street or neighborhood. There was a deep, informally structured network of churches, schools, family businesses, pubs, a social order existing as parallel and as independently as possible under the dominant state. Some residents were teachers, nurses, publicans, or construction workers. The high unemployment rates – reaching 80 percent in some neighborhoods – were passed from generation to generation, as in American ghettos. Alcoholism was rampant. The unemployed lived on the dole, or by odds and ends. The streets teemed with young people with nowhere to go. An alien police force and military vehicles patrolled the road, stopping, searching, chasing, and arresting people. Across the North, there were 34,000 house searches by the security forces in 1976 alone, of a total of 150,000 Catholic households. In the seventies, the vast majority of Catholic homes were raided and searched by the Army which claimed to be protecting them.

The Falls was also a community of organized resistance supporting a vast underground of outlaws, something the Black Panthers dreamed about but could never achieve. An alternative paper, the *Andersonstown News*, and a pirate radio station provided news and opinion from a republican viewpoint. A system of black taxis, like those one sees in gangster movies, replaced the burned-out Belfast buses. A movement to rescue the Irish language was gaining momentum despite sanctions. Drug sales and distribution were effectively blocked by the IRA, which also filled policing functions, sometimes brutally, as the alternative to the RUC. And in spite of the repression and stress, an iron will seemed to triumph over weariness and despair. No one I met in the movement in those days seemed to have any money. Everyone smoked, drank in pubs, and discussed the movement. They were sleepless people whose eye sockets were sunken and dark. They moved from flat to flat, either on operations or to avoid arrest. I met a student leader who explained his grueling lifestyle this way: "I won't sacrifice absolutely everything because then I'd become completely mad. But I have no girlfriend. The life is all based on work. We're a difficult movement for the Brits to penetrate because we work so hard, so many straight hours. You'd have to sell papers, leaflet, picket, and read just to keep up with us. It seems crazy, but I don't want to look in the mirror five years from now and see that the revolution failed. Now's the time, so I do everything I can."

The Provisionals were related to a youth revolution around the world. Years later, Sinn Féin's chairman Mitchel McLaughlin recalled that "we rebelled against the perception of our parents' silence – though I later found out my father had instigated a riot in 1947 and kept quiet about it."[57] In the absence of elders, we in the global protest movements all were "provisionals," that is, we improvised our revolution, mistakes and all, believing that it was the responsibility of our generation alone. But recognizing affinity with this generation of Irish rebels was not enough. The more I uncovered my roots the less I knew where I belonged. I knew I had no role as an outsider in this place where local history was everything. And the blood feuds and faction-fighting were deeply disturbing, since they fit an Irish stereotype and were impossible to rationalize in America. But it was equally disturbing to consider read-justing to America, and Irish America, where Northern Ireland was little more than a caricature of what the Irish thankfully believed they left behind. Assimilation required an amnesia that now made you a stranger in the land of your ancestors. Unless beneath the smooth surface of assimilation there was a hidden, stubborn, independent Irish experience that could be awakened to demand a place for itself in American life.

One day we drove to Derry, on someone's suggestion, to search out a young man named Martin McGuinness, said to be the Provo leader in the Bogside. My wife, Jane Fonda, had flown in from London where she was filming *Julia*. Troy sat on her lap and became a travel guide and adviser on what not to say to British soldiers, who patrolled the streets in full combat gear. We passed through a darkened checkpoint and stopped at the first resting place we encountered, the Everglades Hotel in the Protestant Waterside district, a place with an indoor swimming pool, bar and restaurant, enclosed in barbed wire fortifications. The staff and bar patrons were suspicious about our presence, and we quickly sought our room key. Calling the city "Derry" at the hotel desk, instead of Londonderry, was one of countless ways that we were conspicuous. Even twenty years later, the American media identify the town as Londonderry in deference to the British, despite the fact that a national-ist city council redesignated it as Derry. I am charmed by the name *Derry*, which originates from an Irish word for "oak grove," the place where Columcille once prayed.

We left the hotel politely and expeditiously in the morning, and drove in circles looking for the Bogside. A gas station attendant was kind enough to point us down the hill to the famous Catholic ghetto, and we descended circuitously through ancient gates below the imposing walls where Protestants had defended the old city against Catholic armies in the seventeenth century. At the bottom we entered a flat community of row houses and rain-washed streets where the 1969 street battle with the British army had begun, and where the Bloody Sunday killings occurred in 1972. I had an extreme feeling of vulnerability compared to how I felt in west Belfast, principally because we were entrapped well below the fortified heights. Rising above the walls were British watchtowers. In the midst of this intimidating geography I noticed a huge mural proclaiming "YOU ARE NOW ENTERING FREE DERRY." We were clearly in a community that was not intimidated. Here was an example of the free communities we had dreamed of creating in the sixties. (Some years later, Derry activist Eamon McCann was asked where the idea of "Free Derry" came from. "We were sitting around wondering what to call ourselves and someone had seen a Free Berkeley mural, so we said Free Derry and that was it.")[58]

Lost as usual, we stopped at a pub that mid-morning to ask assistance in finding Martin McGuinness. "And who are youse?" Feeling stupid standing in the dim morning light, I introduced my family and asked if it was possible to tell McGuinness that we were looking for him. The man disappeared, came back again, and said, "Wait here and have something, I'll see what can be done." It wasn't long before he returned with directions to a nearby row of houses on a cramped street below the walls not far from a cemetery. We knocked and the door was opened by Martin's wife, who told us he was returning from church. He soon arrived, a slim, handsome man with blond curly hair and bright blue eyes. The family included his mother, his sister Geraldine and a newborn, Grainne. They were open and friendly, as if this were a normal Sunday-morning drop-in. Martin told Jane that he knew someone in prison who had her picture up on his wall, but he knew little beyond our involvement in the antiwar movement. As we talked, I felt surprised at their cheerfulness in a house that seemed so vulnerable to attack. Then Martin whisked us away to a community meeting in progress.

At a nearby home, we met Joseph McCoughlin, just back from the hospital after a beating by the British army. According to McCoughlin's account, he was stopped and searched the previous night on the bridge we had ourselves crossed over. He was banged up all over – eyes, cheeks, chest and back. His mother carried a huge red welt on her arm from trying to intervene. His white shirt was a dark bloody mess. Troy had never seen blood like this before, and was perplexed at the black smudges where the soldiers had polished their boots on the fallen McCoughlin. I asked Joseph not to throw the shirt away but let me take it back to the USA as evidence. I handed it to Troy to carry.

While in many ways I could relate to these Provisionals, their politics were still confusing to me. They had emerged organically out of the civil rights movement, and then the street fighting against British troops in places like Derry and Belfast. When it became apparent that British troops were not peacekeepers, and would do nothing to prevent murderous gangs of loyalists from rampaging in Catholic neighborhoods, they sought to arm themselves in self-defense. Like sixties rebels everywhere, their theories arose from their experience, not the other way around. Their violence seemed situational, not ideological, and hardly biological. An armed struggle, or at least armed self-defense, seemed the only way to survive with dignity. This option, however, negated the possibility of building alliances with working people or liberals in Protestant communities. Since Protestants at the time were nearly 60 percent of the population, the republican dilemma was how to win a political war against an entrenched majority. The Officials favored calling the war off, which offered no protection against loyalist mobs, paramilitaries, the RUC, and the British army. In the Provo catechism, the solution was to "break the British connection" by blasting the Brits into a decision to withdraw. Once the unionist majority realized that their British lifeline was being cut, so the theory went, the Ulster Protestants would realize they were actually Irish, and adjust. Although this seemed fanciful to me, what was the alternative? To surrender to a police state or wait for the ideological dream of a radicalized loyalist working class? As one Provo told me, "I joined up with what they were calling the right wing. We picked up the gun. The so-called left wing said, But it's not in the book. I said, You stop the Brits with a book and I'll join youse!"

Martin McGuinness and the Bogside residents we met that day were surprisingly candid. They worried about whether the community had the capacity to resist the occupying forces and certain blandishments then being offered to moderate middle-class Catholics. One said, "Not everyone sees the bigger picture. Many of them simply want the inconveniences removed from the streets. One person wanted to know if he could get a British barricade adjusted so it wouldn't cause inconvenience for his car! We still have to educate people to see the underlying problem of the British presence." As in Belfast, their base of support seemed fragile in the face of this challenge. But they were thinking of a long-term settlement as well. The republicans, they reasoned, needed a British agreement to pull out, while the unionist community needed the preservation of majority rule. How to reach a balanced solution in two or three years was the question. No one I listened to that day spoke of the war continuing another two decades.

Still looking ahead, one republican said, "The risk we run is getting the British army out and still having no power. The multinationals are coming in, the debt to international financiers will grow – I am more afraid of the multinationals than the UDR." Du Pont, a major Northern company, had developed a personality test, he said, to cultivate malleable employees. "They demolish their identity before the god of materialism, then turn them into Sunday golfers. Respectability, you see, is very, very important to poor Catholics." Martin added that as the republican movement was becoming more politically astute, the establishment (the BBC, the Church, and educational system) "has been trying all sorts of ways to manipulate us." These were clearly people of a common viewpoint though not a single mindset. They preferred a politics and a sense of community based in nationalism, but saw little or no chance of realizing equal rights peacefully. They accepted that the IRA had a role to play. Martin McGuinness reflected this dualism in his own activity; as he later confirmed, he was an IRA deputy commander during that period (reported in the *LA Times*, May 31, 2001).

I was influenced at the time by Jimmy Breslin's novel *World Without End, Amen*, about Dermot Davey, an Irish American policeman from Queens who visits the North and becomes entranced with a Bernadette Devlin figure named Deirdre.[59] Breslin was one of the first mainstream American columnists to sympathize with the young Provisionals, or at least present them as human beings to an American audience. He also portrayed the contradictions of Irish America through his hero, a cop who dislikes black people but is attracted to an Irish woman with posters of Che Guevara and Black Panthers on her wall. Irishness is disappearing for Dermot until he meets Deirdre.

> The heritage of being Irish is more a toy than a reality. A drink, a couple of wooden sayings, and a great personal pride, bordering on hysterical, in being Irish. *The bloodlines were present. But they were being thinned out by time.* You could count on some help if you were Irish. But there was no way to count on the help lasting forever. Dermot Davey knew the implications.[60]

Breslin captured the revolutionary spark, the manic idealism, and the earthy humanity of Deirdre's generation that I encountered in my 1976 visit. In the novel, Deirdre combines self-defense with a socialist politics that reaches out to working-class Protestants. She is murdered, Breslin implies, precisely for this dangerous fusion. She threatens the manipulated culture of religious sectarianism that keeps Catholic and Protestant apart. She also transcends the stodgy Marxism of the Official IRA. Breslin, however, doubts the possibility that the Provisionals could develop from armed street fighters to a political movement. In the novel, the Provisionals are characterized as older Catholic nationalists trying to manipulate Deirdre's generation into violence, when in fact they were a younger generation tired of the debates of the old. For many Irish Americans like Breslin, the death of Deirdre's politics left little basis for solidarity with Northern Ireland – unless you were a gunrunner or enjoyed singing republican ballads in American pubs.

But if the Provisionals were all such "madmen," how did the current political leadership of Gerry Adams, Martin McGuinness, and republican writers like Danny Morrison eventually emerge? Are they not the same people who were dismissed as tribal killers in their youth? Even during the crazed year of 1976, many of those young Provos were well aware, as James Connolly had written, that there was nothing "elevating" or "civilizing" about what they were doing. Morrison has since written several novels about west Belfast at the time, in which human foibles play a greater role than the pamphlets of Che Guevara.[61] In 1976, the *Republican News* often balanced its shrill reports from the front with reflective essays. These were usually written under the pseudonym "Brownie," now generally acknowledged to have been used by Gerry Adams when he was held in Long Kesh. ("Brownie" may have referred to his shaggy brown hair.) I read these columns with fascination at the time. Some of them were political calls for "active," instead of theoretical, republicanism. But often they were stories of the humanity for which republicans fought. In September, 1976, while I was living in Danny and Sandra's flat, "Brownie" wrote a story ridiculing factionalism in the movement. It described an *ard fheis* (convention) of republican prisoners debating whether to support coalitions with anti-imperialist groups or only with *"true"* anti-imperialist groups. Two prisoners leave the meeting to "reconvene a back-stabbing session in their cell." At the end of the account, "Brownie" acknowledges that his imaginary cellmates, Egbert, Cedric, and "yer Man", didn't even attend the meeting because of disagreements with the chairman.[62]

In another column, on the Irish language, "Brownie" worried about cultural dominance by "tele-colonialism," and quoted Pearse's "rich and soul-satisfying" prospect of Protestant children "learning to curse the Pope in Irish." In other columns, he admitted doubt: "We have seven years of war behind us and perhaps another seven years before us, that is if we are not to be defeated beforehand." And humility: "[active republicanism] means fighting. It's hard to write that down because, God knows, maybe I won't fight again and it will be cast up at me, but it still needs to be said, even by a coward like myself, because at least I will move aside for the fighters."[63]

This seemed to me a very sensible voice amid all the madness. Whereas I couldn't stand ego rivalries and factional power-tripping, this "Brownie" managed to translate it into the humorous stuff of everyday Irish life. But who was reading his columns? The Provo paper had to be printed underground, over the border. Its editors like Danny and writers like "Brownie" couldn't be identified. Sanity and argument would someday open a path for the Provisionals from war to politics. But at the time, picking up the pen of storytelling in the service of the Provos was as treasonable as picking up the gun.

Visiting the Republic, 1976

> What need you, being come to sense,
> But fumble in a greasy till
> And add the halfpence to the pence
> And prayer to shivering prayer, until
> You have dried the marrow from the bone?
> For men were born to pray and save:
> Romantic Ireland's dead and gone,
> It's with O'Leary in the grave.
>> W. B. Yeats, "September 1913"[64]

That September of 1976 I spent a few more days in Dublin with Troy alone, and encountered a Southern Republic that seemed more claustrophobic than charming. Far from trying to support Northern Catholics, or foster a united Ireland by political or nonviolent means, the state was enacting draconian legislation against the threat that the Troubles would spill over to the South. Michael Collins's moment of opportunity to subvert Ulster had arrived fifty years too late, and now the Republic wanted to prevent the North from shaking up its conservative status quo. The proposed laws permitted detention without public disclosure, without the right to an attorney, and without medical care, for seven days instead of the current two. Individuals could be sentenced to ten years for "incitement to join or assist" the IRA. Newspapers could be closed down if they published "inciteful" letters to the editor. Proof of membership in an illegal organization could be based on the word of a policeman, nothing more.

Most people I met in hotels and restaurants, and the media coverage I followed, seemed disconnected from the state of emergency, preoccupied with distractions from the conflict just two hours' drive north. Even by the nineties a survey showed that 75 percent of the Republic's citizens had never spent a single night in the North in their lives.[65] During that week in Dublin, everyone seemed enveloped in the Irish Open or greyhound racing. Yanks like myself were suspected of being simplistic Brit-haters bent on bringing destruction on the Free State from sanctuaries in New York.

The main architect and intellectual defender of this authoritarian stance was Conor Cruise O'Brien, then a government minister, and a writer perceived in America as Ireland's authoritative voice, who wrote for such publications as the *New York Review of Books*. I respected him as an early opponent of the Vietnam war. "Playing a key role in the drive against republicans on both sides of the Atlantic,"[66] he came to meet me in the Gresham Hotel, wanting to set me straight on the Provo question lest I confuse Northern Ireland with Vietnam. He was an absent-minded professor in demeanor, keeping his eyes gazing towards the carpet, where Troy sat quietly playing with toy British soldiers I bought in a Dublin store.

During our talk, O'Brien said several times that he might be considered paranoid, and indeed the scenario he sketched justified such concern. "I know many think I'm obsessive about this, and it's true, I am," he said. His nightmare scenario was the very one I had naïvely believed the Irish wanted: the withdrawal of the British army from the North. "If the British army ever leaves," he said, "the whole place will go up like Lebanon. Sections of the Irish army might go over to the North. That would push the loyalists from mere suppression of Catholics to mass murder. A full-scale war could overthrow the regime in the South." His reasoning was based on the notion that the Irish were more a danger to themselves than anyone else, including their longtime British masters.

I tried arguing with O'Brien that the Northern young people I'd met desperately needed the Dublin government to speak out, not censor what they had to say. And I questioned how he could oppose the American intervention in South Vietnam while welcoming the British intervention in Northern Ireland. The cases were dissimilar, he responded. The United States had no national interest at stake in Vietnam, while the British had a right to be present because the North was a province of the United Kingdom. Wasn't the partition of Ireland imposed by force, I asked, just like the partition of Vietnam in 1954? But I was getting nowhere. I realized that he was comfortable, perhaps like many of his countrymen, with the division of Ireland. Although a living encyclopedia of Irish history, he was also an Anglophile. Instead of wanting to negotiate a political settlement providing the Provisional IRA a space to pursue their goals by nonviolent means, he wanted the Provos stamped out. He would later declare that the revolutionary nationalism of 1916 should be rubbished as a failed exercise in fanaticism and, in time, become a member of Robert McCartney's UK Unionist Party. He was Memmi's perfectly colonized man, resembling the colonizer "to the point of disappearing in him."

I was mistaken to consider O'Brien a fully authentic representative of the South; he was almost a caricature of a self-hating Irish intellectual. Underneath the denial and hostility towards the North I discovered in Dublin was another Ireland, hidden and schizophrenic in nature, that Tim Pat Coogan once described as "genuinely patriotic rather than pub-house republicanism."[67] Writing of the adherents of the dominant Fianna Fáil party in the South, he said: "The late-night Fianna Fáil drinker is quite likely to mutter approvingly about 'the boys' – and then go off without a qualm the next day to vote for some Fianna Fáil measure to curb the IRA."[68] I found this split consciousness in the smallest of episodes. For example, in Dublin I met openly in hotel lobbies with wanted Provos under the eyes of doormen who could have called the gardaí but didn't. A cashier in Dublin, who had moved away from Belfast because she "hated the violence," told me the British government knew all about her family in the North. A friend standing nearby chimed in, "Ah, but there's some things they don't know." The cashier replied laughingly, "Right you are, and they never will."

One night, in a discussion with off-duty journalists and government officials, I listened to endless jokes and stories reflecting the hidden republicanism under the surface of the status quo. One recalled stopping for dinner in a border town only to find his car stolen when he left the restaurant. The restaurant doorman undertook to find the Provos on the chance they had hijacked the vehicle for an operation. After a while, the doorman returned to say he'd spoken with "the lads." It turned out they had hijacked two vehicles that day, but neither fit the description. So, the doorman shrugged, "it must have been a thief." Everyone howled.

It would be a long time, however, before significant Southern support for Sinn Féin would surface. The Republic defined itself more and more as an independent European state. The goal of a united Ireland was only aspirational, no longer meaningful in the daily lives of a majority. As far as I could see, partition had succeeded in turning a geographic border into a mental and cultural border. The North was transformed into another place, a key to the Southern Irish thinking of themselves as civilized and evolved. Additionally, there was the conservatism of the Catholic Church blanketing the Republic. Divorce was virtually illegal, and abortion absolutely prohibited, leaving thousands of Irish women secretly departing for English clinics yearly.[69] The Church was funded and integrated into the educational structures of both North and South. Church-supported censorship extended to certain Irish writers. The ultimate cultural effect was not only to marginalize Sinn Féin's brand of secular republicanism, but to send a counterproductive message to Protestants and unionists that real pluralism was not a likely option for the future. When I arrived in 1976, for example, it had been illegal to sell condoms to married people until quite recently.[70] Despite my Provo view that the British should withdraw militarily, on certain social issues I had to agree with at least the British Labour Party view and oppose the Catholic Church. This was not simply a moral question, but a political one. How could the 900,000 Protestants of Northern Ireland ever be persuaded to enter what they perceived as an inhibiting Catholic state?

I returned to the United States in October 1976, still wondering where I belonged. I had discovered an Irish dimension to my life, but the visit to Northern Ireland left me at a loss. I could identify with the Provo spirit, even defend their armed resistance. But I was alienated from the paranoia, the factions, the blood feuds. As an American, I had no role in the armed struggle or any other struggle in Ireland itself, because I would be considered a blow-in. But political advocacy back in the States was curtailed as well by the demonizing and sanctions against Sinn Féin. As with, Breslin's character Dermot Davey, my republican bloodlines were being thinned out by time. And even if I could sort out where I stood on republicanism, there was the matter of the Church. I wasn't an atheist, and was well aware of anti-Catholic bigotry down through history. But the Irish Church was too much like that of Father Coughlin, and too distant from the Berrigans, for my embrace.

The only options in the USA were (1) to support the reformist politics of the SDLP, which meant opposing the IRA and accepting the presence of the British army as a lesser evil; (2) to become involved in the clandestine, incestuous and infiltrated world of sending money and defending the IRA, which would limit the educational and political organizing I thought to be paramount; or (3) to become a detached Irish romantic, knowing everything about Joyce but nothing in terms of current events.

Not long after I returned to the United States, republican prisoners stepped up their struggle for political status and went "on the blanket," refusing prison clothing, a resistance which built toward the hunger strike crisis of 1981. I wrote letters of solidarity to prisoners and picketed the British embassy in Los Angeles, but felt guilt at not doing enough, and estrangement from Americans who didn't care. I wept in public when the strikers died. Obviously, Margaret Thatcher and the British government suffered a diplomatic public relations disaster. It marked a huge opportunity to speak about the causes of the conflict without having to debate IRA violence. In Ireland itself, tens of thousands of people voted for the hunger strikers in parliamentary elections. It was the beginning of an alternative to violence that eventually would lead to the peace process. But I still noticed an anti-Irish undertone as I tried to get my friends involved. These

Irish hunger strikers, the thinking went, were no Cesar Chavezes or Mahatma Gandhis. Not only were they likely bombers and snipers, but who else except the wild Irish would wrap themselves naked in blankets, smear feces over cell walls, and instruct their loved ones to let them die when they fell into comas? Their steely moral commitment was seen through a biased lens. As with Pearse, the conclusion for many Americans was that the hunger strikers may have seemed idealistic but were Irish psychopaths nonetheless. An Irish-born historian, Padraig O'Malley, writing for the *Boston Globe*, blamed the hunger strikers for manipulating his emotions with their sense of victimhood and "eyes fixed on a star in a galaxy of patriot ghosts," offering their bodies to the "gods of a degenerative nationalism." In a pure expression of self-hatred, O'Malley concluded that "we are our own oppressors . . . We need England. We need it to disguise the sordid and sad reality of our murderous designs on each other." (*Boston Globe*, May 6, 1981)

More than ever, I felt like a stranded Irishman in America. I now rejected the false comfort of assimilation. But neither did it seem effective to be shouting "Brits out!" at Los Angeles bars for Irish immigrants, nor could I join the New Age in its swooning over a Celtic spirituality. The search for my roots only left me a deeper sense of uprootedness. The concept of standing for radical change in both America and Ireland had few backers.

The Eighties: A Political Opening

I was elected to the California state legislature in 1982, beginning a tenure which lasted eighteen years. My ethnicity, while not a burden, was regarded by my voters as a quaint dimension of my character, calling up sentimental associations with a time long past. Most of the Irish of Los Angeles – the great stars of film and stage, the Catholic clergy and lay leaders, the politicians, the union leaders, the police force – had long since disappeared through assimilation into the suburbs. Those who remained – the city still had an Irish Catholic cardinal and mayor in the nineties – focused on very different ethnic constituencies: Latinos in the case of the Church and Republicans of any background in the case of the mayor. Interestingly, while the Irish were assimilating, many others, inspired by the *Roots* phenomenon, were connecting more strongly to their ethnic heritage. One could attend meetings in the seemingly secure Jewish community which focused on the perceived threats of inter-marriage and declining support for Israel. The Latino community was fighting for its identity amid a new wave of nativism similar to that which had faced the Irish a century before. Despite the anti-Latino, anti-immigrant backlash, they were emerging as a majority in the city, and ultimately the state, which once belonged to Mexico. The national dis-course has tended to define the racial identity problem as black–white. But under the Latino umbrella were Salvadorans, Guatemalans, Nicaraguans, Cubans, Puerto Ricans, Mayans, even fifty thousand Belizeans in Los Angeles. There were Native American tribes in my dis-trict, like the Gabrielino, that had been classified as extinct a century before. The Asian population was subdivided among Japanese, Koreans, Chinese, Filipinos, and Pacific Islanders. Among the Jews were Sephardics, Ashkenazis, and Soviet refuseniks. The Armenians were entrenched in Glendale demanding an independent homeland. Blacks included Ethiopians, Jamaicans, Afro-Cubans. Multiculturalism was breaking out. Some fifty languages were spoken in the school district. Los Angeles, I wrote in 1982, was the Ellis Island of the late twentieth century.

The Irish remained potent in their historic strongholds of New York, Boston, Chicago, and San Francisco, but Los Angeles, I believed, repre-sented the American future into which the Irish Americans would disappear. In setting out to recover my own Irish identity I had chosen the challenge of finding its bleached remains in southern California.

The Irish had had an impact on the place, that much I knew. For one thing, the threat of their potential political power led the WASP power structure in the early twentieth century to eliminate partisan elections in the name of "good government." The story of how the Irish machines were blocked in Los Angeles is a case study of how history disappears.

The great Australian writer Thomas Keneally, in his history of the Fenians exiled to Australia, discovered a Los Angeles connection in the person of a distant relative, John Kenealy. The earlier Kenealy was a Fenian ex-convict who planned the successful and sensational rescue of Fenians from the Australia penal colony in 1875. Kenealy ran a three-story dry goods business at 86 Main Street in downtown Los Angeles at a time, Keneally writes, "when Los Angeles looked for all the world like a little town in Australia." Once charged with trying to burn down Cork city, Kenealy went into the fire insurance business in Los Angeles. His business partner's father, W. H. Workman, was the city's mayor, and he built such a powerful immigrant political machine that, in 1911, non-partisan elections were introduced. The effect was that individuals were elected on their reputations instead of, for example, a Democratic Party slate, thus lessening a build-up of the political machines that emerged in New York, Boston, and Chicago. Kenealy died in 1908, eulogized in a front-page *Los Angeles Times* article entitled "Revolutionist Irish Leader Has Passed On." By the century's end, the headline could have summarized the passage of several generations of Irish revolutionists whose descendants migrated into suburban amnesia.[71]

Besides stirring the Protestant establishment into self-protecting reforms, the other hidden legacy of the Famine Irish to Los Angeles was water. It was water that made the growth of Los Angeles possible, water carried through 200 miles of aqueducts and tunnels, draining whole lakes and underground reservoirs to irrigate sprawling subdivisions as far as the eye could see. The builder of the Los Angeles Aqueduct was William Mulholland, a Belfast man born in 1855 who was devoted to finding engineering solutions to the environmental shortages that had plagued Ireland. Mulholland was not simply an engineer, but had the promoter's gift of Irish blarney. With a "lilting brogue" and "flashing Irish wit," according to an enthusiastic history, Mulholland made statements such as, "If you don't get the water, you'll never need it. Because the dead don't get thirsty." Whether it was environmental rape or an engineering miracle, the aqueduct gave birth to Los Angeles through the same muscular determination with which the

Famine Irish built canals, rail lines, and roads across the country. Mulholland himself was a ditchdigger for a time. Unfortunately, he learned that nature cannot be overcome when, in 1928, a dam he built north of Los Angeles collapsed and killed 450 people under a wall of water ten stories high.[72]

In entering politics, therefore, I couldn't very well appeal to an Irish voting bloc comparable to Jews, Latinos, or African Americans, nor could I appeal in an environmental age to the Mulholland tradition of giant engineering projects. The Irish powerbrokers who remained in Los Angeles were part of the business and Church hierarchy. The Hollywood Irish, like Spencer Tracy, James Cagney, John Ford, John Huston and Gregory Peck had all but disappeared. The trade unions were still Irish on the leadership level, but rapidly reflecting their growing Latino base. Films like *Chinatown* had discredited the Mulholland legacy. The building trades were being replaced by an information and service economy. Irish American voters were becoming the haves, often in the face of new minorities battling for their perch in the American dream.

So I faced the classic ethnic dilemma: whether or not to blend in by suppressing my ethnic identity. Deciding that was impossible, I tried to make being Irish relevant in a non-Irish town. I had to broaden my narrow version of ethnicity into a story with more universal application in a city where everyone seemed to be turning inward to their roots while at the same time trying to accept others they barely understood. First, I chose to explain my own rebellious life history as part of an Irish heritage, not just as youthful anger or counterculture leanings. Then I would cite the Irish contribution to making America a better place for working people, enabling parents like my own to become middle-class. That connected the Irish (and the Jewish and Italian communities) sympathetically with the new immigrants from Mexico and Central America organizing for a living wage. I dwelt on overcoming anti-Semitism and racism, knowing that my Jewish constituents still remembered Father Coughlin's tirades, and that blacks, Latinos, and Asians had suffered a disadvantaged status in the labor unions under Irish leadership. In an effort to salvage the better legacies of the Irish from the bitter ones, I tried to contribute my experience to the ongoing debate about race and ethnic relations in Los Angeles.

My opportunity to assert an Irish profile once I was in office was not long in coming. Soon after my 1982 election to the state assembly, Queen Elizabeth II and Prince Philip made an official visit to the state capitol in March 1983. Several members of the legislature spoke on the floor in fawning anticipation. I was surprised, however, to hear one of the assembly's most right-wing members, Pat Nolan of Glendale, denounce the royals for having blood on their hands. Noting that state leaders were planning protocols that included bowing to the Queen, Nolan quoted Ronald Reagan's close adviser Lyn Nofsinger as saying we had fought a war two hundred years before so that we wouldn't have to bow to anyone.

I was impressed, and strolled across the floor to shake Nolan's hand. It was the first conversation between us since my election, which had been heatedly opposed by his party. Unlike myself, Pat came from a large Catholic republican family which never ceased to beat the tribal drum. Like many who came from those staunch Catholic republican families, Pat followed a path to the right, opposing welfare programs, supporting law-and-order, and raising support for Reagan's war in Nicaragua. This was my face-to-face introduction to right-wing American conservatives who shared my view of Northern Ireland but nothing more. What was this phenomenon about? In part it was a logical extension of the narrow Catholic nationalism in Northern Ireland which Jimmy Breslin had described in *World without End, Amen*. The strain of Catholicism that opposed secular liberalism found expression in conservatives like Pat Nolan and, on a national scale, Patrick Buchanan. It was the Catholicism of Father Coughlin, Bishop Sheen, Tom Dooley, and Cardinal Spellman. I couldn't abide it, but I ended up boycotting the Queen with Pat Nolan.

In order to secure the state capitol for the royals, the building was closed to the public, legislators were ordered to take their seats an hour early, and employees were ordered to freeze in place, not even utilize the rest rooms, while the Queen and Philip strolled through the corridors.

Lunch was billed to the governor's campaign contributors. Before arriving, the royal couple stopped at Sutter's Fort, where gold had been discovered in California during the depths of the Irish Famine. The royal party was greeted by whooping members of the Kit Carson Mountain Men in coonskin caps, a fitting tribute to a shared colonial history, before jetting to San Francisco for dinner aboard the royal yacht *Britannia* with the Reagan family. Five thousand Irish Americans protested in San Francisco.[73]

The editorial response of the media to our modest boycott was anger that we would "inject sectarian strife" into the capitol, involve ourselves in foreign policy, and cause embarrassment to the state by the failure to show proper courtesy. I was amazed at the vitriol. The only support statewide came from first-generation Irish.

I had finally added "Irish American" to my sixties persona, and begun the effort to reclaim the nationalist position from the right. In addition, through the "odd bedfellow" relationship with Pat Nolan, I also learned to create Irish bonds across partisan and ideological lines. If we couldn't sort out our differences civilly in America, how could we complain about bloody sectarian and political feuds in the North? A few years later, Pat was indicted in a fundraising scandal and spent twenty-two months in the federal penitentiary. There, among a population heavy with minorities and drug offenders, he converted to a faith-based ministry calling for prison reform, greater emphasis on rehabilitation, and efforts at restorative justice in place of punishment alone. He was no less Catholic, but now the right-wingers didn't fully trust him. Pat Nolan and I eventually would work together on community-based policing in Northern Ireland.

The MacBride Principles

In the mid-eighties I found a more effective legislative approach to addressing the root causes of the Northern conflict consistent with progressive politics in the States. Following the example of Irish Americans in other states, I campaigned for adoption of the MacBride Principles which promoted affirmative action in the hiring of Catholics by American companies operating in Northern Ireland. The concept mirrored a campaign by a black Philadelphia minister, the Reverend Leon Sullivan, who pressured American companies to hire blacks in South Africa. The leverage was billions of dollars in public pension funds invested by states and municipalities in those companies. The anti-apartheid campaign became very powerful, eventually resulting in California – under a Republican governor – divesting some $500 million in pension funds from companies associated with the apartheid regime. The collapse of racial apartheid followed not long after. Along more modest lines, MacBride supporters reasoned that American companies might reform the job discrimination patterns in Northern Ireland or be threatened with eventual disinvestment.

The MacBride Principles were named after Sean MacBride, son of Maude Gonne and John MacBride, originally a fifteen-year-old aide to Michael Collins during the independence war who became chief of staff of the IRA in the thirties, Irish Foreign Minister in the forties, and eventually winner of the Nobel Peace Prize, the Lenin Peace Prize, and the American Medal for Justice. Because of MacBride's international respect, his proposals were taken seriously. What I appreciated was the opportunity to address the root economic causes of the "Troubles" in ways that Americans could understand. If voluntary efforts at affirmative action were encouraged in America, why not in Northern Ireland? There were twenty-five American multinationals – among them General Motors, Ford, TRW, and United Technologies – operating in Northern Ireland where the Catholic unemployment rate was more than twice that for Protestants, and long-term joblessness was chronic.[74] Whether the companies themselves were practicing discrimination was not the central issue. By locating their facilities largely in unionist areas, where nationalists could not travel or work safely, the US firms were perpetuating the sectarian order. By making affirmative outreach efforts to Catholics and nationalists, American companies could be powerful magnets for change. I believed that our human rights ideals should be applied where our dollars were invested, and that strategies that worked effectively for American civil rights and South African freedom would surely succeed in Northern Ireland. Further, I was enthusiastic to make political arguments against subsidized discrimination rather than explaining IRA bombings.

I was truly naïve. With the support of the US government, British officials were waging an all-out campaign to kill the application of the MacBride Principles. The effort was coordinated on every level. A British intelligence agent from MI5 operating out of the embassy in Washington, DC, was in charge.[75] To stop the California legislation I was preparing, the British government hired private lobbyists for the first time.[76] "The pressure in California is extraordinary," commented Paul O'Dwyer from New York. "The Brits who so pride themselves on the persuasive abilities of their diplomatic corps and propaganda machinery have broken down and hired themselves a Sacramento lobbyist to work against the MacBride legislation."[77]

What surprised me most was the vocal opposition to the MacBride campaign by the SDLP leader, John Hume, who visited my home in Santa Monica to lobby against my introducing the legislation. Since I regarded John Hume as a brilliant, passionate, widely respected Irish nationalist, I listened very closely and sympathetically to him. Once again, I felt concerned that I was possibly meddling irresponsibly in the Northern conflict. A burly, disheveled, professorial gentleman, Hume made his points forcefully.

His basic argument was that American investment would be driven away by affirmative action guidelines, and that any foreign investment was better than none. In addition, he said that Northern Ireland's Fair Employment Agency could be strengthened.

His were the same arguments made against affirmative action in the United States, but worse, namely, that private investment in Northern Ireland would be discouraged if corporations were forced to follow guidelines that they already followed in America. The companies had been showered with massive tax breaks and other subsidies, and I wondered why they should receive an additional incentive to avoid American affirmative action guidelines by locating in Northern Ireland. As for the

Fair Employment Agency, it was a mostly timid, understaffed body expressly forbidden to support hiring preferences.

But there was another argument which Hume pursued more vigorously: that the whole MacBride campaign was a ploy by IRA supporters in America and Ireland. In the bitter differences among Irish nationalists, anything that brought legitimacy to Sinn Féin was to be rejected. If you supported the MacBride campaign you were a Provo fellow traveler. On this issue I strongly disagreed. I wasn't sure that "Provo sympathizers" were behind the MacBride campaign. (In 1992, Gerry Adams told me that Sinn Féin had underestimated its importance. The MacBride campaign implied that the partitionist state could be reformed rather than dismantled, a difficult proposition then for republicans. I saw it as a way to challenge the inequality on which the colonial state rested.) The MacBride campaign was supported by the Irish National Caucus, some of whose members had republican backgrounds, though the caucus was broad enough to include US congressmen. It was led by Father Sean McManus, originally from Derry, and, according to a letter I received in June, 1987, from Comptroller Harrison Goldin of New York City, it was supported by the National Council of Churches, the AFL–CIO, Governors Mario Cuomo and Michael Dukakis, and the British Labour Party. And anyway, why shouldn't "Provo sympathizers" be encouraged to work through peaceful pressure tactics towards ending discrimination in the North? If the MacBride campaign was delegitimized because of republican support, wasn't the implication that violence was the only available strategy? If Hume, a devoutly nonviolent man, wanted to end Provo violence, wasn't the best way to join forces in demanding fair employment practices benefiting the unemployed young men and women who were joining the IRA? Our conversation went on for an hour, but to no avail. Hume did not want to challenge the British government over fair employment for fear that American investment would dry up. And he was much more concerned about Sinn Féin drawing support from the SDLP among Northern Catholics than the substance of the issue itself. I was exposed at a new level to the crippling splits among Irish nationalists.

Nonetheless, in early 1987 I sent a letter signed by eighteen legislators to California companies operating in Northern Ireland demanding that they respect the MacBride Principles. I also introduced legislation (AB 1935) designed to throw the weight of California's $546 million pension fund investments in Northern Ireland behind the MacBride Principles. The bill was gradual in approach, declaring an intention not to "diminish the present investment portfolio" nor to "injure the fragile Northern Ireland economy." Pension fund managers were further "encouraged" to make future investments consistent with the MacBride fair employment principles. Should corporations fail to comply with the MacBride Principles, pension managers were "encouraged" to shift those investments to other American firms willing to comply. The hammer in the bill was a requirement for compliance by January 1, 1988.[78]

Never in my eighteen years in the California legislature did I face such all-out and underhanded opposition to a bill. The *Los Angeles Times* called it "mischievous" and repeated the British propaganda that it was "part of a campaign by supporters of the Irish Republican Army."[79] The local *Santa Monica Evening Outlook* slammed it as "Hayden's Folly," and "grandstanding." The same paper claimed that California's economic sanctions on South Africa had proven counterproductive and harmful to blacks.[80] The truth was not that I was meddling in foreign affairs. California's half billion dollars in pension funds was a form of meddling in Northern Ireland in support of the status quo. The meddling was by the British government in the affairs of the California legislature and voters. But the mainstream definition of the Irish conflict prevailed.

The California legislature has a deserved reputation for fairness in the way bills are presented. Both political parties and the public are provided in advance with independent analysis. Procedural subterfuge is frowned upon. But there is an exception when a Speaker or a dominant faction wants a bill killed. Speaker Willie Brown, despite rhetorically supporting my bill, nonetheless sent it to an Assembly Committee on International Trade and Government Relations instead of the committee on pension funds where the antiapartheid legislation was heard. The chair of the trade committee, Assemblywoman Lucy Killea, had quietly told another Democrat that she wanted the measure sent to her committee because she had already rounded up the votes to kill it.[81] That Easter she visited England on a trade mission paid for by the British government. Willie Brown was in the British Isles as well, on a trip paid for by Mars Bars, a subsidiary of a British firm.[82] Brown is notorious for working both sides of any issue. The Irish American columnist Warren Hinckle recalled the time when "thousands of Irish were protesting in front of the British consul's house on Pacific Avenue and Willie worked the crowd of protesters like a genius and then flashed across the street and went into the offending party to work the royalty." Hinckle wryly concluded, "I suppose that's his idea of neutrality."

I knew the bill was in terminal condition when several legislators who originally were coauthors, all of them Catholic liberal Democrats, requested that their names be removed, a development which had never happened to one of my bills before. The Democratic majority leader, Tom Hannigan, spoke to me with a cryptic smile of being invited to tea at the British consulate. Even Pat Nolan, the Republican who boycotted the Queen, who spoke of blood on British hands, sheepishly told me in the legislators' elevator that he "couldn't be with me on this one."

I pondered what to do, and eventually decided to hold an informational hearing of my own and then expose the proceedings of Killea's committee. What irked me was the amused nature of the opposition, including legislators, which betrayed the common attitude that Irish grievances were silly and eccentric while the British agenda was serious and civilized. So I went to work, inviting witnesses from the national MacBride campaign like Father Sean McManus of Derry and Washington DC, Joe Roche from the Hibernians, and Patrick Doherty, the policy guru for the New York City Comptroller's Office. But the most important witness was Oliver Kearney from County Tyrone. Kearney was general secretary of the Licensed Vintners' Federation of Northern Ireland, and an activist in campaigns against job discrimination. He had been fired in the seventies as personnel director of the Northern Ireland housing agency after hiring too many Catholics – too many, that is, from a unionist standpoint (150 in an organization that employed 5,000 people). Kearney was an authentic Northerner with dignified bearing, extensive experience, and an eloquent baritone delivery.

The Sacramento hearings, centering on Kearney's testimony, were televised in depth by the BBC. Kearney explained the mechanisms of discrimination, subtle and overt, in the Northern province. He testified that the MacBride campaign was impelling the British government to add staff and resources to its own Fair Employment Agency, which originally had only five staff to investigate discrimination complaints. One of the agency's board members, the trade unionist Inez MacCormack, had resigned in frustration and helped found the MacBride campaign. Kearney noted the flaws in the British system, especially that corporations could self-certify themselves as "equal opportunity employers."

After the informational hearings were over, the trade committee met and chairwoman Lucy Killea asked if there was a motion in favor of the bill. As previously scripted, the committee members sat in stony silence. No one was willing to move the bill to a vote, which would have meant being recorded aye or nay. This silence was rare; the only other time in eighteen years that I faced this stonewalling was on a bill opposed by the tobacco industry that would have banned "Joe Camel" ads aimed at addicting children to nicotine. The MacBride bill died without the opponents having the courage to vote it down. To force a vote, I later amended the measure to become simply a nonbinding statement of intent. It was defeated on a 2–2 vote with five members once again not voting.

Ten days after the hearing, and three days after the BBC television program, Oliver Kearney once again was fired from his job. His name and address were printed in loyalist paramilitary bulletins and his family received death threats.[83] I felt great guilt and anger. There was further fallout. The Irish republicans in San Francisco, thinking I was too radical and therefore ineffective, asked that their assemblyman John Burton carry a new version of the measure. After laboring for two years, I yielded to the request, hurt by the incessant quarreling and power struggles among the people on whose behalf I thought I was working. The MacBride campaign declined in California for thirteen years until Senator Burton achieved passage of the bill, in watered-down form, in September 2000.

I felt stranded again. What I learned from the whole sorry experience was that the British government, operating in stealth, had more power over the California legislature, even over Irish Catholic legislators, than did the so-called Irish American lobby. Even the much smaller African American community, which had lobbied the antiapartheid legislation, had more clout than the Irish. This wasn't about campaign contributions or voting strength, however. It was about assimilation, about deep, even unconscious cultural affinities with the British viewpoint – or discomfort at being identified as Irish – despite clear and cogent testimony about institutionalized discrimination in the North. It was about divisions among the Irish themselves.

But, as I shall explore in the pages ahead, the issue of basic economic inequality in Northern Ireland would not go away. It was integral to the Northern state itself, even during the peace process of the nineties, despite talk of a "peace dividend." The tragedy was that thousands of unemployed republicans and loyalists fought and died while politicians debated whether the MacBride Principles were too great a burden on US multinationals. Would the MacBride Principles have stopped the killing? Surely not, but at least they addressed the root causes of violence. Republicans fought for equal opportunity, while loyalists fought to preserve relative but fragile privilege. Only an evenhanded policy of assuring decent jobs on both sides of the divide would have ended the zero-sum game by which a Catholic gain was a Protestant loss.

It was not to be. Instead of the MacBride Principles, the British and Irish governments touted their 1985 Anglo-Irish Agreement backed by $120 million in grants from the US Congress. Instead of tackling the issues of colonial inequality directly, the consensus was to "boost morale among moderates" in a new governing arrangement with input from Dublin.[84] "The agreement was clearly aimed at the rise in republican support," wrote Tim Pat Coogan, not at the underlying colonial status that turned hopeless young Catholics into committed IRA members.[85] The real nature of British rule was evidenced in the Stalker affair in the mid-eighties, named after a British police detective, John Stalker, assigned to investigate claims that the RUC collaborated with loyalist paramilitaries in targeting Catholics and republicans. In January 1988, six months after the MacBride hearings in Sacramento, British authorities refused to bring criminal charges against RUC officers implicated in covering up the murder of six unarmed Catholics. In frustration, Stalker went public with a story of harassment and obstruction of his investigation by the RUC.[86]

It was obvious that the killing would continue. The opportunity offered by the MacBride legislation to begin shifting the conflict from a military to a political and economic one was over, lobbied to death. It was a very bad year. The death toll was 106, the equivalent of 25,000 Americans. The IRA, or republican splinter groups, were responsible for seventy-four of the killings. Of the overall total dead, forty-five were classified as civilians.[87] It was clear that the IRA could not be defeated. They were frustrating the British security forces, with all the high-technology weaponry and surveillance systems then available, in a territory about the size of Connecticut. But neither could the IRA win. The British government was not going to surrender and leave its first and last colony. Nor would American public support for Sinn Féin grow as long as the killings dominated media imagery of the conflict. But if the MacBride campaign was rejected, how could an alternative to the stalemate be imagined?

In January 1988, John Hume and Gerry Adams began secret meetings to explore whether there existed a less bloody road to a united Ireland.

Return to the North, 1992

The conflict in Northern Ireland is being managed reasonably well . . . the British, the Irish, the unionists and the nationalists in Northern Ireland all seem to have become accustomed to the present level of violence.[88]

British-funded White Paper on Northern Ireland, 1993

How wrong they were. Change was coming. Bill Clinton, the new American president, promised in his campaign that there would be unprecedented changes in US Irish policy and political opportunities for Irish Americans opposed to British rule. Over the fierce objections of the British government, the milder objections of the Irish government, the initial skepticism of Senator Ted Kennedy, and the unanimous counsel of his foreign policy team, Clinton pledged a visa for Sinn Féin leader Gerry Adams, a peace envoy to the North, and implementation of the MacBride Principles. No longer would Northern Ireland be considered an internal affair of the United Kingdom. At long last, Irish Americans could play a role, as American citizens, in shaping US policy towards the North. In addition, Clinton named Jean Kennedy Smith as US ambassador to the Republic, shattering a tradition of ambassadors "more under the influence of London than independent," as former Irish prime minister Albert Reynolds once described it.[89]

As previously noted, Clinton was responding to an *ad hoc* committee of Irish Americans trying to cobble together a ceasefire with a package of political incentives. They included Niall O'Dowd, editor of a weekly Irish paper in New York, William Flynn, an insurance executive, Chuck Feeney, an international businessman, Joe Jamison, a New York trade unionist, and Bruce Morrison, a former member of Congress. The *ad hoc* committee deserves historical credit for acting in a catalytic role, but it would be an exaggeration to assert that there was an Irish American lobby stronger than the British lobby in Washington. No one in the *ad hoc* group represented institutions like the Catholic Church, the AFL–CIO, or Irish American foundations. Bill Clinton ultimately made and implemented the historic decisions to alter Washington's role in Northern Ireland against tremendous pressures. Was it an affinity for the Northern civil rights movement when he had been an Oxford student? Was it a shrewd strategy to solidify white Catholic votes for a new Democratic Party? Was it payback for the Tories who tried to defeat him in 1992? Was it a realization that Adams and Sinn Féin had to be recognized instead of marginalized, if a settlement were to be achieved? All may have been factors, but an intimate adviser to Clinton told me "this man believes he can reach out to anyone in the world, bring anyone together in the world, and you know what, he's the best at it we've ever seen."[90] The President's pollster, Stanley Greenberg, was never asked to poll voters on the Northern Ireland issue during the 1992 campaign or during the subsequent two years he served in that capacity. Clinton, according to Greenberg, acted from an instinct that he might play a special role in a unique moment.[91]

Immediately after the election, newly-installed Clinton Administration officials and British lobbyists were exerting pressure to force the new President to backpedal from his pledges. I believed that by going to the North, I could bring back an assessment that might convince some in Washington DC that the President was on the right course.

Personally, I wanted my soon-to-be-wife, the Canadian actress Barbara Williams, and my grown children, to see the people and places that mattered so much to me. So the whole family, including Troy (then twenty) and my stepdaughter Vanessa (twenty-four), bundled off to Shannon, arriving in a freezing December dawn in 1992. We piled into a rented car and sleeplessly drove through a menacing fog towards the west. Shortly we reached the remote tower castle where W. B. Yeats had lived and written. The place was completely deserted. The structure, stroked by a mist rising off the icy ground, conveyed an archaic gravity, fitting for a land several centuries older than America. Traveling on, we stopped at a perfect example of the new, tourist-friendly Ireland, Ashford Castle, on the recommendation of a Kennedy family friend in Dublin. The castle and its grand estate contained well-stocked streams, hunting grounds, a golf course, and walking paths. We felt embarrassingly disheveled in the midst of well-dressed couples drinking tea and elegant sportsmen bearing their polished shotguns in the lobby. We slept a few hours, then decided to push on across the deserted west coast, from Connemara to Galway, finally stopping to rest in Sligo close to the border. The exhaustion, the weather, the dangerous one-lane roads, and the madness of my pace left members of my family wondering what sort of vacation odyssey they were taking. Barbara and I slept for the first time in three days while Troy and Vanessa successfully scouted the youth clubs of Sligo.

A Second Visit with Martin McGuinness

It was Christmas season on the snow-covered Derry street when I asked a local resident, as I had sixteen years earlier, if she might get a message to Martin McGuinness. She was an elderly woman in a heavy coat, her white hair wrapped in a thick scarf. She was watching a vehicle burning on a street next to her neighbor's house. The torched car was a victim not of war, but of joyriding. When I approached her, she looked at me carefully. I scribbled my name on a tiny piece of paper which she put in her pocket. "I might be able to do something," she said knowingly. Then off she trudged across the Bogside snow, having instructed us to meet her under the same streetlight in one hour. I felt somewhat ashamed at asking her this favor, but at the same time awed at the simplicity of this resistant community's nature. In his masterful history *The Troubles*, Tim Pat Coogan cites an Irish notion of *uisce fe talamh,* meaning "water under the ground,": "a consciousness of race and place, formed by history and circumstance, whereby one grows up knowing things without realizing where one learnt them."[92] The woman walking resolutely across the Bogside was one of thousands of senior citizens living in a small flat, no doubt a nonperson to the roving surveillance cameras above. But women like her were the "water under the ground" in which those wanted by the police could swim.

We took the opportunity to walk the wet, snow-covered streets of the Bogside. The FREE DERRY mural was still there, now accompanied by vivid, two-story murals about Bloody Sunday and the Battle of the Bogside. The crown forces still peered down from the ancient walls, now with more towers of technology than before. They patrolled the streets in vehicles the color of sharks, each with a metal skirt dropping to the pavement to guard against molotov cocktails. The vehicle windows were tiny and thick, shatterproof. A message was stenciled in red letters on each vehicle's side, inviting potential informants to call a special RUC number. Other vehicles were open-roofed, with army machine-gunners swiveling their weapons in the direction of pedestrians. Barbara, at my suggestion, took photos of an oncoming armored personnel carrier which stopped menacingly in front of her. Soldiers stepped out and demanded her film. We registered a protest to no avail. Now they knew who we were.

Promptly, an hour later, the woman was back, mission accomplished. But first she invited us into her tiny flat for tea. We warmed ourselves in her small, well-kept living room filled with porcelain religious figurines and the glow of a gas fireplace. There she showed us the address of Martin's mother, and said we would find him there shortly. Then she stood up and, for a second time, marched across the darkening streets with us in tow behind her. To an outsider's perspective, the Bogside, especially at night, appears to be a flat expanse of identical streets and row houses arranged like a jigsaw puzzle. Even with proper directions, a visitor (or British soldier) experiences disorientation. We were thankful for our "sentry," and soon we found ourselves sitting in a living room talking with Martin while his mother, sister, and children glanced at an old American movie on television.

When we left the house, after about an hour, there was a small group of individuals working on a car in the darkness, men we assumed to be security. But Martin drove us alone back to our car, and pointed the directions out of Derry to Belfast. Standing in the snow, we said goodbye under a British surveillance tower, the most sophisticated monitoring equipment in the world. He was wearing no coat, only a sweater, which was sparkling with snow. He seemed to want to convey a summary of his experience since the time we had met as younger men. I had asked him if it was strange to stand under the surveillance cameras and listening devices. I imagined an eavesdropping British intelligence specialist being disciplined for missing Martin McGuinness on the street below, or overdosing on thousands of garbled Bogside conversations. "They can never defeat us, you know," he said, smiling. "They can never defeat us." Martin McGuinness was waiting patiently for his adversaries to give up their collective superiority complex and realize that he, like many others born and educated in the Bogside, could hold their own against British gentlemen.

A Meeting with Gerry Adams, Belfast, 1992

Two hours east of Derry on the motorway looms Belfast, a far colder, more intimidating city, an old industrial port looking across the Irish Sea to England. Former linen mills and factories, and the towers of the Harland and Wolff shipyards, loom like dinosaurs' skeletons over the urban horizon, reminders of the booming war economy of an earlier generation. Unlike Derry, where the demarcation is discernible in the walls above and the ghetto below, Belfast's war-ridden neighborhoods bleed into each other. I was reminded of my community-organizing days in Newark, New Jersey, another port city in decline, where the white ethnic working class walled off their Ironbound district, with vigilantes as enforcers, as middle-class whites fled neighborhoods that would become black or Puerto Rican. In the center of Belfast, we took two rooms in the eleven-story Europa Hotel, a plain, functional structure that served as a media headquarters during the war, and carries somewhat proudly the reputation of being the most bombed hotel in Europe.

Since it was dark, freezing, and raining, the cabdrivers were baffled when, in response to their asking our business, we answered "tourism." Not many tourists in Belfast this time of year, they would comment. "That's why it's a good time," we cheerfully answered, never knowing whether it was wise to be honest. As we passed by pedestrians and storefronts, we tried to guess their political sympathies. My family discovered, as I had before them, how racial barriers could be imposed by whites on whites, thus making whiteness itself irrelevant.

At the suggestion of an American friend who'd lived in Belfast, we contacted a north Belfast family of two teachers and their young daughters. As with most Irish people, they were warm and accommodating when I rang them up out of nowhere. We found ourselves in a pleasant home in a mixed neighborhood, a seeming oasis of normalcy in a war zone. The parents were nationalists but not activists, concentrating their efforts on education reform and raising their daughters, who attended a Catholic school. As we talked through the evening, I noted that they spoke of the Falls Road, Sinn Féin, republicans and loyalists, as distant entities rather than familiar communities. The girls, bright and witty, led safe, separate lives lacking any contact with young people from the war zone. I was ready to ask whether my observation was correct when the red beam of an RUC vehicle flashed behind the living-room window curtain. Though the neighborhood remained quiet overall, something clearly was occurring down the street. We saw more RUC cars and an ambulance arrive outside someone's home. After about an hour, they were gone. Then one of the girls came into the living room to report that someone had just been killed down the street. There was something about her low-key tone of voice that was profoundly unsettling. It was hard to believe the truth of what she was saying. Why was she being nonchalant? Was she numb? Was it an understandable response from a child who had never known an alternative to war? Since so many Americans were indifferent to daily reports of atrocities, why was I singling out this young girl?

Down the street, someone apparently in the IRA had shot and killed Stephen Waller, a soldier in the Royal Irish Regiment, in front of his wife as they were watching a soap opera, *Neighbours*, on television.[93] Stephen Waller's father, Archie Waller, was a member of a loyalist gang in the mid-1970s who was murdered in an internal feud. Perhaps the IRA knew something about Stephen Waller that made him a particular military target. Otherwise he was just a uniform. His killing was typical for a year in which ninety-one people died in the conflict, most of them relatively open targets.

A few days before our arrival, on December 13, a Catholic who was widely regarded as a child abuser was killed by the IRA in Derry. A local republican activist, Eamonn McCann, wrote critically of the "savage satisfaction of so many at his maiming and death [which] reflects the cumulatively brutalizing effect which almost a quarter of a century of violence has had on all of us here."[94]

This violence was the result of London's policy of "Ulsterizing" the conflict, as Richard Nixon had "Vietnamized" the Vietnam war to reduce American casualties and antiwar sentiment in the USA. Ulsterization meant deploying the RUC and loyalist paramilitaries against nationalists, and dividing nationalists and republicans with secret counterintelligence campaigns. If the blood that was flowing was Irish, not English, the British army could be positioned as neutral peacekeepers and maintain public acquiescence on the home front. While the IRA managed periodically to stun the British with attacks on the mainland, most of the killing in Belfast was among people residing in adjacent enclaves, widening a cycle of vengeance and vendetta between communities that eventually would have to coexist. The media would report the conflict as tribal and atavistic, exactly the portrayal the British desired. "They can't defeat us, you know," Martin McGuinness had said of the British army. But the British might fund, foster, and perpetuate an unwinnable bloodletting among republicans and loyalists, with civilian casualties inevitable in the dense urban areas, for a very long time. Unless, of course, there was political change, which made the recent American election very important.

A republican security man picked us up at the Europa one morning, and whisked us up the Falls Road to a house where we transferred to a black taxi. We drove a short distance, then turned into a driveway leading to a two-story home at a distance from the road. We entered the living room and met Gerry Adams sitting in a comfortable chair next to a warm gas fireplace.

Gerry Adams is one of those people made larger than life by his historic role. His burden is that his reputation precedes him, a Rorschach test through which others register their feelings about the conflict. He was demonized by the British and unionists for thirty years, suffering internment, interrogation, kicking, beating, and a failed assassination attempt in 1984 (nine months after he was first elected a member of parliament) which riddled his body with five bullets. Fifteen years later, the man who shot Adams still regretted not killing him, saying, "I could see him yelping . . . I emptied the gun at him . . . I think we were set up. [The Brits] weren't worried about Adams – it would have suited them for him to be shot, but they wanted to kill two birds with one stone and lift us afterwards. . . . He was hit in the heart, but he was wearing a flak jacket and that saved him."[95]

The atmosphere around Gerry Adams was not only hazardous but, of necessity, shrouded and secretive, because any association with the IRA and, at times, Sinn Féin, was defined as illegal. Thus, for example, the common allegations that he once was leader of the IRA's Belfast Brigade are based on informants or unnamed sources rather than provable fact, and are denied by Adams without elaboration. Though Adams clearly seemed to be "Brownie" in Long Kesh, he does not take credit for certain of those prison writings which defend or describe violence. Nor can he speak of matters affecting the lives or safety of others. The result is that writers like Fintan O'Toole accuse Adams of being dishonest, and un-authorized biographers like David Sharrock and Mark Devenport declare that his IRA role is a "truth which he himself is bound to deny."[96]

It is a strange journalism that demands that someone like Adams either incriminate himself (and his associates) or have his honesty challenged. By comparison, British officials are rarely if ever accused in the media of being godfathers of murderous gangs or barred from diplo-matic meetings because of their association with the SAS or MI5. In fact, armed British secret agents are lionized in James Bond movies.[97]

Gerry Adams and I are very much of the same generation. He has written that he was gripped by a "youthful, mistaken conviction that the revolution was happening all around us."[98] He was inspired by the American civil rights movement, listened to Bob Dylan, marched against the Vietnam war; "the songs that moved me were . . . the confirmation of a strongly felt reality, a feeling shared across countries, continents and religions."[99] From a strongly republican family, Gerry Adams had been a student and athlete at St Mary's College, then an employee at a pub in Belfast, until the Northern crisis aroused his Irish nationalist instincts. Like many of his generation, his initial foray into politics was community organizing against housing discrimination. He became a member of Sinn Féin, and was first arrested while distributing its newspaper.

When the civil rights movement was met with loyalist pogroms on the Falls Road – mobs literally attacking and burning the houses of Catholics – and the British army became the occupier, Gerry Adams got involved in the "battle of Ballymurphy," a fierce daily resistance from a small west Belfast community of 1,800 families. At this point the youth of Ballymurphy, led by Adams and others, organized barricades and self-defense groups that would evolve into a new generation of republicans. "Bitterness at the violence with which our demands for justice had been met crystallized for many . . . and a steely determination entered many hearts, a feeling that if it was war they wanted, then it was war they would get," he later wrote.[100] At the time, the Provisional IRA was critical of the street fighting because it was dangerously spontaneous and they were not ready to be drawn into armed conflict. They lacked sufficient numbers of trained volunteers and their sparse weapons were limited to old Enfield rifles.[101] But the movement in the streets could not be stopped. Like hundreds of others, Adams, who chaired meetings of the Ballymurphy coordinating committee, lived in a permanent state of emergency far removed from the niceties of life in the South or the States. By his own account, he proposed to marry his future wife, Colette, if they lived through a night curled on a floor under British assault.

His autobiography, *Before the Dawn*, briefly recounts that after a night of British repression, the young Adams collected as many Guinness bottles as he could find at work, for reasons not elaborated.[102] The autobiography is elliptical, painting a graphic eyewitness account of the community resistance to the British without directly revealing Adams's own deeds. He was accused but never convicted of membership in the IRA, interned in 1971 and held aboard a British prison ship, the *Maidstone*, in Belfast harbor, and then in Long Kesh internment camp. In 1972, an early attempt at dialogue took place, in which Adams, along with McGuinness, by then both in their early twenties, were chosen to be on a republican negotiating team flown by British helicopter to secret talks in England. It was obvious from that point forward that Adams was trusted by republicans, including those engaged in armed struggle, to serve as a political and diplomatic representative. But to assume that Sinn Féin was or is simply a shell for the IRA, as unionists continue to do, leaves no explanation for the evolution of the party's sophisticated negotiating teams or large network of candidates and campaign workers.

Now, in late 1992, Gerry Adams was offering us tea on the Falls Road. Across the world Bill Clinton was preparing his inauguration.

Outside the window the deadly Ulsterization policy was grinding on. But the Gerry Adams we met that day was calm, reflective, and, as my wife Barbara observed, a formally courteous man of warmth and humor. He was in a way a kindred spirit, one knowledgeable and supportive of the American New Left, a survivor who had grown up in a movement, and now a man entering his forties with a son born in the same year as my Troy. Since we had never met before, much of the conversation was about the struggles of the past. But there was another purpose I believe he had, to discuss Sinn Féin as a political movement seeking allies in America. Adams wanted Sinn Féin to take off as a political party, a task made extremely difficult by repressive legislation, RUC harassment, and the burden of the IRA's military campaign which Sinn Féin felt obliged to defend. His own political fortunes were low, as the previous year he had lost his parliamentary seat to an SDLP candidate on the strength of unionist votes. Such a setback, however, seemed not to diminish his spirit so much as it intensified his exploration of future strategy.

From the republican perspective, the armed campaign was necessary for two reasons: to defend enclaves like the Falls against the RUC and loyalist paramilitaries, and to pressure the British to withdraw. It was rooted in a tradition whose premise was that physical force was the only language the British understood. So, horrors and all, Gerry Adams's generation upheld that tradition and, in the process, destabilized the Orange state and frustrated the British. But it was clear on the day of our meeting that Adams was seeking to promote a political struggle, the beginning of a peace process. This was not a new idea – Adams had advocated a broader political strategy since the seventies – but there was a new context. Like Martin McGuinness, he was confident that the crown forces could not defeat the IRA or the republican movement. But experience had taught him that neither could the IRA bomb the British out of Ireland. Nor were the unionists, still 55 percent of the population, showing any signs of surrendering their Britishness, dismantling their Protestant state, and recognizing their Irishness on the inside. Therefore, while a certain level of IRA military action was necessary to keep attention to the issue of British occupation, a meaningful political alternative to that violence was becoming urgent. Sinn Féin could not express its political message over the sound of bombs. Behind the scenes, Adams was already discussing a "pan-nationalist" alliance with Sinn Féin's long-time nemesis John Hume, who himself had concluded that only a viable political option, not further British pacification programs, might convince the IRA to end its campaign. In this setting, Gerry Adams was keenly interested in the Clinton Administration's proposed peace plan, and in the potential shape of Irish American politics. He told me that Sinn Féin had not understood the significance of the MacBride Principles campaign as a way to engage Irish Americans in building coalitions that might affect Northern Ireland.

As our conversation continued, we worried about his hectic schedule, but he seemed to enjoy the company and offered us a tour of the Falls. So we climbed into a Sinn Féin-operated black taxi and drove into Ballymurphy, the small estate of his roots. There we saw republican wall murals, including one of James Connolly, an IRA volunteer, Emiliano Zapata, and a black militant wearing an Afro and prison-style street clothes. "You can kill the revolutionary but not the revolution," it proclaimed. Beneath it, mothers pushed babystrollers and young people played dodgeball in a courtyard. Troy, then a street artist in the hip-hop culture, was delighted when Gerry asked him to come paint a mural in Belfast.

We took a long walk through Milltown cemetery, which holds the graves of Belfast's republican dead. The cemetery is a vast place at the top of the Falls Road, with looming Celtic crosses standing like mournful gray ghosts as you enter. Looking down on the cemetery and the Falls is a massive fortress-style RUC barracks with reinforced watchtowers.

Adams wanted to show us the memorial plot where the hunger strikers were buried in 1981. This was a sacred place for him, and for a few minutes he silently paid his own respects. The hunger strikers' graves were just a small plot in the immensity of the place. The wind was freezing, howling. There were only a few family members visiting the gravesites of their loved ones, and none seemed to notice Gerry Adams and his delegation of American visitors, or if they did, they kept the knowledge to themselves as they were used to doing.

We stopped by the Sinn Féin bookstore on Falls Road afterwards, where Adams's latest book of short stories was on sale amid piles of political newspapers, posters of 1916, works by James Connolly and republican historians, tin whistles, T-shirts, coffee mugs, keychains, ashtrays, and Celtic crosses carved out of peat. It was the most heavily fortified bookstore I'd ever been in, located next to the Sinn Féin office. Outside, huge defensive boulders blocked the sidewalk. The building had been subjected to occasional firebombs and even rocket attacks.

Watching him browse, I sensed with full force the dilemma of being an intellectual, a writer, in a state of siege. How to be human in a situation totally dehumanized? How to explore the truth when it was seditious? Perhaps the answer for Gerry Adams, from the time of the "Brownie" articles penned in Long Kesh, was to tell the truth in stories, in fiction, through composite characters, to lead a many-layered life, above all through one's imagination.

Then his driver approached and whispered, or so I thought, that it was time for him to leave the bookstore. It was dangerous to stay too long. The slow-moving pace of the day was over; it was time to say goodbye. In moments he was whisked away while we waited for a black taxi to take us back downtown to Loyal Belfast.

"Unreliable" and a "likeable psychopath" were among the descriptions of Gerry Adams by US diplomats in Belfast to at least one American official sent to bolster the peace process.[103] Michael Mahdesian, an Agency for International Development (AID) official, went to Belfast in 1997 to explore ways to assist ex-prisoners to find employment. "In the early briefings I had from the State Department, a guy from the British embassy was present, James Bevan, the first secretary. There was a total Anglo bias. The Americans in Belfast didn't know what to make of Adams. The 'likeable psychopath' notion meant that you couldn't believe anything he said but he was engaging. But I thought the key point was that Adams was coming from strength, was in the ascendancy. He had the juice. That's why the US went to him."

Neither could the leading American media fathom Adams. "Articulate and enigmatic" and "IRA Chief" were among the descriptions used by the *New York Times* used to describe him during the peace process.[104]

Even when the Irish novelist Edna O'Brien wrote an empathetic piece on Adams for the *New York Times* magazine, it was titled "Ulster's Man of the Dark."[105] "Godfather of violence" was the typical characterization by unionist politicians and Tories. British officials would not shake his hand until 1995, and when they did, we shall see, it was headline news.

None of these descriptions acknowledged the secrecy and security forced upon Gerry Adams's life by a foreign occupation. What was evident, I thought, was a clear-headed, strong-willed man capable of reasoned argument and negotiation. Not "enigmatic" at all, given security issues. Not a godfather but a revolutionary nationalist. The British, with American support, had been trying to demonize and defeat the IRA while supplanting it with the SDLP, an impossible strategy. Here, in Adams, was a realistic alternative, an individual with deep roots and credibility in the world of the armed struggle who proposed a transition to politics, someone who could navigate the whirlpools of the English-speaking world without undermining his anti-British cause. Were London and Washington ready for the political challenge, or did they simply want to defeat the IRA and offer the likes of Adams a face-saving olive branch?

Clearly some would never be convinced to negotiate with the republicans. But others, I was certain, could see the Irish war in the context of the sixties, and understand the merits of making peace with revolutionaries. One of them happened to be in the White House.

On New Year's Day 1993 our family challenged the partition of Ireland that separated my ancestral counties by helping build a bridge over the border at County Fermanagh. It was a day of protest against Ireland's continuing border as others were falling all over Europe. We drove from Belfast through Crossmaglen where we encountered camouflaged British soldiers crouched along hedges against unseen enemies. At the border itself, our vehicle passed through a barricaded checkpoint and we disembarked alongside a narrow stream dividing north from south. On stone ledges someone had scrawled the U2 lyric:

NO Border
NO Cry

Despite it being another freezing day, there were about fifty people digging, shoveling, carrying, and laying stones to create a bridge strong enough for a vehicle to cross into the South. The British had blown up a nearby bridge in an alleged blow against the IRA, which had the practical effect of making it harder for farmers to move their products to market. It was clear to those wading in the icy streambed that the British would destroy our makeshift bridge as well. Bernadette Devlin, now McAliskey, was down in the mud, along with the Belfast priest Father Des Wilson and an assortment of activists from around the North. One of them, whom we would come to know well, was Laurence McKeown, a 1981 hunger striker who was placed back on intravenous feeding at his family's request after entering a coma. Even so, his seventy-day fast was the longest any human being had ever survived. After his release from prison, he became active on behalf of republican prisoners and now he was standing ankle-deep in the mud, passing rocks along to his fellow bridge builders.

There I also met Caoimghín Ó Caoláin, an outgoing, energized local elected official who would later become Sinn Féin's first representative in the Irish Dáil (parliament) in seventy-five years. "Welcome home!" he proclaimed with a smile and a backslap. He gave a quick history of Monaghan's rural economy, showed us the site where a young man was killed by a British sniper from north of the border, and asked about Clinton's new policies, including the potential for investment and tourism. I was beginning to feel roots here at last.

We pitched in with the crowd hard at work on the bridge. At first it seemed mad to freeze ourselves on a project that would soon be wrecked by a British unit, but after a few hours we had suspended our skepticism. The collective spirit, bolstered by the arrival of hot tea, and the sheer determination to open the border, were contagious. We were learning something about the Irish spirit through practice. I understood what indomitable meant.

As darkness neared, everyone stood back for the test: whether a four-wheeled vehicle could actually be driven across our handiwork without spinning its wheels and sinking into the water. The driver gunned his engine and made it across the new bridge on his first try. A shout of happy relief went up from the crowd. The border was open. No more stones would be lifted that day. We could all walk up a hill to enjoy protest songs by a visiting band of Scottish nationalists.

As was often the case during the Clinton years, it was a struggle to carry out a campaign promise. Opposition to Clinton's promises of a peace envoy and a visa for Gerry Adams was growing. No one seemed to want a peace envoy except the President himself, not the British, not the State Department, not Dublin, not Kennedy, not Hume (although the SDLP leader would accept an economic emissary). At stake was a profound policy shift in the "strategic relationship" with London. For the first time since partition, the US government was questioning whether Northern Ireland was the exclusive province of the United Kingdom. In the thrall of assimilation and political realism, Irish American mainstream leadership accepted *de facto* British sovereignty over Irish nationalists in the North. They silently acknowledged the British forces as an inevitable response to the IRA, and sought mainly to reform and humanize partition. The ad hoc Irish American lobby promoting the peace process was a breakaway from the mainstream, and President Clinton seemed willing to go even farther. He was groping towards a new post-Cold War American foreign policy that justified intervention to broker and guarantee peace agreements. Even more alarming to the foreign policy establishment, he was meddling with the Western alliance on behalf of "mere" domestic American interests, namely to cultivate support from Irish American voters.

Isolated in the Oval Office, the President shelved the idea of the peace envoy for two years until December 1994 when he finally appointed Senator George Mitchell, but at first only as an economic representative, not a diplomatic one. In the British view, shared by the US State Department, "it would be intolerable to have an American coming over and treating a sovereign government on the same footing as the political representatives of terrorism."[106]

That left the promise of Adams's visa, which was nearly broken as well. The British lobbied furiously against Clinton giving a "terrorist"

like Adams an American audience and potential fundraising connnec-
tions. Fortunately, John Hume strongly favored the visa as a political
incentive to draw Sinn Féin away from violence. Hume influenced
Kennedy, who in turn weighed in with Clinton. Inside the Administration,
however, none of the national security operatives were willing to lead a
charge for Adams. The Irish Americans within the Administration were
reticent to identify themselves too strongly with an Irish matter. At one
senior staff meeting, they asked Rahm Emanuel, a Jewish adviser to
Clinton, to be the champion of the Adams visa while they remained
silent.[107] "If the guy had been Jewish, there would be no question. We
would be giving him the visa," Emanuel recalls telling the President's
circle. The argument went on for a full year, until finally, on January 29,
1994, the President granted the visa for Gerry Adams to visit New York
for three days. It was to be the first of several trips during the peace
process.

The American media and Irish Americans became entranced by
Adams, almost despite themselves. US Congressman Peter King said,
"They seemed to think he would come through the door with a gun on
each hip. Here was a guy who had been confined to west Belfast and
they treated him like Elvis. We had only the British to thank for
that."[108] At each stop, the press conferences and interviews were more
than the schedule could manage. The press categorized him as a beguil-
ing celebrity rather than a mouthpiece for thugs. He broke their
stereotype of Irish republicans. He was handsome, articulate, a charismatic figure, a rare individual who intriguingly believed his cause was
worth fighting and dying for. "Nothing like a whiff of gelignite for the
charisma, it's better than cologne," quipped a republican activist who
watched, mystified, the sudden frenzy around Adams at a Washington
reception.[109]

The Adams visit also stirred a residual American sympathy for the
Irish cause which had been dampened for a very long time. Neither
censorship nor assimilation had deadened the American Irish on the
inside. In fact, perhaps because of the long denial, the Adams appearances awakened an Irish hunger, a stirring of feelings of affinity they

didn't know they harbored. In most cases, the audience of Irish Americans was hearing the first speech of their lives by a representative of Sinn Féin. Not knowing what to expect on his arrival, Adams soon began to respond to this ache in the audience. He began each talk with a few sentences of greeting in the Irish language. It affected me powerfully each time I heard this introduction, reminding me of a distinct heritage that was lost but could be reclaimed. It triggered a pride that I didn't know I could feel, a pride in knowing that the thing called Irishness was more than St Patrick's Day drinking and jokes about leprechauns.

Adams engaged in friendly banter with Irish emigrants in his audiences who had emerged to enjoy the creation of an Irish space. He joked at the number of elevators he'd seen in America, and that prying food out of a hotel minibar was harder than getting holy water in an Orange lodge. Becoming serious, he quoted Bobby Sands saying that "we shall have our revenge in the laughter of our children," and he evoked a deep response by quietly stressing the unique opportunity of this generation of Irish Americans to help bring peace to the country from which their ancestors had been driven.

He went out of his way to meet with African American leaders; in Santa Monica he sat in a corner for an hour listening to a gang peace activist. I noticed that the affinity went in both directions, that the young African Americans were excited to meet someone "from the IRA," for that seemed to mean they were not "white." The same transracial identification was evident on later Adams trips. Once, for example, on a flight to Canada, while the Sinn Féin team was asleep, I noticed three native women drumming, singing, and talking in seats across from us. The trio called themselves Ulali, and were backup singers for Robbie Robertson. One had been at the Alcatraz Island takeover in 1968, the other two were in their twenties. When they learned who was dozing across from them, their faces lit up. Not long after, they were clustered with Gerry Adams – once again, they identified him as "the IRA," in respect rather than dread – discussing drumming in the Irish and native traditions. I could not describe precisely what I was seeing, but there seemed to be no barriers between them, no racial divide, no amends to make, because in their native eyes Gerry Adams and Sinn Féin were different than the white man, were native people like themselves. As the plane slowly descended into Vancouver, the Ulali trio prayed for the Irish, drumming and chanting all the way down.

Adams and Sinn Féin were closely associated with the African National Congress (ANC) which had fought an armed struggle followed by a negotiated peace in South Africa. So intimate was the involvement that Nelson Mandela successfully encouraged separate planeloads of Sinn Féin and unionist politicians to visit South Africa for an attempted mediation. Former ANC guerrilla leaders met extensively with republicans in Belfast about common issues of negotiating a political agreement with an adversary. A black ANC leader with an Irish heritage, Robert McBride, spoke on platforms with Gerry Adams and Bernadette McAliskey, saying, "History began for me when I became conscious that I was oppressed. History had told us their story, how white people came to Africa and discovered us, civilized us, and formed a covenant with God that gave them the right to rule over us."[110] It was a story with which the all-white Irish audience could easily identify because underlying the surface of racial difference was a common experience of colonial degradation.

I once had occasion to arrange a reception for Gerry Adams by the Latino community in Los Angeles while Sinn Féin and Derry activists were on their way to open an exhibition about Bloody Sunday in Mexico City. There was the same friendly excitement among the many Latino activists present, articulated by state senate majority leader Richard Polanco, who knowledgeably compared the common histories of the Mexican and Irish peoples. In Mexico City itself, the Adams visit was front-page news, comparable to a head of state's arrival. Large, interested crowds attended the Bloody Sunday exhibit which ranged from huge murals to personal items left on the Derry streets when fourteen were shot and killed. Bishop Samuel Ruiz of Chiapas, the defender of the indigenous Mayans and chief mediator between the Zapatistas and the Mexican authorities, came to a private dinner with Adams. At one point I asked a woman art director how so many Mexicans could be moved by the loss of fourteen Irish people twenty-five years ago, when they themselves had lost hundreds in the government repression of the 1968 student movement in Mexico City. She started to cry as she responded, saying, "Fourteen dead we can comprehend, we can see their precious shirts, notebooks, shoes, photographs from that day. The cover-up of Bloody Sunday is being exposed, thankfully. But we've never had an accounting of our dead. They just disappeared. They were shoveled into mass graves. The families know nothing of what happened. So when the Bloody Sunday victims are honored here in Mexico it sends us a message of hope that all the cover-ups will someday be revealed. But in the meantime, we can see and feel our own fallen people in the photos of the Irish dead, you see."

Adams tailored his statements in Mexico to avoid any charge of intrusion into Mexican affairs, but he did call for the cancelation of Third World debt and met privately with groups interested in the lessons of the Irish peace process for Chiapas. He also received an honorary degree from a conservative Catholic academic institution. What I began to realize watching these interactions was that there was a very important possibility for the Irish to assimilate not only into the Western world but into the ex-colonial, indigenous, nonwhite world as well. It was not a question of entering the first by leaving the second behind. It was possible to bridge both; in fact, the African Americans, Latinos, and indigenous peoples were inviting the connection. If the Irish in America had indeed "become white," here was a second chance to be aligned with the nonwhite majority. It was based not only on a common colonial experience, or a common Catholic experience, as I had thought, but in the case of Latinos also on a common Iberian heritage. As Thomas Cahill has noted, the Celtic tribes that gained ascendancy in Ireland around 350 BC were from the Iberian world. In the Irish foundation myth, the sons of Mil came to Ireland from Spain.[111] That would make me, and all the black-haired Irish, distant blood relations of the Spanish and their descendants in Mexico and Latin America. The San Patricios were defending their distant kin when they fought with Mexico against the United States!

Adams the Diplomat

Gerry Adams never slipped from his exhausting, repetitive fifteen-hour daily agenda of portraying Sinn Féin in a rational context, demanding only "parity of esteem" (an Anglo-Irish term for "equality") in open dialogue about Ireland's future. He avoided outright criticism of the IRA campaign, saying that civilian casualties were regrettable and that his hope was to end the violence altogether. Nor was he especially harsh on the British government, simply calling on them to lift their ban on talks with Sinn Féin. On his first American trip, the media, particularly the British media, tried making fun of a Hollywood party that included Sean Penn, Gabriel Byrne, Carroll O'Connor, Anjelica Huston, and Oliver Stone, at the home of Fionnuala Flanagan and Garrett O'Connor. As Hollywood parties go, however, it was a low-key affair of quiet dialogue with an exhausted Adams. Late that night, he changed into a T-shirt for the first time in days and drank half a cerveza. The media spin in London – that Gerry had "gone Hollywood" – was not only fanciful, but backfired by creating the public impression in Ireland and England that the Sinn Féin leader was being applauded by international celebrities. Indeed, to the extent that the goal was to achieve respectability, or at least de-demonize Gerry Adams, the missions became a startling success.

What was remarkable was that the American tours were carried out by a tiny handful of longtime Sinn Féin activists, virtually all of them ex-prisoners. Adams used one or two note cards for his forty-five-minute-long speeches. His assistant Richard McAuley mastered the art of herding reporters into conference rooms and accommodating their adamant requests for individual interviews. Adams kept smiling and never lost his temper. Someone – I never learned who – kept him in clean uniform: a starched white shirt, conservative tie, dark blue or black suit, green prisoners' pin in his lapel. No one could keep up with them. I realized that the secret lay in their long experience of being sleeplessly on the run. Room service and three hours' sleep in a hotel room each night was a luxury compared with the alleys of Belfast or the cages of Long Kesh. In addition, there was something impressively dedicated about the group. There was no drinking, no smoking, no sense that anyone was wide-eyed at the skyscrapers of New York. The mindfulness to detail was uncanny. When the press questioned Adams staying in the Waldorf-Astoria, for example, McAuley quickly pointed out that Eamon de Valera had stayed there seventy-five years before.[112]

Clinton, unlike virtually his entire staff, was convinced early on that he could work with Gerry Adams. To him, Adams was cut from the same (tricolour) cloth as Bernadette Devlin, who was much admired during Clinton's days at Oxford. But Clinton was a master of realpolitik, not a romantic Provo sympathizer. He knew the embarrassment that could be caused if the IRA bombing campaign continued while he was reaching out to Adams. The Administration wanted something extraordinary in return for the visa, a permanent ceasefire by the IRA. While the quid pro quo was not spelled out, it was clear that Adams was expected to deliver the IRA. That way Clinton could protect his credibility and be helpful to the offended British. Wounded profoundly by losing the visa fight, the British now were insisting that Clinton require not only a ceasefire by the "terrorists" but what came to be known as decommissioning, that is, some form of disarmament by the IRA. This, however, represented an intolerable weight on Adams who at the time was trying to convince IRA hardliners that he was not jeopardizing the cause for a speaking tour of the United States. Since the IRA was undefeated after thirty years of battle, it was unrealistic to expect a surrender of weapons through diplomacy. Moreover, the causes of violence would not be addressed through a one-sided call for IRA disarmament. The British army showed no signs of departing; the RUC was still strong-arming nationalists; and hundreds of thousands of weapons were in the hands of loyalist paramilitaries and other unionists. The underlying conditions of unemployment and inequality persisted as well.

Clinton, to his credit, avoided any direct linkage between granting the visa and an IRA ceasefire or gestures towards decommissioning. But his national security advisers clearly wanted to placate the unionists and the

British. In a White House meeting, one of them told me that Sinn Féin would receive less than they wanted, but just enough to prevent them from walking out of peace talks. For the national security circle, the question of Northern Ireland would have been a footnote to European security issues were it not for Clinton's personal involvement.

In Ireland, flashes of war continued, with loyalists launching a rocket attack on the Belfast Sinn Féin headquarters on March 29, a few weeks after Adams's return from his first trip.[113] During the same period, the IRA shot down a British helicopter in South Armagh, stronghold of the republican military campaign.[114] But behind the scenes, the entire republican struggle was shifting ground. The political strategy seemed to be bearing fruit with the new atmosphere in Washington. The Adams visa meant that an articulate Sinn Féin leader could be heard in the American media. Irish American activists could reach out to the largest audience in decades. The political initiative changed Sinn Féin's image and threw the British public relations machinery on the defensive. How could anyone oppose "all party talks" or "inclusive discussions" as Sinn Féin asked? Seeing that the political strategy was working, the IRA on August 31, 1994, announced an open-ended ceasefire to give peace a chance. A vindicated President Clinton granted Adams his second visa one month later, on September 23, and lifted the American government's longtime prohibition on official contacts. In December 1994, when the emboldened President appointed George Mitchell as economic envoy, no one was complaining.

Flying with Adams during this second trip, I decided to ask him the question that worried me most. It was all going too well. The agenda of Washington, London, and Dublin could not simply be to support the growth of Sinn Féin's popularity. They wanted something more: the end of the IRA as a military force without the withdrawal of the British army. I didn't know it at the time, but the Irish prime minister was saying privately that "Sinn Féin will pay a price for going to Capitol Hill. A lot of powerful people went out on a limb for Adams. If he doesn't deliver they'll have him back in the house with steel shutters [Sinn Féin headquarters . . .] so fast his feet won't touch the ground. We're slowly putting the squeeze on them, pulling them in, boxing them in, cutting off their lines of retreat."[115] What if after all the political gains – the favorable public reception of Sinn Féin, the visas and visits, the fundraising, the freedom to organize and lobby in America – the British were not prepared to dismantle the unionist state, the RUC, or the British military occupation? What if this was all a trick to seduce Sinn Féin into a peace process and nothing more? What if the scenario was to allow Sinn Féin to be tolerated, even promoted, as a political minority in a British colony with a unionist majority?

He laughed and said, "Then we'll be into one big crisis." It was clear that he and Sinn Féin had already considered the matter in depth. They were not amateurs in diplomacy, nor naïve when it came to broken promises. The peace process was an experiment, a dynamic, not a guarantee. They knew what had happened before when Irish republicans became divided over accepting a compromise. Neither Gerry Adams nor Martin McGuinness was going to become the next Michael Collins.

The Colonized Economy

I went back to Northern Ireland in early 1995. The Clinton White House had announced a Washington conference to promote investment in Northern Ireland. The President had given a verbal commitment to the MacBride Principles, and I wanted to explore whether and how American investments could work for the disenfranchised. I was thankful that the Administration wanted to focus on the Northern economy, but wary of obstacles to economic opportunity for republicans. There was a well-intended but mistaken notion in the Administration that the Irish North was like the American South in the days of segregation, that civil rights and economic opportunity were the enlightened answer. But of course Northern nationalists were seeking equality as Irish citizens, not as subjects of a colonial power. Northern Ireland was thick with administrative bureaucracies whose power were rooted in London, and whose least desire was to treat Catholics and nationalists as the equal of supporters of the Union. They would resist creating an independent economic base in the ghettos where opposition to British rule was most organized and militant.

I was equally concerned that the US investment strategy might repeat the failures of the assorted "wars" on poverty in which the American government engaged since the sixties. My own experiences in the Deep South, Newark, and Los Angeles had taught me that these antipoverty programs were designed primarily to keep the lid on ghetto violence rather than to root out the underlying conditions. They cultivated a stratum of "safe," assimilated community leaders operating a multiplicity of training, outreach, and service programs that amounted to a new patronage system. But poverty and alienation had remained largely unchanged in the Deep South and Newark, and in Los Angeles the most large-scale racial violence of the century had recently flared once again. The 1992 "uprising," "disorder," or "riot," depending on your definition, claimed fifty-three lives and left $1 billion in property losses. The LA elite promptly announced a plan to "rebuild LA," involving promises of $6 billion in private investment and creation of 75,000–90,000 jobs in five years. Not surprisingly, as soon as the embers of destruction had cooled, the "rebuild LA" effort lost momentum. In one year, it would fold. Fully 70 percent of its funds went to salaries and administration. A *Los Angeles Times* survey revealed that one-fourth of the private firms on Rebuild LA's list of corporate sponsors had no plans at all to invest in the inner city. The chairman of the organization resigned, saying "the obstacles are much more formidable than I thought"; the co-chairman said more bluntly that "what's most discouraging is the business leadership hasn't stepped forward."[116]

The failure of antipoverty efforts in America was occurring against a backdrop of persistent *de facto* segregation in the post-civil rights era. Income and employment gaps between whites and African Americans and Latinos were so significant that, by my calculations, it would take another hundred years to achieve comparable pay at the current rates of progress. Public schools were being "resegregated" in the USA, according to Harvard University experts. Police brutality and misconduct in minority communities continued to be an enduring issue as well, despite numerous blue-ribbon commissions and promises of reform. If such race and class issues remained intractable in America, I wondered, how would Clinton's plans for Northern Ireland be any different? And why would the British allow equal opportunities to Irish nationalists who wanted their independence?

If there was an alternative scenario, I reasoned, it might be found in the working-class ghettos that supplied the soldiers on both sides of the war. A "peace dividend" that provided education, training, and meaningful jobs to young people in those communities was the most plausible alternative to Protestants fighting to cling to declining privileges and Catholics fighting for a new arrangement for their children. It meant a return to the sixties discussions of economic and political strategy among Belfast activists before the military conflict came to dominate the North. Gerry Adams's earliest efforts at improved housing, for example, included alliances with Protestant working-class communities before sectarianism turned rampant.

I made my first exploration of the loyalist Shankill Road in preparation for the White House conference, starting with a community worker named Jackie Redpath, who eventually became a pivotal contact for the White House and delegations of investors. When I asked for a meeting, his reply was somewhat disorienting. "You're fuckin' Tom Hayden! I had a poster of you on the wall in my hippie anti-Vietnam days," he yelled over the phone. He picked me up not long after in a partly operational Volkswagen bug, wearing a blue-and-orange American football fan's parka, and off we journeyed to the Shankill, a community strikingly similar in appearance to the Falls Road except for its fierce anti-IRA murals and anti-Catholic wall graffiti. The road itself is a walking thoroughfare packed with markets, clothing stores, pubs, and community centers, with union jacks, Ulster flags and curbs painted red-white-and-blue. Protestant housing estates feed into the Shankill, separated by small parks and the occasional abandoned area and parking lot. Looming on the horizon are the yellow towers of the Harland and Wolff shipyard, where Protestant fathers once could

guarantee secure employment for their Protestant sons from one generation to the next. But from the late sixties to the nineties, H&W
employment was downsized dramatically, even with significant government subsidies. The fate of the Protestant working class, abandoned by its
employers, resembled that of the white working class perched barely
above blacks and Latinos on the American economic ladder, with
nowhere to go but down – or England.

Jackie Redpath, a thin, red-faced bird of a man, was more liberal in
social attitudes than the average resident on the Shankill Road. While he
thought of himself as British rather than Irish, he was a Dissenter when
it came to religious matters. And as a onetime working-class hippie, he
was open to the global winds of change. Being a pragmatist, he was
organizing a community training and counseling center which he hoped
would be funded by the USA and Europeans. He wanted wealthy Irish
Americans to invest in a hotel on the Shankill.

Jackie was more than willing to work on cross-community projects
with counterparts on the Falls Road. But his basic attitude was one
widely shared with unionists of every shade, and not unlike that of
white conservatives in the USA. His sense was that nationalist grievances were overstated, often whiny, out of date. The truth, he believed,
was that nationalist gains and confidence were on the upswing, and that
what was good for Catholics was bad for Protestants. No statistics on
unemployment rates or Protestant dominance of the RUC could shake
his analysis. Sinn Féin was getting most of the attention now, he reasoned, and the IRA ceasefire would be rewarded with increased
resources. The loyalist ceasefire, which followed that of the IRA by a
month, had received less attention and applause. Jackie was addressing
something real, the loss of privilege, the demise of the Protestant state.
Even if his community wasn't in fact worse off than the neighboring
Falls Road, watching the nationalists rise left a hollow feeling among
those conditioned to look down on them.

We had lunch at a barricaded private club on the Shankill Road with
a group of Jackie's associates who proved to me that Protestants could
down their pints as well as any piefaced Irish Catholic. They were work-

ing-class, pragmatic Protestants mainly interested in restoring and improving the Shankill, and well aware of the potential sources of funding in Irish America and the White House. They could work in cross-community projects and seemed genuinely interested in reconciliation – while retaining their British identity. Some were politically active in loyalist organizations that supported the ceasefire.

> There is more aggression in Protestants than Catholics – it's the frontiersman mentality. God and a rifle. A chunk of them went off to the States in the eighteenth century and were ruthless scalpers of Indians. . . . A tribe of warriors will hold the [Protestant] frontier. Uncivilised and unscrupulous. It is a feature of the withdrawal of the unionist middle classes from politics. The paramilitaries are an army without an officer class. They are lawless. There is no control mechanism – they'd cut a person's arm off with a garden shears.
>
> Unionist political consultant, 1999[117]

> Then again, I have heard people say that the loyalists only did what a lot of other Protestants hadn't the guts to do. Murder is murder. But if anyone took Gerry Adams's life, would any of us shed a tear?
>
> Director, Orange History Museum, Portadown, 1999[118]

> We are, we are, we are the Billy Boys . . .
> We're up to our necks in Fenian blood . . .
>
> Loyalist song

Jackie took me round to meet a young loyalist community worker he named as "Ozo" (his formal name was Alexander Calderwood), who worked on cross-community projects. Tattooed and powerfully built, Ozo could have been cast in Oliver Stone's *Natural Born Killers* were it not for his born-again cheerfulness. We met in his community office, a refitted pub house with pool tables and meeting rooms for youngsters. "Ozo" is a common loyalist nickname, according to the journalist Susan McKay, along with Winkie, Dogs, Hacksaw, Nipper, Spongie, Basher, Spacer, all "sinister cartoon characters."[119] Jackie described Ozo as "the wildest young person I ever met," quite an achievement on the Shankill. He dropped out of school, and committed dozens of crimes before killing a west Belfast Catholic at age seventeen. The Catholic victim was dropped on the Shankill Road by a loyalist cabbie, and Ozo did the rest, crushing his skull with a cinder block. Ozo had recently been released from Long Kesh after twelve years. "You'll find he's very interesting," Jackie said.

Like a number of loyalists in prison, Ozo went through a born-again Christian experience. These individuals had killed, or risked their lives, for their Protestant faith, only to find they were treated with official disdain by their prison guards and by respectable Protestant society. As paramilitaries and prisoners, some like Ozo began to feel like cannon fodder for the Orange political elite. Betrayed by the Protestant state, they were born-again in their prison catacombs. From their ranks came a significant impetus for the loyalist ceasefire that followed that of the IRA.

I didn't hesitate to shake his hand warmly, although he was the first Catholic-killer I'd ever knowingly spoken to. While people like Jackie and his partners were key to the organization of any new order, I realized that Ozo and the men who fought the war were its foundation. Ozo seemed used to telling his story, and willingly obliged on camera. He was still in daily contact with old comrades in the loyalist paramilitaries, he said, but was also involved in dialogue with former IRA prisoners. He was organizing workshops between loyalist and nationalist youth, and wanted to take them on trips to the United States. He and Jackie wanted me to contact the US consulate to urge a visa for Ozo and his kids, which I agreed to do. I asked Ozo how he imagined the peace process to work. He offered a straightforward class analysis of the war.

At the end of the day, it's the working-class people of both communities who have fought the war and not the people up the social ladder, so it's the working class alone who can end it. There are some here [in the hardline loyalist ranks] who keep accusing the "hard men" [the paramilitaries on ceasefire] of going soft. These are saying "No, No, No" and "Never, Never, Never." But they didn't fight, and they've never gone without food on their table or clothes on their back.

The people up the social ladder should let these ceasefire talks have a chance. The important thing is that nobody's been killed in eight months.

There it was, the elusive dream of the Irish left, in which working-class solidarity would triumph over sectarianism, something like a Klan member becoming a labor movement organizer. Those like Ozo would never become republicans, they might define themselves as British, but they were finished being cannon fodder for those "up the social ladder." Ozo was in a minority, but he was not alone. The problem of sectarianism, like racism, might be reduced if working-class Protestants could shift the blame for their plight from the IRA to those "up the social ladder." It wasn't Irish republicans, for example, who downsized manufacturing jobs for the loyalist working class.

But religion and nationality (like race in America) always seemed to trump class consciousness. Sectarian bigotry was planted in young Protestants in deprived areas like Ozo's. They thought the Catholics, the IRA, the Taigs, whatever they were called, were winning. It was like a game, a soccer match. Once, in a changing area of north Belfast, where Catholic homes had been burned and gutted on the edge of a Protestant estate, some kids approached me carrying a sign that simply said "Drumcree." They wanted to sell me a soft drink and have their picture taken. They were perhaps ten years of age, tousle-haired, cute as they posed. As I snapped the shutter they smiled and shouted "fuck the pope." Another time, in the loyalist Fountain section of Derry I came upon a mural depicting an Ulster Freedom Fighter (UFF), in a death mask contorted with hate, a tattered Union Jack in one hand and a blood-dripping sword in the other. Behind the UFF man the Catholic Bogside was burning up, the Free Derry mural covered with smoke. On the ground was a beheaded Catholic. "We Determine the Guilty, We Decide the Punishment" was emblazoned above the mural. I stopped at a corner store beside the mural to buy some film, when three young teenagers approached me, wearing jogging clothes with Adidas emblems. "Take our picture, Mistah, take our picture?" They posed in front of the UFF mural, two of them standing at military attention while the third raised his fists and shouted, "Long live Hitler!" They were the next generation of Ozos.

On the Falls Road, just moments from the Shankill, the thirty years' war had left a network of strong community leaders demanding their right to participate in community economic development. Most, though not all of them, were from republican backgrounds. Many were the wives, ex-wives, sisters, and cousins of republican prisoners or victims of violence. Having resisted British troops, armored cars, helicopters, shootings, beatings, and the incarceration of perhaps half the male population, they were self-confident despite their second-class status.

Their problem was one of risen people in a falling economy, something akin to the thousands of American blacks elected after the Southern civil rights movement who inherited structural poverty and unemployment. While deindustrialization created job loss among Protestant workers, it also demoralized the Catholics. In 1991, 28 percent of Catholic males were officially unemployed in the North, with many more defined as no longer seeking work, and in ghettos the jobless percentage was far higher. Few were employed in top government positions, and fewer still in security occupations, while the public sector represented 63 percent of Northern Ireland's GNP. Catholics were typically nurses, teachers, unskilled workers, pub owners. In addition, they were subject to systemic discrimination and, if associated in any manner with republicans, excluded from any government grants.[120]

I visited with the revered community priest, Father Des Wilson, who along with others was trying to restore the ancient Conway Mill to a new center of community development. The building, which housed numerous republican community groups as well as a furniture store and black-cab repair shop on the first floor, was a several-story nineteenth-century linen mill with broken windows, cold cement floors, and an elevator that didn't work. You could look through cracks in the wall at British soldiers working out in modern facilities in the adjacent barracks. The mill was astir with community service activity but was denied any government funding during the conflict, including funds from the International Fund for Ireland (IFI), which received millions from the US government. Instead, large sums were targeted to the North Howard Street Mill just across the street, which was controlled by the Catholic Church hierarchy. The funds were expended according to official policy, expressed in the 1985 Anglo-Irish Agreement that "disbursements shall be consistent with the economic and social policies and priorities of the respective governments."[121] The bulk of the IFI funds came from the US Congress and, although subsequently reformed, the program was widely condemned as a one-sided, corrupt "runaway gravy train," rather than an incentive for peace, in the eighties.[122] Northern Irish youth were sent for vocational training to a McDonald's in Chicago, among other "vocational training" programs. In those years, hotels and golf courses were renovated, a skydiving club was funded, and hundreds of thousands of dollars went to bookie shops and bars.[123]

How could private or public investment, especially well-intentioned investment, ever reach this community where British rule enforced second-class status? If liberal solutions were inadequate to address poverty in the United States, what sort of solutions were possible in a place like Belfast? If the British government was opposed to the targeted investments envisioned by the MacBride Principles, what was the alternative? Was the much-touted market approach of Bill Clinton's "new Democrats" and Tony Blair's New Labour capable of ending the long-term unemployment that had been reinforced by a unionist agenda? Or were the governments interested only in the ceasefire and not the economic roots of the conflict?

Geraldine McAteer, Eileen Howell, Niamh Flanagan, Jean Lundy, Ruth Taillon, and Deirdre McManus were among the Falls women ready to assert themselves in peacetime community development. So was Laurence McKeown, Deirdre's mate, the surviving 1981 hunger striker whom I had first met bridge-building along the border. He dreamed of counseling and cooperative ventures for ex-prisoners. There was Jim Neeson, seeking to turn the black cabs into a self-sufficient venture. Máirtín Ó Muilleoir and Robin Livingstone were turning the *Andersonstown News* into a competitive weekly with ambitious plans for expansion. Tom Hartley was improving the Falls Park through the Belfast City Council. Once-forbidden Irish-language schools, started in 1971 by two brothers, Seamus and Sean McShane, were a growing force. They all were determined to overcome the exclusion of the republican and nationalist community from decisions regarding economic and social development. In the absence of private investment or government programs, they had developed the concept of "community trusts" to "regenerate" places like the Falls. Different from paternalistic American antipoverty programs, the independent trusts would renew the community "physically, socially, and in spirit." While funding grants were necessary for start-up purposes, the notion was to achieve maximum community control through local banking and spin-off enterprises like Jim Neeson's renowned black taxi fleet. The underlying notion, consistent with their whole struggle, was to advance national self-determination, not become social workers for the United Kingdom. An initial step was to demand inclusion in the upcoming White House conference.

There was one idea for community development coming from the outside which was attracting great interest, a proposal for a new branch of the University of Ulster on the "peace line" between the loyalist and republican communities. Thinking it was a great idea for employment training in the peacetime economy, as well as an assurance that west Belfast might be stabilized, I made an appointment to see its proponent, Dr Wallace Ewart, whose office was in the suburbs of Belfast. An affable academic entrepreneurial type, Ewart saw an opportunity to attract funds to what he called a "peace university" with a range of programs similar to an American community college. I suggested that an ivory-tower model was inappropriate in communities that had fought a war for their identity, and that he should include community leaders on the Falls and Shankill in all phases of the planning process.

At his suggestion, we drove into Belfast to observe the site. What fascinated me was that Dr Ewart immediately became lost in the streets between the Shankill and Falls roads, just as befuddled as I had been on my first visit to Belfast in 1976. As I helped him find his way, I realized this was a case study in the continuing cluelessness of the authorities. Dr Ewart, with his niche in the United Kingdom educational system and his admiration of American community colleges, was in charge of planning a university in a war zone with which he was unfamiliar. But he seemed well-intentioned, and I resolved to help him through the obstacles when I got back to America.

One person who needed no directions around Belfast was a youthful columnist for the *Andersonstown News* and elected member of the city council, Máirtín Ó Muilleoir. At thirty, he literally was a child of the Troubles which he chronicled. Slender, bespectacled, rushed, wry, Ó Muilleoir was a groundbreaker inside the unionist-dominated dome of power at Belfast City Hall. As an elected Sinn Féin councillor, he and his allies were demonized like no politicians I'd ever met. He wore a flak jacket to every council meeting. The Sinn Féin office inside City Hall was bombed in 1994. One of his colleagues, Alex Maskey, shot in the stomach at home, was called "leadbelly" by the jeering daughter of Ian Paisley when he returned to City Hall.[124]

This petty and lethal arrogance was rooted in the unionist assumption that City Hall was an impenetrable bulwark of Orange power. The earliest campaigns of Sinn Féin in local politics were categorized as only "a new dimension in urban terrorism" by the *Sunday Times*.[125] Opining that Sinn Féin knew "they will never persuade the Catholics to vote for them at the ballot box," the *Sunday Times* went on to confide that unnamed military intelligence experts expected Belfast republicans to use the control of food "to force the Catholic community to support them."

These stereotypes seemed radically at odds with Máirtín Ó Muilleoir. We met at Cultúrlann, a converted Presbyterian church on the Falls Road which served as an all-purpose center including an Irish-language school. Ó Muilleoir was no longer a Sinn Féin member, which was due, I sensed, to his independent journalistic spirit. He was busy defining a new Irish identity and development strategy, based on culture, beyond traditional rhetoric. "Our ambition must be to leave the war mentality for the artists' vision," he began. "There needs to be a post-ceasefire explosion of creativity to build on. Look around at this place, an Irish-language school, bookstore, theater, summer festivals, all in an area where people weren't supposed to have a culture."

In Ó Muilleoir's vision, the model for Belfast would be Barcelona, not New York, London, or Dublin. He was attracted to regions of unique cultural identity emerging in Europe. "The Europeans are easier to deal with than the Brits. They are more used to proud, assertive nationalists and cultural diversity. The Brits don't have any of that. If we could be 10 percent of Barcelona! Franco tried to repress them and take their language. Yes, they are still on the land of Spain but they have their own language, their own regional government, their own television, industry, and finance. People come there from all over the world."

As to economic development, Ó Muilleoir scorned the "offer of drab, dead-end jobs with no quality of life." Belfast, he told me, is where Irish republicanism was born. "If we can keep the energy of the last twenty-five years, we can give a dream to the city. We can build on pride in identity and culture. *It's been criminal till now to be Irish in our own country. Now we can be Irish to the world.*" Ó Muilleoir predicted (correctly) that Irish filmmaking would boom in peacetime. In the previous year, he said, thirty films had been made all over Ireland compared to only seven in England. A $10 million investment in a Galway-based Irish-language television network would employ people in "trying to make the Irish language profitable." He noted the explosion of Irish popular culture globally. Had any other small nation produced the likes of U2, Sinead O'Connor, Van Morrison, Black 47, the Cranberries, the Chieftains, Jim Sheridan, Gabriel Byrne, Liam Neeson, Fionnuala Flanagan, Paddy Doyle, and Seamus Heaney? All these figures existed globally through the horizontal stage of international media, yet all were distinctly Irish nationals. Their universal appeal lay in articulating their national roots, not in abandoning them.

Ó Muilleoir saw a key role for Irish Americans in creating an economic base through culture. "We have to build bridges with those people abroad who have supported us through the years of strife. When Americans come here, it won't be for McDonald's. Will those who fought to help us win the right to a job now buy the products we make? If they know about them, I think they will."

Ó Muilleoir was the embodiment of a new global Irish identity that bypassed the clichés of assimilation, neither clinging to parochial Catholic nationalist pride nor blending meekly into the English-speaking world. He also sought an alternative to the traditional notions of economic growth, one based on the growth of creativity and culture. And despite his understandable Belfast boosterism, he opened the possibility of being Irish anywhere on earth, transcending national physical boundaries.

On one point I felt particularly challenged, however, that of the importance of the Irish language. How could one fight for "Irish identity" without including the ancient language in reclaiming that identity? I was becoming painfully aware that all my innermost thoughts and verbal communications were in the language of my colonizer. The unionists had pronounced the Irish language as "dead," or "the language of leprechauns." Not that the English language wasn't perfectly functional in the modern world. But being functional was the problem, an idiom that made adaptation and assimilation successful. I realized that language, far from being neutral, was a mode of achieving dominance, not only over market and diplomatic transactions, but psychically as well. Our immigrant ancestors were commanded to become fluent in English not simply for survival, but to shed their "backward" culture for a modern one.

With the near extinction of the Irish language after the Famine, the deep oral culture of the Irish disappeared or became the diminishing stuff of folklorists. A 1900 article in the *United Irishman* lamented that "by turning our backs on our language, [we] have lost the power that our memories would give us. . . . [These memories] teach us the work of the centuries. . . . [It] is a priceless heirloom, for the loss of which no amount of commercial success can compensate."[126] This organic mode of thinking, still known as *dinnseanachis* – in which every place and thing had a subjective presence and story – was replaced by a modern form of consciousness that emphasized ego and materialism. I recalled a story attributed to Seamus Heaney about a class of Irish-speaking children learning English. Instructed to write about the sparrow, a bird well-known in Irish folklore, one youngster began his sentence in English by writing, "The sparrow is a migratory bird," a correct description of the bird's mechanical nature, but ended the sentence with the phrase, "and he have a roundy head," showing an Irish sense of subjective relatedness with the bird.

A Brian Friel character in the play *Translations* similarly scoffs at English as suitable mainly for commerce. Gaelic, on the other hand, is "full of the mythologies of fantasy and hope and self-deception – a syntax opulent with tomorrows. It is our response to mud cabins and a diet of potatoes."[127] Was my lifetime command of English preventing me from the expression of distinctly Irish emotions? I bought some Irish-language tapes and dictionaries at Cultúrlann to take home with me. They still remain on my bookcase, unopened, as dust-laden perhaps as some inner recesses of my soul.

The Greening of the White House

The White House Conference for Trade and Investment in Northern Ireland, held in Washington May 24–26, 1995, was the first gathering of all parties in one place in the history of the "Troubles." One of its highlights was the first meeting, albeit behind closed doors, of Gerry Adams and the frosty British Secretary of State for Northern Ireland, Sir Patrick Mayhew. But the larger action took place in conference workshops and receptions where republicans and unionists were treated as equals. Invitations were hard to come by, and I was pleased that the White House made efforts to include the community leaders from the Falls and Shankill roads among the respectable corporate and government leaders in attendance. It was their first trip to America, their first recognition as parties to the peace process, the first collaboration with others who had always been alien and threatening. It was one of the Clinton Administration's finest moments, which culminated in a euphoric party on the White House lawn under a dramatic electrical storm.

I happened upon Jackie Redpath hanging around the refreshments table. He was buoyant, perhaps a bit stunned, to be welcome in the midst of the dread "Irish American lobby" which loyalists believed was in command of the White House. I instructed him in the technique of waiting in front of the rope line where eventually President Clinton would work the crowd. We waited uncomfortably for an hour before the President appeared, gave an enthusiastic speech, and, as predicted, began shaking hands and exchanging small talk with each individual along the rope. All types of Irish and Irish Americans, including members of Congress and big contributors, holding cameras and autograph books, started pushing us, from behind, into the frozen phalanx of Secret Service agents. Clinton approached, then reached out to Congressman Peter King, bantering that he wished more in the Republican congressional majority were like him. Then suddenly Jackie Redpath, shored up by myself, was standing face to face with the President. I introduced them and Jackie, determined to seize the moment, invited Clinton to visit the Shankill Road. "I will, I promise to," Clinton responded eagerly, then was gone. Jackie needed a drink.

I sat on the lawn as the rain began to clear, amazed at the celebration of coexistence between old enemies. Ozo hadn't made it, but there were at least twenty from the Falls and Shankill roads. It may have been raining, but Sinn Féin was in from the cold, its leaders circulating easily in the crowd. The SDLP contingent was proud of the power-sharing they long had championed. Dublin officials circulated in delight. Ethel Kennedy was greeting people with her daughters Kathleen and Courtney, now married to an Irishman until recently imprisoned by the British. Unionist politicians, though stiff and nervous amid so many Irish Americans, were busy passing out business cards and posing for White House photos, though trying to steer clear of handshakes or photos with glad-handing republicans who, according to Mayhew, had to pass through a "period of decontamination" before becoming acceptable.

The British and Irish press, which had been obsessed with whether Adams and Mayhew shook hands (they did, briefly and privately), took notes in amazement at the history being made all around them. Mary McGrory apologized to anyone who would listen for having opposed the Adams visa and personally upbraided the Sinn Féin leader on an earlier visit.

I had a late dinner during the conference with the prime organizer, Undersecretary of Commerce Charles "Chuck" Meissner and his key aide, Virginia Manuel. Neither had any background in Northern Ireland, which by this time I was prepared to consider an asset. There was no ethnic baggage, no guilt, only an American idealism laced with a can-do approach. Like his boss, Secretary of Commerce Ron Brown, Meissner came from the civil rights activism of the sixties. Like myself, he noted with pride, he came from a liberal Midwestern campus, the University of Wisconsin. His wife, Doris Meissner, was administrator of the US immigration service, where she knew all about visas for Irish immigrants.

Perhaps it was the shared idealism of the sixties, or a common irreverence for conventional wisdom, but Chuck Meissner and I became good friends. He had enormous practical wisdom about getting things done in Washington and the private sector, which I lacked. I could brief him on Northern Ireland in ways that the US intelligence services never would. We talked for hours, floating on the feel-good atmosphere of the conference, and he invited me to accompany him as an adviser on his first business mission to the North, scheduled in a few months. He completely identified with the inclusion of the community groups in places like the Falls Road, not caring about their controversial republican backgrounds. "Economic development doesn't work anymore unless the community buys in," he said. If the British didn't like it, well, far better to include the community groups in building peace than making war. As our conversation wound down, he suddenly had a vision based on my mentioning the proposed Belfast university campus. "The campus is a great idea," he said, "but we should have something there like the independent student unions that we had in Madison and Ann Arbor, remember?" Gesturing enthusiastically, he said, "I see a shovel and the President, and the

President turning over the ground where the campus will be. And I'll raise a couple of million from Irish America, and we'll build the William Jefferson Clinton Student Union on that spot, a whole free speech and peace studies center, a space completely independent of the government."

That October of 1995, I accompanied Meissner as he pursued his dream across Northern Ireland. He and Virginia had managed to recruit an odd cross-section of business people to come along, including Diana's California Cookies, a Spokane water systems firm, Land O'Lakes butter company, and the Data Technology Group of Cambridge. Each would be involved in matchmaking with a related Northern Ireland firm. The whole group would be hosted like visiting royalty and, behind the scenes, Chuck and Virginia would meet leading political representatives. The itinerary included Belfast, Derry, Monaghan, and a final evening at the ambassador's residence in Dublin.

I worried, looking at the schedule prepared by diplomatic officials, that the delegation would be presented with a sanitized version of the North, one which, ironically, I had never experienced. My task was to brief Chuck and the delegates informally on realities that were being avoided. The highlight of my week was to sneak Virginia off to a social drink with Danny Morrison, Laurence McKeown, and Deirdre McManus at a republican pub under the RUC barracks on Falls Road. From there – at midnight – we walked across the street into pitch-black and windy Milltown cemetery to see the hunger strikers' graveplots, then walked down the entirety of the Falls Road, past Sandy Row, where we left one reality behind and entered that of the Europa Hotel, where country-and-western music blared from the bar across a lobby filled with partying unionists. Like Chuck, Virginia knew nothing about Ireland before taking the assignment. She came to the Clinton world from a fundraising background. She was a Catholic woman of Irish descent, never before engaged in Irishness. But now she was taking it in, embracing the women from each community, with the same energy as her boss. Rather than being frightened of republicans, she met individuals like Danny Morrison with curiosity and respect, attitudes they had rarely encountered from an official.

During the Meissner trip, we visited with republicans, unionists, community workers, John Hume, members of the Alliance Party, British civil servants, and Northern bankers and businessmen. The unionist mayor of Belfast, Hugh Smyth, was on especially good behavior with the Americans, even including Sinn Féiners in his receptions and briefings. The American presence was a great outside equalizer, I realized more strongly than ever. The only touchy moment came in the massive dining chamber of Hillsborough Castle, when the delegation was asked by Baroness Jean Denton, minister of the economy, to rise and toast the Queen. I remained seated quietly at my table, joined thankfully by a couple of odd nationalists who made the invitation list. The Americans, including Chuck, took the incident with great merriment later as I escorted them to some working-class pubs.

Six months later, in April 1996, Chuck Meissner and Ron Brown were killed when their US plane crashed into a mountain on a mission to Bosnia. Others would continue his maverick legacy, most notably Virginia Manuel and the President's friend James Lyons at the International Fund for Ireland, but the community development advocates had lost a kindred spirit at the highest level. Everyone in Ireland who knew Meissner was stunned. That such a man, not himself Irish, could be so devoted to Ireland was deeply appreciated across all the divides. That he should die so absurdly, while on a humanitarian mission, was also understood all too well.

In late summer 1998, I was invited officially to observe what the phone caller termed the "sod turning" at the new Belfast university, now referred to as the Springvale Educational Village. I sat in a covered enclosure on a green Belfast field thinking of Chuck Meissner. Bill and Hillary Clinton joined Tony Blair and his wife Cherie in welcoming everyone to west Belfast. Gerry Adams, the MP for the area who would normally be the host, was sitting on a side bench next to Senator George Mitchell. Adams was acknowledged for his leadership in the peace process by the President and Prime Minister, but not allowed a few words of welcome and greeting. The US government, through James Lyons, was promoting the university with a $5 million grant. The British government, which had delayed approval as a bargaining chip in the peace process, was at last on board. A shovel with a silver blade was produced. Two young people, one Catholic and one Protestant, spoke of their hopes for the future. Then they started to enact Chuck Meissner's dream by turning the sod where the new campus would grow. Even the Prime Minister and President took a turn. As the shovels turned the sod, I imagined gravedigging transformed into groundbreaking.

Afterwards I gave Jackie Redpath and David Ervine, the Progressive Unionist Party leader, a lift to their side of town. Ervine, by now a member of the new Assembly and a loyalist supporter of the peace process, had been imprisoned for allegedly carrying a bomb in a stolen car. When I dropped him at his office, he muttered with black humor that he would probably be shot for attending the university groundbreaking with Adams.

As I write, the Springvale campus still remains engulfed in controversy over how much it will open its ivory tower and serve the community. Leaders from both the Shankill and Falls roads, as well as independent educational reformers, continue to insist that the campus adjust to the community instead of the other way round. West Belfast leaders in 1998 blasted Wallace Ewart for being "patronizing" and "derogatory" for describing the community as an "educational underclass" locked into welfare dependency. While the tempers flared, however, all parties were talking. There was certainty, however, that the "peace campus" would open its doors. As for the William Jefferson Clinton Student Union, only time would tell.

In 1999, five years into the peace process, there would still be no economic "peace dividend." In the beginning of 2000, while the Springvale campus moved forward at a snail's pace, the largest single investment in west Belfast was a new $3.5 million RUC barracks atop the Springfield Road. The Mackies manufacturing plant, where President Clinton had proclaimed a new era, was now in receivership. McErlean's, the doughnut shop where Clinton shook hands with Gerry Adams, was closed too. In 1999, the unemployment gap between Catholics and Protestants in the workforce was "stubbornly resistant to change," according to an independent study. British government labor statistics for 1994–97 showed increases of Catholics among the longterm unemployed. Catholic males were 2.9 times more likely to be unemployed than Protestant males, up from 2.4 before the original ceasefires. Harland and Wolff was 94.3 percent Protestant, with just sixty-nine Catholics among 1,150 employees. The Bushmills distillery was 91.2 percent Protestant. Only six firms had located in west Belfast since the 1994 ceasefires.[128]

Most astonishingly, the largest foreign investors in Northern Ireland, eighty-nine American firms representing an increase from forty when Chuck Meissner began his mission in 1995, were employing fewer Catholics in 1999 than before the ceasefires. The Catholic percentage of the US workforce in the North fell from 43.6 percent in 1993 to 39.4 percent in 1998.[129] One major Northern employer, the Irish American William Farley, owner of Fruit of the Loom, had begun moving his operations to the British-controlled tax haven in the Cayman Islands.[130]

This would have been Chuck Meissner's nightmare. With all the attention to Northern Ireland, how could it have happened? One answer was that the strategic emphasis of British and US policy was to secure the end of violence, not the end of poverty and inequality. It had been the same after "urban disorders" in the United States. Once the rioting subsided, once the blue ribbon commissions made their reports, the status quo re-emerged amid even greater cynicism. The authorities in Northern Ireland knew that neglect of the underlying conditions might breed a new cycle of violence, but that was irrelevant compared to making the ceasefires permanent and decommissioning the IRA. From the official viewpoint, any termination of hostilities, moreover, would bring economic dislocation, not rebirth, since security service layoffs would increase unemployment among Protestants. So would any equalizing of job opportunities in the public sector of the Protestant state. There was a "peace dividend" for the well-to-do, on the other hand, reflected in the gleaming Waterfront concert hall, adjacent office development, nine new hotels (and a facelift for the Europa), all designed to send a message to investors and tourists that the place was booming not with bombs but profit opportunities.

Even Irish American businessmen, try as they might, couldn't make a decisive difference in the status quo. One of the most influential of them, the software magnate John Cullinane, created a network of Friends of Belfast and helped secure 140 jobs in software development through Liberty Mutual.[131] Another, the billionaire Chuck Feeney, preferred low-key grants to groups like restorative justice centers operated by former republican prisoners. One of the most inventive, Art McCabe of Lowell, Massachusetts, envisioned the conversion and redevelopment of British and RUC barracks combined with a nationalist-oriented "enterprise zone" investment strategy. McCabe, whom I met in 1997, embodied the model of a pro-nationalist entrepreneur – a cultural capitalist – sought by Máirtín Ó Muilleoir in Belfast. He attempted to attract investors with an interest in strengthening the Irish heritage. He brought community theatre from the Falls Road to an old immigrant museum in a New York synagogue. He sought to restore places like Conway Mill while at the same time rehabilitating the riverfront mills in Lowell and Fall River, where my ancestor Bridget McKenna was born amid thousands of Famine survivors and immigrant textile workers. He refused to give up, but met repeated rebuffs from the Northern Ireland bureaucracy.

One major obstacle was the policy departure of both Tony Blair and Bill Clinton from the social welfare traditions of John Maynard Keynes and Franklin Roosevelt. The British government's "partnership for peace" policy was sanctifying the "spirit of market liberalization" as the central premise of the New Labour and New Democratic platforms. The result for the working class and urban poor had already been depicted graphically in the film *The Full Monty* where unemployed workers spin through the revolving doors of so-called "retraining" schemes while actual job opportunities become downsized. The mayor of Belfast extolled Taiwan and the "Asian tiger" economies as "an economic model to emulate."[132]

But neoliberalism was not the root reason for the lack of an economic peace dividend in the ghettos. After all, the Southern Republic was experiencing the so-called Celtic Tiger phase of economic growth during the same period. Setting aside comparisons with Taiwan and Singapore, and disregarding the significant poverty left in the tracks of the Celtic Tiger, it was nonetheless the greatest economic growth since the creation of the twenty-six-county state. The Republic was becoming a low-tax, low-wage, skilled labor platform for multinational corporations seeking entry to the emerging European Community. Just twenty miles west of Dublin was a new high-tech valley. Microsoft was pressing CDs. Broadband infrastructure was sprouting. Hewlett-Packard and Intel employed 2,000 workers each. Monster.com had arrived, and the MIT Media Lab was coming.

The difference between North and South was not a simple matter of differential taxation or exchange rates. Nor was it only the absence of durable peace. The central problem, as always, was the British and unionist desire to keep Northern Ireland colonized and therefore a dependent part of the London-based economy. Who ever heard of a colony outstripping its mother country economically? In the North, inequality – intentionally uneven development – was institutionalized for the 43 percent of Northerners estimated to be nationalist and/or Catholic. The economic development agencies such as the Industrial Development Board (IDB) were dominated by a unionist ethos that gave preference to investments in pleasant Protestant areas like Craigavon, a mainly Protestant town created in the sixties offering 100-acre parcels of land for industrial development – where many nationalists would fear to go. Even the most educated nationalist classes were excluded from senior decision-making circles in business or government. The flow of investment into Northern Ireland was a subsidy of partition, including its purpose of keeping nationalists contained in the United Kingdom. British laws concerning discrimination against Catholics were considerably weaker than those of the United States; official British policies, for example, expressed the surreal hope that workplace discrimination and harassment be reduced by a "spirit of cooperation" and "without recourse to legislation" in order to spare business "excessive burdens imposed by anti-discrimination laws."[133]

Sinn Féin strategists in fact believed that economic considerations would impel the Northern business elite towards a united Ireland, not out of nationalism but because it was good for business. Indeed, they could cite the chairman of the Ulster Bank, Sir George Quigley, as an advocate of economic unity. "With a single market in Europe it would be ludicrous not to regard the island of Ireland as a single market . . . there are commercial opportunities which should be taken wherever they exist . . . the mental map of people all over Ireland must be enlarged," Quigley has noted.[134]

However, applying the vision of a borderless world to Ireland, even for commercial purposes, would be a threat to partition and the United Kingdom. At the time of the White House conference, only 44 percent of Northern firms exported to the Republic at all.[135] The perceived rationality of enlarging markets conflicts with the barricaded nature of the colonial state. The solution might have been a strict application of the MacBride Principles requiring American investors to target areas of historic discrimination and economic disadvantage, Catholic and Protestant as well. Instead, the US supported a hollowed-out MacBride approach, allowing an American firm – encouraged by official development authorities – to locate in a unionist area with a unionist workforce, and to comply with MacBride simply by extending "outreach" programs to Catholics. The Northern state refuses to undertake MacBride enforcement policies such as contract compliance, ensuring that the MacBride Principles will not achieve significant increases in Catholic employment.

As a result of these colonial and laissez-faire assumptions, it was certain that the next generation of loyalist and republican youth would be pitted against each other not simply by issues of loyalty and faith, but by a downsized, increasingly competitive economy that disadvantaged the Protestants unless the Catholics were kept in their place. The only alternative to this grim future would require a return to the forgotten themes of James Connolly, trade unionist, nationalist, and martyr, who believed in anticolonialism, nonsectarianism, and democratic socialism. Connolly wrote that "the currents of revolutionary thought in Ireland, the socialist and the nationalist, are not antagonistic but complementary." If that was asking too much in the New World Order, even a return to the post-war Marshall Plan interventionism of the 1940s might have bridged the gap. But the apostles of corporate globalization were relegating Ireland to the new chessboard of capitalism, where unionists and nationalists could vie with each other and both compete with Poland or Singapore.

Instead of changing the inequalities of the market, the authorities were concentrating on a major alternative approach similar to the civil rights period of the American sixties. They were devoting their energies to what became the Good Friday Agreement.[136]

The Handshakes at Stormont, October 13, 1997

Three years after the first IRA ceasefire, all parties were finally prepared for the talks which led to the Good Friday Agreement. In the interim, the IRA briefly returned to its bombing campaign, killing two, wounding 100 and causing tens of millions of dollars' worth of property damage in the Canary Wharf section of London in February 1996. "Oh fuck, it was like the Kennedy assassination around here, like the end of the world," Jackie Redpath told me in a Shankill pub a few weeks later. The IRA blamed the British government for eighteen months of delays and for imposing decommissioning as a new condition in the talks. In June they blew up Manchester city center. Though not reaching pre-1994 levels, violence continued to erupt until July 1997 when the IRA announced the "unequivocal restoration of the 1994 ceasefire." The British and the unionists had failed to achieve decommissioning. For their part, the Irish republicans took a step that would have been unimaginable a few years before. They returned to Stormont, the hated site of British rule, for talks that would lead to an assembly in a still-partitioned state of Northern Ireland.

On October 13, there would be the first meeting of Sinn Féin and a British prime minister since 1921. On the Falls Road, the sun was out but the temperature was cold, a little like the talks themselves, hopeful but stalemated. I went to the Conway Mill to follow the Sinn Féin delegation to the Castle Buildings at Stormont.

Conway Mill still lacked furnishings, its upper windows remained cracked. The only recent improvements appeared to be security monitors and buzzers. Otherwise its long-broken chairs, piled newspapers, stained rugs, and metal desks remained intact. Posters leaned ready against the walls ("All Party Talks Now!," "Disband the RUC," "Remember the Women of 1916"). All of it in perfect contradiction to the rolling greens and marbled imperial pillars of Stormont just outside the city.

When I arrived at 9 a.m., the leadership was holed up in planning for the historic day. Mitchel McLaughlin had driven in from Derry, Pat Doherty from Donegal. Gerry Adams, Martin McGuinness, Gerry Kelly, and Siobhan O'Hanlon were already there. I was sipping a poisonous instant coffee when Gerry Adams strolled in, looking fit, smiling, charged-up. After all, it had been seventy-six years since the last meeting with a British prime minister. The media in Belfast and London were obsessed with whether Blair and Adams would shake hands. Or was Sinn Féin still contaminated? They could not imagine asking the question the other way around, i.e. if Gerry Adams was going to shake hands with a British prime minister who oppressed and colonized the nationalist population.

We took five vehicles to the Castle Buildings, a complex of modern offices behind the massive façade of Stormont itself. The all-party talks would take place in a three-floor maze perfectly designed for delegations to be quartered and separated. There was an eerie, formal atmosphere to the building, deepened by the fact that David Trimble and the various unionist delegations had refused to greet or acknowledge the Sinn Féin delegates. This caused a moderate paranoia in the hallways, coffee lounge, restaurant, and especially the bathrooms, where at any moment one might be challenged to make eye contact, nod, smile, or say hello, with other eyes carefully observing.

The Sinn Féin strategy was to be unfailingly polite, light-hearted where appropriate, and show willingness to shake hands and do business. The result was an awkward impasse as the delegations waited for

Blair's arrival. To kill time, I went with Pat Doherty, Sinn Féin vice president, to the third-floor lounge for coffee and doughnuts. Pat is a genial, fiftyish engineer from Glasgow and Tyrone, a longtime political organizer,[137] whose brother Hugh was part of the IRA's Balcombe Street gang captured in a London siege in the early seventies. I carried a small camera inside my coat to record the occasion. The lounge entrance was a hazardous passage where adversaries might brush against each other, and where one's place in the coffee line required subtle negotiation. The men's room entrance was worse.

Crossing the lounge with coffee in hand, I glimpsed Hugh Smyth, former lord mayor of Belfast, whom I had once visited at City Hall. At the time, Smyth was wooing an Icelandic tourist delegation to choose Belfast over Dublin and, in an expansive mood, he had asked my wife if she wished to wear his royal-red official robe with an ermine collar (she could not refuse). I decided to approach him and reintroduce myself. The circumspect Pat Doherty remained at a distance, holding his coffee, encouraging me to take the step.

Smyth was surprised to see me but remembered our previous conversations with Chuck Meissner. Americans, with our naïve informality, seem able to drift across divides in the North unlike the Irish. Smyth waved me to have a seat. He was having coffee with three men I assumed to be delegates when one of them came into focus, a grizzled, pipe-smoking elderly gentleman. He extended a tattooed hand, and said in a deep voice, "Oh yes, Senator, it's grand to see you and won't you have a seat? I am Gusty Spence."

Gusty Spence? I was face to face with the loyalist figure who, in a certain sense, had begun and ended the war for Ulster. In 1966, as a member of the Ulster Volunteer Force (UVF), he supported a proclamation declaring that "known IRA men will be executed mercilessly and without hesitation [while] less extreme measures will be taken against anyone sheltering or helping them, but if they persist in giving them aid, then more extreme methods will be adopted."[138] In June 1966, Spence was in the Malvern Arms pub off the Shankill Road when four Catholics came in for a late-night drink. Spence drank and talked with them. At about 2 a.m., he and others from the UVF shot the Catholics as they left the pub, killing one named Peter Ward. Spence was convicted of murder in an incident widely seen as the beginning of the Troubles.[139] He spent eighteen years as a loyalist paramilitary leader inside Long Kesh, released in 1985. In October 1994 Gusty Spence was chosen to announce the loyalist ceasefire that followed that of the IRA, expressing "abject and true remorse" to the victims' families.[140]

Gusty knew somehow that I had once tried to meet him through Jackie Redpath, and seemed eager to chat. Across the lounge, Pat Doherty drank coffee and watched the goings-on.

To ease into the issues at hand, I began telling Gusty about a book on the Great Hunger I was editing. In unionist mythology, there was no Famine in Ulster because Protestants were an industrious people protected by a providential God. In the unionist view, the Famine befell Catholics because of their backward sinfulness. But new research by Christine Keanely was uncovering evidence that the majority of deaths in the Lurgan workhouse, for example, were of Protestants. I was wondering if I should be choosing this subject as a conversation opener when Gusty replied, dragging on his pipe, "Oh, yes, the Famine struck us too, that's just part of the truth that hasn't been told." I felt relieved and, with the preliminaries over, I asked Gusty how he viewed the talks.

In American gang terminology, I guessed, Gusty would be defined as an "original gangster," or "OG," a term of respect for an elder, the kind of person who might mediate disputes. I guessed correctly. Gusty leaned over confidentially to say, "I'm here to cover their backs," meaning that his authority with the loyalist paramilitaries could help the unionist delegation manage any tough compromises without fearing reprisal. A good man to know, I figured. Gusty carried an attitude of confidence, as if certain that the talks would eventually yield a positive result.

Pat Doherty now strolled over from his side of the lounge, ostensibly and politely to ask if I wanted to return back to the second floor (since I could not possibly find my way). I could feel him hovering on the edge of the unionists' space, and I started to respond when he extended his

hand to Gusty, who promptly shook it. Then he carefully and delibera-
tively shook the others' hands, as if permitted by Gusty's gesture. I asked
Pat to sit down. The unionists agreed and passed him the coffee cake.
The discussion resumed, and I became aware that the personal was also
the diplomatic, that every gesture had meaning, however indirect. Gusty
became jovial, telling tales about the enjoyable times he'd spent in
Dublin, the names of pubs and shops he frequented, all to suggest a comfort level and familiarity with Irish ways. Pat, who resided over the
border in Donegal, told a little story in turn about a neighbor who
would give up a united Ireland for a "nine-county Ulster." Everyone
laughed. He had implied that Sinn Féin could be flexible, that if the
Ulster that the UDA and UVF defended was restored to its original size
before partition, it would have a Catholic majority. I could barely keep
up with the subtlety of their banter. This was the peace process at a fundamental one-on-one level.

After a short while, we arose to return to the respective offices. I
stood, shook hands all around, and asked Gusty if he might allow a
photo for a souvenir. No problem, he waved, allowing Pat to click off a
few shots of us together. Then, probing in a nonchalant way, I asked to
take one of Pat and Gusty. Pat nodded that it would be fine. Gusty
paused and then shook his hands in the negative. I thought Gusty was
perfectly happy to do it, but that perhaps he had to watch his own back.
The public handshake was a bargaining chip to be extended across the
table later.

I went to the cafeteria for lunch, a comparatively open space where
Americans, British, unionists, SDLP, Sinn Féin, the Women's Coalition all
stood in the same lines. But Sinn Féiners like Gerry Kelly ate by themselves. Once a legendary escapist from Long Kesh, Kelly was now
wearing an elegant tailored suit and complaining wryly that "incarceration" of the diplomatic kind in Stormont was more difficult than
incarceration in Long Kesh because there was no escape. On this day,
Kelly was preoccupied with something called "sufficient consensus"
which had crept into the talks, suggesting that either side could simply
veto any proposal they disliked. This would mean the only agreement

possible would be an agreement to talk on and on. Across the table, Martin McGuinness, the lead negotiator, shared the suspicion that the British strategy was to stall. At least the food was better than in a prison, McGuinness acknowledged. He winked and said, "It's all par for the course," with understatement.

Two hundred reporters crammed the parking lot below. Tony Blair's huge green helicopter was on approach. Gerry Adams was arriving by car. At 2:45 Blair was in the building, planning courtesy calls on each of the delegations separately. Sinn Féin would be last. This required adroit scheduling by advance men for the Crown, since everyone was on the second floor. As I sat inside the door, the Secretary of State Mo Mowlam suddenly appeared. Not one for protocol, she waved at "the Shinners" and continued down the hall to John Hume's office. About 3:15, Blair himself materialized from next door, smiling, shaking hands, seeming fit and trim, making sure to stare away from the Sinn Féin office just feet away. It was not yet time.

I turned to Martin McGuinness, who was standing there watching the diplomatic choreography. On the wall behind him was a poster of the 1916 Rising with a soldier's uniform draped on a chair. How do you feel at this exact moment? I asked. "They are no better than us, you know," he replied with a tense smile. As he spoke, Gerry Adams whisked into the side room to huddle with his colleagues before meeting Blair. I looked in to record the moment, and found them sitting around a table laughing at themselves. They posed for a photo, and Adams suggested I slip into the meeting with Blair. "If you can't, we'll leave the blinds open." Then the seventy-year wait was over. Abruptly, they stood and headed for the appointed meeting with the Prime Minister.

A security officer told me the Unionist Party had registered a complaint about my taking pictures. I guessed that Gusty Spence had been too informal. The halls were empty now, the day darkening, as Sinn Féin met the British government in a plain meeting chamber on the first floor. I went outside to photograph the photographers. Inside, I later learned, Blair shook hands, was engaged and listening carefully. Accompanied by seven aides from the British side, the Prime Minister alone did the talking for his government. Adams took Blair's hand, wished him a Celtic *céad míle fáilte* (welcome), and expressed the hope he would be the last prime minister "to rule over my country." The two men talked together for half an hour, and agreed to talk again. Adams, by now a careful student of negotiating arts, said the Prime Minister would have to "get into our heads" if the talks were to progress, just as Sinn Féin now had to get into the psyche of unionism. If the Prime Minister had gone through Gerry Adams's life experience, he would be an Irish republican, Adams told him. Barriers were broken, if not bread, and the meeting came to a cordial end.

At 4 p.m., Blair and his delegation strode out to meet the freezing press, making a well-rehearsed statement about the importance of non-violence by all parties, a commitment to democracy by all parties, before being drowned out by howling questions about whether there was a handshake. The Prime Minister stood, as if unprepared, or perhaps unable to answer, the only question that seemed to matter. Did you shake his hand? Did you shake his hand? What was it like? Can you tell us how you felt? Blair was strangely mute for a man fluent in soundbites. I wondered if the reality of what he'd done was overwhelming the symbolism. History was holding his throat. He made a sound, then caught himself, then failed to answer again. "Well, Sinn Féin is a party to the talks . . . treat them as any other party . . . the importance of the commitment to nonviolence . . . treat them as he would any other human beings. . . ." He simply could not acknowledge that he shook their hands. I was stunned. Then Blair was gone.

As I drove down the seemingly endless driveway away from Stormont, Blair's chopper was already lifting off for England. He'd gone from Stormont to a short appearance in east Belfast to reassure his unionist base. I speculated whether he told them there was no handshake. The phrases "no surrender," "no handshake," were running through my mind, when I turned on the radio. There was a live radio report that the Prime Minister had been threatened by a loyalist mob in east Belfast. As he smilingly strode toward a department store to shake hands, the broadcaster said, loyalists jeered him, pushed, pelted him. They yelled that he had blood on his hands. They were wearing sanitary gloves to express their disgust at the contaminating handshake made in private. Siobhan O'Hanlon, listening to the radio, quietly said, "Well now, maybe he can feel a bit of what we've been going through all along."

Good Friday

The Good Friday Agreement of April 1998 recast the contours of Irish identity and illustrated the importance of Irish Americans reclaiming a role in Northern Ireland.

A fatal melancholy had long surrounded the diplomacy concerning Northern Ireland, perpetuating the stereotype that the Irish Troubles were insolubly rooted in character. The warring parties were too far apart for politics to replace the gun, it was said. A conflict that was centuries old could not be resolved on the short-term deadlines of statesmen in Washington, London, and Dublin.

Casting the conflict in these terms, of course, served a useful purpose in Anglo-American circles. The premise of incorrigible tribalism justified the British claim to be a civilized mediator while reinforcing the melting-pot mythology, namely that the Irish were primitive, tribal, a separate people from the modern Irish Americans who reached civilization through the Atlantic crossing to assimilation. The legacy of shame and self-hatred cauterized the Irish and Irish Americans against identifying with Northern Ireland. Unless they were born in Belfast or Derry, few Irish Americans read the news from the North and felt a solidarity. Even fewer looked at the media images of masked IRA men and recognized their ancestors in the Molly Maguires or the Ribbonmen.

An Israeli friend, Meron Ben-Veniste, once summarized to me the approach of government officials to such deadlocks. As former deputy mayor of the divided and disputed city of Jerusalem under Mayor Teddy Kollek, Ben-Veniste dropped out in frustration and began a comparative study of Jerusalem and Belfast. Intrigued, I asked Ben-Veniste what he'd learned and his reply stayed with me. "That politics is the art of managing the insoluble," he said and shrugged.[141]

I preferred to find a total paradigm shift, but in the short run managing the insoluble was the negotiating agenda. In Northern Ireland, the war was stalemated. The British army could not defeat the IRA and the effort to colonize the Irish nationalists into identity with unionism was an utter failure. But neither could the British army be driven out, nor could the unionist majority be resettled elsewhere in the British Isles. Any liberal hope of reconciliation in the foreseeable future was utopian. To "manage the insoluble" meant creating a new space in which contradictory loyalties could be expressed more effectively than through violence. Tony Blair, in a discussion with US congressmen, tried to describe this as a public relations problem since, he said, "the differences of substance between [the unionists and republicans] were not as great as often thought." For Blair, therefore, it was "a presentational dilemma," "since the two sides needed to present the outcome in different ways."[142] But it would take more than a gimmick to transform the war into a purely political conflict.

The real interest of London was not as a mediator, but to preserve Northern Ireland as a province of the United Kingdom. In 1993 the British had declared they no longer had a "selfish strategic or economic interest" in the Union, a statement intended to encourage the talks process. Gerry Adams couldn't obtain a clear answer, however, to the question of whether a comma followed "selfish". If not, the Brits were only declaring the lack of "selfish strategic" interest, not an "unselfish strategic" interest. They had a continued aspiration to be a great power, which required that they be a credible guarantor of the rights of the pro-British population of the North. Further, with the decline of their former empire, the British were locked in an identity crisis. Where did their decline stop? What were their boundaries? If Northern Ireland was lost, what would prevent Scotland and Wales from becoming independent?

Blair's project was to reverse England's decline without the pretension of restoring its empire, to create what became known as a "cool Britannia." Like Bill Clinton, he was man of the sixties, had worn his hair long, indulged in the counterculture. Blair had married a Catholic professional, a young lawyer with a keen interest in human rights. While neither willing nor able to surrender a part of the United Kingdom, Blair wanted to end discrimination against Northern Catholics. He believed he could decouple colonialism from religious discrimination. All his colonial subjects would be equal regardless of religious background, at least until a majority of them voted their consent to join a united Ireland – a prospect at least a generation away, long after Blair's tenure in office.

This approach to modernizing partition still placed Blair in tension with most of the unionist community because of its privileged position through the Orange Order and related institutions in Northern Ireland. Extreme and politically popular Christian fundamentalists like the Reverend Ian Paisley ranted against the Catholic Church as "the whore of Babylon." Whether they shared Paisley's prejudice, the more moderate unionist community knew that to destroy discrimination against Catholics would undermine their state of privilege. They hoped that an agreement would disarm the IRA, protect the Union with Britain, and yield only token and gradual concessions to the nationalist community.

Irish nationalists could not settle for another generation of token reform. The Northern Catholic middle class, raised in the sixties, was no longer content to be second-class professionals, nurses instead of doctors, clerks instead of managers. John Hume's moderate SDLP was threatened with loss of its middle-class base to a peacetime Sinn Féin if it appeared to be delivering anything less than first-class opportunities for its constituents. That forced the SDLP in a direction at greater odds with the colonial state.

For the Dublin government, the peace process presented a special paradox. It would have to abandon the rhetorical nationalism at the heart of the twenty-six-county state – its constitutional claim to the territory of Northern Ireland. The claim was never acted on, but maintained a link with the 1916 generation. As a concession to London and the unionists, Dublin was being asked in the peace negotiations to accept partition by yielding its claim to the North, which would remain part of the UK until a majority voted otherwise. On the other hand, the Republic would be expected to become more assertive in its diplomatic role in the North, at least if republicans were to be convinced that political pressure was more effective than the armed campaign. Dublin could no longer wash its hands of the North but would have to speak out on claims of injustice and participate more meaningfully than ever in new cross-border institutions. More important, Dublin would be lifting censorship and allowing a peaceful and confident Sinn Féin to compete politically for elected office in the twenty-six counties, an opening that would threaten the monopoly of the Fianna Fáil party over historically republican constituencies in the twenty-six counties.

As for Gerry Adams, Martin McGuinness, Sinn Féin, and especially the IRA, the prospect of any compromise was treacherous as well. The honored dead in Milltown cemetery had shed their blood for a united Ireland, not a mere presence at Stormont. Without saying so, Sinn Féin would be breaking its most hallowed tradition by participating in the partitioned state. An equally sacred republican credo was never to put down the gun until the British were gone from Ireland. The compromise in the works would at best create a kind of binational state within the North, people of both traditions being treated equally. But could a colonial system built on the backs of nationalists be reformed in such a way? Some republicans saw the opportunity to convulse unionism by making it yield its historic privilege. Others wondered if they were selling out the republican aspiration for national self-determination through a united Ireland for representation in a Northern "statelet" they historically condemned as illegitimate. It was crucial for them that cross-border institutions become a peaceful bridge to reunification, and that Northern nationalists not only achieve equality in the North but be empowered by electing representatives to the Southern government as well.

The Parades Crisis

Reality in Belfast was as grim as ever as the May 1, 1998, deadline for the peace talks approached. Since 1995, the North had been shaken as local nationalist communities resisted clamorous Orange Order parades through their communities. Some in Sinn Féin were unsettled by the eruption of street militance which threatened to derail the talks. The North nearly disintegrated in 1996 when the RUC and British army clubbed and arrested nationalists in Portadown to allow an Orange parade from the Drumcree church down the nationalist Garvaghy Road. Rioting erupted all over Northern Ireland and Sinn Féin activists found themselves urging people to stay in their homes. On the other hand, the Orangemen saw a Sinn Féin conspiracy everywhere and Ruth Dudley Edwards wrote that the residents' groups were only "transmission belts" for IRA subversion, and that nationalist residents of Garvaghy Road "would have to go well out of their way to be offended" since only sixty-six out of 900 houses, by her count, had windows from which the parade would be visible. Edwards was either in denial or counting on public ignorance of the history of the Orange Order in Portadown for the previous two centuries. As for David Trimble raising a triumphal salute with Ian Paisley when the RUC forced an Orange march down the road in 1995, she wrote that Trimble "has a great capacity to look crosser than he is."[143] Trimble was chosen leader of the Ulster Unionist Party based on his behavior on the Garvaghy Road that year.

In 1998, the parades flashpoint in Belfast was the lower Ormeau Road, where Troy, remembering Gerry Adams's suggestion, had decided to paint murals in the marching season. About five hundred nationalist families clustered on a few blocks of the road, between the River Lagan and the Queen's University neighborhood. Most of them were refugees from earlier forms of ethnic cleansing, which included threats, intimidation, arson, and shootings. The neighborhood was neglected and poor, even though many people worked. Women, for example, took long early-morning bus rides to make one or two pounds per hour cleaning houses. The community was fighting blight. There was a single petrol station, which the authorities initially opposed with claims that it would be used for making molotov cocktails. In addition, there was a grocery store, pub, church, a storefront community center, and an Irish-language school. There, early in 1998, I met Gerard Rice, a former republican prisoner, now working with the youth in social programs. Gerard, I found, was a barometer to whether the peace process meant anything at all on the ground.

He lived with his wife Lucy and several children around the corner from the community center, in a completely barricaded house with a steel-reinforced door. The neighborhood could cope with poverty, he said, but felt unprotected against loyalist gunmen who could carry out a drive-by shooting and disappear in less than a minute, as two UFF assassins had in February 1992, killing five residents, including a fifteen-year-old boy.[144] On July 1 of that year, only four months later, loyalists marched by the same Ormeau Road location holding five fingers aloft in a gesture celebrating the murders.[145] Gerard represented an interesting new model of republican leadership that was emerging while Sinn Féin was absorbed in the Castle Buildings at Stormont. Gerard was not opposed to the peace talks, but neither was he willing to trust his fate to diplomatic discussions. In some ways, his new role was more hazardous than being an IRA volunteer. He was unarmed, visible, in the streets, an irritant to the RUC, still demonized by the loyalists. Gerard reminded me of Amiri Baraka's "living inside someone who hates me" when he said of the proposed peace accord, "At the very least it has to recognize that I am Irish and I am trapped here. I should be able to say I'm Irish without persecutions and assassinations." Another former Volunteer said bluntly, "Northern nationalism is locked into a state where one can only hope for benign tolerance at best or total hostility at worst. The diplomats are talking about giving the unionists, who are less than 20 percent of the island's population, a veto over life for nationalists here."

The people of the lower Ormeau Road, living in such a small cosmos, tended to know who the assassins were. Late on the night of January 18 that year, their volunteer sentries had watched a silver van with blackened windows and a new license plate (TAZ 9413, they told me) pull up to a taxi stand with the back doors facing the cabs. A resident called the RUC. A minute later, residents listening in on the RUC band heard the police radio report the existence of the silver van. The occupants of the van pulled away immediately.

The next night, the RUC closed their checkpoint on the Ormeau Road at 7 p.m. Thirty minutes later, eyewitnesses said, the identical silver van pulled up next to the cab of Larry Brennan, a fifty-two-year-old driver waiting for customers. Brennan was a Catholic engaged to a Protestant, Dorothy Creaney, who was determined to go ahead with the wedding despite loyalist death threats. As Brennan sat behind his wheel, a resident saw two local loyalists she claimed to recognize shoot him dead. The silver van drove off. Even though the names of the loyalists were given to the police, no one was ever charged for Larry Brennan's death. The newspapers, including the *New York Times*, utilized intelligence sources to spread the story that it was a "tit for tat" killing in response to the killing earlier in the day of a senior loyalist by a republican splinter group. The implication was that the impossible Irish were driven by vendettas once again, and that an innocent taxi driver had suffered the penalty. The media failed, however, to ask if the RUC had received a report about the silver van the night before, which would indicate that the Brennan murder was not in response to the day's earlier killing.[146]

A few days after Gerard Rice and I first met, he drove me an hour southwest to visit the residents of Garvaghy Road in Portadown. This was an even scarier place, reminding me of the back roads of Mississippi where civil rights workers could be halted and lynched with the knowledge of local sheriffs. One friend of mine said her hands perspired every time she drove on the motorway near the place. The Orange Order was founded in Portadown in 1795, and ever since the town has been considered the Orange citadel of Northern Ireland. During the annual July "parades season," the Orangemen in sashes, suits, and bowler hats had marched behind fifes and drums through Catholic/nationalist communities in a demonstration considered triumphalist and intimidating. The parades led to violence on many occasions before the nineties, but were now the focal point of a deepening struggle for power as the peace talks deadline neared. In essence, the proposed agreement would recognize majority (Unionist) rule, but strip the majority of its triumphalism and its antinationalist RUC. Otherwise it would be just another agreement on paper.

In her first month as Northern Ireland Secretary, Mo Mowlam approved the brutal use of the British army to allow "Orange feet on Garvaghy Road" as the Orange Order insisted. Now the confrontation had become year-round. The loyalist paramilitaries had been led until recently by Billy Wright, aka "King Rat" or "King Billy," who was killed in prison by a republican faction two months before my visit, in December 1997. Billy Wright was responsible for some thirty-five intimidation killings of Catholics across the North. According to the reputable *Sunday Business Post*, that "such a small group, in a highly visible loyalist population with its own links deep into the security forces and operating in the most policed and intelligence-sensitive terrain in Europe, could for at least nine years carry out random slaughter on this scale and remain in business itself raises important questions."[147]

The Garvaghy Road itself is an uninspiring sight, simply a mile-long blacktop ribbon running through modest housing estates on either side. At one end a tunnel connects to the loyalist-dominated civic centre where Catholics shop at a Dunnes store on the edge. At the other end it turns off to a small rural road to the Drumcree church, a cold gray hilltop edifice where the annual Orange parade begins with a church service. The nationalist residents were incensed by the Orangemen, comparing their 1,000 annual marches in Northern Ireland with "having 300,000 Ku Klux Klan marches through black communities in your country."

The leader of the group I met in a tiny community center was Breandán Mac Cionnaith (whose insistence on his Irish name infuriated the local Orangemen). McKenna, in the English version, was an independent elected councillor for the community. While not a Sinn Féin representative, he was, like Gerard Rice, a former republican prisoner; he had been convicted a decade earlier as an accessory in a bombing in Portadown. He lived with his wife and daughters in an inconspicuous two-story flat just off the Garvaghy Road. Brendan, like Gerard, was a marked man because of his leadership and associations, and could travel nowhere beyond the Garvaghy Road without risking his life. On that day of "sightseeing," however, he drove us to a loyalist neighborhood to photograph bloodthirsty "King Rat" graffiti, and to the entrance to the Drumcree church.

I visited the nearby two-story home of the Hamill family, whose twenty-five-year-old son Robert had been stomped to death by a loyalist

mob the previous April 27, 1997. His family was in the process of col-
lecting thousands of signatures petitioning Mo Mowlam to investigate
the case, not only to bring justice but to serve notice that such killings
would be taken seriously. Theirs was a somber, dimly lit living room with
the quality of a funeral parlor. There was a photo of Robert, a big, smiling fellow with a ring in his ear, who was described as apolitical and who
left behind a wife and three children.

I was stunned at RUC radio transcriptions and public relations documents regarding Robert Hamill's murder obtained by a bright,
dedicated local attorney, Rosemary Nelson, through Irish Watch, a
British-based human rights group. Several RUC officers in a Land Rover
observed the killing of Robert Hamill and took no action. Hamill and his
friends were returning on foot from a party when a loyalist gang inter-
cepted and attacked him. The press releases subsequently issued by the
RUC showed a pattern of cover-up. On April 27, shortly after the attack,
the press release declared that "police moved in to separate rival factions . . . [and] police themselves came under attack," a common RUC
theme. On April 30, however, as public attention was drawn to a slowly
dying Robert Hamill in a local hospital, the RUC story changed to a
"police Land Rover crew in Portadown town centre were alerted to a dis-
turbance and immediately intervened to gain order and prevent assaults,
[but] these officers were unable to contain the situation." On May 7, the
RUC acknowledged that the attack on Robert Hamill was unprovoked,
not a case of drunken Irish factions brawling. "It now appears clear that
four people, two couples who had left a social event at St Patrick's Hall,
were set upon by a large crowd. The two men in the group of four were
knocked to the ground and viciously beaten." On the following day,
Robert Hamill succumbed to his injuries. After Robert's death, the RUC
arrested and interrogated six young men, holding just one from the "large
crowd" they now were admitting had "viciously beaten" the young
men.[148] The Hamill family called for suspension of the RUC officers, one
of whem, they said, had taught karate to the boy who kicked Robert to
death. Mo Mowlam agreed to look into the situation. Twelve weeks after
his death, Robert's wife gave birth to their third child, a girl.

This was the atmosphere on the streets of Northern Ireland as the deadline for a peace agreement neared. Back in east Belfast, I talked with a worried Jackie Redpath, who said "the spiral back to conflict can be rapid, like water going down a bath, because the hope destroyed is worse than the hope you never had."

During the same week, a former US ambassador to London wildly accused Jean Kennedy Smith, Clinton's appointee to the Dublin post, of being "an ardent apologist for the IRA."[149] While the charge was flatly untrue, it exposed the widening breach between traditional American policies and the direction in which the Clinton Administration was heading.

That month I met with the Northern Ireland Secretary of State, Mo Mowlam, in Hillsborough Castle. We had first talked in 1997 during an official visit she made to Los Angeles, at the Counsel General's estate in a wealthy LA neighborhood, where a handful of Ulster unionists, businessmen, and liberal Catholics were invited for tea. Mo was considerably Americanized by having attended university in the States, where she was attracted to the women's, peace, and civil rights movements. I came to tea not knowing what to expect, and was disappointed by a conventional briefing on the "bright prospects" for investment and peace in the North. When I asked some critical questions, however, she was willing to discuss other issues informally. The official secretaries were taking careful notes on everything that was said.

Now she invited my wife and me for a briefing at a critical moment in the peace process. When we arrived at the royal castle on February 13, 1998, she wasn't there. Instead the door was opened by a friend of hers from London, an actor, who said he was instructed to entertain us. He was on holiday with his partner, another actor, from London. Within two minutes I accidentally triggered a security alarm when I searched for the light switch on a darkened wall. The crown forces were reassured everything was fine, and we explored the royal chambers on the first floor. Upstairs someone was cooking informally, and I sat down to prepare notes for my meeting with Mo.

It was a critical point in the peace talks because Mo was pondering whether to expel Sinn Féin due to the IRA having allegedly shot a loyalist and a drug dealer the previous week. Under the British interpretation of the agreement, political parties to the talks could be punished with suspension or exclusion for any ceasefire violations by armed groups associated with them. Clearly, I thought, Sinn Féin wasn't encouraging the IRA to kill anyone on the streets at this point in the process. Expulsion would throw a roadblock in the peace talks and encourage republican hardliners in their view that negotiations were a trap. The previous year, in May 1998, the RUC's chief constable acknowledged that all units of the Combined Loyalist Military Command had broken their ceasefires. But it was twenty months later, after at least five loyalist-sponsored killings in a two-week period, that a brief suspension of a loyalist party occurred. By contrast, Mo's government was proposing an indictment of Sinn Féin only four days after the latest killings. The rush to judgement was odd because of the nature of the two killings attributed to the IRA as well. One victim, Brendan Campbell, was a suspected drug dealer who once threw hand grenades and sprayed a machine gun at the Sinn Féin office in Belfast. The other was Robert Dougan, allegedly a member of the UDA's south Belfast hit squad. After the spree of loyalist killings of innocent Catholics in early 1998, graffiti on the Falls Road had become critical of the IRA for failing to respond – as the much smaller INLA had done.[150] Whatever the real stories, it appeared that the IRA was under pressure to maintain its traditional role or see the rise of other factions. An astute analysis by *Sunday Tribune* security writer Ed Moloney described the republican problem as follows:

The history of the republican side of the peace process is one of a vicious cycle: British obstructionism sapping grassroots republican confidence in the process [and thus] forcing internal concessions to the IRA which both limit Sinn Féin's room for manoeuvre and appear to vindicate the sceptical view that Provisional republicans can never be brought to democratic politics.[151]

Suddenly Mo breezed in like a tornado. She threw off her coat, scarf and wig (she was a cancer survivor), in that order, sat down in a deep cushioned chair with her legs up, and poured herself a glass of scotch. All the while her official secretary, a young man, stood by with a notebook and pen in hand. Wasn't Sinn Féin discharging its duty to discourage such killings? I asked her. Wouldn't their expulsion risk the process blowing apart? Didn't she know that Gerry Adams and Martin McGuinness were fully participating in a process that would lead away from guns? She seemed to believe that the Adams–McGuinness leadership wanted peace, and even admired them. But the "Shinners," as she called them, would have to be expelled the next morning, with assurances that they could rejoin the peace process if the IRA violence subsided. I was watching the real power in Northern Ireland at work. From inside the castle, after consulting the Prime Minister in 10 Downing Street, London, this hard-drinking, barefooted, bareheaded Englishwoman in front of me could expel an Irish nationalist party from peace talks on Irish soil. The only difference between Mo and previous lords of the castle was that she was openly eccentric and definitely likable – and, as events would prove, she was too dovish, too independent, for the British establishment.

I asked a few more questions about the peace talks generally. Did she believe it possible to achieve a binational and democratic Northern state? "Sure, why not?" she answered quickly. "Sometimes a settlement seems so close. Reform the North with our equality agenda. Create cross-border institutions, some with executive powers, some not." Did she agree that equality in the North meant Irish national rights, not simply civil rights within a United Kingdom? "Yes, there should be an opening to achieve a united Ireland sometime in the future. There will be a Catholic majority someday. Everybody knows that." She spoke fondly, maternally, of "Gerry and Martin" and "the Shinners" she was disciplining in the morning. Perhaps she was preparing a "decent interval," as Henry Kissinger had tried in South Vietnam, between the peace talks and the reunification of Ireland. Although she had approved the British army and RUC brutalizing the Garvaghy Road residents to put "Orange feet on Garvaghy Road," just as she now was approving the expulsion of Sinn Féin, my feeling was that her heart wasn't in it any longer. I was surprised at her frankness. Her secretary was observing and faithfully recording this entire scene.

Not long after, Sinn Féin was reinstated and, on Good Friday, the historical agreement was reached. It did not surprise me some eighteen months later when, after constant complaining by the unionist parties, Blair dumped Mo and replaced her with a new Northern Ireland Secretary, Peter Mandelson, whose subsequent unilateral suspension of the Assembly almost wrecked the agreement. The last time I spoke with Mo, she was calling to exchange views on one of her new government assignments, the regulation of genetically modified food.

Sinn Féin could be brought in from the cold in exchange for the ultimate dissolution of the IRA. That was the position of the national security staff in the White House and the State Department. The President's foreign policy team, starting with Secretary of State Madeleine Albright, was Europe- and NATO-centered. For example, in an interview on the "high points" of the Administration's global achievements – just after the President's third trip to Northern Ireland – Albright neglected even to mention the Irish peace process, while noting Bosnia, Kosovo, North Korea, the Middle East, Russia, China, Afghanistan, Cuba, and coping with the bombings of Nairobi and Dar es Salaam.[152] Northern Ireland was a peripheral issue compared, say, to the Balkans. Why do you spend so much time on Northern Ireland? I once asked James Steinberg, a National Security Council (NSC) deputy, Albright protégé, and a presidential point person for Northern Ireland. "It's important to the President," he replied. It was clear to the strategic thinkers that Northern Ireland was part of the President's political agenda, a place where he could receive adulation, one of his few legacies. But maintaining the US–British axis in NATO was too valuable to be ruptured over equality for Irish nationalists. The White House advisers' plan, as the talks deadline approached, was to "keep Sinn Féin locked into the process, offer them too little to make them happy but just enough to keep them from walking out."[153] Internal polling in Ireland showed that a compromise peace agreement would receive popular backing in a referendum across the island and that, the strategists believed, would force Sinn Féin and other political parties to accept it.

I didn't share their obsession with the "special relationship," and tried to argue that in the wake of the Cold War, America should adopt the role of peacemaker rather than policeman of the world. The planet was bleeding with conflicts that could no longer be described in the old Cold War terms which allowed the US cynically to rationalize supporting "our" dictatorial regimes against Moscow's. The conflicts now were about finding political and negotiated alternatives to violence as ways to cope with poverty, exploitation, and racism. The promotion of peace processes like the one in Northern Ireland, I felt, should be a central foundation of national security policy. I suspected that the President himself agreed, but his advisers preferred to look at the Irish issue as one of Clinton's pet political projects. As evidence of this, the policy was determined out of the White House, not the State Department. The President had redefined Northern Ireland as no longer an internal matter of the UK but also no longer under the jurisdiction of his own State Department. This decision made the peace process even more urgent since it might not survive past the President's second term.

Despite the novelty of the President's approach, his own technicians used a conventional negotiating model, once described (in another context) as drawing up "a plan that gives each side exactly half of what it wants."[154] The adversaries were defined as the two religious "tribes," not Irish nationalism versus British colonialism. Therefore the British were not a "side" that would receive "exactly half of what it wants," but a special ally with which the United States had only tactical disagreements. Beyond that misunderstanding, the half-a-loaf formula was transparent to everyone. It encouraged the unionists to play their "Orange card" by threatening to leave the talks if they were unhappy. As the later referendum would show, barely half the unionist constituency supported the Good Friday Agreement, compared to 99 percent of nationalists, so the authorities tried continually to appease them. It was wishful thinking on the part of the White House, Senator Chris Dodd and Fintan O'Toole that the same David Trimble who had danced a jig with Ian Paisley on the Garvaghy Road could become "the Hume of the unionists."[155] The comparison was misguided, particularly since Hume had devoted his entire life to opposing the kind of adamant sectarianism through which Trimble rose to power.

Former Senator George Mitchell most faithfully represented the President's instincts. Like Clinton, he approached the issue from outside the conventional State Department box. Like Clinton, he had discovered his Irishness late in life. He was raised to think of himself as a Lebanese American, and only at midlife did he become interested in an Irish immigrant ancestor who walked from Canada to Maine. He grew up with none of the inferiority complexes of Irish Americans, who felt they had to demonstrate repeatedly to the British that an Irish American can be "fair." Mitchell thus served as a powerful bulwark against pro-British State Department influences over the negotiating process. Most important, he was an empathetic individual, a serious listener, and an experienced negotiator. When I interviewed him late one night at the Europa, it was clear he'd developed a passion for Northern Ireland that transcended any narrow view of US interests. His new realization that he could do something to end the conditions that drove his ancestor to America kept him on task during the loneliest hours.

The final framework of the Good Friday Agreement, reached after thirty-six sleepless hours on April 10, 1998, was a perfect example of "managing the insoluble." For the British and the unionists, it preserved the United Kingdom, as Blair put it, into the lifetime of his grandchildren. It established an assembly and executive branch that would govern from the seat of British rule at Stormont. The Dublin claim of sovereignty over the North would be lifted. Because of the mechanism of proportional representation, it was clear that Trimble would be the prime minister (or "first minister," as the agreement named the office). The North would be incorporated into a new "Council of the British Isles" with Wales and Scotland.

But Irish nationalism was given recognition as well. The implicit deal was that in exchange for the ceasefire, Sinn Féin would no longer be ostracized. Visas, fundraising in America, and future investment were the rewards Clinton gave initially. The Good Friday Agreement enshrined the validity and equality of the Irish national identity for citizens of the

North, in effect promising a binational democratic arrangement subject to majority (Protestant) will for an indefinite period. The means of achieving equality were left to an array of commissions on equality, human rights, the Irish language, judicial reform, and policing, with deadlines for implementation. Based on its electoral strength, Sinn Féin would be allocated two portfolios in the executive. There would be no requirement of oaths or allegiance to the Crown. At the last moment an agreement was reached to release all prisoners of war within two years.

Sinn Féin carefully avoided calling the agreement a final settlement. Instead of a united Ireland there would be "cross-border" institutions on noncontroversial issues such as health and waste management. According to the *Sunday Tribune*, however, "An all-Ireland trade promotion body which would have supported the development of home-based industrial and service companies on both sides of the border was the major casualty of the negotiations."[156] The Dublin government would receive an expanded consultative role in the North. In republican movement terminology, echoing Michael Collins, the Good Friday Agreement was a stage, a transitional step, towards the goal of a united Ireland. With the IRA's ceasefire in place, Sinn Féin at last had an opportunity to achieve its goals peacefully and politically. Sinn Féin strategists wagered that, in the absence of IRA violence, their share of the Catholic middle-class vote in the North and the Fianna Fáil vote in the South would increase significantly. They also believed that unionism would be shaken as the scaffolding of Protestant privilege was torn down. They would be proven right: their vote in both the North and the South rose substantially, while unionism became gripped by paralysing tensions. But Sinn Féin's crisis was also political, since the agreement depended on political will in London, Washington, and Dublin, capitals not known for their stability or sympathy. The Good Friday Agreement was not a legally enforceable treaty, as its later suspension by the British would reveal.

While the republican consensus was strong, not everyone in the movement was pleased. Seeing the agreement as a sellout, new armed groups – variously called the Real IRA and Continuity IRA – already began to initiate action. Six months after the agreement, on August 15, 1998, the

Real IRA catastrophically botched an operation in Omagh, causing a 500-lb bomb to explode without an accurate warning, killing twenty-nine and injuring 310.[157] The splinter organization suspended operations temporarily, but it was clear that intermittent republican violence would continue in spite of the IRA ceasefire. Many others, while against the resumption of violence, were adamant in opposing any yielding of IRA weapons as long as the loyalist paramilitaries, the RUC, and the British troops were in place. Why should the IRA surrender in a war they didn't lose? they asked.

Others in the republican movement went along with the leadership strategy but with political misgivings. Many could not accept a modernized form of partition open to Catholics. They stood firmly for a thirty-two-county united Ireland. Others, like Máirtín Ó Muilleoir, believed that "it's a pity that the nationalist side didn't indicate earlier that they would have been willing to sign up to less than a United Ireland so that we could have had a healthy debate on the other options – including my old hobby horse, repartition."[158] If majority consent was required to end the Union – a proposal that guaranteed the Protestant/unionist grip on the North indefinitely – then why suffocate the nationalist majorities in Belfast, Derry, south Armagh, Fermanagh, and Tyrone? Why couldn't they – or all nationalists, for that matter – be represented somehow in Irish political institutions in the South? They could not vote in the election for President of Ireland, for instance, even though the President herself, Mary McAleese, had been born in the North and, indeed, was a former law student of David Trimble.

Since the primary strategic objective of London, Washington, and Dublin was to end the IRA military campaign – no nation-state could tolerate the presence of an armed rebellion threatening the official order – the security issue was the most contentious. Enormous pressure was placed on Adams and McGuinness somehow to put the IRA on a leash. At key moments, powerful Irish Americans joined the British demands "to keep up the pressure on Sinn Féin not to go back to violence" and give "comfort to the Ulster unionists," as Blair requested in his Washington meetings with the Irish American lobby.[159] There was no comparable pressure to "keep the British from going back to violence" and give "comfort to the unemployed Catholics of the North."

The Good Friday Agreement contained three crucial, interrelated points on security arrangements, though the overwhelming focus always seemed to be on forcing the IRA to effectively dissolve its military capacity. On decommissioning, the agreement required of Sinn Féin (and other parties) a "good faith" effort to "use any influence they may have" to achieve decommissioning of all paramilitary arms within two years. Decommissioning itself was not defined. If it meant IRA disarmament, there would have been no agreement at all. Instead the term was what the Irish call a "fudge," an ambiguity needed to facilitate compromise. Generally, decommissioning meant "out of commission," which could mean weapons verifiably not in use. Under this formula, the IRA would never surrender arms to the British, but could allow an international commission created by the agreement to verify that its arsenal was out of use. A further ambiguity concerned the nature of weapons to be decommissioned. Bombs manufactured from fertilizer and small arms could never be prevented except by creating a peaceful alternative. But the IRA also had supplies of missiles, rocket launchers, and automatic weapons obtained on international markets. Those arsenals represented the military capability that the USA, London, Dublin, and especially the Unionist Party wanted destroyed. Their desire for such decommissioning arose from one of two delusions, either that Sinn Féin could order the IRA to disband in the absence of an overall demilitarization of all parties, or that the IRA had been defeated and was simply looking for a respectable way out. Getting officials with a deeply ingrained superiority complex to understand that they could not defeat the IRA was the challenge for Sinn Féin.

Compared to IRA decommissioning, two other basic reforms of the security situation were ignored or deferred, another reflection of the British assumption of superiority and legitimacy against the IRA "bandits." First, the British were obligated to publish a plan for troop reductions, removal of security installations, and ending of emergency powers. While far from the original "Brits Out" demand of the republicans, the provisions clearly intended British demilitarization to levels of a "normal peaceful society." Finally, the agreement called for a "new beginning to policing" based on human rights norms and achieving the confidence of those most alienated in the past. While not the nationalist proposal to "disband the RUC," the policing reforms clearly envisioned the end of the RUC as an occupying army.

These elements of the agreement were deeply opposed by the British security establishment and army, as well as the RUC and Unionist Party. An exception was Michael Oatley, the former MI6 operative who had negotiated periodically with Sinn Féin since the seventies, and who helped convince Tony Blair that the deal was sound. Acknowledging that the ceasefire was initially opposed by many within the IRA, Oatley advised he had "no doubt at all" about the commitment of Adams and McGuinness to "finding a political way forwards." Prophetically, he blamed "picadors" in the British establishment, including *The Times*, the *Daily Telegraph* and right-wing Conservatives, for thrusting barbs into the flanks of the IRA so that "the animal eventually, with reluctance, will charge."[160]

Shortly after the passage of the Good Friday Agreement, the divisions in the North reached violent proportions once again over the Garvaghy and lower Ormeau roads. In July 1998, Barbara, Troy, and I were there as international observers among some 100 US, Canadian, and European activists, lawyers, church workers, and one member of the US Congress, Donald Paine, an African American I had known from civil rights days in Newark.

The crisis in Portadown had intensified each year since 1995, and now became a rallying point for the loyalists opposed to the three-month-old Good Friday Agreement. The RUC and the British army were assigned the task of blocking the narrow road and fields below the Drumcree church that separated the growing Orange tide from the nationalist community. On the lower Ormeau Road where Troy was painting wall murals, the tiny neighborhood was also readying for an all-out assault from the loyal orders. If the loyalists broke through the security lines, the ensuing bloodshed and havoc would have threatened not only the Good Friday Agreement but also the structure of the North as a whole.

In the week prior to the peak July 12 marching day, loyalist paramilitaries burned ten Catholic churches and attacked scores of nationalist homes across the North. Tony Blair and David Trimble denounced the arson and posed for photos in charred church ruins. But would they, could they, stop the angry loyalists gathering by the thousands at Drumcree? Trimble lobbied to overrule a Parades Commission decision that the parade should be prevented in the interests of peace. Blair, to his credit, deployed British troops to block the road. Arrayed against them would be up to 50,000 Orangemen and paramilitaries with guns. Could the British army, deployed in a thin line behind barbed wire, stop a charge? Would they shoot an Orangeman? And what of the RUC, whose members lived in unionist communities? Would they shift from their role as armed guards of the Protestant state to defenders of nationalists and republicans?

We tried sleeping in a home overlooking Garvaghy Road one night, but were kept awake by low-flying British helicopters and our own guilt at taking the beds of residents who needed their rest more than we did. Early the next morning, I was stunned to see the numbers of people wearing orange sashes or carrying union jacks filling the field in front of the British line. Since the parade down the Garvaghy Road wasn't permitted, why were the loyalist throngs allowed to gather in such force? They were bringing in food, tents, blankets, and ominous bags that contained fence cutters, petrol, and countless devices to be used in a siege. I knew that if a hundred nationalists in twenty cars with such equipment tried to caravan into Portadown they would be stopped, turned back, and probably arrested. Yet the Brits and RUC allowed this Orange army to gather and deploy overnight, intent on forcing their parade down the road. The security forces were now vastly outnumbered and could stop a loyalist charge only with lethal force, which might escalate to war right across the North.

I drove with two Dublin journalists across Portadown to the Orange hall, surrounded by newly arrived contingents of Orangemen preparing to march. The tension reminded me of walking into Mississippi courthouses in the early sixties. I felt that thousands of eyes were on my back, that unknown numbers of weapons were in the crowd. Yet we got inside the Orange hall to meet David Jones, the Orange Order's Portadown spokesman. He was slightly agitated given the developing situation, but tried to answer calmly why he refused to meet Brendan McKenna and seek a compromise. Jones reiterated the Orange Order's position that Brendan had committed violent acts and that "not enough time has passed" to soothe Orange feelings. In effect, the Orange Order was asserting the right to choose the nationalists with whom they would negotiate. It was a bizarre condition to impose since we were surrounded by scores of loyalists who, I was sure, had committed plenty of violence themselves. One of the Orange advisers at Drumcree was the Reverend Kenny McClinton, who was the main orator at the funeral of "King Rat," Billy Wright. McClinton was a convicted double killer for loyalist terror gangs, who had advocated beheading Catholics and sticking their heads on poles in the 1970s, and who admitted involvement in the most "macabre" and "heinous" forms of torture.[161] Was it fine to talk with him but not with Brendan McKenna? The conversation was becoming a scene, as Orangemen with camcorders approached.

We exited the hall and walked briskly through the Orange crowd, and drove around town to the Drumcree church itself. There, atop the hill, we briefly stood amid thousands of loyalists taunting and advancing on the barbed wire behind which the British and RUC stood at passive attention. Some of the loyalists were applying wire cutters while others were pacing off the length of the British line. Back at the church entrance, a largely middle-class Protestant crowd watched and waited. Among them, however, was a knot of Adidas-clad loyalist youth, including a tattooed fellow with shaved head who wore a T-shirt and blue running shorts. He was muttering something under his breath, keeping his head down, and briskly leafleting bystanders or the windshields of cars. Sensing that we didn't belong, he kept his batch of leaflets to himself as he passed us. I took one off a car and examined its content, which included a photo of Blair standing next to a Catholic priest in one of the burned-out churches. The leaflet was a celebration of church-burning, citing Deuteronomy 7:5

and Revelation 18:9 and 19:3. "Thus shall ye deal with them," it read; "ye shall destroy their altars and burn their graven images with fire. . . . And the kings of the earth, who have committed fornication and lived deliciously with her, shall bewail her, and lament for her, when they shall see the smoke of her burning . . ." In large letters it ended, ". . . THEY SAID, ALLELUIA, AND THE SMOKE ROSE UP FOREVER AND FOREVER." I'd never been in a place like this before and felt alone and vulnerable. But what I was experiencing was only a moment in the fanatical fury that faced Garvaghy Road residents every day, and undoubtedly had taken the life of Robert Hamill.

I drove the hour back to Belfast and, sensing an impending disaster, started faxing off letters to the President and American civil rights leaders. The White House was now involved in promoting cooling-off "talks," but that moment was past. The Drumcree issue was being used as a weapon to wreck the Good Friday Agreement and bring down the newly formed Assembly. Whether Clinton and Blair were receiving reliable intelligence was unclear. But I was certain that the British army and RUC could not (or would not) hold back what was coming. I did not understand their defensive passivity in the face of the massive buildup in front of their eyes. Seemingly no roads were closed to the loyalists still bringing in supplies. If the lines were breached, the IRA might have little choice but to stage diversionary actions across the North. More British troops would be sent as "peacekeepers." Demilitarization and RUC reform would be scrapped.

In this mood, Barbara, Troy, a friend, and I hurried out for dinner in Belfast, looking for a restaurant near the university. As we walked one block from the Europa through the loyalist area Sandy Row, I noticed a vacant lot filled with tires, kindling wood, and discarded furniture. In its center a young man seemed to be methodically setting the whole lot on fire. He and a couple of friends watched as a small blaze billowed in the dusk. It seemed odd that no RUC were at the scene, so I walked over to inquire what they were doing. The young man, perhaps fifteen years old, was setting fire to a mattress when I approached him. Trying to humor him, I asked if he was cold or setting the fire for another purpose.

He was quite willing to talk as he kept about his business. "Drumcree," he answered with an expressionless mask.

I persisted. "Drumcree? I was just down there. What is the connection between the fire and Drumcree?"

"To get our people down the Garvaghy Road," was the terse reply.

"Really? What's the plan?" I asked nonchalantly.

"We're going to burn everything around the city centre."

"And why do you think that will get people down the Garvaghy Road?" I asked.

"Oh, ay, it will work because we will burn the whole place. They will give in later this week," he said.

He seemed as confident as he was humorless, clearly believing in his contribution to pressuring the government to allow the march at Drumcree. The scary thought was that there were hundreds like him around the city, and thousands around the North.

We left him at his task, and continued to the restaurant three blocks away. Inside, it was a trendy establishment with well-dressed professionals drinking wine and eating California cuisine. They seemed utterly disconnected from the arson and mayhem down the street. By the time we finished our meal, the Sandy Row lot was ablaze. A firetruck was there, hosing the flaming perimeter. Two or three RUC Land Rovers had arrived, the officers standing in line and holding plastic shields as a growing crowd of loyalist teenagers threw rocks in their direction. There was no apparent plan to prevent Belfast from burning. Just as the young man had announced, the carjacking and rioting went on through the night.

A political crisis became inevitable. The defiant enemies of the peace agreement were threatening to destabilize all of Northern Ireland, using the marching issue as a pretext. If the authorities pushed the march down Garvaghy Road there would be a violent nationalist response on the lower Ormeau Road. It was July 9. Knowing nothing else to do, I wrote Clinton, Blair, and Mo Mowlam, saying the situation was like Little Rock, the President's home town, or Mississippi, where presidents Eisenhower and Kennedy were forced to intervene with force against "no surrender" segregationists who burned buses, bombed churches, killed civil rights workers, and resisted the desegregation laws. In this case, the fragile structure of the new state promised by the Good Friday Agreement was being overthrown.

At 4 a.m. on July 12, loyalists threw a molotov cocktail into the home of a Catholic woman, Chrissie Quinn, in the town of Ballmoney, County Antrim. Her three small boys were burned to death. I faxed Mo Mowlam:

> Now that three children are dead, burned in their sleep . . . I urge you to stand firm against the Orange Order . . . the weight of world opinion is with you. You must disperse the Orangemen from the streets back to their lodges where they can examine their consciences. . . . If you stand firm, I believe this crisis will be defined by historians as the end of the long war, and the end of loyalist terror against the new government created by the Good Friday Agreement . . .

And I faxed another note to the President:

> Troy called early this morning from lower Ormeau Road saying they've sealed the streets, and asked me to do something. Moments later I learned that three children were burned to death by the loyalists overnight.
>
> For God's sake I urge you to speak out forcefully against the apocalypse of sectarian anti-Catholic violence that is being fomented by the Orange Order before it is too late.
>
> The children are dying and there is worse to come unless the Orange marchers at Drumcree are dispersed, and Monday's parade at lower Ormeau Road is banned as well.
>
> It is your Good Friday Agreement, Mr President, that the loyalists are out to destroy, even if it means taking innocent lives in the process. I know you are being advised to be protective of David Trimble lest the Orangemen tumble him. The same call for solicitude and patience came from Southern governors in your Southern United States in the 1950s and 1960s. But there comes a time to understand

the impatience of nationalists under mortal siege . . . and to insist that the Orangemen shall not pass until they examine their consciences and accept nationalists and Catholics as brethren under both God and the Good Friday Agreement.

The test of wills at Drumcree, however, was over for now, as the Orange leaders realized the moral and political disaster caused by the dead Quinn boys. Whether they took it to heart was open to question. Certainly the Reverend William Bingham was deeply ashamed, preaching that "no road was worth a life." The media communicated Bingham's sorrow around the world, but failed to report that he was jeered and attacked by loyalists immediately after the sermon. At Drumcree, the Orange leadership firmly denied that the boys' deaths had anything to do with the confrontation. The leaflet with the biblical quotes invoked to celebrate the burning of Catholics was still circulating at a Drumcree rally a week later.[162]

My summer recess from the legislature over, I rushed back to Sacramento with worries about Troy on my mind. He was moving from one place to the next on the lower Ormeau Road, staying up till all hours frenetically painting murals opposing the imminent loyalist march down the road.

Some were blunt: WHAT IS IT ABOUT NO THAT YOU DON'T UNDERSTAND? Another was elaborate, featuring a big-footed Orangeman beating a drum as he marched past a locked-up nationalist community depicted only by eyeballs staring from the darkness. The mural was called A POSTCARD FROM THE EDGE, *Having a wonderful time! How was your summer?*

To appease the loyalists for prohibiting the Drumcree march, the government was insisting that the lower Ormeau Road be cleared for the Orangemen on July 13. I knew the drill. The Royal Irish Regiment (RIR) and the RUC would arrive before dawn to barricade all the side streets, preventing people from leaving their block. Then the protesting residents would sit nonviolently to block the street. A band of perhaps fifty Orangemen, banging loudly on huge Lambeg drums, would march across a bridge that separates the Lower Ormeau area from a loyalist community. The RUC, backed by Land Rovers, pointing guns with gas grenades and plastic bullets, protected by shields, would forcibly remove each person sitting in the street until the path was cleared for the march.

The residents were meeting to decide their response. It was rumored that Sinn Féin wanted a token march to proceed in order to preserve the peace agreement (which, ironically, promised to eliminate sectarian and triumphal parades). The British, with tacit White House support, wanted the lower Ormeau Road march to "balance" the prohibition on the Garvaghy Road. Bullet-proof vests were being urgently sought for residents' leaders who would be in the streets. Finally, given the death of the Quinn children, the Lower Ormeau residents, with bitter reservations, decided to allow the Orange march on the condition that it be absolutely silent and take no longer than fifteen minutes. They further decided to shame the march, nonviolently. Troy and others went all over Belfast buying up huge rolls of black cloth to make flags of shame that would be draped from every window for five blocks.

I was pleased that Troy had lived through the siege and made his small contribution. Whatever else he chose to do in life, his Irish roots were planted.

But the loyalist marching season of 1998 never ended. Marches, rallies, rioting and vigils for Drumcree continued in Portadown through the year, as the issue remained the magnet for opponents of the Good Friday Agreement. Loyalists even included "traitorous" RUC officers as targets for their attacks, accidentally killing one with a pipe bomb. Then, on March 15, 1999, attorney Rosemary Nelson was killed by a sophisticated explosive device attached to her car, as she was leaving her home in the Portadown area. The lawyer for Robert Hamill's family, I had attended a press conference with her during the Garvaghy Road siege. She had complained previously to the authorities of RUC threats to kill her, and received no protection. Her murder was the second time that a prominent human rights attorney had been assassinated at home by loyalists. The first victim was Patrick Finucane, who was shot in 1989 while at home in north Belfast with his wife and three children. Rosemary Nelson had testified before the US Congress in September 1998 that "no lawyer in

Northern Ireland can forget what happened to Patrick Finucane," and a United Nations Special Investigator concluded that the RUC "engaged in activities which constitute intimidation, hindrance, harassment or improper interference" towards lawyers for republicans or nationalists. The Finucane investigations had produced substantial evidence that RUC officers shared intelligence files with loyalist paramilitaries, that they knew of the planned hit on Finucane and did nothing to prevent it, and that one of the loyalists' most aggressive killers was a British agent. Nevertheless, nothing was done as the plot against Rosemary Nelson unfolded. Nine days after her mutilation, the pro-police Commission for Police Complaints responded to her earlier request for aid. In a modest but rare rebuke of the RUC, the Commission identified sixteen "serious concerns" about her case, including findings that RUC officers were "hostile, evasive, disinterested [sic] and uncooperative," and that several exhibited an "ill-disguised hostility to Mrs Nelson."[163]

By comparison, a British paratrooper named Lee Clegg was acquitted that March of the killing of a Belfast teenager despite the judge's description of Clegg's testimony as "untruthful and incapable of belief." And ten days after Rosemary Nelson's murder, the young man accused of stomping Robert Hamill to death was acquitted.[164]

That summer of 1999 I returned to Garvaghy Road, where one incident of sectarianism would be engraved permanently in my memory. As the Orange Order marchers approached us, an Irish American activist named Shannon Eaton was sitting on the wall of a cemetery snapping pictures. She was out of sight as the loyalists arrived, giving fingers to the nationalists and shouting epithets. RUC officers in full body armor with German shepherds stood facing a few score nationalists while their backs were turned to the menacing crowd. "Get over here, Blondie," the loyalists were shouting at someone. "You Fenian whore, why don't you pray to the Virgin Mary, you fucking cunt? . . . I'm going to strangle you in your rosary beads." Where was Shannon?, I suddenly wondered. Then, only seconds later, she came stumbling through trees, head bleeding, with an RUC officer holding her arm. Just out of my eyesight, the loyalists had attacked her, dragging her off the wall. As she blacked out, she had seen one of them trying to drive a pole into her face. Two teenagers and an older Catholic woman pulled her back into the cemetery before the RUC arrived.

Shannon was vomiting as she was pulled into an RUC Saracen, shouting, "I want to see my American friends." I ran over with several others to prevent her from being arrested, and to provide emergency assistance. She was allowed to sit on the grass under the supervision of medics and human rights observers. None of her assailants was arrested.

I walked over to the RUC officer, a woman, who'd walked Shannon away. I asked her to go back to the wall to search for the shattered parts of Shannon's camera. Then the unexpected happened. The officer seemed to be trembling as we walked. "Assholes, the assholes," she exclaimed. I didn't know if she meant everyone in the confrontation, or the loyalist mob. It turned out she meant her fellow RUC officers, who had seemed to react with nonchalant indifference. "I'm ashamed," she told me, still shaken. Then she went back to her professional demeanor, helped find the broken camera, bagged it for Shannon, and disappeared into the ranks of officers.

The Role of Police in War and Peace: The Patten Commission

It was plain that radical reform of the RUC was a minimum requirement to achieve the stated goals of the Good Friday Agreement. The RUC, 94 percent Protestant, emerged from a war mentality designed to preserve an undemocratic social order. With 12,692 personnel and 159 installations in January 2000, the RUC was a powerful institutional obstacle as it faced the prospect of becoming a dinosaur. A goal of the peace agreement was to transform it from the security force of the colonial state into a professional police service in a democratic society.[165]

Orchestrating this "new beginning" of RUC reform was assigned to a commission headed by the Right Honorable Christopher Patten, former governor of Hong Kong. That Patten's previous mission was to lower the Union Jack over a former colony was not the assurance the unionists were looking for. Patten was a progressive in the colonial mode, a genteel version of Mo Mowlam. His mandate, however, was limited to preparing a report and recommendations, a task which took nearly eighteen months spanning the violent marching seasons of 1998 and 1999. The other eight commissioners included one moderate Catholic, Dr Maurice Hayes, and two Americans, a New York academic and a former public safety official from Massachusetts. They held packed, intense public hearings all across the North, and added visits to several other countries, including Britain, Canada, South Africa, Spain, and the United States, where they visited Los Angeles.

Curious at what lessons they might take back from LA, I contacted Patten and asked him to meet with local civil rights attorneys who had labored for police reform since the Watts rioting of 1965 – the same span of time as the "Troubles" in Northern Ireland. We had our experience with prestigious commissions – one headed by CIA director Allen Dulles in 1965, the other by future Secretary of State Warren Christopher in 1992 – which, despite significant reforms, had failed to remove the conflicts which led to the largest American urban rioting of the twentieth century. The Los Angeles Police Department (LAPD) had had an African American chief since 1993, and 43 percent of the force was black, Latino, Asian, or women officers – by coincidence matching the percentage of nationalists in the Northern Ireland population as a whole.[166] Plainly, Los Angeles had failed to end the festering antagonisms between police and the inner city (as demonstrated by the so-called "Rampart" scandal – involving widespread beatings, framings, and planting of evidence by paramilitary "crash" units at the Rampart Street precinct – which flared in September 1999 and led to federal intervention). If anything, civil rights advocates in Los Angeles felt they should be studying the "new beginning" prophesied in Northern Ireland.

On January 21, 1999, the Patten Commission, absent one member, held a private two-hour meeting with civil rights attorneys I brought together in Los Angeles, including a former California attorney general, John Van de Kamp, civil rights attorney Constance Rice, Amnesty

International attorney Paul Hoffman, and LA County's police ombudsperson Merrick Bobb. The meeting was held where the Patten commissioners were staying, a breezy inn in Agoura Hills, an over-whelmingly white area of suburban Los Angeles County with a large residential population of police officers. Their trip was clearly designed by someone to avoid direct experience of the areas of Los Angeles which most resembled the Falls Road.

Earlier in the day the Patten commissioners received a briefing from the chairperson of the police commission appointed by the Mayor of Los Angeles, and heard that the LAPD was making great strides. The LA Commissioner failed to share that the LAPD's inspector general had quite recently been removed because she demanded independent access to police files. We pointed out that police departments routinely engage in high-powered public relations campaigns, classify internal documents, and operate with organizational cultures based on codes of silence. Affirmative action over three decades had resulted in appointment of an African American chief but with African Americans, Latinos, Asians, and women clustered at the lower rungs of the police ladder. A pattern of "racial profiling" and "at-risk youth profiling" was the center of con-troversy, with police refusing to turn over crucial data on the targets of their street frisks and stops. The lack of independent investigative powers for the inspector general, who had an office with only seven profes-sional staff, was another battleground. And the result? Half the African American and Latino youth populations of Los Angeles had been stopped and/or arrested and incarcerated at some point during their lives. The total number of inmates in state and local facilities across California was 240,000, the highest per capita incarceration rate in the USA. The country as a whole had an incarceration rate of 600 per 100,000 compared to 105/100,000 for Northern Ireland.[167]

Patten was committed to listening, rather than previewing any rec-ommendations of his commission, but he choked loudly at hearing the size of California's inmate population. The group listened carefully. At evening's end, John Van de Kamp spoke for the Los Angeles delegation in urging the commissioners to take full advantage of the "new beginning." Connie Rice urged them to dispose of the "organizational culture of war" which made police departments view the world as a conflict between civilization and subversives. I tried to stress that independent neighborhood complaint centers were among the confidence-building measures that were still lacking in Los Angeles. All of us tried to note that Northern Ireland didn't have thirty-five years for gradual police reform, the time span of the slow-moving Los Angeles effort.

The key difference that was being blurred, as usual, was that Los Angeles, and the United States as a whole, was a democratic place with elected officials who appoint police chiefs and legislate law enforcement reforms. Whatever significant progress had occurred in four decades usually resulted from independent lawsuits based on constitutional principles or political pressure from voting constituencies. Northern Ireland still lacked any such democratic accountability. It was a province of the United Kingdom whose Royal Ulster Constabulary, as the title implied, was appointed and accountable to the Northern Ireland Office. If the nationalist majority in Belfast demanded a local police force, their local city council was powerless to create one. If they wanted an independent investigation of RUC complicity with paramilitaries, only Her Majesty's Government could establish one. If they demanded American-style constitutional protections, they would learn that the British government had no constitution in place – though they would be assured that British acceptance of European human rights standards was imminent. Apart from his good liberal intentions, Chris Patten had been a servant, and a Right Honorable one, in the regime that controlled the province of Northern Ireland from Westminster. While the nature of the Patten Commission created an appearance of impartiality, of detachment, of being a civilian inquiry, in fact it was only an advisory body which could never question the state itself.

The final Patten Report, issued six months later in September 1999, followed exactly a model of police reform consistent with the underlying colonial presence. The British went on a public relations and political offensive seeking support in the United States. Mo Mowlam must have called her entire American Rolodex, myself included, urging support for the Patten Report as the "best we can do under the circumstances." She was specifically concerned that Sinn Féin not hold out for deeper reforms, for fear that the whole package would disintegrate.

The vision spelled out in the Patten Report – human rights, a new beginning, a police service in place of a police force – sounded better than its practical application. The core proposal was for a growth of the Catholic percentage in the service to a "goal" of 29–33 percent in a decade, accomplished through an annual process of 50–50 recruitment.[168] Given the bureaucratic slowness of institutions, this would be relatively rapid progress. But it still meant that the percentage of nationalists in the population would still be significantly greater than the proportion of nationalists in the police service in the year 2010, perhaps twice as high. By the Patten formula, the police service would not be half Catholic for twenty years. Would that convince republicans, or nationalists as a whole, to support the decommissioning of the only "police service" – the IRA – that guarded their neighborhoods against loyalist attack? Not likely. According to RUC statistics, there were 139,588 licensed weapons in the hands of Northern unionists in 1998, an actual increase from the previous year, one gun for every seven unionists, an arsenal that would not be affected by decommissioning in the least since they belonged to individuals rather than paramilitary groups.[169]

The Patten proposals rested on religious definitions more than political ones. Thus the solution could be interpreted to propose more Catholic participation in keeping the colonial law-and-order. At the same time, Patten proposed removal of "Royal" from the name of the service, consistent with the Good Friday Agreement's ban on oaths and symbols of the Crown. But little in Patten explicitly recognized the need for nationalists to have confidence that their political loyalties would not be suspect. A possible solution – to allow community-based "restorative justice" structures to take the place of both the IRA and the RUC in nationalist areas – was rejected as a possible "front for paramilitaries." At the same time, it was decided that longtime membership in the Orange Order was not in itself a disqualification for a police officer. There would be no tribunals or sanctions against RUC officers with past records of brutality continuing on in the new force. The weapons used to fire plastic bullets – which had killed seventeen people, including eight children, by 1999 – would continue to be used for crowd control in more sophisticated and potentially lethal form.[170]

The Patten Report revealed again where the imbalances lay in the observance of the ceasefires. The report noted that loyalist violence continued on a far higher level than republican violence during the first eleven months after the Good Friday Agreement. Excluding the Omagh bombing by a republican splinter group, the Patten figures attributed sixty-four shooting incidents and fourteen bombing incidents to republican groups, compared with ninety-six shooting incidents and 122 bombing incidents by loyalist groups.[171] In the single month of June 1999, after the Patten Report was finished but not yet released, Portadown loyalists attacked a mixed-marriage couple by hurling a pipe bomb into their home, killing fifty-nine-year-old Elizabeth O'Neill, a Protestant who had lived in the house with her Catholic husband for twenty years.[172] Pipe bombs were thrown at several other houses in Portadown and Belfast during a single week.[173]

The Patten Report, in keeping with the British (and, I believe, US) negotiating strategy was less than Sinn Féin desired and expected from the process, but a proposal that couldn't be rejected. On the other hand, the unionists, loyalists, the Northern Ireland Police Federation, and most Conservatives in Westminister joined in adamant opposition to everything from the name change to proposals for accountability. Once again, they threatened to collapse the entire Good Friday Agreement unless they had their way. Or, some thought, they wanted to exchange Patten implementation for IRA decommissioning. While this was never part of the deal, the thought of the IRA decommissioning its capacity to defend nationalist communities – demanded by May 22, 2000 by David Trimble – when it would be at least another decade before Catholics might make up 30 percent of a reformed RUC was difficult to take seriously. The replacement for Mo Mowlam, Blair political confidant Peter Mandelson, would soon insist on more compromising of the Patten proposals to appease unionists. By January 1, 2001, there was little tangible sign of the new beginning in policing Northern Ireland, aside from some initial efforts to recruit Catholics. Even the concept of reform was too much for the Police Federation, implying as it did that something was wrong with the RUC's law enforcement. At the time of the report, exactly 977 of 13,300 RUC officers were identified as Catholic – down from 10 percent in the 1960s and 21 percent in 1923 at the creation of the Northern Ireland state. At some future point, however, it appeared that the policing, decommissioning, and demilitarization agendas would have to be settled simultaneously, or not at all.

If the RUC was beyond reform, except in the most gradual and unenforceable terms, what was the status of the British army? Was there any vision of its departure from Northern Ireland beyond the abstract commitment to plan for demilitarization "if the security situation allows"?

At the time of the Good Friday Agreement, there were 13,000 British troops stationed in the North. While the discourse from London, Dublin and Washington focused on extracting decommissioning and statements that "the war is over" from the IRA, no one was asking the parallel question: was the war over from the British military perspective? Public discourse continued to define the IRA as bandits, irregulars, guerrillas, rebels, and the British as the authorities entitled to exercise sovereignty. Furthermore, according to public discourse, the British army wasn't involved in a war at all, but only playing a security role in Ireland's age-old "troubles." It was seen as crucial that the British army and the RUC were perceived as having won this unacknowledged war against the IRA and thus preserved the Union. Any peace agreement linking IRA decommissioning with British demilitarization, therefore, was outrageous to British security officials by implying moral, political, or military equivalency between the official security forces and the subversives. The British military establishment turned mutinous in 2000 and threatened Blair with resignations if there were any such linkage. ("Military figures today launched a pre-emptive strike against suggestions for token decommissioning by the IRA and the Army. . . . The government refused to comment on specific allegations of a 'revolt' by military chiefs." *Belfast*

Telegraph, February 22, 2000) Their alternative, supported by David Trimble, was "no guns, no government," that is, if the IRA didn't begin decommissioning, Sinn Féin should be denied the seats they were entitled to in the newly established executive cabinet at Stormont.

The embarrassing problem with these British army and unionist scenarios was that they were demanding what they had failed to achieve on the battlefield. The military chiefs and the Northern Ireland Office ("the securocrats," as nationalists called them) couldn't admit this failure; their superiority complex made them believe that the IRA was losing the war and suing for peace.

I had suggested in the *Andersonstown News* that the alternative to the "no guns, no government" scenario, if pushed to the maximum, would be "no government, no peace." In other words, if the British securocrats insisted too much on decommissioning, there would be a collapse of the new institutions and a return to violence. I knew that Sinn Féin was committed to ending the military conflict, and that the IRA was supportive of any political alternative that truly ended the system of undemocratic privilege. But many republican activists were absolutely opposed to any form of decommissioning until the war was really over – if then. "The Brits and the politicians assume we'll take half a loaf," went a typical comment, "but they don't understand us at all. We don't need half a loaf. We don't even need to eat."

My belief was that the parties should orchestrate a simultaneous, three-level endgame, reflecting the stalemated nature of the military conflict. On the same date, the Patten reforms would be accelerated to install trustworthy police units in all nationalist communities, complete with community liaisons and restorative justice mechanisms for nonviolent offenses. Second, the British army would announce a timetable to dismantle fortifications and begin loading its combat units aboard ships and helicopters. Third, the IRA would order its active service units to cease operations in England, dump arms or put its offensive weapons beyond use, to be verified by the de Chastelain commission. It would retain a self-defense capacity indefinitely, or until loyalist weapons were put out of use as well. Proposals for linkage along similar lines were floated in the media, drawing immediate threats of resignation from Britain's top general, who was fiercely opposed to "a gesture of demilitarization alongside terrorist groups in Ulster." ("Gen. Sir Charles Guthrie, the Chief of the Defense staff, threatened to resign this week if the government continued with plans to involve the army in a gesture of demilitarization." *The Daily Telegraph*, February 26, 2000) I also heard from certain republicans in south Armagh, who flatly said "never" to any idea of decommissioning. "Not one bullet, not one ounce" (referring to Semtex) was sprayed on walls in republican communities.

Heart of the Matter: South Armagh

South Armagh, where my ancestors surely walked the hills, holds a place in Irish – and British – imagination infinitely larger than its modest scale. Nestled on the border against Louth and Monaghan, its mountainous beauty and cultural legends are background to its military history as the center of a long resistance to successive invaders, an enchanting place with a "loric landscape" of undulating beauty. One can see as many as eight counties of Ireland from its hilltops. The nearest cities, Newry and Dundalk, are small in comparison with agricultural valleys and fields, lakes that multiply toward Cavan in the west, and the mountains and passes that have long demarcated the Northern planters' strongholds from the native Irish to the south and west.

In a rural area of only 23,000 residents, most of them republicans, 123 British soldiers have been killed since 1971, not to mention scores of RUC officers, by one of the most successful guerrilla movements in the twentieth century. A journalist with access to RUC and British security sources, Toby Harnden, says "no other part of the world has been as dangerous for someone wearing the uniform of the British Army."[174] When the Northern Ireland Secretary, Merlyn Rees, called south Armagh "bandit country" in 1975, he was using an image rooted in centuries of occupiers' frustration.

Winston Churchill and David Lloyd George had no particular wish to include south Armagh in the partitionist state. In fact in 1925 the Boundary Commission recommended south Armagh be incorporated in the South on the grounds that British units would be "unfortunately situated if fighting took place."[175] But south Armagh was incorporated nonetheless, and indeed proved to be "unfortunately situated," something like a fishhook in the throat of the Union.

I visited south Armagh several times after the signing of the Good Friday Agreement, believing it to be the key indicator of whether the war would end, as envisioned in the Good Friday Agreement, or would someday resume. Harnden, a *Daily Telegraph* bureau chief now with the *Washington Post*, described the people of south Armagh as having a "defiant abnormality," a choice of term that locates their resistance in a peculiar mindset apparently unlike any other.[176] They considered themselves Irish, more captives than citizens of Northern Ireland. They did not recognize the border that winds invisibly through their farms and fields, except for purposes of the illicit commerce that adds to their stereotype. "The border has no currency" in south Armagh, said journalist Nell McCafferty.[177] Crossmaglen, the heart of south Armagh, "would do your head in, if you're not used to it," she added.

> Most people in Crossmaglen work south of the border, just a few miles away. . . . They bring home wages in Irish punts. They pay punts for goods in Crossmaglen, which are marked in Irish prices. The goods themselves are bought in the Republic. You can always, if you are off your head, pay British money at British prices for these goods, but you will pay more.

My sense is that the people of south Armagh are classically Irish, not "abnormal." Unconquered, they were occupied, but never assimilated. If they were "fierce," it was because they survived one foreign occupation after another. They were rural, undistracted by the rootless consumer society. If they were parochial, it was because they were local. They watched the same Ulster news propaganda, the same British programming, the same American soaps, as everyone else on the island, but they were less affected. In short, they seemed to know who they were. They produced "the boys that beat the Brits", as one of them said. The "abnormality", it could well be added, was the British presence in the area.

The people of south Armagh descend from legendary "bandits," that is, the numerous secret societies formed by the native Irish after dispossession from their lands at the hands of foreign "bandits." In legend, their history can be traced to Cuchulainn, the hero of the Ulster sagas, whose warrior image is depicted in Belfast murals and repeated in children's stories in Irish-language schools. Reading the epic Irish myths of battles against invaders on the adjacent Cooley peninsula, or on the fog-covered Slieve Gullion that looms over south Armagh where Cuchulainn received his name, one might be drawn to the parallel with the "traditional heroic ideal" of American Indians described by the theologian Thomas Berry:

> The Indians have never accepted human life as ordinary, as something that can be managed in a controlled or painless manner. They realize that life tests the deepest qualities within the human personality, qualities that emerge in heroic combat not merely with others, but also within oneself and the powers of the universe.[178]

Just south of Slieve Gullion I explored the three-story tower of Moyry Castle, whose stone ruins sit on a grassy hilltop just off a one-lane road known only to the locals. The fortress, still containing old stone watch-towers with small turrets, propelled me back and forward in time. It was a freezing day, and I tried to imagine crown forces peering through their small apertures into woods that harbored the wild Irish natives they so feared. The power and vanity of the imperialist motivation was beyond me. Four hundred years before my arrival, in 1600, on this spot, Lord Mountjoy defeated the Irish Gaelic forces, securing the valley known as the Gap of the North below me. Now, with my camera's zoom lens aimed from the castle's entrance, I could photograph a new British "castle," a watchtower atop the adjacent hill, still monitoring south

Armagh for the wild Irishmen of the south Armagh IRA brigade. In 1989, two RUC officers were killed in an IRA ambush in this place, one of them the most senior RUC official killed in the war.[179] From Moyry Castle, the seventeenth-century watchtower, I could see across the horizon to most of the fourteen watchtower bases built there by the British since the 1970s. The British had confiscated homes, community centers, farmlands, and sports grounds to construct perhaps the most elaborate high-technology fortifications in the world. The irony that they were repeating a failed history must have weighed on their effort to deny it.

My hosts in south Armagh were an association of farmers and residents, whose purpose after the IRA ceasefire and Good Friday Agreement was to draw public attention to these British watchtowers as evidence that the conflict was far from over. Their organizing secretary, Toni Carragher, was a driven, fashionably dressed woman who worked in Newry and lived with her husband, a farmer named Peter Carragher, and their mischievous eight-year-old son, also Peter, in a sturdy two-story residence on the Glassdrumman Road five minutes from the south Armagh center of Crossmaglen. She took photos with a professional eye, ran a one-room office from her study, and coordinated outreach to the outside world, including Dublin ministers and members of Congress in Washington.

Her husband Peter fit the stereotype of the solid republican farmer rooted in south Armagh over many tangled generations. Indeed, one explanation for the IRA's success in this small area was the scarcely broken chain of family relationships to the land going back to ancient times. Looking at Peter I sensed the fusion of nationalism and the land question, the personal with the political. From his kitchen door I saw a flat stretch of farmland which, at a point invisible to the outsider's eye, crossed over the border into the South. Surveying his domain, he said bluntly, "The British are not welcome here, and they never have been. They cannot operate anywhere around here, except if there is a ceasefire. Instead of digging in, they need to dismantle the installations and go."

Down the Glassdrumman Road a few hundred yards from the Carragher farmhouse stands a huge watchtower known to the British as

Golf Three Zero, constructed apparently to surveil the nearby border farm complex of an individual considered by the authorities to be the leading IRA figure. The fourteen towers collectively are meant as patrol bases, lines of defence, and means for surveillance of suspicious ground movement. Under them are submarinelike complexes each holding as many as thirty-two British soldiers. They are continuously supplied by a fleet of droning helicopters, which also serve in combat. While they are ominous in appearance, and create considerable speculation about surveillance technology, the fact is that the watchtowers symbolize the fact that the British forces are pinned down. They are physical evidence that the British army has been fighting a war – not mediating some tribal troubles – for thirty years without success. It is widely believed, at least by the security establishment and the media, that south Armagh is not only the headquarters of the IRA but also the bomb factory that produced the 1996 Docklands explosion that ended the first ceasefire, and a base of the dissident IRA faction that set off the Omagh bomb.

I tromped through the fields of watchtowers one day with a local farmer named Henry. The feeling of being watched from below ground through tinted towers above was unsettling. The watchtowers were desolate in appearance, though beehives of intelligence agents and soldiers swarmed just below them in the bunkers. Henry, like many residents I spoke to, complained that their cattle were stampeded and traumatized by the continual low-flying helicopters, that uncontrolled runoff was polluting the streams and fields with garbage and toxins, and that the watchtowers were permanent confiscations that proved the British would never leave. I dropped in on one family living in a stucco home just yards below a huge tower built on the land their parents had owned. Two children were watching television action figures, and a baby was fussing, as we talked in a kitchen in the line of sight from the watchtower. Another elderly couple lived next door to the corrugated wall of a base at the center of Crossmaglen. As we sat for tea on their outdoor patio, the noise and vibration of military helicopters just 100 feet away was ceaseless. The RUC base overlooking the Crossmaglen square resembles a heavily protected structure from outer space, with coils of barbed wire and thick screens overlaying its surveillance apertures. Below on the street, shoppers visited McNamee's bakery, Lee's optician's, and a local pharmacy. (The RUC station on the square was removed in 2001, but not the larger base behind it.)

I spent an evening with Jim McAllister, who is described in Harnden's book – which is disliked as inaccurate by local republicans – as "the authentic voice of republicanism" in south Armagh. I wanted to know how Irish legends and culture affected local people, particularly those who played a part in the struggle. In the Western world today, as in Ireland during the Gaelic Revival a century ago, there is a surge of interest in Celtic spirituality and culture that is largely unconnected with nationalist struggles for jobs, housing, police reforms and independence. I wanted to know whether Irish republicans in south Armagh involved in the military or political struggles had time for explorations of this past that surrounded them.

"The legends and the culture are a background influencing the character of people around here," said McAllister. Take the Gaelic language, he explained, "even if they don't speak it, it's always there inside the English language. If a baby's crying, for example, people will always say things like 'What's on that child?' Even the names of places are Gaelic, they would mean nothing in English. Camlough means 'crooked lake,' so we say 'Camlough lough,' meaning the 'crooked lake lake.'" As many as seven hundred Irish words, he guessed, were circulating inside the English language. McAllister, an elected member of the local council, recalled a debate with a unionist member, whose surname was Kennedy, over whether the town should have an Irish-language office. When the unionist vehemently objected, McAllister called him a "a Kennedy," explaining amid laughter that the name means "misshapen head" in the Irish tongue.

The Cuchulainn saga, McAllister went on, was also a background to local life, "maybe the way you Americans think of the Founding Fathers." Cultures can distort but never erase their founding myths, he said, noting that "even computer games with action figures are like the Cuchulainn myth. And you can get all the Irish sagas on the internet!"

The epic stories do "give us a knowledge of who we are, that we're not a made-up people, not a newly created people, but a people trying to re-create ourselves, what Gerry Adams (and Connolly before him) calls the reconquest of Ireland. Colonialism decries local culture, it even makes it illegal. The Catholic Church did it too, stamping out or co-opting our old traditions. The magic wells became holy wells and then they became church sites. No way was Saint Bridget a Christian, she lived before Christ!"

People remain very superstitious but won't necessarily admit it, he continued. The signs are in folkways and humor, for instance in the practice of leaving certain bushes and trees littered with little notes petitioning for cures, in avoiding cutting down lone bushes that belong to faeries for fear of losing a farm, or in the common joke that goes, "I don't believe in faeries but they're there, you know."

At the Lough Neagh funeral of an IRA Volunteer several years previously, McAllister said, thousands of people walked around a Celtic cross in a counterclockwise direction, to the consternation of surrounding British soldiers and helicopters. "As we were walking, a cow came up from the lake and gave birth to a calf," he recalled incredulously. "Ardbo, or sacred cow, was a place on the shores of the lake where the first people arrived from the Middle East, all very poor, because they'd lost everything, when all of a sudden a cow came from out of the lake. They discovered they could get milk there, and they stayed. That sacred cow kept the tribe alive."

When I asked if there was a new Celtic revival, McAllister said, "Look at the language, which IRA prisoners learned in prison, shouting out one word after another as lessons. Now many people are giving their infants Irish names, and new housing estates Irish place names." He warned that "There's also Gaelic language without politics" being promoted along with "regeneration" schemes to "soak up youth who would have joined the IRA or been unemployed." As for the Slieve Gullion, access to its cultural resources was blocked by the British army. "Kids can't go up there because of the army. You can't have a successful Celtic revival without removal of the British presence," he said.

What interested me in this encounter was the contrast between Jim McAllister and the stereotype of south Armagh republicans as fanatics or thugs. If Jim McAllister were living in the former Soviet Union or contemporary China, his status as a member of a captive minority would be called a human rights violation.

Harnden's account, which professes to be "not intended to be a work for one side or the other,"[180] is often weighted towards security sources. For example, he recounts the arrest, "confession" and sixteen-year imprisonment of republican Pat Thompson without mentioning Thompson's testimony that he was beaten bloody, taken to a hospital, and physically coerced to sign a statement. Instead the author cites the Crown prosecution who claimed Thompson's confession was made "quite freely."[181] Relying on information from security sources who have been unable to define, detect, or defeat the IRA is inherently hazardous and borders on the irresponsible.

It is virtually impossible to access the hidden culture of republicanism in south Armagh, but certain factors are clear. One source told me why the republicans had succeeded in turning south Armagh into a quasi-liberated zone. He observed that the area was 99 percent nationalist in the first place, which meant "the whole struggle from day one was republicans versus the British army." In Belfast, by contrast, the large unionist population guaranteed the British an ally to gather intelligence and conduct Protestant–Catholic sectarian wars. Residents of south Armagh simply didn't "go into the barracks" (join the RUC). Files on south Armagh republicans, three hundred of which had recently been found in an Orange hall in County Antrim, were gathered by the police, not by neighbors. Even with watchtowers and devices that allegedly could read a business card at 600 meters, he said, south Armagh was impregnable. "It's been said we are the nerve center of the armed struggle against British rule, which is true. This will be the last British outpost in Ireland."

He believed British intelligence was flawed by arrogance. "The Brits' mistake is that they underestimate us," he said. "We may not be college graduates, we may not look smart, but the people here are very, very intelligent." He added, "Every armed action was meant to grow from politics, to make the English public ask, how many more of these must we go through. The media would hide the facts, but the IRA could bring the war to their front doors. They are still talking about the Brighton bomb." He was referring to a bomb fitted with a twenty-four-day timer which an IRA unit concealed in the Grand Hotel in Brighton; it blew up on October 12, 1984, during a Conservative Party conference, and Prime Minister Thatcher was nearly killed. In a chilling communiqué, the IRA stated: "Today we were unlucky, but remember, we have only to be lucky once."[182] "When they write the military history, they'll see that the brains behind that were second to none," he said.

He discussed how south Armagh republicans would judge the Good Friday Agreement. First, would it advance British withdrawal? So far it hadn't. The British were refurbishing their fortifications and claiming new security threats as justification. There would always be "security threats" so long as there was a British military presence in Ireland. In any event, the British bases and watchtowers were ineffective in stopping military action by new republican groups or the Provisional IRA in the event the agreement collapsed.

Second, the agreement was an instrument to "internationalize the movement to expose unionism," he said. By that measure, Sinn Féin commanded a larger audience than ever before and the unionists, especially at Drumcree, were exposed as bigots to the whole world. So far, however, the presence of the British army remained largely invisible, and south Armagh was ignored as a tribal backwater by most public officials and the media.

Third, the agreement would be valued if it "divides unionism" between pro-agreement unionists and diehard opponents like Paisley. A new alignment in Irish politics between pro- and anti-agreement forces might transcend the divide along sectarian lines. "Of course, what is bad for unionism is not necessarily good for us," he observed. The Good Friday Agreement could collapse, the Paisleyites could become the Protestant political majority, excessive concessions could be given Trimble to keep him afloat, or feuding loyalist paramilitaries could unite in the renewed killing of Catholics.

No republican I met in south Armagh mentioned a single reform the

Good Friday Agreement had delivered. "The only change here is the ceasefire by the Provisional IRA," one person said. "And the Brits are taking advantage of it." Investment and tourism were chilled by the presence of the helicopters and fortresses. The Patten proposals were dead on arrival in south Armagh. Republicans scoffed at a 30 percent Catholic RUC; instead, they would settle for nothing less than a "thirty-two-county Irish police force." They wanted no part of Northern Ireland.

One meeting more than any other illustrated the gap between British and Irish perceptions of south Armagh. In November 2000, a delegation of British members of parliament (MPs) came to Crossmaglen on a fact-finding tour. The meeting occurred upstairs at a social services agency overlooking the square. Below us stood a huge monument to the IRA, an iron statue of an ancient Irishman glaring across the square at the RUC barracks. The British MPs – including Helen Jackson, Valerie Davie, Jenny Tonge, and Chris Leslie – were acting in the composed, objective, almost disconnected manner that makes Irish nationalists consider them perfidious. The community activists, including Jim McAllister and Toni Carragher, were giving back in the manner that the Brits find unreasonable. I took notes on the rapid-fire discussion, which went like this:

MP: "We are amateurs here, not experts; our purpose is to hear your views. What are the solutions as you see the situation?"

Local Activist: "There are fourteen hilltop outposts here, which we believe are being used long-term for military training purposes. Demilitarization is in the Good Friday Agreement. What are you doing about it?"

MP: "We want to be helpful. We thought the Good Friday Agreement was a way forward. What has to be done? Tell us."

Local Activist: "The IRA have put away their guns. Why are the outposts still here? Listen to us and stop picking your nails!"

MP: "I would love to see a united Ireland, but the thing is, there are hundreds of thousands here who desperately want to stay British – what is the answer?"

Jim McAllister: "Unless you implement the Good Friday Agreement in full, it's worthless. And if it fails, the loser will be constitutional politics, because people will go back to the old ways."

MP: "But the Good Friday Agreement makes a constitutional change. Under the agreement, Northern Ireland is part of the United Kingdom. That's at the heart of the agreement. That's what the negotiations were about. What are you asking us to do now?"

How blithely patronizing were these MPs, how deeply in denial of their own responsibilities. Jim McAllister told them flatly that "to move forward, the British have to recognize their fault, their responsibility, not act like they are somehow assisting the Irish as a neutral mediator." But it was exactly that message the MPs were blocking out. When the meeting broke up, signaled by an NIO officer tapping his wristwatch, I was convinced that the British had no intention of abiding by the Good Friday Agreement, except for portions favoring their position. But if that was the case, if Irish nationalists were supposed to continue "living inside someone who hated them," who could rule out a "return to the old ways"?

As I kept returning to south Armagh, sifting the ancient myths, the elusive family links, and the shadowy contemporary conflict, I discovered that the hunger striker Laurence McKeown was building a house there for his family, in the tiny township of Mullaghbawn, the place in Irish myth where the young man Setanta was renamed Cuchulainn and became the defender of Ulster. Mullaghbawn, described as a "very wild and disloyal place" by a district inspector in the 1920s, seemed no less wild and disloyal now, a flat, green valley of dispersed houses linked by the narrowest of roads, all in the shadow of Slieve Gullion. There Laurence was steadily constructing a two-story granite home at the very base of the mountain. When I asked why he and Deirdre had chosen the site, they invariably said it was "beautiful" or a "good place for the children." As Jim McAllister had suggested, they placed no emphasis on the historic or cultural significance of Slieve Gullion. Yet the mountain was hardly a background; indeed, it was their backyard. I guessed that they were re-enacting the ancient Irish warrior myth naturally, not like wanderers seeking their roots.

There was more to learn from the arc of their lives. Both Laurence and Deirdre had been involved in the thick of the conflict for two decades. Deirdre had joined a revolutionary socialist group as a young woman, and evolved from there to leadership in the many efforts to regenerate west Belfast through community trusts, especially those promoting alternatives for young people. She and Laurence lived for years in the heart of Ballymurphy, the densely populated housing estate where fierce resistance against the British army was waged from the first days of the "Troubles." There they raised their two small daughters Caoilfhionn and Orlaith. From her small front yard, and when walking to her office up the road, Deirdre looked every day into a huge graveyard. For several weeks in 1998, just across her sidewalk, a mound of flowers marked the burial site of Terry Enright, a respected community worker involved in sports and environmental projects with Deirdre. Yet Deirdre carried on, unbroken. She looked forward to moving to rural Mullaghbawn after thirty years in west Belfast, and to getting involved with Sinn Féin in community organizing. Her life, like the struggle itself, was moving into a new phase. Instead of war interrupted by temporary ceasefires, it looked more like peace occasionally interrupted by the violence. It was time to build a new family life in a new Ireland.

The story of Laurence epitomized that of some 15,000 republicans who had been incarcerated over three decades. At the age of nineteen, on August 2, 1976, Laurence was arrested as the British government commenced its criminalization program and, incidentally, during my first visit to Belfast. More than anything else, the British policy exposed the fundamental identity question at the heart of the conflict: were those who violently resisted British rule a criminal caste of primitive Irishmen, or were they genuine Irish nationalists fighting an occupier? The little-recognized irony was that republican prisoners like Laurence behaved like "animals" to assert their dignity as humans. Ordered to wear the prison garb of common criminals, they refused, were stripped naked, locked down, and thrown blankets to cover themselves. Thus they became known as "the blanket men." Prisoners who rejected criminal status were placed "on the blanket." Next they were denied access to toilets, and were given chamber pots instead. When their guards refused to empty the pots, the prisoners poured urine out the cell doors and threw their feces out the windows. When the guards threw the feces back into the cells, the prisoners decided to smear them on the walls.

In these appalling conditions, widely interpreted as a fight between barbarians and civilization, began a five-year campaign for status as political prisoners that culminated in the hunger strikes of 1980 and 1981. When a hunger striker died in July 1981, the *Daily Mail* called it a "battle to achieve political status for thugs," and opined that the IRA ordered Joe McDonnell to starve to death because "to the IRA Joe McDonnell is worth more dead than alive."[183] In fact, according to Laurence and Gerry Adams, the IRA Army Council was against the hunger strike.[184] Laurence volunteered for the hunger strike to the death which began on March 1, 1981. Bobby Sands died on May 5. Laurence started fasting on June 29, after three more prisoners had died. On a certain level he also died, passing into a coma after seventy days. His family, however, chose to intervene as is allowed when prisoners lose consciousness, and he slowly returned to the world of the living. For many months, he could not keep his balance when walking around the prison yard. When we first met in late 1992, it was sixteen years after his arrest and conviction, eleven years after the hunger strike, and six months after his release from Long Kesh. He was six feet two inches tall, his head was closely shaved, he seemed gaunt and his eyes were sunken. Whether it was the myth or the man, you couldn't look at Laurence without being reminded viscerally of his experience.

During his imprisonment, he had obtained a BA degree, and subsequently achieved a PhD at Queen's University in 1998, writing his thesis on the experience of republican prisoners. He immersed himself as well in a republican ex-prisoners' self-help organization, Coiste na n-Iarchimi. Laurence titled his thesis *Unrepentant Fenian Bastards: The Social Construction of an Irish Republican Prisoner*.[185] Unrepentant, yes. But a criminal, a thug, a terrorist? Laurence was the living contradiction of the Anglo-British stereotype of their Irish adversaries. Though perhaps exceptional, he was also representative of the maligned IRA volunteers incarcerated during the war. His story – and theirs – was rooted in a long tradition of rebellion passed on in saga, song, and sacrifice. What is often overlooked is how the republican prisoners' story has foreshadowed both the course and the possible ending of the conflict itself.

The hunger strikes of 1980–81 were like a set-piece battle against British rule, a confrontation to the death, very much in the spirit of Terence MacSwiney, the IRA leader and Mayor of Cork, who fasted for seventy-three days to his death in 1920, asserting that "victory is won not by those who inflict the most but by those who can endure the most."[186] Afterwards, however, a phase of demoralization and confusion set in. The strikers had failed to achieve all their demands. Tensions erupted between families. It appeared that war and imprisonment would continue without end.

In this context – roughly like the military impasse prefiguring the 1993 peace process – the republican prisoners adopted a new, more flexible strategy of working within the prison framework with the same ultimate objective of liberation. To unify their ranks, they moved to the "conforming" wings, where demeaning prison work was expected. They secretly sought to make it necessary to segregate the republicans in special blocks without provoking a negative response from the British. They subverted prison work by using toolmaking equipment to make and smuggle out Irish handicrafts like Celtic crosses. The concrete factory in the prison became known as "the independent republic."

They learned Gaelic, often one word at a time. They held political education classes, and developed democratic give-and-take in place of hierarchical lectures. They formed poetry workshops, and transported their writings on toilet paper "bangled" deep inside their rectums. They created a book fund and communal arrangements to share food and tobacco. They studied the educational techniques of Paulo Freiere where the "students" are the "teachers." They published a prison journal for themselves and the outside world. (One of its articles, on gay rights, was yanked in the American edition and replaced by a Gerry Adams appeal for funds.)

The first editorial in their journal reflected their evolution from a mainly military mindset: "The state is not sustained by force alone," it began. As Laurence later wrote, after the hunger strike, "we knew that head-on confrontational, physical battles were not the way to wage prison struggle . . . we could achieve our goals through exploiting inconsistencies in prison rules, divisions within the prison hierarchy, the fears, anxieties and emotions of prison guards on the ground, and by intellectually undermining the prison rules."[187]

While benefiting from these accommodations to the prison system, the republican prisoners never retreated from resistance or co-ordination with the IRA. The prison officials were more amenable to accommodation rather than repression because the IRA was targeting their personnel on the outside. Using tactics of surprise, the prisoners achieved an unprecedented mass escape in 1983. They held one of the H-blocks for two hours, seized a lorry and broke out of Europe's most high-security prison: of thirty-eight escapees, nineteen got away. Fourteen years later, in March 1997 (during the peace process itself), an escape tunnel over 100 feet long was accidentally uncovered in Long Kesh. On December 10, 1997, another republican prisoner escaped in the disguise of a woman attending a holiday party. The prisoners' movement's greatest victory, however, was the Good Friday Agreement's promise to release them all, a clear recognition that their "crimes" were political in nature.

By analogy, the republican movement in general has reached a consensus that "confrontational physical battles" are no longer the way to wage the struggle for freedom. Just as the prisoners chose to work within the system, hollowing it out as they advanced step by step, so the republican movement has chosen to enter the very institutions they formerly attempted to shatter. The military struggle appears to have been necessary to force the institutions of state and police away from their policy of "criminalization" towards one of political acceptance of Irish nationalism. But, in the process, those same institutions of the colonial state have undermined their own purpose. To use a prison metaphor, the republican movement is achieving what gains are possible within the system while still tunneling their way beyond partition.

And that, perhaps, is why Laurence, Deirdre, and their children live at the base of Slieve Gullion. They are far from retired from the struggle. They have tunneled their way into the "independent republic" of south Armagh, and await the fall of London's empire in the North as a whole.

Back to Danny Morrison's

Danny Morrison had a solution. The IRA should detonate ten pounds of Semtex in the quarry on Black Mountain above Belfast and when the Ulster Unionist Party say it isn't enough, add ten pounds more. And when the unionists ask how can they know that another ten pounds isn't hidden away for future use, General John de Chastelain could supervise and weigh 100 pounds dug up in a Kerry bunker and blow it up in front of television cameras. And when unionists are still suspicious, claiming that if NASA was able to fool the world by simulating the moon landings in the Nevada desert, what could the Irish American lobby not do with digital cameras, the IRA could surrender its AK47s, 12.7s, RPGs, Semtex, detonators, coffee jars, and beer kegs, and throw in the staff of *An Phoblacht* for good measure . . .

We were laughing around the dinner table in his Falls Road home. The decommissioning demand would never end, he predicted, because the British and unionists need to triumph. "They want to say, You lost, we won, you were wrong, we were right, you murdered, we defended," he said, "and if they can't win, they want decommissioning to cause a split within the nationalist community." That was it, I thought. A split among republicans over the Good Friday Agreement would be accompanied by bloodshed, which in turn would serve as a rationale for the continued British military presence, once again to save the Irish from themselves! The fundamentals hadn't changed.

At the table was the ninety-year-old father of Rita O'Hare, the Sinn Féin activist I'd met in Dublin on my first visit twenty-four years ago. Rita was unable to visit her father in Belfast for fear of being charged with taking part in offences in those former times. Her dad, in excellent physical and mental condition, lived not far from Gerry and Colette

Adams. He was a Belfast Protestant who had long ago married an Italian Catholic who came to Belfast to open an ice cream store.

Danny was now married to Leslie Van Slyke, a BBC reporter from Toronto. As they lit candles, turned on a stereo, poured themselves some wine, and served up pasta, I savored the contrast to the earlier time when a Morrison home life was an impossibility. I still slathered my food with ketchup mixtures, but otherwise the quality of life was improving. Yes, the conflict continued; Danny's son, Kevin, now twenty-three, the same age as his father when we first met, had not so long before been kicked in the groin by the RUC and hospitalized for not leaving a dance in a timely manner. But there was no going back. Life was changing and it could not be stopped.

Danny had just published a prison diary, *Then the Walls Came Down*, mainly consisting of personal notes to Leslie during the years in Long Kesh. The title was drawn from a Traveling Wilburys song:

> And the walls came down
> All the way to hell.
> Never saw them when they're standing,
> Never saw them when they fell.[188]

In the diary, Danny was dreaming about listening to the song while in bed with Leslie, then his girlfriend. He wakes up to the melody and realizes it is five in the morning in Crumlin Road jail, in October 1990. The diary is a reflection on the personal dilemmas of republicanism, issues usually never voiced, whether, for example, love and marriage are sustainable in a time of war, and what happens to individuals if they are not.

Danny's journey began as a romantic, not a revolutionary. When he was eighteen years old waiting on tables, he devoured *Anna Karenina*, *Wuthering Heights*, and the writings of Graham Greene. The experience of British occupation made him a propagandist instead. His first marriage collapsed, perhaps from the strains of the time. In prison he returned to his own personal "troubles," those of the heart. In an essay on "Love and Jail," he wrote:

Just to the side of the struggle, out of sight, lie the corpses of marriages and broken relationships shed by the despairing, those who simply couldn't take it any more. . . . [For] someone struggling desperately to hold onto love, no appeal to the happiness of the past or to the promised rosiness of the future can allay . . . the pain and desolation of the present.[189]

The lives of republicans were "completely and indefinitely subordinated to the pursuit of the struggle," he wrote resignedly. The personal "troubles" were repressed amid the larger "Troubles," but at huge, and invisible, psychic cost. This suffering takes many more forms than marriages collapsing when a partner is imprisoned for years. Danny recalled a young imprisoned loyalist on the A wing at Long Kesh, who was arrested for "gross indecency," that is, for having a fifteen-year-old boyfriend. If it had been a fifteen-year-old girlfriend, Danny noted, "he would be a hero among his mates." Instead, they beat and verbally abused him. But the young prisoner fought back, shouting out the personal scandals of the other loyalist prisoners. The authorities would not move him, and "he was eventually overwhelmed by abuse and hatred." One night he crushed his cell lightbulb, ate the glass, was taken to hospital, and never seen again. In response, Danny wrote a short novel pondering the legitimacy of such a relationship and the "wrathful, intolerant and hypocritical response of society." The book, *On the Back of the Swallow*, is still read across Ireland.[190]

The prison diary is a book about the *personal decommissioning* that still lies ahead for tens of thousands in Northern Ireland. And because of its tensions, not in spite of them, it is about the irrepressible humanity of Irish people in the struggle against oblivion. One might think, therefore, that Danny Morrison would be welcome in the United States, where he has been invited to lecture at Harvard University as well as other institutions. But Danny Morrison has been rejected for a visa to the USA. He is a "security risk" because, in 1983, he tried to enter America illegally from Canada to attend an Irish American dinner. He was deported immediately. Today, when he applies for a visa waiver at the US consulate in Belfast, he is informed that the FBI opposes his entry. If he rejoined Sinn Féin, however, he would be admitted to the US because Sinn Féin members receive waivers in the interests of the peace process. The absurdity is that Danny Morrison was first banned from America because he was a Sinn Féin member and now is banned because he is not.

The FBI still demonizes republicanism and, according to Morrison, informed the US consul that he is "against the peace process." Danny Morrison refuses to surrender his hard-won identity as a writer. The issue is an important one, since Morrison would humanize the lives of Irish republicans perhaps like no one else, raising questions about why the war was fought in the first place, and how far America has strayed from the time when Thomas Emmet aided Thomas Paine.

PART III

Recovering the Irish Soul

We soon got the idea that "Italian" meant something inferior, and a barrier was erected between children of Italian origin and their parents. This was the accepted process of Americanization. We were becoming Americans by learning how to be ashamed of our parents.

Leonard Corello[1]

I was born in 1941, but my black soul is much older than that. Its earliest incarnations occurred eons ago on another continent somewhere in the mists of prehistory. Thus, there are two selves: one born a mere fifty-eight years ago; the other, immortal, who has lost sight of the trail of his long story. I am this new self and an ancient self. I need both to be whole. Yet there is a war within, and I feel a great wanting of the spirit. The immortal self – the son of the shining but distant African ages – tells the embattled, beleaguered, damaged self, the modern self, what he needs to remember of his ancient traditions. But the modern self simply cannot remember and thus cannot believe. The modern self has desperately tried, but the effort has been only marginally fruitful. Maliciously shorn of his natural identity for so long, he can too easily get lost in another's.

Randall Robinson[2]

I see now that there's no point in Ireland getting the six counties back, if Irish culture has been totally forgotten and destroyed. That will have meant that they've won in the end. So I'm going to try to get as involved as much as I can.

Shane MacGowan, cofounder of the Irish rock band the Pogues[3]

I visited the Jewish museum in New York and was very impressed. I also visited the tenement museum, excellent, real history, real lives. Why is there not a museum about the Irish in New York? All they seem to do is clap themselves on the back by having parties with dignitaries. Irish America wants to forget their poverty or else just remember it in a begorra-ish way. It was the real Irish people who made America, the people who helped build the Brooklyn Bridge, the people who lived through the Orange riots in New York, the people who struggled to raise twelve children in the tenement blocks of Orchard Street. And yes we have come a long way over there but let's put it down permanently and create a museum about the Irish, good and bad, successful and not so successful, but the reality. It upset me that there is no permanent exhibition to the Irish in New York. Is there one anywhere? I feel that it has something to do with the inability to come to terms with who they really are and that they still wear the weights of their ancestors many generations later.

Niamh Flanagan, west Belfast, September 2000[4]

Prologue

Over the centuries, an independent Irish identity has been forged in efforts to resist confiscation, discrimination, forced emigration, and assimilation into British and WASP cultural standards. The nationalist and human rights struggles in Northern Ireland over the past thirty years are the latest chapters in this long quest for an unfettered Irish identity. The so-called "Troubles" are a continuation of the Irish saga, not a deviation. Those who sentimentally respect Irish rebels in the distant past, however, all too often ignore their incarnations today. Those who delight in leprechauns or revel in Celtic spirituality without ever visiting Northern Ireland are the hollowed Irish, perpetuating the only version of Irish identity the masters will allow.

A degrading anti-Irish sentiment today is still ubiquitous. I was listening to Nora Casey of the *Irish Times* one morning on Pat Kenny's RTÉ Radio One (November 15, 2000) express her total frustration at Irish stereotypes on British television. The soaps, she complained, were all about drunken, wife-beating Irishmen, or characters on *EastEnders* going back to Ireland with trinkets for the natives. One media outlet called for listeners to send in the 100 best Irish jokes, one of which was "Have you heard the one about the latest ethnic minority?" Another, defended by an editor of the *Sunday Telegraph*, asked, Why did the Irish get all the potatoes and the Saudi Arabians get all the oil? Answer: Because the Irish had first choice.[5] "There are five million Irish in Britain," she exploded. "We lose two-thirds of them in every generation: one-third don't care, one-third identify as British, and one-third remain Irish. The top, most successful Irish businesses here [in Britain] don't want to be identified as Irish. I want my children to grow up with heroes and heroines, not thinking Irishmen are drunken, layabout wife-beaters." This rage was coming from a very successful Irish professional, who sounded very much like African American professionals in America. She was discussing a phenomenon of the past that is still current. The 2.5 million Irish immigrants living in England, the largest immigrant minority in Europe, have mortality rates 30 percent higher than other citizens, and much higher rates of schizophrenia and depression. A report in the *British Journal of Psychiatry* concludes that "the Irish experience of colonialism and racism makes them distinctive among Britain's white population."[6]

Robbie McVeigh was angry too. A PhD from a Protestant background, he was the butt of anti-Irish attacks while studying at the London School of Economics. After being stopped once by a policeman and questioned for having a Nelson Mandela book in his car, he became so frightened on a trip to Ireland that he threw away possessions like a Starry Plough button that might seem "suspicious." "Even now it is hard to explain how debasing the experience was, but the crucial thing was that they made me forget that I had done nothing wrong."[7]

In America, assimilation often makes Irish Americans the butt of their own jokes. On my fortieth birthday, a friend of mine hired leprechauns to host a celebration of my Irishness. In my closet I have a T-shirt with a drawing of the popular potato-head character, inscribed, "Mr Potato Head goes to Ireland." When we're not indulging in self-hating jokes, our distorted sense of Irish pride is channeled into drinking or reducing our Irishness to lay religious activity, St Patrick's Day parties and cheering for Notre Dame.

In our long day's journey towards success, Irish Americans are in danger of becoming lost souls. We are trading our real identity for a new and trendy, commercially packaged "heritage." As Marilyn Halter points out, "shopping for an ethnic identity has become big business for contemporary consumer society."[8] We may climb the corporate ladder – by some estimates, one-third of American CEOs are Irish Americans – but these material gains are often achieved at the expense of deeper spiritual benefits. We can ignore Northern Ireland as a place apart, or we can act to end the cycles of injustice and denial that have forced millions of our own people to leave their country. We can become a permanent caste of Reagan Democrats, adopting the same superior pretensions and free-market nostrums that doomed our own ancestors to catastrophic suffering, or we can learn from our origins to identify with the landless, the hungry, the poor, and the immigrants in our own country and abroad. We can reap the privileges of being white or, remembering the shame of being classified as simians and asking what is whiteness but privilege?, we can transcend the superficiality of our skin color to join in solidarity with the majority who are darker than ourselves. We can dismiss the underclass in our own cities as hopeless, inebriated, violent incorrigibles, we can dismiss as inferior the two billion people living on wages of one US dollar per day, and in doing so live lives of perfect denial of our own origins. Or we can see ourselves mirrored in the roughened, unkempt, tearful faces of today's persecuted, and act to alleviate their suffering as we once hoped others might do for us. We can keep grasping for self-esteem and respect through an institutionalized, almost fossilized, Church that has too often joined with the powers that oppress, that has too often dismissed or demonized the interests of women, Mayans, Jews, Muslims, or the unconverted wretched of the earth, the rebels and revolutionaries, the homosexuals and free thinkers, or we can join the renewal of spirituality, including Catholic spirituality, by identifying with religious dissenters, liberation theologists, goddess and nature traditions, and the deeply creation-centered spirituality of Brigid and Colomcille that infuses the original Irish character.

A novel by Irish expatriate Sean Kenny, *The Hungry Earth*, explains the choice each must make between denial and the truth.[9] Kenny's hero is a Dublin yuppie banker named Turlough whose modern life is falling apart. His career is stagnant, his marriage is empty, and he is sunken in a desultory affair with someone at work, when suddenly he inherits a cottage in the remotest western part of Ireland. Thinking of selling off the cottage for debt relief, or perhaps using it for weekend dalliances, Turlough makes a visit, during which he stumbles and, in a common Irish theatrical device, finds himself catapulted back in time to his ancestors' lives during the Famine. Drawn towards that hidden past, he quits the bank, leaves his marriage and girlfriend, and becomes an eccentric Irishman involved in studying folk culture, seeking lost artifacts, calling in to radio shows to complain about the deliberate amnesia towards the past, all while waiting, Yeats-like, for the next trance to reveal the identity of his ancestor buried in the graveyard beside the cottage. In his dream-state, he encounters landlords, big houses, starving peasants, bumbling social workers, and a hard-edged "bandit" who robs, kills, and even eats human flesh to survive the catastrophe. In the climactic ending, Turlough becomes free when he embraces the fact that in part he owes his very existence to an Irish rebel who, in desperation, became a cannibal so that later generations might live.

One of Kenny's important lessons is that we must embrace and turn around the stereotypes imposed on us, not simply hide them or feel obliged to overcompensate for them. For example, when I once heard David Trimble pontificating on the need for Sinn Féin to be "house trained"[10] before being allowed into peace negotiations, a statement which followed the British government's earlier insistence on "decontamination," I heard the echo of my master's voice down through the ages and realized one reason to be Irish: someone should occasionally go into the Big House and shit on the master's rug. If the reader cringes at this statement, so do I. But why do we cringe? It is the master, after all, who calls us dogs. The Trimbles are without shame. If we cringe, is it because the master is in our psyches? Do we not have to purge the master's contamination of ourselves? Can that be done politely?

I am not suggesting that we become our stereotypes, but that we let the master know we will not accept them. This means our closet doors of shame must be opened, that we must not settle for a superficial respectability, for an Irish version of becoming an Uncle Tom. We must not be ashamed to say we come from a rebel tradition. We must not seek respectability by rhetorically denouncing the IRA or washing our hands of the Irish conflict. That amounts to collaborating in the British and Anglo project of killing our roots. While no one who is a principled pacifist or critic of armed strategies need defend the IRA, it is just as important that Irish people stop trying to prove they are house-trained.

Our "triumph in the English-speaking world" – adapting the subtitle of Thomas Keneally's fine book on the nineteenth-century Fenians – is not goal enough.[11] The native always wants to prove he is the match of the colonizer – in everything from business achievement to war to Nobel prizes, to Olympic gold medals. This is a necessary catharsis for the colonized as well as a valuable learning experience for the colonizer. But an equally important, and more lasting, triumph, is when the colonized feel no necessity to prove anything. Having proven themselves equal by emulation of the colonizer's ways, the colonized can focus on the restoration of their culture, history, identity, and interests because they are inherently important, not to prove something to the doubting world. Something like this awakening is occurring in Ireland and the Irish Diaspora today, in ways large and small.

Mary Robinson, a human rights lawyer who became Ireland's first elected president in the nineties, next became the United Nations Commissioner for Human Rights, for example. She won the post in part because the United Nations recognized that the Irish are unique in the so-called First World for having been degraded and brutalized as a colony of the British. It is impossible to imagine a British prime minister being appointed to the same position. As Irish president, she wept in empathy during a visit to Ethiopian famine victims. She traveled to Boston to commemorate the first memorial to the Great Hunger. As UN Commissioner she has reached out to Mayans in Chiapas and Palestinians in the occupied territories. Her successor as president of Ireland, Mary McAleese, another human rights lawyer, has followed in Robinson's path. In addition to the conventional roles of touting the

Celtic Tiger, tourism, and investment, she made a 1998 Australian visit where she was "mobbed by descendants of Irish orphan girls who were sent to Australia between 1848 and 1850 to work as virtual slaves. She then removed a stone from the barracks where the slave girls were sent, and dedicated the construction of a sculpture to recall the Famine."[12]

These are vivid examples of the Irish ability to assimilate into the larger world represented in the halls of the United Nations – that is, the vast majority of people on the planet. There is no intent here to diminish the achievement of the Irish in the English-speaking world – the prizes for literature and film, the Book of Kells, and other contributions to the Western religious heritage – but an intent only to note the relative lack of attention to the possibility of contributing to humanity by assimilating into the cultures and nations that have experienced famine and colonialism.

Thomas Cahill's wonderful best-seller *How the Irish Saved Civilization* unconsciously applies a Eurocentric limit to the notion of civilization. In his very first sentence, Cahill writes that "the word Irish is seldom coupled with the word civilization."[13] When I read this introduction I was stunned. Was he serious, or cunningly ironic? "If we strain to think of 'Irish civilization,'" he goes on, "no image appears, no Fertile Crescent or Indus Valley, no brooding bust of Beethoven."[14] Our "one moment of unblemished glory," he declares, is when we "took up the great labor of copying all of Western literature." Irish monks, he says, preserved the written literature of Western culture and established centers everywhere in Europe where civilization could flower once the "barbarian hordes" had retreated. In one sweeping introductory page, Cahill ignores the Ulster sagas, Irish literature, and 1916, the first twentieth-century anticolonial revolution. He apparently eliminates Joyce, Yeats, and Shaw as major influences on "Western literature." He fails to ask how the Irish have also tried to save themselves from Western civilization as constructed by the Romans and British, and makes no reference to the continuing lack of civilized norms under British rule in the North today.

But Cahill's book underscores the potential Irish contribution to the larger world. With 70 million Irish people around the planet, with a heritage of traveling the globe without colonial ambition, the Irish are uniquely situated to dissent from Western corporate globalization on behalf of the poorer cross-section of humanity. This is precisely what Anglo-Saxon establishments on both sides of the Atlantic fear. They need to keep Ireland, even a united Ireland, loyal to the New World Order, and Irish America white and conservative. Deviation by either the Irish or Irish Americans, or both in concert, would break up the consensus of rich nations that now claim to speak for the Western world. Too much questioning of the assimilation myth, in the view of Professor Allan Bloom, leads to a "weakening [of] our convictions of the truth or superiority of American principles and our heroes."[15] From this point of view, the assimilation of Irish Americans is not enough. The ultimate goal is the assimilation of Ireland as a whole into the American-led global order.

The Republic: Corruption or Reform?

In the Irish Republic, change is under way. Institutions of Church and state are weakening from chronic corruption and public skepticism. Persistent scandals have rocked the Catholic Church, including a 1992 admission by the very bishop who welcomed the Pope to Ireland in 1979, of fathering a child, and a 1994 case of sexual abuse that caused a "flood of allegations against priests and Christian Brothers." In 1999, a County Leitrim priest called the Olympic athlete Sonia O'Sullivan a "slut" for having a child out of wedlock in violation of Church teaching on faith and morals.[16] In that same year, the *Sunday Times* published an analysis comparing Irish priests to an endangered species.[17] In all of 1999, only one man was ordained as a priest in Dublin. In the same year, twelve serving priests died in Dublin and six retired. Half the capital's 5,550 diocesan clergymen were over sixty years old, while only one in five was under forty. "There has been a loss of faith in all our institutions – banks, politicians, and the church – and that affects religious practice," said the public relations director of the Dublin diocese, seeking to explain why Mass was "no longer fashionable."[18]

Indeed, the banks and politicians themselves were enmeshed in a seemingly permanent politics of corruption. By 1999, publishers were rushing out books on Ireland as "a scandalous country," including an A-to-Z directory of scandal called *This Great Little Nation*.[19] Campaign slush funds, contributions from developers to the entire Dublin city council, and offshore tax shelters in the Cayman Islands were all scandals that reflected what Fintan O'Toole called "the gap between church and State on the one hand and the reality of Irish life on the other," where "living in the Republic meant having to get used to a kind of systematic hypocrisy, in which saying one thing and doing another was the definition of well-adjusted behaviour."[20]

Many observers detected a deeper social corruption that could not be blamed on elites alone. Despite the Celtic Tiger boom, there was rising popular antagonism to immigrants arriving from Africa and Asia, as well as entrenched indifference to Ireland's indigenous "travellers," a tragic moral irony since the Irish depended historically on being welcomed in other lands. In addition, there was pervasive social anomie from the wrenching adjustment to the fast lanes of wealth and consumption. "In banks, financial institutions and high tech companies, in almost every walk of life, employees now work long hours without paid overtime. The roads are full of commuters before seven in the morning, and the buses and trains are still carrying an exhausted workforce home to domestic dissatisfaction twelve hours later. . . . Are we a nation, or have we sold our soul to become a jobs park, a small industrial estate on Europe's continental bypass?" asked reviewers of a July 2000 study for the *Sunday Independent*.[21]

The peace process, however, has enabled a revival of the republican spirit across Ireland. Northern elections in 2001 made Sinn Féin the largest nationalist party for the first time, with a slight edge over the SDLP. Perhaps more remarkably, a September 2000 poll showed Gerry Adams to be the most popular politician in the Republic, one indication that citizens of Southern Ireland are still Irish on the inside.[22] Adams's rating was 57 percent, four points ahead of the Irish prime minister, Bertie Ahern. Until the Good Friday Agreement, Sinn Féin was politically invisible in the South, showing popularity ratings as low as 1–2 percent. But the peace process and Good Friday Agreement, including the end of official censorship, made it possible to hear the Sinn Féin message and vote for a new Ireland. For the moment, Sinn Féin leadership effectively represents the aspiration for national reunification in both North and South. All the decades of censorship and denial, all the promotion of a consumer society, all the roaring of the Celtic Tiger, had not erased the aspiration for national reunification in the South. "Our vote is hidden under the Fianna Fáil vote," Gerry Adams once told me. I thought him either clairvoyant or mad at the time, since there were no signs of any such sentiment in the polls. But he was right. Sinn Féin is rapidly expanding across the South in areas that have been traditionally republican but marginalized; in areas of urban and rural poverty with ineffective representation by other parties; among middle-class liberal nationalists; and among idealistic young people. Of course, the peace process will force Sinn Féin to consider divisive questions which have been deferred in wartime – reproductive rights and the separation of Church and state, for example. It is by no means certain either that an elected Sinn Féin bloc will be acceptable to the traditional Dublin establishment. For example, Garret FitzGerald, the architect of excluding Sinn Féin during the war, is now opposed to their participation during the present peace. His argument reveals much about the Dublin elite's mentality: Sinn Féin's presence in elected office would interfere with the Dublin regime's "constructive" relationship with Northern unionists. "For the sake of Northern Ireland," FitzGerald asserts, "it is still too soon for this to happen."[23] Despite FitzGerald's resistance, it is altogether possible that the party will become a critical minority in the Dáil (parliament) with enough votes to determine whether a governing coalition rises or falls. In that scenario, Sinn Féin could bargain for a more aggressive policy towards the North as the condition of its support of a regime in the South. That would be difficult, if not impossible, for the unionist politicians to accept – a Sinn Féin-influenced foreign ministry! – but might give Northern republicans a truly viable possibility of taking the gun out of Irish politics. The other option, remaining in opposition but with growing popular support, would position the party for the future.

Either scenario might also give the US Administration and Congress an anxiety attack. The American strategic interest is that the Irish Republic become a loyal and obedient handmaiden of Washington's global military and economic policies, not a supporter of peace and human rights movements against NATO and the World Trade Organization. It is ironic – and telling – that a public warning against Southern Irish independence was issued at the beginning of the George W. Bush Administration by a Republican US congressman with sympathetic ties to Northern republicans. Representative Benjamin Gilman (R-NY) warned against Dublin allowing issues such as "nuclear weapons, capital punishment, the US embargo on Cuba, and the European Union's anxiety about US trade and investment goals" to interfere with building a partnership with the United States. He went on to urge that "the new, prosperous and pro-business Ireland . . . assist our communication with the European Union – that is, serve as the *American gateway* into Europe's distant, complex and diverse institutions."[24] The message was straightforward: with George W. Bush and the Republicans controlling the US government, if you want our continued support of the peace process, we expect you to toe the American line. In thanks for our diplomacy in the North, we expect you to tone down your support for nuclear disarmament, to end your opposition to the death penalty, and to the US embargo on Cuba, and to become an American facilitator in Europe. Gilman's letter echoes the Reagan era when a US State Department official wrote a memo saying, "To be very frank, I don't believe we should allow ourselves to be used by the Irish, particularly since the Irish have not been supportive of our interests in Central America."[25] These American assertions are not only a challenge to Ireland's national right of self-determination but could lead to a conflict between Washington and the Catholic Church, whose policies on nuclear weapons, capital punishment, poverty, hunger, and immigration are markedly different from those of the State Department. Indeed, if the Catholic Church wishes to recover its credibility among Irish (and many

Irish American) Catholics, it need only register its opposition to these inhumane and arrogant American demands.

What is reflected in Gilman's polite but unmistakable diktat is an attempted continuation of longterm efforts to prevent Irish dissent from upsetting the US–British strategic design for the world. In their first official meeting, Prime Minister Tony Blair told President Bush that additional levels of American involvement in Northern Ireland by an American president weren't necessary.[26] During the Cold War, Irish American Democrats – together with the State Department and British intelligence – saw Sinn Féin as a radical threat, even a "second Cuba" in the making. After the Cold War, the new concern among US and British officials was to disarm the IRA and invite electoral nationalists to become junior partners in institutions like NATO and the World Trade Organization, a process already well under way. The peacetime threat from Sinn Féin arises from its opposition to US–British wars like that in Kosovo, and its opposition to transforming neutral Ireland into an arm of NATO under the guise of a "partnership for peace." Since most Irish nationalists are already inclined to oppose these US policies, the addition of Sinn Féin to the national chemistry causes a paranoia in high places that a united Ireland will begin to look too much like an Amnesty International and Greenpeace office combined. An analysis of British intelligence notes blatantly that "M15 and the RUC Special Branch clearly have a major role to play in the continuing political struggle against the republican movement."[27] Therefore the assimilation of Ireland itself into the American–UK global economic and security arrangements is a high priority for the Western establishment just as the assimilation of Irish immigrants into the mainstream was a high priority for American leaders like James Conant in the 1920s.

In fact there is a burgeoning school of conservative thought, promoted in such journals as *American Outlook*, which openly advocates "the Anglosphere" as the cultural underpinning of the new global order.[28] The historian Francis Fukuyama opines that "a well-conceived assimilation policy will become a necessity for coping with cultural diversity," and that "no one should feel ashamed" about seeming "to enjoin a certain degree of cultural uniformity."[29] Kevin Phillips, author of *The Emerging Republican Majority* (1969), which sought to incorporate Irish Americans into the Nixon Republican Party, now joins the chorus for the Anglosphere, whose "core thought is a kind of English revivalism." Whether conceived as a return to the past or as a new model of mono-culturalism, the emphasis on the Anglosphere is a denial of the Irish heritage and of the heritage of former British colonies. Phillips notes this problem and counsels that the Anglosphere be made "more attractive and accommodating" to the Irish and other such groups, without suggesting how.[30] The assumption is that the Irish, as white English-speakers, should bond with the British legacy against a hostile world. There is no sugges-tion that the British should withdraw their Anglosphere from Northern Ireland.

It will be impossible to erase Irish identity fully under the pressure of globalization. The Dublin minister of arts and culture, Sile de Valera, criticized the European Union in 2000 for "impinging on [Irish] identity, culture and tradition."[31] Then, in a shocking rebuff to globalization, 54 percent of Irish voters in the Republic rejected EU expansion in a June, 2001 referendum. A "yes" vote on the Nice Treaty, which cannot be implemented without the support of all fifteen members of the EU, was supported by the major political parties, the business elite and the Church establishment. In a heavily biased headline, the *LA Times* declared that "Irish Leaders Faulted for Voters' EU Rebuke," as if the Irish establish-ment had failed in its duty to control the primitive nationalist instincts of the Irish masses.[32] But the issue was a fundamental one of sovereignty and democracy. Should the Irish people, on the crest of their greatest nation-alist achievement in eighty years, now accept the notion of the globalizers that we are living in a post-nationalist era, or not?

Those who said no to the EU arrangement included a former attorney general in Dublin arguing that the EU would leave little or no role for democratically elected institutions, and that Irish self-determination would effecively be nullified.[33] Significantly, the only Irish parties to oppose the treaty were Sinn Féin and the Green Party. As Danny Morrison declared, "the people who came out and voted 'no' in the

South form the real conscience of the Irish nation and are saying that despite the purported benefits of membership in the European Union, their souls, their sovereignty, are not up for sale. The world has to remain a rainbow coalition of independent and good people, and if 'nationalism' means denying the bad people the authority to aggrandize power, and in our name to bomb people and nations we do not know or understand, who are of no threat, then 'nationalism' has to be for us."[34]

In the same electoral period in which Southern voters rejected the EU treaty, Northern voters elected Pat Doherty and Michelle Gildernew of Sinn Féin as abstentionist MPs, making Sinn Féin the North's largest nationalist party with an especially powerful loyalty among young voters. Ruth Dudley Edwards, the maverick pro-loyalist Dublinite, complained that most voters didn't care about Sinn Féin's terrorist background; to them, she wrote, "Sinn Féin is cool; Sinn Féin is sexy; Sinn Féin is the future."[35]

Notwithstanding the whines from those for whom the tables are turned, Danny Morrison is right in declaring that the future of the Irish soul is at stake. While it may be centuries older than the United States, and deemed to have an intrinsic value, Irish culture – like other indigenous cultures – is an impediment to the establishment of a single world monoculture. If an Irish dimension is to be preserved in the global order, the Irish themselves will have to define and retain what it means to be Irish in the face of an American-dominated economic and cultural empire. While it is the ancient British foe that dominates the North, it is a new reality that American multinationals have the greatest economic influence in the South. The recent surge of Irish nationalism and cultural distinctiveness bodes well for the survival instinct in Irish character. But the failure to deal deeply and fully with the legacy of the Famine and the Troubles is a serious challenge. The insular culture of denial may leave the Irish with no basis for identification with thousands of mostly African immigrants seeking refuge in Ireland.

And what of the Irish Americans in this new world order? Will they identify themselves with the elitist ethos of the World Trade Organization and seek to impose a corporate, aesthetic, and security monoculture on the rest of the world? Having been assimilated in America, will they join in America's assimilation of Ireland?

If Irish Americans were to become half as supportive of Irish Northern nationalism as Jewish Americans are of Israel's interests, the British army would be on transports flying home. That day has not come. The sprawling suburban world of Irish America is becoming steadily more conservative, more Republican. If it is true that one-third of American corporate CEOs are of Irish descent – as Father Andrew Greeley and Tim Pat Coogan claim – they are not using that muscle to break up economic inequality in Northern Ireland. The Catholic Church will issue statements supporting the peace process, or issue protests against extreme cases of British brutality towards Northern Catholics, but seem to reserve more venom for gays, lesbians, and goddess worshippers than for the Orange Order or even Ian Paisley.

Great possibilities for renewal lie in Celtic music, art, music, theatre, and film. But, contrary to unionist myth, entertainment careers in America are not advanced by romanticizing the IRA. Most Irish and Irish American careers succeed in exactly the proportion that they avoid the "Troubles." John Lennon, an Irish working-class lad from Liverpool who dreamed of retiring to an Irish village and who never wavered from his peace-and-love message, nevertheless attracted the organized wrath of the US intelligence agencies and the immigration service when he was suspected of sending funds to the IRA after Bloody Sunday.[36] The extraordinary Belfast artist Van Morrison, who provided a moving performance on President Clinton's first visit, has generally avoided taking controversial positions on the thirty-year war in his hometown. According to a Morrison biography, *Celtic Crossroads*, the Belfast singer "rarely alluded directly, either in songs or interviews, to the civil war that had engulfed his birthplace. . . . Like James Joyce or Samuel Beckett, he had chosen exile, cunning, and silence. . . . Nevertheless, the psychic death of his native land darkly shadowed his work, and made evocations of a paradise glimpsed in childhood unbearably poignant." The Irish band U2 has similarly tended to place greater emphasis on global justice than on taking controversial stands on colonialism in the North. Their moral and political interests, particularly the Jubilee 2000 project to end Third World debt, are profoundly Irish in character. But like James Joyce and so many of Ireland's greatest artists, they have tended to avoid a direct taking of sides in the most controversial issue of Irish identity, the lasting British presence in the North. Of Ireland's contemporary artists, Sinead O'Connor has taken great risks to dwell on the psychic meaning of amnesia towards the Famine and the North, describing Ireland as a macroexample of child abuse. In carrying out what amounts to a passionate personal intervention against the psychic effects of colonialism and clericalism, she has experienced a classic case of backlash. Instead of dealing with its own secret shame, elements of the Irish public have projected their anger on Sinead O'Connor instead. In turn, she has acted out her emotions more and more self-destructively – for example, by tearing up the Pope's picture on national television – which further isolates her as the alleged cause of her own problems.

Sinn Féin support in America depends heavily on Republicans in Congress who tend to oppose affirmative action, immigrant rights, poverty programs, livable wages, and environmental limits on polluters. As often happens, what is good politically for Northern Irish nationalists – building the broadest support from all quarters – is not necessarily progressive for America. Thus, many powerful organizations and movements – the women's movement, for example – remain on the sidelines in the American debate over Northern Ireland because they believe, for the most part correctly, that Northern nationalism is antichoice. The national civil rights coalition pays little attention to Northern Ireland because Irish Americans are either removed from civil rights issues domestically or involved in a negative way as law enforcement officials. The American Jewish leadership is involved in constant dialogue with African Americans and Latinos, but not with Irish Americans because of strong memories of Catholic anti-Semitism and the continuing sense that the Pope has failed to understand the magnitude of the Vatican's historic legacy.

Nevertheless, there is a progressive Irish American tradition that is being reawakened by the struggle in Northern Ireland and by a growing interest in cultural and ethnic diversity in America. I believe that assimilated Irish Americans remain Irish on the inside, in the same sense that the Irish in the twenty-six counties are potential Sinn Féin voters, women's liberationists, or environmental radicals. Many of the deepest Irish traditions – of rebellious nationalism, of women as heroines, of shamanism and druidism, of a spirituality centered in nature – remain to be tapped in the collective unconscious of the Diaspora. Ireland is the only country on earth with a musical instrument, the harp, for a national symbol, and a special status for bards and poets from the days of the high courts to the current policy of requiring no taxes from writers. These are historic values at odds with what Yeats called "the greasy till." Assimilation may threaten, corrupt, and sometimes trivialize these values, but it will never destroy them because they have endured in the Irish character for centuries. They are easily translatable politically into themes of fighting for the underdog, for human rights, peace, environmentalism, and putting the quality of life ahead of the quantity of possessions.

White Americans, including Irish Americans, will have to reassess how they fit in an American society in which whites are becoming the minority. In California, where in 2000 the majority were people of color, there are signs of a white backlash in voter-approved initiatives to ban affirmative action, deny public services to illegal immigrants, and prohibit bilingualism. However, the backlash was hardly uniform in white communities, where 40 percent voted against the initiatives. The realities of a multicultural state cannot be avoided or wished away for much longer. The Bush Administration, like unionist politicians in the North, may engage in a holding action against the future, but nevertheless is forced to make symbolic affirmative-action gestures in its cabinet appointees. The anxious desire to resist ethnic diversity in the name of a "common" American culture – which turns out to be a WASP culture – cannot prevent the emergence of a new multicultural America with multiple identities and ethnicities, including a kaleidoscope of biracial hybrids. White people will have to ask themselves where they fit into this multicolored country. Breaking them away from their vapid whiteness is part of the answer. The official census category of "white, non-Hispanic" must be stricken as an unfounded embarrassment, and replaced by a range of ethnic options for all Americans. The peaceful and positive transition from a white America to a nonwhite America is impossible without whites coming to see themselves not in terms of skin color but in terms of their own ethnic heritage.

Without censorship, Sinn Féin – and Irish nationalists generally – will continue to play an important role in enriching what it means to be Irish in America, and an American in the world. Gerry Adams can continue drawing audiences of 1,000 students on campuses and giving media interviews in America for as long as his schedule allows. There is an excitement to hear the Sinn Féin leader just as there was for Bernadette Devlin at the beginning of the conflict. Sinn Féin is already the catalyst for a historic revision of the American role in Northern Ireland, modifying the colonial power of London. In making Northern Ireland a domestic American issue, not simply a garrisoned province of the British, a new opportunity for Irish America to pressure Washington has been created. By defining its role as a mediator, the US government creates an incentive for Irish Americans to move the center of debate towards Irish nationalism as a counterweight to the British. This process continues the reversal of assimilation for the Irish American community.

How far the reversal can and should go is a question worth asking. I sometimes think that the deepest fear of the British and Anglo-American establishments is that the American people will come to remember what the British did to the American colonies. There was a revolution, not a cricket match. Yet I cannot remember anyone in my life being angry about the British inflicting death and destruction on Americans who wanted nothing more than their freedom. It is as if Americans would prefer to forget we fought the British, as if it was something necessary but regrettable, a family trauma or Freudian rebellion best forgotten. This sanitizing of the American Revolution is the necessary underpinning of the celebrated friendship and strategic partnership between our two countries. Why dredge up the past, scratch old wounds? The question might very well be reversed: Why cover up the past? Why would the Americans strike for independence were it not for British atrocities that made the relationship insufferable? Could we not learn from what the British did to us to understand what the people of Northern Ireland may be going through? Would it be worth recalling that the American colonists became republicans at the same time, and for the same reasons, as the United Irishmen?

An example of British concern over how Americans historicize the American Revolution is a review by David Gritten, a London critic, of the films *The Patriot* and *Braveheart*, both starring Mel Gibson, which appeared in the *Los Angeles Times* of July 12, 2000. In *The Patriot*, which deals with the American Revolution, the British shoot the Gibson character's son, execute injured rebels, and burn down a church with rebel villagers inside, making the British "seem a decidedly scummy bunch" in Gritten's view. The portrayal of the British army is "offensive," he declares, and he finds it "hard to imagine any other ethnic group being represented in this way with such impunity." In *Braveheart*, he objects to the notion that the Scottish rebel William Wallace took arms against the English because they murdered his wife. "But in the end, those horrid Englishmen execute our hero brutally," he comments. Is Gritten saying the Americans, or the Scottish people, had no meaningful or valid grievances that justified their violent rising against the British? "The problem may be our accent," Gritten speculates.

> Anyone speaking as we do must be cold and snobbish. There may be a grain of truth there: as a people we're certainly reserved. We have emotions; we just tend not to share them with others. We're not interested in locating our inner child, and we certainly don't want to do group hugs. Englishmen do not speak of chasing their dreams.

He readily adds that he's not blind to English faults either. Their soccer hoodlums are "appalling." Public life is "boorish." "Customer service in England? Lazy, surly, resigned – it is a cause for shame." Customer service? What about England's historic responsibility for spreading imperial havoc around the world? If Gritten's rant seems an isolated one, consider a warning from the British Home Secretary, Jack Straw, in

2000, that continued challenges to English identity could create a violent nationalist backlash. The minister noted that the English "propensity to violence" was "very aggressive" and could boil over if too much nationalism flared in Northern Ireland, Wales, and Scotland.

Breaking the assimilationist mold will mean more than merely lobbying for implementation of the Good Friday Agreement. It will mean reconstituting our national myths, the stories we teach our children and which guide our lives. If Irish Americans identify with the 10 percent of the world which is white, Anglo-American and consumes half the global resources, we have chosen the wrong side of history and justice. We will become the inhabitants of the Big House ourselves, looking down on the natives we used to be. We will become our nightmare without a chance of awakening from its grip.

We should ask ourselves, who wanted to keep the closet of Northern Ireland closed to us, and why? Why was the truth kept from those of us in America, and what was the fear? And then we should recover what has been hidden inside us. We should stop trying to please those we feel are superior to us, and start reclaiming the Irish dimension of our lives. We should green our souls, our spirits, our minds, our lives. If Irish America goes green, there goes white America.

Imagine the Irish American self as an architectural "dig," if you will. On the upper surface is a family living in a suburban house. Just below is that family, in an earlier time, living in a New York tenement with the sewage running through. Digging deeper in time and place, that same family is found in the dark, fever-ridden chamber of a coffin ship, and further down, standing in the blackened rubble of a cottage somewhere in Ireland. Still excavating our racial memory, we see our ancestors feeding their families, playing music, and telling stories in a village community. And before that distant time, we see horsemen, soldiers, bards, queens in robes, vast stone ceremonial structures. All of these lives, over all the centuries, are inside us, our repressed ancestors. Like archeologists of human identity, we must uncover, preserve, and learn from all these past selves. "Once we were kings," say the Maoris of New Zealand. So too were the Irish. To ponder what this means, a traveler might spend a day at Newgrange, in County Meath, in the valley of the River Boyne.

I first went there a few years ago on the coldest day I have ever experienced. The human settlement of this valley 5,000 years ago was a heroic achievement, like that of the native people first settling North America, and yet these ancestors of ours were classified as primitive. I thought of what I owed those people as I climbed a gradually ascending hillside towards a structure built of large, interlocked granite boulders, perhaps the "greatest collection of megalith art in the world."[37] How had these early people pulled such colossal stones – some weighing many tons – from the riverbed below? How had they known to fit them so seamlessly together? What dream led them to accomplish this task, which must have taken many years?

So little is known about Newgrange (it is named, prosaically, for the "new grange" of a nineteenth-century landlord farmer) that pre-conceptions tend to dominate. The long-held British "scientific" view was that a foreign race must have built this magnificent site because the native Irish were incompetent to do so. According to historian Martin Brennan, the authorities "could not conceive that the monuments were indigenous constructions of the native Irish." An enlightened British army engineer, General Charles Vallancey, explained the monuments as "caves of the sun" and described the druids as "revolutionary prophets" in the observation of time, much like the Mayan people. He was ignored.[38] During the Celtic revival, the poet George Russell (A.E.) wrote that the monuments were "a greatness we are heirs to, a destiny which is ours though it be yet far away."[39]

Another misconception was that Newgrange was only a "passage grave," or sepulchre, used exclusively for the burial ceremonies of an elite. Finally, less than two hundred years ago, a small rectangular aperture was discovered above the entrance to the chamber, perfectly placed to admit the light of the rising sun on the solstice dawn, December 21. The beams of a dying sun would also enter a related structure at nearby Dowth. Newgrange may have been serving this purpose for 5,000 years, long before the sun rose and the sun subsequently would set on the British empire.

While sites like Newgrange are still a mystery, it is clear that these Irish ancestors lived at an extraordinary time in the evolution of what it means to be human. Like the Mayans, they divined the heavens, invented astronomy, linked the rhythms of the universe to their planting and harvest seasons. They may have worshipped the sun, whose first rays announcing the end of winter flooded through the aperture to light the spiral wall carvings within the chamber. In folk tradition, the mounds were not considered graves primarily, but the abodes of the native Irish gods; the *tuatha de danaan,* "lords of light," lived in these structures, and the goddess of the Boyne, the source of wisdom, lived nearby. In this place, the hero Amairgin, the bard of the Milesians from Spain, recited his poem:

> I am wind on the sea
> I am ocean wave
> I am roar of sea
> I am bull of seven fights
> I am vulture on cliff
> I am dewdrop
> I am fairest of flowers
> I am lake on plain
> I am a mountain in a man
> I am a word of skill
> I am the point of a weapon
> I am the God who fashions fire for a head.[40]

These were a formidable people. And yet, as I have quoted Thomas Cahill, if we strain to think of "Irish civilization," no image appears. If the wondrous achievement of Newgrange can be distorted and disregarded, the task of restoring Irish memory is indeed a large one. As another example, the Irish founding saga, the *Tain*, was never fully translated into English until recent times. This was not an accident. Unlike the Irish scribes who saved and translated the works of Western civilization, the intellectual establishment was apparently in no hurry to make an Irish creation myth accessible to the world. But just as Newgrange was built by countless people over countless generations, one stone at a time, so too can the reconstruction of our Irish identity be achieved as well.

We can start by reinhabiting our Irish self in simple ways. Read Irish history, novels, and poetry. Listen to traditional Irish music. Learn a few words in the Irish language. Observe the old calendar of festivals, based on the seasons of solstice and equinox. Give your child an Irish name. Save St Patrick's Day from those who think that getting drunk makes you Irish. Visit Ireland, and include south Armagh, west Belfast, and the Bogside, not just the castles, golf courses, and pubs.

We can build Irish content into our institutional life. If you are religious, ask for the observance of Saint Brigid's feast on February 1, or for a discussion of the "pagan" Irish contribution to Christianity. Ask your church social justice committee for a meeting on Northern Ireland. If you are a parent, question why the school curriculum sanitizes the Famine experience, and ask your school board for new curriculum materials. If you are civic-minded, ask why there is no Irish museum, no Famine memorial, virtually anywhere in the United States.

If you are involved in government or commerce, invest in Irish-owned companies or purchase from them wherever possible. Join or form an Irish American political club in your congressional district. Invite speakers on Northern Ireland and Irish history. Demand that your congressmen speak out for police reform, jobs, and the peace process in the North. Connect your local club to national Irish American lobbying groups.

If you are Protestant, demand that your denomination denounce the Paisleys and the Orange Order as sinful and bigoted. Identify with rebels like Wolfe Tone, Thomas and Robert Emmet, and Henry Joy McCracken. If you are Catholic, be tolerant on issues like abortion and gay rights which are litmus tests of whether a united Ireland will promote diversity and pluralism.

Make amends to those in your community – Jews, African Americans, feminists, or gay people, for example – who may harbor deep feelings of distrust or ill-will based on historical experience with Irish Americans. Learn their perceptions of Irish racism, anti-Semitism, and sexism. If the amends are accepted, ask them to include human rights in Northern Ireland on their agendas for social change and begin interfaith and inter-group dialogue on local problems in your community.

And keep dreaming, as I try to. Irish culture should not be commod-ified or made to disappear under the homogenizing pressures of a far younger society, the United States of America. As Americans, we need our country to become more internationalist by assimilating into the dreams of its immigrants, including the Irish dream which is one of spirituality, poetry, and learning in everyday life. As Irish people, we must not allow our homeland to become only a platform for the multi-nationals or a heritage theme park.

In my dream I am taking a handful of soil from Emmet Garity's grave in Sullivan Township, Wisconsin, and my Nannie's grave in Oconomowoe, and my parents' graves too, and I am packing up that soil of the dead to be carried back to Ireland. In this dream, others are pick-ing up blackened shale from the old coalfields of Pennsylvania, still others are packing up rocks from the railroad beds in Chicago, and some are retrieving stones in mineshafts in Montana. And granite from cathedrals built by immigrants, and brick from tenement buildings. Some of us are taking the seeds of oaks and wildflowers. I see a loric landscape slowly emerging in America, a landscape with plaques of remembrance instead of one prostrated to malls and surveyors' dulling gridlines, a map becoming alive with reclaimed Irish stories.

In this dream, I see Irish people reclaiming invisible Irish graves, hold-ing services, planting gardens. I see those same people gathering the rubble of ruined fever hospitals, the battered soil of old Famine roads, the rocks of the coast, the seeds of plants and flowers from abandoned village fields. I see Irish-Australians, Irish-Canadians, Irish-Mexicans, Irish-English, Irish-Spaniards, Irish-Latin Americans, gathering up their sod of memory as well.

In this dream Irish from all over are migrating home. They come in ones and twos and in groups. When they arrive, they leave their sod and stone in a field, which in time becomes a field of flowers, a hill, a grave-yard, an oak grove, a mountain, a place to bury pain and grow our history until memory surpasses forgetting and the sod of the dead becomes the fertile soil of awakenings.

Afterword

On the Fourth of July, 2001 anniversary of America's independence struggle against British colonialism, I visited Stormont, site of continuing British rule in Ireland. I thought of the thousands of Irish immigrants to America who shed their blood for an independence their descendants back home still had not achieved.

Across a conference room table was London's newest Minister of State at the Northern Ireland Office in charge of police, prisons and parades, a personable woman with the very Irish name of Jane Kennedy. She had consented to meet with a delegation of American observers of the Orange parades in places like Lower Ormeau Road and Garvaghy Road. "Happy Fourth of July," she began, smiling, as if it were a shared holiday rather than a celebration of British defeat. She went on to say that "my first task is to learn," because her "involvement in Northern Ireland [was] limited." She described how impressed she was "by the police officers' efforts to improve Northern Ireland," and explained that she was shocked by the church burnings in the North because such sectarianism had vanished in England. (In the next week, three English cities were rocked by riots and firebombs over the status of Asian immigrants.)

As she went on, I was increasingly struck by her lack of knowledge, bizarre (or so I thought) for an official in charge of security issues. She kept looking at, or deferring to, the bureaucrats from the Northern Ireland Office for confirmation of her answers to questions. Although her own government was banning inflammatory parades scheduled that week for Drumcree, Minister Kennedy claimed encouraging progress regarding the parades issue, "so that parades can go ahead in an atmosphere of mutual respect." In Derry, she began to say, talks were in progress involving the loyalist Apprentice Boys. Then she checked herself and asked the bureaucrat at her elbow, "I believe that's their name, isn't it?"

It might seem to have been a small slip, but by analogy it was like a White House official in charge of legislation forgetting the name of the Republican or Democratic party. But there was no indication of embarrassment or worry about the sheer ignorance on display from Her Majesty's Government. I remember a resigned senior republican leader commenting on the comings and goings of British secretaries – four since the 1994 ceasefires – that "we have suffered fools for a very long time in Ireland."

Minister Kennedy was now claiming credit for the RUC being able to patrol the streets routinely without the British Army with its negative "psychological impact." That this "achievement" was related to the IRA's continuing ceasefire didn't factor into her analysis. Under questioning, she admitted one spot where the British Army continued to patrol, south Armagh. "As long as the threat remains," she asserted, "the Army will be there." If the mere existence of the south Armagh brigade was a "threat," I thought, she has no idea of how long the Army will be patrolling.

It dawned on me that Minister Kennedy was of Irish lineage on the outside but thoroughly British on the inside. The assimilation had been completed. The colonizing process had succeeded. In Memmi's terms, the colonized had "disappeared" into the colonizer.

The entertainment section of the Belfast press that week showed the full scale of British and American film "tele-colonialism." In addition to their British soaps, movie-goers could watch *Shrek*, *Pearl Harbor*, *See Spot Run*, *Dracula 2001*, *Autumn in New York*, *The Mummy Returns*, and *Spy Kids*. There was an interview with Angelina Jolie in the *Belfast Telegraph* promoting her film *Tomb Raider* about the video-game heroine Lara Croft. I had known Angelina as a young girl, a friend of my kids, who attended a progressive summer camp with which I was involved. I was sure she was a person of conscience. She did manage to slip in that "Lara has been raised in England, but she's not uptight," a comment that slightly gratified me. But in the US–Hollywood global market, social commentary is not for sale. The interviewer was obsessed with what the article called "the breast question," i.e. the comparison between Angelina's breast size and that of the curvy action figure she played. It turned out that Angelina wears a 36C and Lara a 36D. "Personally, I wouldn't want those breasts", Angelina revealed. (*Belfast Telegraph*, July 3, 2001)

Reading the interview, I felt I was out of touch with the world. The night before I had been staring at a Lara Croft advertisement for a popular soft drink on the Lower Ormeau Road, in which the curvy robot was beckoning her youthful audience to have the energy for her. Below the cyber-babe was an IRA tricolour mural. Next to it another mural showed a silhouetted Orange man with a "stop" line drawn though him. They faced across the river in the direction of loyalist marchers and RUC vehicles.

Whatever erosion of Irish identity was being inflicted by American entertainment culture, serving to distract attention from the everyday oppression of British rule, it wasn't having the desired effect on the people of the Ormeau Road that night. They were out in force to await and, if necessary, block a loyalist parade which included 100 Orangemen up from Portadown. Gerard Rice, the residents' association leader, and his wife Lucy had to lecture and push back youngsters who wanted to confront the "peelers" (the longtime Irish term for the royal police force) or any loyalists bent on invading their neighborhood.

One reason the youngsters on Ormeau Road were steamed and unresponsive to the Lara Croft advertisement was that on the morning of the Fourth of July a nineteen-year-old Catholic teenager named Ciaran Cummings was shot and murdered by loyalists as he waited for his lift to work in County Antrim. A caller to the *Irish News* from the loyalist "Red Hand Defenders" said they killed Ciaran, an ordinary Catholic boy, in retaliation for the election of two Sinn Féin council candidates in Antrim. The nationalists who voted Sinn Féin, the caller declared, were "going to have to pay the price for it." He hung up with the slogan "God save Ulster." (*Irish News*, July 5, 2001)

To the world media, it was just another example of "unfathomable" Irish violence, the sectarianism which, according to Minister Jane Kennedy, had vanished from England. But even the dogs on the street knew better. To keep Irish voters from expressing themselves as republicans – revealing that they were Irish on the inside – elements of loyalism were inflicting death as the punishment for voting Sinn Féin. There was another motive as well. If loyalist paramilitaries started killing innocent Catholics, the IRA would have less interest in decommissioning gestures during the crucial round of peace talks starting that same week. Better, from the loyalist viewpoint, the IRA might be provoked into breaking its ceasefire and retaliating, which would lead to Sinn Féin being expelled from the fragile Stormont government.

In fact loyalists were going crazy at the political success of Sinn Féin. In north Belfast, an elected official from Ian Paisley's Democratic Unionist Party (DUP) refused to shake the hand of his elected Sinn Féin colleague, Gerry Kelly. In Strabane, south of Derry, an elected Sinn Féin town council chairman shook hands with a Paisleyite vice-chairman. When the photo appeared in the papers, the loyalist vice-chair issued a statement "retracting" the handshake. In Magherafelt, County Down, where another Sinn Féin representative was elected to chair the town council, the Paisleyite vice-chairman refused to be elected and take his position if the Sinn Féin council members voted for him, which they did. After twenty-four hours of negotiations, the grumbling loyalist took his position.

The old order was crumbling. Suddenly loyalists were expected to sit down and negotiate with nationalists, instead of simply imposing their customary annual 2,400 parades on Catholic streets, 1,100 in July alone. Worse, Sinn Féin candidates were being elected to scores of municipal council seats in a province that was originally gerrymandered to loyalist interests. Sinn Féin now had four abstentionist members of parliament, including the first republican woman, Michelle Gildernew, since Countess Constance Marklevicz in 1918. The new electoral map was becoming "green all the way round from Derry City to the mouth of Strangford Lough, with that nationalist hue digging into mid-Ulster as well," reported the *Irish Times* (June 11, 2001).

It must be remembered that the nationalist population and vote in Northern Ireland still hovers around 43 percent, not a majority for now or the near-term future. But the very fact of expanding nationalist pride and power in any part of Northern Ireland is intolerable to many loyalists. Because Sinn Féin was spreading into County Antrim, nineteen-year-old Ciaran Cummings had to die.

These realities are far from the conventional understanding of the Northern Ireland conflict. On June 22, the Associated Press reported that the British Army was keeping "Roman Catholic and Protestant rioters" apart at great injury and risk to the Army. ("Mobs in Belfast Attack Police During Street Riots," June 22, 2001, in *LA Times*) In the week that Ciaran Cummings was shot on a street corner, the loyalist paramilitaries (the Ulster Freedom Fighters, code for the Ulster Defense Association) withdrew support for the Good Friday Agreement (July 10, 2001 announcement). The IRA, which supports the Good Friday Agreement, remained on ceasefire. Yet all the drum-beating over decommissioning was obsessed with the IRA weapons which remained silent, not the loyalist weapons which were being used. President Bush, the *New York Times* and the *Los Angeles Times* issued calls for IRA disarmament.

As these words were written, the British and Irish governments were once again engaged in frantic efforts to save the institutions of the Irish peace process from collapse. No one can predict, but I believe the process will survive and limp forward, not simply because of the diplomatic effort, but because Irish republicans are gaining more support and saving more lives through the political process with all its snares than they could by returning to armed struggle. Sinn Féin was supposed to be "confounded" by the era of peaceful politics, and their "capacity to win a sympathetic hearing from the gullible abroad removed," in the fantasy of the London *Times* (April 6, 1998). Quite the opposite has happened. Instead of political power growing from the barrel of a gun, in the case of the IRA it has grown from guns remaining silent.

It is possible, however, that loyalist rage at Northern nationalism's rise will lead to more killings and perhaps eventually an IRA response. The problem, and the threat of violence, will remain, however, as long as Ulster's loyalists see themselves as British on the inside with privileges protected by the Crown, instead of Irish citizens with cultural ties to Protestantism or British culture.

Irish people will not wait. They are finally free under the Good Friday

Agreement to express their Irishness without criminal sanction. In Belfast on the Fourth of July, I listened to an Irish-language musical group perform at Culturlann, the Irish cultural center grown up in a former Presbyterian church. Enjoying themselves at one table were the lookalike brothers Sean and Seamus McShane, both around sixty years of age, who took matters into their own hands at the beginning of the "Troubles." After the loyalist mobs attacked Bombay Street in west Belfast in 1969, the brothers physically rebuilt thirty-one homes with funds raised by Bernadette Devlin from the United States. They took their electricity from the lampposts. For their efforts, they were called communists and Provo terrorists. In 1971, they started an Irish school, at a time when it was an offense to send one's children there. Not done, they built the first, small Irish-language community when it seemed both impossible and criminal.

On the Fourth of July the McShanes were smiling at their successors singing in Gaelic at Culturlann. Meanwhile, at the next table their protege and partner, the entrepreneurial Máirtín Ó Muilleoir, had obtained a printing press for the *Andersonstown News* more sophisticated than that of the *Irish Times*, and with his colleague Robin Livingstone, whose little sister was killed by British soldiers in 1981, was dreaming up a nationwide Irish language paper. Imagine, I thought, the North redeeming the South instead of the other way round. The Irish spirit long hidden on the inside was flowering in the outside world now with escalating energy.

"Something like an inspiration occurred in the public life when the ceasefire occurred," said the poet Seamus Heaney in a 1995 speech at Queens University. (The text is from the journalist Kelly Candaele). "Not only in the public life but in the most guarded recesses of the individual psyche as well. People felt that little unforeseen excitement which brings a whole person to life." Connecting the person to the political work of peace, Heaney went on: "(It is) the kind of excitement that starts poetic writing. And just as the work of poetry depends upon the successful completion of turning an original excitement into a sustained and resourceful composition, a process where every minor point of verbal nuance becomes in the long run a point of major importance, it's the same I will say in the work of peace building."

The key lesson Heaney recalled learning at the very beginning of the "Troubles," when immersion in the Irish language and Irish modes of thought were both tempting and subversive, was the experience of "an elsewhere of potential that felt at the same time like a somewhere being remembered."

That is an eloquent and Irish way of summarizing the theme of this effort to make sense of our experience. To feel Irish on the inside is to have access to "an elsewhere of potential," a legacy lost in repression and shame, that is also "a somewhere being remembered," a place we have been, the ground of meaning almost made a graveyard, both physically and spiritually.

The Irish Canadian novelist, Jane Urquhart, has written a novel called *Away* about this same "somewhere being remembered." It ends with a synthesis of Irish and universal consciousness.

> Then she saw the world's great leavestakings, invasions and migra-
> tions, landscapes torn from beneath the feet of tribes, the Danae
> pushed out by the Celts, the Celts eventually smothered by the
> English, warriors in the night depopulating villages, boatloads of
> groaning African slaves. Lost forests. The children of the mountain
> on the plain, the children of the plain adrift on the sea. And all the
> mourning for abandoned geographies.

Would the Jane Kennedys ever feel Irish on the inside? Not likely, I thought, but more and more Irish people were part of Heaney's "some-where being remembered." I felt complete, at home, in Belfast on the Fourth of July.

Tom Hayden
Belfast
Fourth of July, 2001

Epilogue to the Paperback Edition:
The Way We Were

... a motley rabble of saucy boys, negroes, and molattoes, Irish taigs and outlandish jack tarrs ...

> John Adams, lawyer for British soldiers accused in the 1770 Boston Massacre, describing the original American rebels gathered at the Boston Custom House.[1]

An Irish American told me this story at a book signing in Lowell, Massachusetts, a cradle of the Famine Irish: "My grandfather was one of four. His mother was a cleaning lady who gave up the other three children to wealthy Protestants whose homes she cleaned. My grandfather stayed a poor Irishman, which was a source of endless bitterness. If his mother had only abandoned him, he thought, he would have been better off."

In a question and answer session at Merrimack College, also in Massachusetts, an Irish American woman remembered this story of her grandmother, an Irish-born woman living in the American South: One day she sat down in the back of a bus "for no particular reason". The black riders were discomfited. The white bus driver demanded that she move to the front. But the more he threatened her, the less she would budge. Finally, she blurted out that the Irish had once been treated as second-class citizens and she wasn't going to treat others that way.

Both these Irish Americans confided to me that they had forgotten, or suppressed, these anecdotes until the give-and-take discussion of *Irish on the Inside* triggered the memories' return. I mention these stories, among many I have heard, because of what they illustrate about the Irish. The first is about instilled shame. The grandfather would have preferred to be abandoned by his mother than to remain Irish. We can only imagine the poverty and humiliation that made him feel this way. The second story is about the instilled sense of justice that comes with the Irish experience. The woman on the bus acted from an inherited instinct that made her flare up against participating in racial discrimination against others.

Irish on the Inside triggered a flashback for a friend named Sean in Belfast as well. As a child, he recalled, he watched an Ulster television program called *Romper Room*, something akin to *Sesame Street*. On the program, a teacher named Mrs. Adrain pretended to peer through a magic mirror (the television screen) to name the children who watched the show. Sean ran home every day to watch Mrs. Adrain recite, "Romper Bumper Bumper Boo / Tell me, tell me, tell me do / Magic mirror tell me today/ Did all my friends have fun at play?" After this "magic chant," Mrs. Adrain would call out Anglo names like Simon, Richard, Rebecca, and Samuel, but never Sean, Seamus, or Bridget: "she never saw me no matter how close I went to the TV." Still haunted by this experience, Sean, now a father, wrote me that Mrs. Adrain "would not see my kids today either – Kevin, Una, Grainne or Sean. This is how insidious British/Unionist assimilation remains in our country. But today my children look into the eyes of Irish republicans and this is the only magic mirror they want to be reflected in."

How many other stories are there like these instances of recovered memory? I am convinced there are countless ones buried in Irish hearts and that a unique phase of Irish cultural recovery is now underway. Most of the repressed memories are personal, like those recounted above. But equally significant is the retrieval of historical truths from a long period of war, repression, and organized misinformation regarding Ireland itself and the melting-pot mythology of Irish America. This recovery is in part the fruit of the Irish peace process, which has thawed a repressive climate in which any serious critic of British policy was smeared for offering justification of the Irish Republican Army's armed struggle. For example, the peace process has produced a new public inquiry into the 1972 killings of thirteen Catholics during "Bloody Sunday" and two feature films on the subject. Not by coincidence, the last half-decade has produced many more books, memorials and cultural events related to the Great Hunger than during the previous eighty years since partition.

The original edition of *Irish on the Inside* ended with a fanciful dream about a Famine memorial made of soil, sod, stones, artifacts, and flowers, a place to reflect on why the Irish were starved and its meanings for current generations. The eminent revisionist historian at Oxford University, Roy Foster, seemed to become apoplectic over this vision, denouncing it as "demented" and "alarming" in a review in the *New Republic*.[2] I was not alone in my sentimental imagining, however. Just such a living monument, a reconstructed Irish potato field crossed with a burial mound, was opened in 2002 in New York's Battery Park City, on a simple plot covered with sixty-two native plants including nettle and blackthorn, stone from each of Ireland's thirty-two counties, limestone from Kilkenny and fossils from the Irish Sea. The quarter-acre site, exactly the size of the tiny plots decreed under Britain's infamous 1847 Gregory Clause, sits atop a limestone base adorned with quotations from the Famine period which resonate in today's world of famines and dispossession.[3] The visitor can walk a simple dirt path to the memorial's highest edge and view both Ellis Island and the Statue of Liberty.

What does it mean that it took 150 years for Irish Americans to construct a moving and respectful memorial to their own immigrant past, or that the first Famine Museum opened in the south of Ireland, in County Roscommon, in 1997? There is a delayed reaction to certain collective traumas, perhaps because grieving and drawing lessons are only possible when a certain succeeding generation feels safe with the traumatic legacy. Even today, such memorials, books, and public school curricula on the Famine meet with jeers about victimization and calls to get on with modern life. But of course it is hard to process grief and anger when the victimizers are either still in power or wait 150 years to make a minimal apology, as British Prime Minister Tony Blair did in 1997, and it is doubly difficult to get on with modern life when famine still haunts the planet for the same reasons – arrogant superiority, indifference to poverty, and allegiance to *laissez-faire* economics – that dominated

Trevelyan's era. The modesty and detail of the New York Famine Memorial not only draws the visitor into the silence of history but seems a way for the dead to communicate to the living. Like the individual stories hidden in the Irish psyche, this Memorial is "inserted into the modern world almost as if it were an offering."[4]

All this seems sadly lost on Foster, whose serious contributions to Irish history and the biography of William Butler Yeats are tarnished by his obsession with attacking Irish republicans, writers like Frank McCourt, and anyone who he finds guilty of demonizing the British on behalf of Catholic nationalist dogmas.

It's not that these purported dogmas must be preserved without revision. Foster and his fellow revisionists argue, for example, that insisting on accusing the British of "genocide" is a prime example of one such nationalist dogma. The British government similarly lobbies against any reference to "genocide" in American school curricula on the Famine. Obviously, such a volatile charge should be tested against a rigorous standard of proof, not simply folkloric tradition. For example, one claim that seems false in the nationalist tradition is that the foodstuffs produced and exported from Ireland during the Famine years were sufficient to feed the Irish people. Nationalist historians such as Cormac Ó Gráda, Christine Kinealy and James Donnelly have accepted that additional provisions would have been needed to stem the starvation. But what light does this cast on nineteenth-century British intentions? That the British policies were "more effective than is sometimes allowed", as Foster writes in *Modern Ireland*?[5] Noting that "much retrospective condemnation has been heaped on Trevelyan's shoulders," Foster holds a softer view: that "government policies were by no means passive, and certainly not careless, but they were generally ill-founded."[6] In his gentle critique, Foster illustrates the broad tendency of revisionism to view the nineteenth-century British establishment as consisting of "genuinely good men . . . by no means indifferent to Irish needs."[7] Foster seems to store more venom for Irish nationalists, and certainly for *Irish on the Inside*, than he has ever mustered towards Charles Trevelyan. It is worth noting how closely Trevelyan came to advocating, if not racial genocide, the mass death or forced emigration of millions of Irish peasants when he wrote that "we are advancing by sure steps towards the desired end" and that "we must not complain of what we really want to *obtain*."[8] Trevelyan was directly applauding the fact that smallholdings "have become deserted owing to death or emigration or the mere inability of the holders to obtain a subsistence from them in the absence of the potato . . . ," and the prospect that "if small farmers go, and their land-lords are reduced to sell portions of their estates to persons who will invest in capital, we shall at last arrive at something like a satisfactory settlement of the country."[9] Trevelyan was the minister responsible but he was hardly alone; in 1847, *The Economist* opined that "it is no man's business to provide for another," while the *London Times* asserted that "something like harshness [was] the greatest humanity," leaving John Mitchel to claim that "Ireland died of political economy."[10] The echoes of these commentaries in today's discussion of corporate globalization are so disturbing that it is no wonder that some would prefer the past to be forgotten. Even the scale and uniqueness of the Irish famine continues to be downplayed by revisionist historians. Yet historian Amartya Sen has concluded that "in no other famine in the world [was] the propor-tion of people killed . . . as large as in the Irish famines in the 1840s."[11] Cormac Ó Gráda has carefully calculated that "with the likely exception of 1918–22 in the Soviet Union though, the proportionate cost in lives of the Irish famine was much greater, distinguishing it from most, though not all, historical and modern famines."[12]

If the label of genocide makes Foster uncomfortable, would ethnic cleansing do as a summary of the British establishment's position? Or perhaps John Milton's seventeenth-century call for a "civilizing conquest" over the "savage customes" and "true barbarisme" of the Irish?[13] Why is a writer like Foster so given to such boisterous polemics but unable to select a harsher phrase than "ill-founded" for policies so catastrophic? In another passage, Foster describes the calamity as simply a "subsistence crisis that was beyond the powers either of the existing state apparatus or the prevalent conceptions of social responsibility – in Ireland at least."[14] The British government could have taken more affirmative steps, as the

Belgians did during their 1867 famine, as Foster himself admits, but they were "not up to the challenge."[15] Foster's conception of the historical limits of British "social responsibility" is quite lenient and forgiving, therefore, especially when he agrees that it was laced with a widespread bias against the "feckless" Irish who deserved retribution.[16] Cormac Ó Gráda has shown Foster wrong in his claim that there were no deaths from starvation in Killaloe, County Kildare. According to Ó Gráda, Foster's history ignored 113 deaths recorded in Killaloe's temporary fever hospital, and the drop in population in rural Killaloe parish from 2,948 in 1841 to 1,666 in 1851.[17] These are the kind of omissions that would lead Foster to lacerate a nationalist historian.

In one passage Foster denies that the Great Hunger was a "watershed" in Irish history ("as a literal analysis, it does not stand up to examination"[18]) by using the peculiar argument that the same disasters frequently took place in the preceding centuries – an admission that makes the failure of British "social responsibility" seem all the more deliberate. Foster then reverses himself and acknowledges that the crisis of the 1840s was a unique, transformative one after all, because the rate of population decline – 2.2 million in five years, including probably one million deaths – reached "undreamt of levels."[19]

What could be Foster's reason for devoting so much energy to promoting revisionism? As he tells reporters, he was raised in a Protestant enclave in County Wexford where the surrounding Catholic nationalism was claustrophobic for him.[20] But why such determined, almost swaggering, persistence in trying to prove the British less responsible for events which were catastrophic by any account? And why the difficulty in understanding those who claim that the Famine memory is so often lost to a cultivated amnesia? As Brendan Bradshaw has pointed out, the citadel of revisionist historians produced only one academic study of the Famine in the fifty years between its founding in the 1930s and the late 1980s.[21] Kinealy's research shows that during that period, 'When the revisionist approach was in the ascendant, only two major books were produced on the Famine".[22] That paucity of material suggests that denial or avoidance were cloaked in the gowns of academia.

The function of Foster's revisionism is to undermine the nationalist and republican case against British rule in Ireland, especially among Irish Americans. Truly objective efforts at revision, or conceptual bridge building, between the "two traditions" seems an entirely worthy enterprise. But Foster's intent, expressed discreetly in his academic work and polemically in his public commentaries, seems more to purge his perceived enemies than, say, clarify the nature of British colonialism. His classic *Modern Ireland* (1982), written in the midst of the Troubles, ends with a condemnation of the tendency to be "more" or "less" Irish, an absurd preoccupation at a time when Northern nationalists were not permitted to be Irish at all. Foster wrote that he wanted to reduce "the sense of difference" and make being Irish into a "simple national, or residential, qualification."[23] Was Foster criticizing the British or the unionists for their fundamental refusal to recognize the simple national and residential identity of Irish people in the Six Counties? It took ten more years of war before the British and the unionists (reluctantly) agreed to allow equal rights for those of Irish nationality in the Good Friday Agreement. Foster wasn't among those marching to support the rights of nationalists, but arguing against those credentials being too "aggressively displayed."[24] In the name of "cultural maturity," his book proposed a new European identity and a "less restricted view of Irish history," code words for making the Irish identity more agreeable to the British.[25]

Eamon Delaney continued in the same diversionary vein as Foster in the *Irish Times*, claiming that the central theme of *Irish on the Inside* is what revisionists and neo-conservatives call the "MOPE" theory – that the Irish are the Most Oppressed People Ever.[26] Such intentional marginalizing may not have been new to Delaney, a former Irish diplomat assigned to the New York consulate in the early nineties when Irish American republicans were being demonized. Completing the purge was Ian Buruma in the *New York Review of Books* where I was accused of perpetuating a lethal "blood lust" on behalf of identity politics.[27] (Times and fashions change. In 1967, the same editors of the *New York Review of Books* lusted excitedly themselves over the drawing of a Molotov cocktail that accompanied my account of the Newark riots they published.)

One example of the kinds of association considered romantic and far-fetched by these reviews is the claim in *Irish on the Inside* that Che Guevara had Irish roots. It's apparently a great day for the Irish when any visiting celebrity, movie star, presidential candidate or golf pro is discovered to have a trace of Irish blood, but an occasion for concern and denial when an international socialist revolutionary is claimed. Yet Che's Irish connection was not fabricated, only forgotten. Shortly after *Irish on the Inside* was published, Che's daughter, Dr. Aleida Guevara, visited the Galway coast where a castle, a restaurant, and a hanging site are named after the eighteenth-century Lynch family from which Che descended. His daughter spoke at pro-Cuba meetings across the country.[28]

Irish on the Inside was reviewed thoughtfully and constructively in the *Los Angeles Times* (Frank McCourt),[29] the *New York Times* (Andrew O'Hehir),[30] the *Washington Post* (Thomas Flanagan),[31] *Publishers Weekly*,[32] and the *Irish Democrat*[33] and *Irish America*,[34] not to mention my favourite Irish paper, the *Andersonstown News*,[35] so the question arises: why such passionate differences among such credible observers of the Irish condition? It appears that even though the shooting and killing has diminished in Northern Ireland, the underlying conflict over Irish and Irish American identity has intensified. Those who are uncomfortable with the changing currents in Irish politics, particularly the emergence of mass public support for republicanism, and the increasing emphasis on multicultural diversity in American politics, are hostile to the analysis presented in this book, while those who identify with the challenges to the status quo in Ireland and North America are interested or supportive.

To summarize my viewpoint, the dominant alliance in the new world order is that between the United States, which is the sole superpower, and the United Kingdom, no longer a superpower but still the mother culture from which mainstream American culture derives. Together they promote an "Anglosphere" of cultural and economic hegemony, a worldview of the WASP backed by the use of military force. Of course, the two countries share a history of conflicts as well as consensus dating back to the American colonial experience. In Northern Ireland, the US has been more sympathetic to Catholic nationalists because of its own large Irish American population. Nevertheless, the US has always supported the state interest of the UK in maintaining its colony in Northern Ireland. Having failed to demonize and defeat Irish republicanism over the past three decades, the UK and US have opted for what Foster calls a "face-saving *modus vivendi* established for the troublesome Six Counties that will incidentally split the republican movement."[36] Sinn Féin has decided to shift its focus from the military stalemate to a political challenge towards these arrangements. In terms of domestic American politics, this means an elite strategy of detaching Irish Americans from support for the republican struggle in Ireland, and assimilating them into an embrace of an upwardly-mobile WASP value system rather than identification with minorities and immigrants based on a sense of common heritage. The revisionist project of defining a "modern" Irish identity that is somehow beyond nationalism and unionism parallels the neo-conservative project of preserving the melting-pot mythology against the pressures of multiculturalism. Collective and individual memory of degradation, discrimination, humiliation and rebellion is seen as a threat to the stability of the US–UK power arrangement.

Northern Ireland is one example of the legacy of the British empire which the US is steadily inheriting. According to Foreign Secretary Jack Straw, "Britain caused many of the world's current crises, ranging from the Indian subcontinent to the Middle East and Africa, India, Pakistan – we made some quite serious mistakes . . . The odd lines for Iraq's borders were drawn by Brits. The Balfour Declaration and the contradictory assurances we were giving to Palestinians in private as they were being given to the Israelis – again, an interesting story for us but not an honourable one."[37] An essential characteristic of the strategy of empire is to preserve power by dividing the loyalties of colonial subjects. The cultural occupation of the colonized mind becomes more significant over time than the military occupation of their lands.

Tom Clancy's *Patriot Games* (1987) captures the divisive strategy of defeating Irish republicans and assimilating Irish Americans. The novel's hero is Jack Ryan, played in the screen version by Harrison Ford. A former marine officer lecturing in London, he saves members of the royal family from an attack by a republican splinter group. The Queen visits Ryan in the hospital, curious that an Irish American would risk his life for such a purpose. Ryan's answer encapsulates Clancy's favourable view of what Irish Americans have become:

> " . . . Where I come from, we – that is, Irish Americans – have made out pretty well. We're all in the professions, business and politics, but your prototypical Irish American is still a basic police officer or fire-fighter. The cavalry that won the West was a third Irish, and there are still plenty of us in uniform – especially the Marine Corps, as a matter of fact. Half the local FBI office lived in my old neighbour-hood. They had names like Tully, Sullivan, O'Connor and Murphy. My dad was a police officer half his life, and the priests and nuns who educated me were mostly Irish, probably. Do you see what I mean, Your Majesty? In America we are the forces of law and order, the glue that holds the society together – so what happens? Today, the most famous Irishmen in the world are the maniacs who leave bombs in parked cars, or assassins who kill people to make some sort of political point. I don't like that, and I know my dad wouldn't like it. He spent his whole working life taking animals like that off the street and putting them in cages where they belong. We've worked pretty hard to get where we are – too hard to be happy about being thought of as the relatives of terrorists . . . I guess I understand how Italians feel about the Mafia."[38]

Tom Clancy's Irishman perfectly personifies the assimilation process at full throttle, a form of self-administered brainwashing. Starting as an external plantation (literally, the plantation of Ulster), the planting process is also psychic, growing into a disgust with one's own kind. In time, the colonized protect the colonizers by proudly policing anyone who reminds them of their former selves. The former rabble becomes the glue.

The September 11, 2001 slaughter of some 3,000 American civilians reinforced the foundations of this identity in several ways. A significant number of the victims were Irish Americans who had climbed the ladder of success in the world of financial services. But a disproportionate number of the firefighters and police who died were Irish Americans as well, displaying the physical courage and devoted loyalty for which the Irish are famous. Whereas before 9/11 these firefighters and cops were forgotten men, locked in an ancient ethnic patronage system, or tarnished with racial controversies, their deaths vaulted them to iconic status in the nation's official war on terrorism. Their willingness to sacrifice without qualms or criticism was promoted as a new standard of unquestioning patriotism for all Americans.

The war on terrorism led by the US and Great Britain consolidated this new patriotic order, casting a net of suspicion far beyond the Al Qaeda networks. Rupert Murdoch's *New York Post* editorialized against Gerry Adams as "Osama's Soul Brother."[39] Civil liberties and human rights considerations became secondary or irrelevant in foreign policy. One of the early casualties was Mary Robinson, the former Irish president who served as the United Nations human rights commissioner. Robinson, as I have noted, represented a positive alternative model of global Irish assimilation – linking her Irish experience to the cause of preventing torture and promoting human rights across the world. The US government pressured the UN to force Robinson's resignation in July, 2002. "Our position has basically been that anybody would be an improvement," said a satisfied State Department official when she was removed.[40] Her "insistent questioning of aspects of the war on terrorism after Sept. 11 . . . won her the lasting enmity of officials in Washington."[41]

The Irish peace process suffered serious erosion in the post 9/11 climate as well. The Bush family and administration, with close ties to the earlier Tory government of John Major, would have resumed a more pro-British posture after the Clinton years in any event. But the 9/11 atmosphere generated greater pressure on the IRA to decommission its stockpiles or face US and British consequences in the war on terrorism. Where Bill Clinton had wrenched the Northern Ireland portfolio away from the pro-British State Department in order to shape the Good Friday Agreement, Bush immediately restored the primacy of the State Department Anglophiles. Equally important but little noted was Bush's Republican Party alliance with Christian fundamentalists wed to extreme loyalists in Northern Ireland. For example, Bob Jones University, which in 2000 still prohibited inter-racial dating when Bush made a campaign appeal during his intense South Carolina primary with Senator John McCain, counted the Rev. Ian Paisley among its doctoral degree recipients.

The peace process itself unleashed a dynamic that the British and Americans could not entirely control, however. The compromise made by Irish republicans was in effect the acceptance of Northern Ireland as a partitioned entity in the United Kingdom, at least for the foreseeable future. But the provisions of the Agreement requiring equality, civil liberties, police reform, British demilitarization, and cross-border institutions in a context where the guns were silent challenged the core nature of the Northern state and created space for the expansion of Sinn Féin's constituency and mandate. If the Agreement was implemented, the North would become a bi-national state internally with decision-making links to the South, a transition which would undermine unionist privilege and weaken the link with Britain. The moderate center envisioned by the British and the US steadily disintegrated as the SDLP lost votes to Sinn Féin and David Trimble's Unionists declined in equal measure to Rev. Ian Paisley's Democratic Unionist Party (DUP). By 2002, the majority of Unionist/loyalist voters were opposed to the Good Friday Agreement because of its equality provisions. Loyalist paramilitaries enjoyed free rein in attacking Catholic children attending Holy Cross School in Belfast. Over 500 bomb attacks were inflicted on nationalists between 2001–2002 by loyalist paramilitaries seeking to intimidate strongly republican communities like Short Strand and, incidentally, provoke the IRA to break its ceasefire.[42] Faced with the rising political popularity of both Gerry Adams and Ian Paisley, the British government in 2002 once again displayed its colonial hand and suspended the Stormont Assembly to consider renegotiating the Agreement itself.

While little was heard from London or Washington about the unabated terrorism of loyalist paramilitaries, a concerted campaign was intensified against Sinn Féin and the IRA despite the continuing republican ceasefire. The IRA may have provided ammunition for this UK–US diplomatic assault in one case – that of three Irishmen arrested with false passports in Colombia, and charged with providing weapons training for the guerrillas there. As of this writing, the Colombian trial has been suspended and the three men remain in prison. Then came wild accusations and arrests of alleged IRA members for rifling security files in Castlereagh and Stormont. In several of these cases, the evidence seemed fabricated, non-existent, or based on informant's testimony, but whatever the final truth, none of the evidence suggested that the IRA had yet broken its ceasefire or Sinn Féin its commitment to the peace process. (On July 4, Prime Minister Blair, separating himself from his security bureaucracy, admitted there was "no doubt at all that the leadership of Sinn Féin are committed to this process and want to make it work."[43]) The Good Friday Agreement did not prohibit the IRA from consulting with other revolutionary organizations, obtaining intelligence information on police or army movements, or raising funds – any more than British intelligence was prevented from spying on republicans, or British troops prohibited from training in South Armagh, or, for that matter, bombing Iraq. This was a public-relations disaster for republicans, especially among disappointed sympathizers in Dublin and Washington who hoped that the IRA would decommission or disband without similar steps by the British army or unionist paramilitaries. Characteristically, Danny Morrison responded for Northern republicans with a commentary in the *Guardian*:[44]

> True, the IRA, because it exists, does not make it easier for unionists. But that's life . . . the IRA continues to exist because nationalists still

feel vulnerable. But it can only return to armed struggle if the institutions and forces of the state attack nationalists or deny them their
rights, which thus begs the question of unionists and the British: is
the war over? If it is over, why do you want the Special Branch? Why
do you not make the police service acceptable to nationalists? Why
are the forces you support still bugging houses and cars, gathering
intelligence, targeting republicans, recruiting informers? Can you
guarantee that you will not go back to internment, censorship, the ill-
treatment of prisoners, shoot-to-kill operations? Can you assure us
that you will cease your double standards which give political cover
and encouragement to loyalist paramilitaries . . . Because you have a
past does not mean that you cannot have a future. Here is the hand
of friendship. Tell us that the war is over.

More sophisticated questioning of Sinn Féin came in seemingly objective
books on Gerry Adams and Martin McGuinness by accomplished journalists Ed Moloney, Liam Clarke and Kathryn Johnston, citing extensive
sources in the security services and among unnamed republicans.
Moloney's work, *The Secret History of the IRA* depicts Adams as a sinister and duplicitous, though effective, leader who kept his peace strategy
secret from his republican constituency, and even from the IRA Army
Council which Moloney says he chaired, through fifteen years of private
dealings. Somehow, according to Moloney, Adams managed this svengali
manoeuvring at the very heart of the IRA while lacking military credentials and qualities of personal bravery, especially in comparison with
McGuinness. But on the other hand, Clarke and Johnston claim to know
that McGuinness "wasn't much of a fighter" either, and may have been
protected by the British authorities as a man with whom they could
negotiate.[45] Both books seek to define Adams and McGuinness as leading dual lives, on the one hand promoting themselves as public
personalities while hiding their responsibility for the IRA's darkest deeds.
According to these accounts, McGuinness leads a charmed life, while
Adams has "clearly bewitched" Edna O'Brian who wrote a profile in the
New York Times magazine.[46] Lapsing into the oldest stereotype,

Moloney writes that Irish America was "intoxicated" and "made drunk" in the excitement over Adams's visa in 1995.

The danger is that these highly-promoted "insider" biographies promoting classic stereotypes will become definitive sources, even though they don't compare with more objective works by Peter Taylor,[47] Deaglan de Breadun[48] or Tim Pat Coogan.[49] In addition, there are works by former republican prisoners which provide far richer insights into the republican imagination and experience. Danny Morrison's several novels about life in occupied West Belfast are anything but dogmatic. The hunger striker Laurence McKeown's insightful history of how IRA prisoners developed non-military approaches to struggle is not even available for sale in the US.[50] There is also the case of Patrick Magee, charged with bombing the Brighton Hotel and nearly killing the Tory Party leadership in 1984. Magee earned a doctoral degree in prison for a thesis analyzing some 700 works of fiction on the Troubles – not the profile of a violent sociopath. Published as *Gangsters or Guerillas?* (2001), Magee's book analyses how all republicans, not simply Adams and McGuinness, have been constructed and manipulated as incorrigible terrorists in the vast majority of fictional depictions.[51] Magee's work is testimony to the fact that a onetime "terrorist" can be a thoughtful academic under other conditions.

The implicit notion that a voluntary army like the IRA and its supporters might be led like remorseless automatons by one or two manipulative individuals is even rejected by one of Moloney's most solid sources, Brigadier General James Glover, an intelligence specialist who commanded British land forces in Northern Ireland in the late seventies. In an internal document referenced by Moloney, the British expert wrote that "our evidence of the caliber of rank-and-file terrorists does not support the view that they are mindless hooligans. . . ."[52] In summary, the view that the IRA has been an isolated band of misfits, or that the Adams–McGuinness leadership secretly negotiated the Good Friday Agreement behind the backs of the republican faithful, is refuted by any number of eyewitness histories and, of course, the public fact that the Agreement was thoroughly debated and ultimately supported by 98 percent of the nationalist vote. As for the allegations concerning Adams or

McGuinness's association with brutal atrocities in the past, the hazy evidence presented tends to be circumstantial. It is virtually unavoidable that an urban guerrilla war caused civilian casualties and unforgivable atrocities, for which its leaders hold responsibility. What is more remarkable – and unaccounted for in these works – is that men like Adams and McGuinness were able to survive, transform and lead a militaristic organization into such a unified and political peace strategy, while largely avoiding British and US conspiracies to foment bloody internal divisions.

Not that everyone was enthusiastic about the peace agreement on the republican side. Significant longtime IRA members, unable to support the agreement's implied endorsement of partition, withdrew to form dissident factions with armed capabilities. They have been blamed for the catastrophic Omagh bomb explosion of August 1998, among several other incidents. However destructive, their actions failed to wreck the peace process or seriously divide the republican movement (and North Ireland's official police ombudsman uncovered evidence that the Special Branch may have failed to act on intelligence in its possession before the Omagh blast).[53]

One respected left-wing (Trotskyist) critic, Eamonn McCann of Derry, celebrated Moloney's book as describing how the Adams–McGuinness leadership was trapped within "conventional bourgeois politics," leaving "no fundamental contradiction between the politics of the Provo leadership and of the British ruling class."[54] This stinging critique, however, fails to acknowledge that the British "ruling class" had to be bombed, pressured and politically outmanoeuvred to arrive at the minimum provisions of the Good Friday Agreement. A common claim is that the main provisions of the Good Friday Agreement could have been achieved in the 1974 Sunningdale Agreement while saving thousands of lives. But this hypothesis ignores the fact that the British government yielded to a loyalist general strike in 1974, and that the Sunningdale blueprint included no place for Sinn Féin, no release of IRA prisoners, no commitments to equality, no visas to the United States, and so on.

McCann is quite right that Sinn Féin, like the African National

Congress and other revolutionary movements, has departed from its early socialist rhetoric into acceptance of neo-liberal market incentives for business investment. Even here, however, ideology leads McCann too far. If Sinn Féin panders to the multinational corporations, as he claims, why does Sinn Féin oppose corporate globalization and the Treaty of Nice, and place emphasis on the priority of finding government solutions to poverty across Ireland? These are hardly the goals of the British ruling class. McCann's ideological dilemma has been his support of a hypothetical working-class revolution as a higher strategic priority than fighting a nationalist war against the link with Britain. McCann's concern over how Sinn Féin deals with class politics in a time of globalization is already a subject of intense debate among republicans. Having fought for a nationalist dream, they are unlikely to give it up for token inclusion in the new world order.

As of 2002, Sinn Féin continued to make historic progress on the electoral front in spite of attacks from every conceivable direction. Its electoral mandate in the North surpassed that of the SDLP and appeared to widen. The party's inroads in the South were further evidence that significant numbers of voters remained Irish on the inside, not revisionist, West Brit or European. Sinn Féin candidates won five seats in the Irish parliament in the May 2002 elections, the electoral equivalent of Ralph Nader's Green Party winning some twenty-five congressional seats in an American election. That gave the party a position of influence in the South for the first time in sixty years, and it came narrowly close to achieving a key role in the balance of power in Dublin. The most interesting triumph was that of Martin Ferris in Kerry, who defeated a former Irish foreign minister, Dick Spring. Ferris, as the media persistently informed every voter in Ireland during the election, was a forty-seven day hunger striker in the seventies and a convicted IRA gunrunner who was captured on the Boston trawler *Marita Ann* in 1994. As if those credentials were not unconventional enough, the police arrested Ferris and his campaign manager on the eve of the election for a supposed vigilante assault on drug dealers four months earlier. The charges, which backfired, were dropped after the election and Ferris now sits in the Irish Dáil analyzing the budget of a state he has spent a lifetime opposing. Previously condemned for abstaining from the Irish state, now he is feared as the enemy within.

In the election's aftermath, the attacks on Sinn Féin grew even more hysterical. The Sinn Féin machine "threatens to become unstoppable" claimed the *Scotsman*.[55] "There goes the neighbourhood," lamented Ellis O'Hanlon in the *Irish Independent*.[56] "Our Democracy is Now in Peril" announced an *Independent* headline for a commentary by noted revisionist historian Ruth Dudley Edwards who concluded that "the fascist jackboot is at the door."[57] Reading these distorted diatribes, I began to realize a fundamental aspect of the anti-republican, revisionist agenda. Thirty years of Irish McCarthyism have allowed a build-up of wildly inaccurate stereotypes towards republicans and northern nationalists. The years of exclusion and censorship allowed the distortions to achieve a level of credibility, as well as fashion. Those who disagreed were demonized by the accusation that they were Provo sympathizers. However, the peace process mandated an Irish *glasnost*, or openness to previously forbidden ideas, for which mainstream opinion leaders were unprepared. While Sinn Féin entered the political process with ideas as its new weapons, establishment Ireland (and its allies in England and the US) responded with foaming over-reactions not unlike the red-baiting that plagued US politics for decades.

In context, however, the Irish vote was very understandable and far from revolutionary. The moderate Fianna Fáil Prime Minister, Bertie Ahern, was elected overwhelmingly in a vote for the status quo. Additionally, under enormous pressure, Irish voters reversed themselves and approved the Nice Treaty, thus accepting inclusion in the expanding European Union. Sinn Féin's growing strength was centered in pockets of high-poverty, border counties, and among younger anti-establishment voters. In part, the Sinn Féin vote was against the relative decline of the "Celtic Tiger" economy after a decade of boom. In the previous year, firms like Gateway and Dell slashed dot.com jobs, the number of Irish workers employed by multinationals declined 20 percent, and the gap between rich and poor grew to be larger than any developed country besides the United States.[58] What shocked the political establishment – since every major party had announced before the election that they would not include Sinn Féin in a governing coalition – was the reappearance of strong support for a party that was considered dead and forbidden for some decades. Now Sinn Féin is the only nationalist political party on both sides of the border, thus actively representing a "united Ireland" constituency. Its leader, Gerry Adams, remains the most popular of opposition party leaders. It could lay claim to being a party of peace and Irish reunification, able to influence policy in Stormont, the Dáil, the White House and Westminster. If that is not a revolution, it is an alternative, a center of hope in a time of terrorism.

Among Irish Americans, the process of redefinition has continued to accelerate as well. The leading example is the emergence of a strong Irish–American constituency pushing for official American involvement in securing peace and justice in Northern Ireland. This constituency is broadly-based enough to influence politicians in both parties. Even the Tory-leaning President Bush, who during the 2000 presidential campaign disparaged Bill Clinton's peace strategy as meddling in Northern Ireland, has recognized the popularity of Clinton's policy and reversed his position on the Agreement, at least for public consumption. But with the reality of Bush's retreat from Clinton's policy of independence, it will be increasingly important for Irish Americans to educate and pressure the Administration to embrace the Agreement as a policy framework, not weaken it by concessions to the British and unionists.

Will this new Irish American lobby continue developing an assertive voice in national affairs, or will the blood lines, as Jimmy Breslin once called them, be thinned into a pale token of our potential? The efforts of neo-conservatives to reinforce "traditional values" at the expense of cultural diversity are intensifying. The potential of Irish American peace activists will depend on how this deeper quarrel between Anglo assimilation and rainbow-style multiculturalism plays out. If most Irish Americans choose to blend into the white conservative culture, they will lose the empathy necessary to support peace and justice in Northern Ireland. If, on the other hand, Irish America sees itself as a distinct community with historical ties to the disenfranchised, the desire to make a difference in the Irish peace process will expand.

Perhaps nothing reveals the emergence of a post-Famine, post-colonial Irish temperament better than the scandal that was ripping apart the Catholic Church in the new millennium. While it stemmed from the Church's hierarchical, patriarchal nature and affected Catholics of all ethnic backgrounds, the scandal was difficult to separate from the Irish and the Irish-Catholic experiences. The Church in both countries has played a key role in shaping a conservative Irish culture based on obedience to authority in all spheres of life. The same culture cultivated a piety based on guilt and redemption. These norms always conflicted with the rising culture of democratic values, especially the exclusion of women. The sixties saw the rise of liberation theology in Latin America, and the worldwide liberalization loosed by *Pacem in Terris*. By the eighties, the Vatican's advocates of orthodoxy prevailed once again, but could not prevent a pattern of institutional scandal from leaking out to the media and the Catholic public. In Ireland, individual clerical scandals were accompanied by films and revelations about systemic abuse of young people in the Church's "industrial schools" and girls' reformatories. One film touched a deep nerve in 2002, Peter Mullan's *The Magdalene Sisters*, which depicted the banishment of thousands of young girls to Church-run commercial laundries – de facto workhouses – for violations of the Catholic moral code including flirtation, "looking pretty," being raped, and becoming pregnant outside of marriage. Some 30,000 girls worked without pay seven days per week with only Christmas Day off, were repeatedly beaten and punished, and forced to pray in every waking hour. One million people – one of every four Irish people – saw *The Magdalene Sisters* in the first month the film was released, despite Vatican denunciations that it was an "angry and rancorous provocation."[59] Almost overnight, decades of Irish shame and denial were being confronted, including cover-ups by the Archdiocese of Dublin and collusion by state officials. The reform spirit even entered sectors of the Church itself; for example, when the Vatican ordered a Benedictine nun not to speak at a 2001 conference in Dublin on the ordination of women, 128 Benedictines signed a letter of opposition and the Vatican yielded.[60]

In the US, a pattern of long-standing sexual abuses and cover-ups burst into public attention, raising questions about the tradition of celibacy, the exclusion of women and married priests, and the closeting of homosexuality. In heavily-Irish cities like Boston, lay Catholics demanded unprecedented accountability in the face of these institutional cover-ups; in a typical example, an Irish Catholic woman, Anne Barrett Doyle, joined a lay Catholic reform coalition, admitting that she "had enjoyed being part of this little club and had not fought against [her] sub-servient role."[61] The scandal sometimes spread from sexual cover-ups to allegations that Church privileges could be purchased. For example, in Los Angeles, Cardinal Roger Mahoney drew protests when his new $200 million Cathedral was found to include 1,270 basement crypts and 5,000 niches as burial sites for wealthy parishioners such as former Mayor Richard Riordan, with price tags as high as $50,000.[62] At the time, seventy-two of the Cardinal's current or former priests in the Archdiocese were under criminal investigation, and not long afterwards several of his ranking lieutenants mysteriously resigned.[63] A similar rage was spreading in Ireland, where the Archdiocese of Dublin agreed to a police investigation of sexual abuses after congregants heckled a cardinal with unprecedented shouts of "it's too late!" during Mass.[64]

The new militancy of these lay Catholic reformers stood in absolute contrast to the silence and denial that suffocated my Catholic child-hood in Royal Oak, Michigan. In my parents' world, the Church was beyond any scrutiny; in fact, the idea of scrutiny itself was beyond scrutiny. And if there was any wrongdoing it was felt proper to the keep the matter quietly closeted for fear of embarrassing not only the institution but one's own status. My lasting image of my mother is that of a woman with hushed lips. Now such lips are protesting against invisibility and abuse. An exodus of the Catholic faithful is not likely in either America or Ireland, but a fundamental renovation of the Church is on the agenda, a call to celebrate democracy as well as Mass.

This liberalizing trend among Irish Catholics is a positive development in the face of rising religious fundamentalism elsewhere. The leadership of progressive women, whether activists like Anne Barrett Doyle or more visible figures like Mary Robinson, is a powerful challenge to the patriarchal paradigms that have dominated Irish-Catholic consciousness for centuries. While far from settled, the reform movement among American Catholics has the potential to retrieve the Catholic social justice tradition from conservative control. For the Irish, the challenge to rigid Catholic nationalism may strengthen the possibilities for a more inclusive and egalitarian concept of a united Ireland. Unionists like Paisley and Trimble, each in different ways, have benefited from rallying Northern protestants against the Catholicism to their South (Paisley railing against 'Popery' and the "Whore of Babylon" while Trimble accused the South of being a "pathetic, mono-cultural, mono-ethnic state" which has no reason to exist "except Catholicism and anti-Britishness"[65]). But if the edifice of traditional Catholicism disintegrates in the South, unionism will be faced with an invitation to a non-sectarian future that will be increasingly difficult to oppose. Gerry Adams once said that, while a Catholic himself, he preferred the more democratic processes of Presbyterianism. If not quite the United Irishmen's revolutionary republic of Catholics, Protestants and Dissenters, the new Ireland that is developing will be more open to diversity and reconciliation than ever before. Who knows, there may even be a place for lapsed Catholics like myself. The question then will be whether unionism can fare without a Protestant state or whether its ultimate commitment is to sectarian dominance.

The restoration of the Irish American past has been enriched by recent explorations of the street gangs formed by Irish immigrants in the Five Points neighbourhoods of New York in the nineteenth century. Patrick Tyler's *Paradise Alley* (2002)[66] follows Peter Quinn's *The Banished Children of Eve* (1994)[67] in resurrecting the story of the Famine Irish in New York. The history of this period is virtually a creation story of Irish America, or certainly Irish Catholic America, because these were the first arrivals in the unprecedented wave of immigrants after the Famine.

This two-decade period between the Irish Famine and the American Civil War was the crucible in which the new Irish political and racial loyalties were defined. Yet little if any scholarship has been devoted to the study of how these complex attitudes came to exist, and what lessons might be learned from history to address the continuing problems of race, class and status today. Tyler's novel highlights the little-remembered story of how Irish immigrants and runaway slaves lived, and often cohabited, in the same tenements, how blacks were described as "smoked Irish" and Irish were classed as "white niggers." This inter-racial genesis of Irish America is whitened out of the ethnic history, as is its demonic twin, the rise of Irish racism to secure self-esteem and polit-ical-economic advantage. Tyler's chief protagonists are an inter-racial couple in Five Points, contending with the furies of a lynch mob. Another is an Irish prostitute whose services were available to black as well as white men. She is targeted by one Irish male who complains bitterly that "it wasn't right, having to share even our whores" with the Africans. Tyler's imaginative novel thus opens the closet doors to the way we really were as America's first urban underclass. It is little wonder that when these sons of Ireland were faced with conscription into the Union Army while the sons of privilege could pay $300 for a substitute draftee, they revolted in the streets of New York.

Martin Scorsese's epic *The Gangs of New York* brings the same era to the movie screen for the first time. As the *New York Times* reviewer acknowledged, "there is very little in the history of American cinema to prepare us for the version of American history Mr. Scorsese presents here."[68] In an understatement, the reviewer described the conventional version of history – what I have called the melting-pot mythology – as "the usual triumphalist story of moral progress and enlightenment." Instead, the review went on, the film "places the immigrant urban work-ing class at the center of the American story," which he describes as "a fairly radical notion."[69] Scorsese's gritty history conflicts with the melt-ing-pot myth that the Irish made it in America by hard work and piety. The romanticized tale permits Irish Americans, like Jewish Americans and Italian Americans, to incorporate a romanticized criminal past into their immigrant success stories, and still draw a sharp line between themselves and today's Crips, Bloods, Mexican Mafias, and Latin Kings. One irate letter I received for *Irish on the Inside*, for example, said "your willingness to ascribe my heritage to a familial tie to 'Mad Dog' Coll is vulgar, and your recent realization of 'Irishness' as key to some link between the Irish and 'people of color' [are they the same as colored people?] is simply stupid – a sign you've never been forced to mix."[70] Scorcese's accomplishment enables us to see the roots of present-day respectability in this "vulgar" past; indeed, his shanty Irish embody a certain nobility. The film makes it possible to look in the historical mirror and see that the Irish, and other white ethnics, come from pasts not dissimilar to the minority youth being criminalized and demonized as scapegoats today.

Some will question whether Scorcese merely recycles the stereotype of the Irish as a pathologically vendetta-ridden violent rabble. Some of the Irish gangs were driven by nationalist pride, not simply by vengeance or criminal activity. The name of one of the most notorious gangs, the Plug Uglies, was an Americanized reference to Ball Oglaigh, or "Irish Volunteers," the Fenian movement, according to Danny Cassidy of the New University's Irish Studies program.[71] The conflict between the nativist/protestant working class, represented by Daniel Day-Lewis, and the Irish immigrants is plainly manifest in the film. The Day-Lewis character, Bill the Butcher, eerily resembles modern loyalists like the "Shankill Butchers." He proclaims that "fear preserves the order of things." The Irish characters are characterized by an innate spirit of vengeance, it is true, but as one of them bitterly observes, 'We never thought the war [against landlords and the British] would follow us" to New York, "but it was waiting for us" in the form of anti-Irish bigotry. To be historically balanced, Scorcese should have included the Fenian movement, the Land League, and other Irish working-class struggles of the time. Nevertheless, the manipulated divisions of the urban working class along religious and racial lines are piercingly depicted by Scorcese as a tragic birthmark on American society.

The future now depends on whether America's estimated 20 million

Irish descendents continue the quest for respectability at the price of shunning this "shameful" and "vulgar" past in New York's slums, a past which remains present in Belfast and even Dublin today. (When I escorted the African American actress Alfre Woodard and her family to Belfast's Lower Ormeau Road in 2001, one impression was unexpectedly familiar to her: "Those people are sooo ghetto.") The drive for assimilation fosters blind forgetfulness and encourages instead an identification with the norms of the former oppressor.

With respect to Northern Ireland, this means a serious revisionist distortion of American history to erase any parallels between our legitimate eighteenth-century revolution and the one still continuing in Ireland today. However, since the parallels are so precise, what suffers is America's understanding of its own history. Our revolution against England becomes a brief, almost bloodless, fairy tale in this time of an Anglo-American alliance. Yet it was a "motley rabble" of "saucy boys," including "Irish taigs" and "molattoes," who confronted the British Army in the incident known as the "Boston Massacre" which exactly foreshadowed "Bloody Sunday" in Derry two centuries later. In addition, American patriots carried out acts of "terrorism" against loyalists in that era far beyond anything the IRA has ever been accused of contemplating. Mobs of republicans calling themselves the "Sons of Liberty" destroyed loyalist printing presses, stole loyalist cattle, tarred and feathered loyalist partisans, and physically forced thousands of loyalists into Canada. If these American colonists, many of them Irish, were justified in carrying out such intimidation and terror to gain their independence, who could deny the right, at least in principle, of Irish people to reunify their nation today over the objections of a 20 percent loyalist minority? The Good Friday Agreement is far more generous towards today's loyalists than those who opposed the American revolution, granting them a veto over the aspirations of the vast majority of Irish citizens. As Gerry Adams has said, "It is not our intention to put unionists into the political space that nationalists and republicans have long sought to escape from."[72] Given these parallels, one can see the importance of fostering false consciousness among Irish Americans, including Tom Clancy's fictional characters, about their own origins. One might even describe revisionism, as Tim Pat Coogan has, as history becoming a form of counter-insurgency.[73]

Simultaneously, the strategy of assimilation encourages middle-class Irish Americans to identify with the successful "haves" rather than join in coalition with the "have nots." As Republican pundit David Brooks has noted with satisfaction, 19 percent of Americans described themselves as part of the richest one percent of the population in a 2000 survey, and another 20 percent said they expected to be in the future.[74] The prospect of upward mobility is thought to be more satisfying, even intoxicating, than any affirmation that their destiny and interests are shared with the poor and marginalized. This is why so many white ethnic Democrats become Republicans. Many successful Irish Americans are distanced from poverty and starvation today precisely because they are distanced from their own past. But as new generations of the Irish become more secure, and as American identity becomes more contested racially and ethnically, the pull of a genuine Irish heritage could become stronger. And if the upward mobility of the middle classes is choked by the re-emergence of a dynastic upper class there will be a time when more Irish Americans will opt for an identity with their roots for a sense of where they belong. It is interesting that the former Republican strategist, Kevin Phillips, who invented the political realignment in the sixties that led the phenomenon of 'Reagan Democrats," now writes angrily about the rise of a new political aristocracy, and that *New York Times* essayist Paul Krugman condemns a "new gilded age" that threatens to destroy the middle-class ideal that once made ethnic attachments seem outdated and purely sentimental.[75] In these conditions, the Irish rebel heritage might still emerge from within the shadows of memory to enrich American democracy and create a bridge of empathy to the disenfranchised of the earth.

Notes

Part I Irish on the Inside

1. Eavan Boland, "The Dolls Museum in Dublin," in *In a Time of Violence*, Manchester, Carcanet Press Limited, 1994.

2. Personal interview with the author.

3. Nathan Glazer and Daniel Patrick Moynihan, *Beyond the Melting Pot: The Negroes, Puerto Ricans, Jews, Italians and Irish of New York City*, Cambridge, MIT Press, 2nd edn, 1990.

4. Roddy Doyle, *The Commitments*, London, Minerva, 1987, p. 9.

5. Thomas Keneally, *The Great Shame, and the Triumph of the Irish in the English-speaking World*, New York, Doubleday, 1999.

6. James Connolly, "Harp Strings," *The Lost Writings*, ed. Aindrias Ó Cathasaigh, London, Pluto Press, 1997, pp. 89–90.

7. Thomas Cleary, "In Search of the Irish Soul: Essays on the Evolution of the Irish Mind," unpublished manuscript, 1997, pp. 8, 338.

8. Quoted in Cleary, p. 4.

9. Fintan O'Toole, *The Ex-Isle of Erin: Images of a Global Ireland*, Dublin, New Island Books, 1997.

10. Ronald Takaki, *A Different Mirror: A History of Multi-cultural America*, New York, Little Brown, 1993, p. 139.

11. Peter Quinn, "In Search of the Banished Children," in Tom Hayden, ed., *Irish Hunger*, Dublin, Wolfhound Press and Boulder, Roberts Reinhart, 1997, p. 154.

12. Sean O'Callaghan, *To Hell or Barbados: The Ethnic Cleansing of Ireland*, Kerry, Ireland, Brandon, 2000, p. 15.

13. Lerone Bennett, Jr, *The Shaping of Black America*, Chicago, Johnson Publishing, 1975, p. 50.

14. Ibid., p. 51.

15. O'Callaghan, p. 79.

16. Ibid., pp. 128–9.

17. Bennett, p. 48.

18. See David Wilson, *United Irishmen, United States: Immigrant Radicals in the Early Republic*, Dublin, Four Courts Press, 1998, cover page.

19. Colm Tóibín, *The Irish Famine*, London, Profile Books, 1998, p. 40, quoting economist Amartya Sen.

20. Paul Cowan, *An Orphan in History: Retrieving a Jewish Legacy*, New York, Doubleday, 1982.

21. Charles Johnson and Patricia Smith, *Africans in America: America's Journey through Slavery*, New York, Harcourt and Brace, 1998, p. xi.

22. Cecil Woodham-Smith, *The Great Hunger: Ireland 1845–1849*, Harmondsworth, Penguin, 1991 (first published 1962).

23. Conversation with Tim Pat Coogan, Dublin, 1997.

24. See James S. Donnelly, "The Great Famine and Its Interpreters, Old and New," in Hayden, p. 123.

25. Ibid., p. 119.

26. Ibid., p. 121.

27. Mary Daly, *The Famine in Ireland*, Dublin, Dublin Historical Association, 1986, p. 113.

28. Robbie McVeigh, "The Last Conquest of Ireland? British Academics in Irish Universities," *Race & Class*, Vol. 37, No. 1, July–September 1995, p. 116.

29. Cited in Luke Gibbon, "Unapproved Roads, Post-colonialism and Irish Identity," in Trisha Ziff, ed., *Distant Relations*, New York, Smart Art Press, 1995, p. 63.

30. Hayden, p. 17.

31. Gibbon, pp. 62–3.

32. Morrison's quote cited in Peter Quinn, "An Interpretation of Silences," *Eire Ireland* magazine, spring 1997, p. 17; Moynihan's quote from Glazer and Moynihan, pp. 247–8.

33. *Oxford History* quote from Joy Hakim, ed., *Oxford History of the United States*, London, Oxford University Press, 1991, p. 29; Thatcher quote from *Endgame in Ireland*, a Brook Lapping production for BBC2, RTE (Ireland), June–July 2001.

34. *Nation*, October 2, 2000, p. 13.

35. Correspondence with Stephen Arditti, director of state governmental relations, University of California, September 12, 2000.

36. Mark Levy and Michael Kramer, *The Ethnic Factor: How America's Minorities Decide Elections*, New York, Simon and Schuster, 1972, p. 138.

37. *Sacramento Bee, San Francisco Chronicle*, October 9, 1997.

38. Tim Pat Coogan, *Wherever Green is Worn: The Story of the Irish Diaspora*, London, Random House, 2000, p. 369.

39. Niamh Flanagan, conversation with the author, Belfast, 1999.

40. Glazer and Moynihan, p. 247.

41. Jorge Casteneda, *Compañero: The Life and Death of Che Guevara*, New York, Vintage, 1997, p. 4; Paco Ignacio Taibo, *Guevara, Also Known as Che*, New York, St Martin's Press, 1997, p. 3.

42. Jon Lee Anderson, *Che: A Revolutionary Life*, New York, Grove Press, 1997, p. 67.

43. See Kathryn Mills and Pamela Mills, eds, *C. Wright Mills: Letters and Autobiographical Writings*, Berkeley, University of California Press, 2000, p. 6.

44. Ibid., pp. 21–3.

45. Ibid., pp. 55–7.

46. Marcia Graham Synnott, *The Half Opened Door: Discrimination in Admissions at Harvard, Yale, and Princeton, 1900–70*, Westport, Conn., Greenwood Publishing Group, 1979, pp. 40–44, 245.

47. Takaki, p. 161.

48. Edwin Teale, ed., *The Wilderness World of John Muir*, Boston, Houghton Mifflin (1954) 1982, p. 316.

49. Interview with the author.

50. Albert Memmi, *The Colonizer and the Colonized*, Boston, Beacon Press, 1991.

51. William Kennedy, *Very Old Bones*, New York, Penguin, 1997.

52. John Duffy Ibson, *Will the World Break Your Heart? Dimensions and Consequences of Irish-American Assimilation*, New York, Garland, 1990, p. 126.

53. I am indebted to Tom Hyde, an Irish genealogist in Dublin, for the research cited here into my family history, utilizing previous data compiled by Lineages, Inc., and material from a cousin, Heather Flanagan, in Wisconsin, the genealogist Theo MacMahon in County Monaghan, and archives in Cavan, south Armagh and Louth. I wish to also thank the historian Harold O'Sullivan in Dundalk, County Louth.

54. For life expectancy and other information on Irish immigrants, the best source is Kerby Miller, *Emigrants and Exiles: Ireland and the Irish Exodus to North America*, New York, Oxford University Press, 1985, p. 319.

55. Jacob A. Riis, *How the Other Half Lives*, New York, Dover Publications, 1971, p. vi.

56. Miller, p. 319.

57. Noel Ignatiev, *How the Irish Became White*, New York, Routledge, 1995.

58. In addition to Ignatiev, see the excellent works of Theodore W. Allen, *The Invention of the White Race*, London, Verso, 1994, and David R. Roediger, *The Wages of Whiteness: Race and the Making of the American Working Class*, London, Verso, 1991.

59. Michael Padden and Robert Sullivan, *May the Road Rise to Meet You*, New York, Penguin, 1999, pp. 101–2.

60. Coogan, *Wherever Green*, p. 327.

61. Ignatiev, p. 12.

62. Ibid. p. 59.

63. Quoted in Peter Quinn, "Closets Full of Bones," in Hayden, p. 239.

64. Ibid.

65. James T. Farrell, *Studs Lonigan*, Urbana-Champaigne, University of Illinois Press, 1993, p. 735.

66. Conversation with the author, Dublin, 1997.

67. Farrell, p. iv.

68. John McGahern, *Among Women*, Faber & Faber, London, 1990, p. 68.

69. Brendan Kennelly, "My Dark Fathers," in Hayden, p. 246.

70. Ibid., p. 243.

71. Gearoid Ó hAllmhurain, *A Pocket History of Traditional Irish Music*, Dublin, O'Brien, 1998, p. 75.

72. Terry Eagleton, *Heathcliff and the Great Hunger: Studies in Irish Culture*, London, Verso, 1995.

73. Kennelly, p. 244.

74. Peadar Livingston, *The Monaghan Story: A Documented History of the County Monaghan from Earliest Times to 1976*, Enniskillen, Clogher Historical Society, 1980, p. 211–22.

75. Ibid., p. 218.

76. Ibid., p. 217.

77. Glazer and Moynihan, pp. 261–2.

78. John Corry, *The Golden Clan*, cited in Monica McGoldrick, John K. Pearce, and Joseph Giordano, *Ethnicity and Family Therapy*, New York, Guilford Press, 1982, pp. 148, 154.

79. Miller, p. 534.

80. *Detroit News*, January 30, 1939.

81. For a history of Father Coughlin, see Sheldon Marcus, *Father Coughlin: The Tumultuous Life of the Priest of the Little Flower*, New York, Little, Brown, 1973.

82. McGoldrick *et al.*, pp. 310–39.

83. Brochure, Shrine of the Little Flower, Royal Oak, Michigan, 2000.

84. Mary Gordon, *Final Payments*, New York, Ballantine, 1978, p. 28.

85. *Detroit News*, June 11, 1973.

86. Emmet Larkin, "The Devotional Revolution in Ireland, 1850–75," *American Historical Review*, June 1972, Vol. 77, No. 3, pp. 625–52.

87. Michael Coffey and Terry Golway, eds, *The Irish in America*, New York, Hyperion, 1997, pp. 48–55.

88. Neal R. Davison, *James Joyce, "Ulysses" and the Construction of Jewish Identity: Culture, Biography, and "the Jew" in Modernist Europe*, Cambridge, Cambridge University Press, 1996, pp. 21, 68–9.

89. See *Irish America* magazine, December 1997–January 1998, pp. 36–7.

90. Davison, pp. 68–9.

91. *Irish America*, December 1997–January 1998, p. 37.

92. Memo to author from Harold Brackman, September 22, 1997.

93. Robert Fisk, *In Time of War: Ireland, Ulster and the Price of Neutrality, 1939–45*, Dublin, Gill & Macmillan, 1983, p. 48.

94. McGoldrick *et al.*, p. 314.

95. Quoted in McGoldrick *et al.*, p. 17.

96. Ibid., p. 315.

97. Peter Gavrilovich and Bill McGraw, *The Detroit Almanac: 300 Years of Life in the Motor City*, Detroit Free Press, 2000, pp. 47–9.

98. Ibid., p. 48.

99. Andrew Greeley, *The Irish Americans: The Rise to Money and Power*, New York, Harper & Row, 1981, p. 122.

100. McGoldrick *et al.*, p. 314.

101. Miller, pp. 414, 498.

102. Ibid., p. 497.

103. From a sermon by Sheen in the 1950s. Quoted in Ibson, p. 20.

104. *Los Angeles Times*, October 9, 1999.

105. Garrett O'Connor, "Alcoholism in American-Irish Catholics, Cultural Stereotype vs. Clinical Reality," paper, December 3, 1993.

106. Niall O'Dowd, "The Myth and the Reality," *Irish America*, October 1988. John Waters, *An Intelligent Person's Guide to Modern Ireland*, London, Duckworth, 2001.

107. O'Dowd. See also Richard Stivers, *The Hair of the Dog: Irish Drinking and Its American Stereotype*, New York, Continuum, 2000.

108. Greeley, p. 173.

109. Derek Wilson, *Dark and Light: The Story of the Guinness Family*, London, Orion, 1998, p. 66.

110. O'Connor.

111. Eugene O'Neill, *Long Day's Journey into Night*, New Haven, Yale University Press, 1984, p. 31. See also the discussion by Ibson, pp. 180–87.

112. O'Neill, p. 93.

113. Lacey's observations are in Hayden, p. 87.

114. For a discussion of parallels between Irish goddesses and Molly Bloom, see Maria Thymoczko, *The Irish Ulysses*, Berkeley, University of California Press, 1994, p. 114.

115. Quoted in Hayden, p. 88.

116. J. J. Lee, *Ireland 1912–1985: Politics and Society*, Cambridge, Cambridge University Press, 1989, p. 6.

117. McGoldrick *et al.*, p. 314.

118. Eamonn McCann, *Dear God: The Price of Religion in Ireland*, London, Bookmarks, 1999, p. 59.

119. Joe McVeigh, *Renewing the Irish Church*, Dublin, Mercier, 1993, pp. 73–4.

120. Joe McVeigh, *The Wounded Church: Religion, Politics and Justice in Ireland*, Dublin, Mercier, 1989, p. 29. See also Matthias Buschkuhl, *Great Britain and the Holy See*, Dublin, Irish Academic Press, 1982.

121. McVeigh, *Wounded Church*, p. 26.

122. James Joyce, "Fenianism" (1907), cited in Davison, p. 39.

123. O'Faolain, quoted in McGoldrick *et al.*, p. 17; Moynihan, quoted in Ibson, p. 54.

124. Oscar Handlin, *Boston's Immigrants: A Study in Acculturation*, Cambridge, Harvard University Press, 1959, p. 131.

125. Ibson, p. 34.

126. Wole Soyinka, *Myth, Literature, and the African World*, Cambridge, MA, Cambridge University Press, 1976, pp. 1–2.

127. Clyde W. Ford, *The Hero with an African Face: Mythic Wisdom of Traditional Africa*, New York, Bantam, 1999, pp. 23, 145.

128. Ibid., p. 7.

129. David. A. Wilson, *United Irishmen, United States*, p. 67.

130. Glazer and Moynihan, p. 240. See also Daniel Cassidy, "The Real Black Irish," *Irish Herald*, September 1997.

131. David A. Wilson, *United Irishmen, United States*, p. 139.

132. Ibid., p. 67.

133. For this account of Paine, see David Dickson, "Paine in Ireland," in David Dickson, Daire Keogh, and Kevin Whelan, *The United Irishmen: Republicanism, Radicalism, and Rebellion*, Dublin, Lilliput Press, 1993, pp. 135–50.

134. Jack Fruchtman, *Thomas Paine, Apostle of Freedom*, New York, Four Walls Eight Windows, 1994, pp. 433–44; see also Eric Foner, *Tom Paine and Revolutionary America*, New York, Oxford University Press, 1976, p. 261.

135. Dickson, p. 149.

136. This account of the San Patricios is from James Callaghan, "The San Patricios," *American Heritage*, November 1995, pp. 68 ff.

137. Michael Hogan, *The Irish Soldiers of Mexico*, Mexico City, Fondo Editorial Universitario, 1997, p. 243-4.

138. Ibid., p. 243.

139. *La Jornada*, March 22, 1995.

140. Kevin Kenny, *Making Sense of the Molly Maguires*, New York, Oxford University Press, pp. 14, 24.

141. Ibid., p. 37.

142. See Fox Butterfield, *All God's Children: The Bosket Family and the American Tradition of Violence*, New York, Avon, 1995, p. 97.

143. William H. A. Williams, *'Twas Only an Irishman's Dream*, Urbana-Champagne, University of Illinois, 1996, pp. 148–9.

144. T. J. English, "The Original Irish Gangsters," in Coffey and Golway, p. 113.

145. Ibid., p. 118.

146. The only biography of Mad Dog Coll is Breandan Delap, *Mad Dog Coll, An Irish Gangster*, Cork, Mercier Press, 1999, pp. 20–27.

147. Dick Lehr and Gerard O'Neill, *Black Mass: The Irish Mob, the FBI, and a Devil's Deal*, New York, Public Affairs, 2000, pp. 20, 24.

148. Coogan, *Wherever Green*, p. 294.

149. Eric Foner, manuscript to myself.

150. Foner ms. cited.

151. Miller, p. 537.

152. Ibson, p. 202.

153. Ibid., p. 105.

154. Ibid.

155. Kenneth O'Donnell, *"Johnny, We Hardly Knew Ye,":* Memories of John Fitzgerald Kennedy (with David Powers and Joe McCarthy), New York, Little, Brown, 1970, p. 358.

156. Glazer and Moynihan, p. 250.

157. Ibson, p. 124.

158. Quoted in ibid., p. 126.

159. James Carroll, *An American Requiem: God, My Father, and the War That Came Between Us*, New York, Houghton Mifflin, 1996, p. 178.

160. James Carroll, *Prince of Peace*, Boston, Little, Brown, 1984, p. 301.

161. Jack Newfield, in conversation with the author. See also Jack Newfield, *Bread and Roses Too: Reporting About America*, New York, Dutton, 1971.

162. Edwin Guthman and Richard Allen, eds, *Robert F. Kennedy: Collected Speeches*, New York, Viking, 1993, pp. 107-8.

163. Ibson, p. 170.

164. Coogan, *Wherever Green*, pp. 288, 300.

165. Ibid., pp. 299, 301.

166. Glazer and Moynihan, p. 282.

167. Kevin Phillips, *The Emerging Republican Majority*, New York, Doubleday Anchor, 1970, p. 172.

168. Greeley, p. 37.

169. Glazer and Moynihan, p. 226.

170. John Conroy, *Unspeakable Acts, Ordinary People: The Dynamics of Torture*, New York, Knopf, 2000.

171. Obtained by the author through a US Freedom of Information Act request, 1976.

172. Tom Hayden, *Reunion*, New York, Random House, 1988, p. 304.

173. Peter Quinn, Introduction to William Riordan, *Plunket of Tammany Hall*, New York, Signet Classics, 1995, p. xvi.

174. Miller, pp. 322-3.

175. Marcus, p. 44.

Part II Going North

1. *Irish News*, March 15, 1999.

2. Obtained through the Freedom of Information Act, 1976.

3. 1922 extract from the *Limerick Leader*, quoted in Helen Litton, *The Irish Civil War*, Dublin, Wolfhound Press, 1995, p. 105.

4. Ibid., pp. 134-5.

5. Brian Friel, *The London Vertigo*, Loughcrew, Gallery Press, 1990, p. 10.

6. Roddy Doyle, *A Star Called Henry*, New York, Viking, 1999.

7. Ibid., p. 314.

8. Ibid., p. 327.

9. Alan Riding, "Chipping Away the Blarney: Ireland Lauds a Novelist Who Dismantles National Myths," *New York Times*, September 22, 1999.

10. Doyle, p. 342.

11. Fintan O'Toole, *The Ex-Isle of Erin: Images of a Global Ireland*, Dublin, New Island Books, 1996, p. 13.

12. Jack Holland, *The American Connection: US Guns, Money and Influence in Northern Ireland*, Dublin, Roberts Reinhart, 1999, p. 118.

13. Andrew Wilson, *Irish America and the Ulster Conflict, 1986–1995*, Belfast, Blackstaff Press, 1995, p. 112.

14. Ibid., p. 116.

15. Quoted in ibid., p. 140.

16. See "US Furor Over Five Jailed Irish-Americans," *Christian Science Monitor*, August 18, 1972; Shana Alexander, "The Patriot Game," *New York*, November 22, 1982; and "British, US Intelligence Helped Arrest," *Irish Times*, January 2, 1984.

17. Wilson, p. 159.

18. Holland, p. 138.

19. *New Statesman*, October 7, 1994.

20. *New York Times*, June 1, 2000.

21. Niall O'Dowd, in *Ireland on Sunday*, July 9, 2000.

22. Conor O'Clery, *The Greening of the White House*, Dublin, Gill & Macmillan, 1996, p. 240.

23. See Holland, p. 130.

24. *New Statesman*, October 7, 1994.

25. Wilson, pp. 84–5.

26. Jon Wiener, *Gimme Some Truth: The John Lennon FBI Files*, Berkeley, University of California Press, 1999, pp. 200–203.

27. Wilson, p. 109.

28. Wilson. See also Jo Thomas, "Bloody Ireland," *Columbia Journalism Review*, May–June 1998; Roger Faligot, *Britain's Military Strategy in Northern Ireland*, London, Zed, and Dingle, Brandon, 1983; Liz Curtis, *Ireland and the Propaganda War*, Belfast, Pluto, 1998.

29. Emerson and Lewis are quoted in Holland, pp. 198–9, 203.

30. Wilson, p. 62.

31. Ibid., p. 77.

32. Don Mullan, ed., *Eyewitness Bloody Sunday*, Dublin, Wolfhound Press, 1997; Trisha Ziff, *Hidden Truths: Bloody Sunday, 1972*, Santa Monica, Smart Art Press, 2000.

33. Christopher Hitchens, *Blood, Class and Nostalgia: Anglo-American Ironies*, New York, Farrar, Straus & Giroux, 1990, p. 123.

34. Quoted in ibid., pp. 119–20.

35. *USA Today*, February 23, 1993.

36. Quoted in Tim Pat Coogan, *Disillusioned Decades: Ireland 1966–87*, Dublin, Gill & Macmillan, 1987, p. 184.

37. Ibid.

38. Transcript quoted in the *Irish Times*, February 17, 1998.

39. *Irish Times*, November 11, 2000.

40. *Protestant Telegraph*, April 17, 1976, cited in *An Phoblacht*, May 22, 1976.

41. Frank Kitson, *Low Intensity Operations*, London, Faber, 1971, p. 87.

42. *Sunday Times*, March 13, 1977.

43. Quoted in *Republican News*, August 21, 1976.

44. Quoted in Ruth Dudley Edwards, *Patrick Pearse: The Triumph of Failure*, Dublin, Poolbeg Press, 1990 edition, pp. 236–7.

45. Ibid., p. 237.

46. Bik MacFarland *et al.*, "POW 742," *Something Inside So Strong* (album), Belfast, 1999.

47. Desmond Maguire, ed., *Padraic Pearse: Short Stories*, Dublin, Mercier Press, 1968; Dermot Bolger, ed., with Eugene McCabe, *Padraig Pearse: Selected Poems*, Rogha Danta, Dublin, New Island Books, 1993.

48. Bolger, ed., p. 12.

49. Published in Loreto Todd, *Green English: Ireland's Influence on the English Language*, Dublin, O'Brien Press, 1999, p. 143.

50. Don Mullan, *The Dublin and Monoghan Bombings*, Dublin, Wolfhound Press, 2000.

51. For access to Belfast republican papers, thanks to Yvonne Murphy, Librarian, the Linen Hall Library Political Collection, Belfast.

52. David McKittrick, Seamus Kelters, Brian Feeney, and Chris Thornton, *Lost Lives: The Stories of Men, Women and Children Who Died as a Result of the Northern Ireland Troubles*, London, Mainstream Publishing, 1999, p. 669.

53. Sydney Elliott and W. D. Flackes, *Northern Ireland: A Political Directory, 1968–99*, Belfast, Blackstaff Press, 1999, pp. 392–3.

54. McKittrick *et al.*, p. 670.

55. *Republican News*, September 1976.

56. *Republican News*, August 1976.

57. Mitchel McLaughlin, conversation with the author, Derry.

58. Panel discussion, West Belfast Festival, August 2000.

59. Jimmy Breslin, *World without End, Amen*, New York, Viking, 1973.

60. Ibid., p. 78. My emphasis.

61. Danny Morrison, *West Belfast*, Dublin, Mercier, 1989; *On the Back of the Swallow*, Dublin, Mercier, 1994; and *The Wrong Man*, Dublin, Mercier, 1997.

62. *Republican News*, September 1976.

63. *Republican News*, May 1976.

64. In W. B. Yeats, *Collected Poems of W. B. Yeats*, London, Macmillan, 1950, pp. 120–21.

65. Davis Sharrock and Mark Davenport, *Man of War, Man of Peace: The Unauthorized Biography of Gerry Adams*, New York, Macmillan Pan Books, 1997, p. 365.

66. Wilson, p. 112.

67. Coogan, *Disillusioned Decades*, p. 31.

68. Ibid., p. 68.

69. Ibid., p. 95.

70. Ibid., p. 95.

71. Thomas Keneally, *The Great Shame, and the Triumph of the Irish in the English-speaking World*, New York, Doubleday, 1999, pp. 598–600.

72. John Barnes, *Irish American Landmarks*, Detroit, Visible Ink Press, 1995, pp. 453–6.

73. *Los Angeles Times*, March 5, 1983.

74. Data from Senate Office of Research, Sacramento.

75. *Irish News*, May 22, 2000.

76. Conversation between British lobbyist Donald Burns and the author, November 18, 2000.

77. *San Francisco Chronicle*, column by Warren Hinckle, May 13, 1987.

78. AB 1935, 1987, in Assembly archives, Sacramento.

79. *Los Angeles Times*, May 19, 1987.

80. *Santa Monica Evening Outlook*, May 21, 1987.

81. Author's conversation with Assemblyman Patrick Johnston, April 21, 1987.

82. See Warren Hinckle, "Curious Stew of Irish, Sacramento Politics," *San Francisco Economist*, May 13, 1987, and "Free Speech in US, but not N. Ireland," *San Francisco Examiner*, June 23, 1987.

83. *San Francisco Chronicle*, June 23, 1987.

84. *Los Angeles Times*, February 6, 1988.

85. Tim Pat Coogan, *The Troubles: Ireland's Ordeal 1966–1995 and the Search for Peace*, London, Hutchinson, 1995, p. 183.

86. Elliott and Flackes, p. 456.

87. McKittrick *et al.*, p. 1,057.

88. Extract from a 1993 Research Service Report on Northern Ireland, a semi-official briefing paper for members of Congress, which was subsidized by the British government. Quoted in O'Clery, p. 28.

89. Quoted in Clery, p. 83.

90. Rahm Emanuel, conversation with the author, November 23, 2000.

91. Stanley Greenberg, conversation with the author, March 4, 2001.

92. Coogan, *The Troubles*, p. 113.

93. McKittrick et al., p. 1,304.

94. Ibid.

95. Interview in Susan McKay, *Northern Protestants: An Unsettled People*, Belfast, Blackstaff Press, 2000, p. 98.

96 Sharrock and Devenport, p. 37.

97. Another example of this double-standard was the liberal journalist Mary McGrory, who became venomous at a dinner with Adams in a Washington suburb when the Sinn Féin leader was allowed to visit America. "He smiles a lot," she wrote in apparent disapproval of his politeness. "He is silky, turning surly only when asked about fronting for an organization that shot fathers on their front doorsteps." At the dinner in question, she asked Adams if it was "really necessary" to kill people in such a way, to which he replied, "No it wasn't, and I regret that." This wasn't enough for McGrory, who started demanding that Adams say "permanent" in speaking of the IRA

ceasefire. Finally, according to the dinner host, he said, "Permanent. Permanent. Permanent. There!"(O'Clery, p. 179). Here was an Irish American columnist, in the midst of an IRA ceasefire and clearly at the most hopeful moment in recent Irish history, still finding it necessary to attack an Irish political leader working for peace in a manner she never would display towards a British official. Earlier, she had opposed the Adams visa, writing that it "encouraged all the wrong people" and "brought Clinton eight days of coruscating stories in the British press" (ibid., p. 132). Only much later, after the Good Friday Agreement was signed, did she admit in the *Washington Post* that she was wrong (ibid., p. 240).

98. Gerry Adams, *Before the Dawn: An Autobiography*, New York, William Morrow, 1996, p. 93.

99. Ibid., p. 94.

100. Ibid., p. 143.

101. Ibid., p. 144.

102. Ibid., p. 101.

103. Michael Mahdesian, deputy for Humanitarian Response, US AID, in conversation with the author, February 20, 2001.

104. Sharrock and Devenport, p. 328; see, for example, "IRA Chief Eases Stand on a United Ireland", *New York Times*, October 31, 1994.

105. *New York Times*, February 1, 1994.

106. O'Clery, p. 30.

107. Rahm Emanuel, conversation with the author.

108. O'Clery, p. 109.

109. In Conor O'Clery, *The Greening of the White House*, Gill and Macmillan, Dublin, 1996, pp. 132, 179. The quip from the activist mentioned in the previous paragraph came in conversation with the author, 1999.

110. *An Phoblacht*, September 21, 2000.

111. Thomas Cahill, *How the Irish Saved Civilization*, New York, Doubleday Anchor, 1995, pp. 79–80.

112. O'Clery, p. 109.

113. Elliott and Flackes, p. 67.

114. Ibid., p. 66.

115. O'Clery, p. 106.

116. *Los Angeles Times*, November 18, 1993.

117. McKay, p. 51.

118. Ibid., pp. 129–30.

119. Ibid., p. 96.

120. Excellent research is done by the West Belfast Economic Forum, based on field interviews and Northern Ireland Office data. See also Maura Sheehan and Mike Tomlinson, *The Unequal Unemployed: Discrimination, Unemployment and State Policy in Northern Ireland*, Aldershot, Ashgate Press, 1999. US investments are monitored by the Investor Responsibility Research Center, Inc., in Washington DC.

121. Dr Maura Sheehan, "The International Fund for Ireland: Some

Findings on its Patterns of Expenditure," paper produced by the West Belfast Economic Forum, 1995.

122. John A. Barnes, "US Wallets Pay for Those Smiling Irish Eyes," *Wall Street Journal*, March 16, 1990.

123. Ibid.

124. Máirtín Ó Muilleoir, *Belfast's Dome of Delight: City Hall Politics 1981–2000*, Belfast, Beyond the Pale, 1999.

125. *Sunday Times*, August 3, 1976.

126. William Rooney, cited in Maria Tymoczko, *The Irish Ulysses*, Berkeley, University of California Press, 1994, p. 262.

127. Cited in Todd, p. 140.

128. Data provided to the author by IRRC, Washington DC, March 1, 2000, and West Belfast Economic Forum.

129. IRRC data.

130. *Irish Times*, September 4, 1998.

131. Correspondence with the author, February 29, 1996; Jim Fitzpatrick, "North American Networking," in *Corporate Northern Ireland*, by Johnstone Media, Edinburgh, 1998, p. 125.

132. Quoted in the *Andersonstown News*, June 6, 1998, p. 21.

133. *Partnership for Equality: The Government's Proposals for Future Legislation and Policies on Employment Equality in Northern Ireland, . . .* March 1998, pp. 10, 34, 46.

134. George Quigley, *Corporate Northern Ireland, 1998–99*, p. 91.

135. Ibid., p. 91.

136. See Sheehan and Tomlinson.

137. Pat Doherty was one of four Sinn Féin MPs elected in the June 2001 parliamentary elections. The others were Gerry Adams (for a fourth term), Martin McGuinness (for a second term) and Michelle Gildernew.

138. Peter Taylor, *Loyalists*, London, Bloomsbury, 1999, p. 41.

139. Ibid., pp. 42–3.

140. Ibid., p. 233.

141. Conversation with the author, Jerusalem, 1982.

142. *Irish Times*, February 17, 1998.

143. Ruth Dudley Edwards, *The Faithful Tribe: An Intimate Portrait of the Loyal Institutions*, HarperCollins, 1999, pp. 296, 301, 319.

144. Elliott and Flackes, p. 178.

145. Ibid., p. 381.

146. *New York Times*, January 20, 1998.

147. *Sunday Business Post*, January 4, 1998.

148. Royal Ulster Constabulary press releases, April–May 1998, provided by Irish Watch, London.

149. *Los Angeles Times*, January 20, 1998.

150. See "Killers Who Stalk the Peace Process," *Sunday Times*, February 15, 1998.

151. *Sunday Tribune*, February 15, 1998.

152. *Los Angeles Times*, December 24, 2000.

153. James Steinberg, conversation with the author.

154. *New York Times*, January 21, 1998.

155. The "Hume of the Unionists" comment was made by Senator Christopher Dodd; see *Irish Times*, February 17, 1998.

156. *Sunday Tribune*, April 19, 1998.

157. Elliott and Flackes, p. 377.

158. *Andersonstown News*, April 18, 1998.

159. Transcript in the *Irish Times*, February 17, 1998.

160. *Sunday Times*, October 31, 1999.

161. Martin Dillon, *God and the Gun: The Church and Irish Terrorism*, London, Orion, 1997, pp. 23, 33, 34.

162. McKay, p. 175.

163. All this information on Rosemary Nelson is in the *New York Times*, May 2, 1999.

164. Elliott and Flackes, p. 137.

165. Figures from *A New Beginning: Policing in Northern Ireland, the report of the Independent Commission on Policing for Northern Ireland*, hereafter referred to as the Patten Report, September 1999.

166. Merrick Bobb, Mark Epstein, Nicolas Miller, and Manuel Abascal, *Five Years Later: A Report to the Los Angeles Police Commission on the Los Angeles Police Department's Implementation of Independent Commission Recommendations*, Los Angeles, May 1996.

167. Marc Mauer, *Race to Incarcerate*, New York, New Press, 1999, p. 21.

168. Patten Report, p. 83.

169. Moya St Leger, writing in the *Irish News*, August 4, 1999.

170. *Irish News*, August 4, 1999.

171. Patten Report, p. 75.

172. McKay, p. 363.

173. *An Phoblacht/Republican News*, June 10, 1999.

174. Toby Harnden, *"Bandit Country": The IRA and South Armagh*, London, Hodder and Stoughton, 1999, p. 14.

175. Ibid., p. 146.

176. Ibid. p. 252.

177. *Sunday Tribune*, February 20, 2000.

178. Thomas Berry, *The Dream of the Earth*, Sierra Club, San Francisco, 1988, p. 190.

179. Harnden, pp. 102–3.

180. Ibid., p. 2.

181. Ibid., p. 79.

182. Jonathan Bardon, *A History of Ulster*, Belfast, Blackstaff, 1992, pp. 753–4.

183. Quoted in David Beresford, *Ten Men Dead*, HarperCollins, London, 1987, p. 307.

184. Gerry Adams in Beresford, p. 344; also in Adams (*Before the Dawn*), p. 288. Adams wrote to Bobby Sands saying "Bobby, we are tactically, strategically, physically and morally opposed to a hunger strike." When it went forward, he nevertheless chaired Sinn Féin's hunger-strike committee and built support for both the strike and a solution.

185. Published as *Out of Time: Irish Republican Prisoners, Long Kesh, 1972–2000*, Beyond the Pale Press, Belfast, 2001.

186. See Frank Costello, *Enduring the Most: The Life and Death of Terence MacSwiney*, Brandon Publishers, Kerry, 1995.

187. McKeown, p. 176.

188. Quoted in Danny Morrison, *Then the Walls Came Down*, Dublin, Mercier Press, 1991, p. 110.

189. Ibid., p. 272.

190. See note 61.

Part III   Recovering the Irish Soul

1. Leonard Covello, cited in Philippe Bourgois, *In Search of Respect*, Cambridge, Cambridge University Press, 1996, p. 30.

2. Randall Robinson, *The Debt: What America Owes to Blacks*, Dutton, NY, 2000, pp. 13–14.

3. Shane MacGowan and Victoria Mary Clarke, *A Drink with Shane MacGowan*, New York, Grove Press, 2001, p. 244.

4. Correspondence to author.

5. Stuart Reid, in *American Spectator*, May 1995.

6. *Irish Times*, February 16, 1998.

7. Robbie McVeigh, "Nick, Nack, Paddywhack: Anti-Irish Racism and the Racialization of Irishness," manuscript provided by the author.

8. Marilyn Halter, *Shopping for Identity*, Schocken, New York, 2000, p. 8.

9. Sean Kenny, *The Hungry Earth,* New York, Roberts Rinehart Publishing, 1995.

10. *Irish Times*, June 3, 2000.

11. For details of Keneally's book, see Part I, n. 5.

12. *Irish Times*, September 3, 1998.

13. Thomas Cahill, *How the Irish Saved Civilization*, New York, Doubleday Anchor, 1995.

14. Ibid., p. 3.

15. Quoted in Arthur Schlesinger, *The Disuniting of America: Reflections on a Multicultural Society*, New York, Norton, 1998, p. 62.

16. Eamonn McCann, *Dear God: The Price of Religion in Ireland*, London, Bookmarks, 1999, p. 6.

17. *Sunday Times*, August 1, 1999.

18. *Irish Times*, August 1, 1999.

19. See *Sunday Independent*, October 31, 1999.

20. *Irish Times*, May 13, 2000.

21. *Sunday Independent*, July 2, 2000.

22. *Belfast Telegraph*, September 21, 2000.

23. *Irish Times*, July 9, 2000.

24. "Irish–US Links at Risk in Post-North Agreement Era," *Irish Times*, December 23, 2000; my emphasis.

25. *Ireland on Sunday*, July 9, 2000.

26. *Los Angeles Times*, February 24, 2001.

27. *New Statesman*, October 7, 1994.

28. See *American Outlook*, March–April 2001.

29. Quoted in ibid., p. 25.

30. Quoted in ibid., p. 29.

31. *An Phoblacht*, September 21, 2000.

32. *LA Times*, June 10, 2001.

33. John Rogers, *Irish Times*, May 19, 2001.

34. Danny Morrison, "A New Day Dawning," *Belfast Telegraph*, June 11, 2001.

35. *Irish Times*, June 11, 2001.

36. Jon Wiener, *Gimme Some Truth: The John Lennon Files*, Berkeley, University of California, 1999, p. 198; also Jann Wenner, *Lennon Remembers*, NY, Verso, 2000, p. 151, in which Lennon says, "I hope we're a nice old couple living off the coast of Ireland or something like that, looking at our scrapbook of madness."

37. Martin Brennan, *The Stones of Time*, Rochester, Inner Traditions International, 1994, p. 72.

38. All in Brennan.

39. Ibid., p. 31.

40. Mary Low, *Celtic Christianity and Nature: Early Irish and Hebridian Traditions*, Blackstaff Press, Belfast, 1996, p. 10.

Epilogue to the Paperback Edition: The Way We Were

1. Howard Zinn, *A People's History of the United States*, New York, Harper & Row, 1980, p. 67.

2. *New Republic* Online, December 5, 2002.

3. *New York Times*, July 16, 2002.

4. *New York Times*, July 16, 2002.

5. Roy Foster, *Modern Ireland, 1600–1972*, London, Penguin, 1988, p. 325.

6. Ibid., p. 327.

7. Kevin B. Nowlan, in *The Great Famine, Studies in Irish History, 1845–52*, New York, R. Dudley Edwards and T. Desmond Williams, 1957, p. xi.

8. Charles Trevelyan, cited in Christine Kinealy, *The Death-Dealing Famine*, London, Pluto Press, 1997, p. 3.

9. Ibid., p. 3.

10. Cormac Ó Gráda, *Black 47 and Beyond: The Great Irish Famine in History, Economy, and Memory*, New Jersey, Princeton University Press, 1997, p. 3, 4, 5.

11. Cited in Ibid., p. 3.

12. Ibid. p., 5.

13. John Milton, cited in Norah Carlin's "The Cromwellian Reconquest of Ireland, 1649–51," in Bradshaw *et al.*, *Representing Ireland: Literature and the Origins of Conflict, 1534–1660*, Cambridge University Press, 1993, p. 216.

14. Foster, p. 320.

15. Ibid., p. 325.

16. Ibid., p. 325.

17. Ó Gráda, p. 206.

18. Foster, p. 318.

19. Foster, p. 324.

20. Interview with Foster, *Boston Globe*, September 15, 2002.

21. James S. Donnelly, "The Great Famine and Its Interpreters, Old and New," in *My Irish Hunger*, Dublin, Wolfhound, 1997, p. 118. See also Brendan Bradshaw's "Nationalism and Historical Scholarship in Modern Ireland," *Irish Historical Studies*, xxvi, no. 104 (November 1989), pp. 320–51. Also Kevin Whelan, "Come All Your Staunch Revisionists – Towards a Post-Revisionist Agenda for Irish History," *Irish Reporter*, 11 (second quarter, 1991), pp. 23–25.

22. Kinealy, p. 3. Also see her *This Great Calamity, The Irish Famine, 1845–52*, Dublin, 1994, pp. xv–xxii.

23. Foster, p. 596.

24. Ibid.

25. Ibid.

26. Eamon Delaney, "Cliches Abroad," February 1, 2002.

27. *New York Review* of Books, April 1, 2002.

28. Brien McDonald, "Memories of Che, a Revolutionary Son of Ireland," *Independent*, March 21, 2002.

29. *Los Angeles Times Book Review*, January 6, 2002.

30. *New York Times Book Review*, February 24, 2002.

31. *Washington Post Book Review*, February 17, 2002.

32. *Publishers Weekly*, cited in Amazon.com, June 28, 2002.

33. Joe Jamison, *Irish Democrat*, July 30, 2002.

34. Tom Deignan, *Irish America*, December/January, 2002.

35. Martin O Muilleoir, *Andersonstown News*, January 11, 2002.

36. *Boston Globe*, September 15, 2002.

37. *Times*, November 15, 2002.

38. Cited in Patrick Magee, *Gangsters or Guerillas?* p. 142 (see note 51, below).

39. Reported by Sinn Féin representative Rita O'Hare.

40. *Los Angeles Times*, July 23, 2002.

41. Ibid.

42. See letter to Tony Blair by Gerald P. Lally, Irish American Unity Conference, May 21, 2002, e-mail: editor@iauc.org.

43. *New York Times*, July 5, 2002.

44. *Guardian*, October 14, 2002.

45. Liam Clarke, Kathryn Johnston and Martin McGuinness, *From Guns to Government*, London, Mainstream Publishing, 2001, pp. 42, 254.

46. Ed Moloney, *A Secret History of the IRA*, New York, Norton, 2002. For Edna O'Brian reference and the "intoxication" of Irish Americans, see p. 42.

47. Peter Taylor, *Provos, the IRA and Sinn Féin*, London, Bloomsbury, 1997.

48. Deaglan de Breadun, *The Far Side of Revenge: Making Peace in Northern Ireland*, Cork, Collins Press, 2001.

49. Tim Pat Coogan, *The IRA: A History*, Roberts Rinehart, Boulder, 1994; *Wherever Green Is Worn, The Story of the Irish Diaspora*, London, Random House, 2000.

50. See my review of McKeown's book, *Out of Time, Irish Republican Prisoners in Long Kesh*, 1972–2000, Belfast, Beyond the Pale Publications, 2001, in the *Los Angeles Times Book Review*, August 12, 2001.

51. Patrick Magee, *Gangsters or Guerillas? Representations of Irish Republicans in 'Troubles Fiction,'* Belfast, Beyond the Pale Publications, 2002.

52. Moloney, p. 174.

53. "Top Flanagan Aides Dispute His Version of Omagh Bomb Inquiry," in the *Guardian*, May 22, 2002.

54. *The Nation*, November 18, 2002, p. 44.

55. *Scotsman*, May 20, 2002.

56. *Irish Independent*, May 19, 2002.

57. *Independent*, May 19, 2002.

58. *Los Angeles Times*, January 5, 2003.

59. "Film Breaks Silence on Irish Asylums," *International Herald Tribune*, November 29, 2002. Also see BBC News, November 8, 2002.

60. *The Nation*, August 19–26, 2002.

61. Ibid.

62. *New Times*, August 29–September 4, 2002.

63. Ibid.

64. *New York Times*, December 31, 2002.

65. *Irish News*, November 23–25, on Trimble speech in Chicago. Trimble's "pathetic" remark was in March, 2002, to the Ulster Unionist Council.

66. Patrick Tyler, *Paradise Alley*, New York, Harper Collins, 2002.

67. Peter Quinn, *The Banished Children of Eve*, New York, Viking, 1994.

68. *New York Times*, December 20, 2002.

69. Ibid.

70. Correspondence from Leo Bradley, Coffin Library, Kimball Union Academy, Meridian, New Hampshire, 2002.

71. Conversation with author, 2002.

72. Speech to conference on peace and reconciliation, Dublin, January 14, 2003.

73. Tim Pat Coogan, in public forum with myself, Dublin, 1997.

74. *New York Times*, January 12, 2003.

75. *New York Times Magazine*, October 20, 2002.